4/26/ 2009

Dearest Rev. Jay & Christina SMN.

Congratulations !
At the starting point of this long journey
as a minister and his wife,
we wish you " Joy & Gladness"

♡ Choi Family
(Paul. Lauren, Matthew, Andee
Karen

SERMONS
on WOMEN *of the*
❦ BIBLE ❦

Other Sermon Collections
by Charles H. Spurgeon

Sermons on Men of the Bible

Sermons on Jesus and the Holy Spirit

Sermons on Prayer

Sermons on the Death and Resurrection of Jesus

Sermons
on WOMEN of the
BIBLE

CHARLES H. SPURGEON

HENDRICKSON PUBLISHERS

Sermons on Women of the Bible

Hendrickson Publishers, Inc.
P. O. Box 3473
Peabody, Massachusetts 01961-3473

ISBN 978-1-59856-284-2

Printed in the United States of America

Cover Art: Julius Schnorr von Carolsfeld's (1794-1872) depiction of Ruth staying with Naomi as Orpah abandons her. Courtesy of the Pitts Theology Library, Candler School of Theology, Emory University.

Library of Congress Cataloging-in-Publication Data

Spurgeon, C. H. (Charles Haddon), 1834-1892
   Sermons on women of the Bible / Charles H. Spurgeon.
         p. cm.
   ISBN 978-1-59856-284-2 (alk. paper)
1. Women in the Bible—Sermons. 2. Sermons, English—19th century.
I. Title.

   BS575.S57 2008
   220.9'2082--dc22

                                          2008031

Contents

Women of the Old Testament

thou bring not my son thither again. The LORD God of heaven, which took me from my father's house, and from the land of my kindred, and which spake unto me, and that sware unto me, saying, 'Unto thy seed will I give this land'; he shall send his angel before thee, and thou shalt take a wife unto my son from thence. And if the woman will not be willing to follow thee, then thou shalt be clear from this my oath: only bring not my son thither again."
—GENESIS 24:5–8

bestowed much labor on us. Salute Andronicus and Junia, my kinsmen, and my fellow prisoners, who are of note among the apostles, who also were in Christ before me. Greet Amplias my beloved in the Lord. Salute Urbane, our helper in Christ, and Stachys my beloved. Salute Apelles approved in Christ. Salute them which are of Aristobulus' household. Salute Herodion my kinsman. Greet them that be of the household of Narcissus, which are in the Lord. Salute Tryphena and Tryphosa, who labor in the Lord. Salute the beloved Persis, which labored much in the Lord. Salute Rufus chosen in the Lord, and his mother and mine. Salute Asyncritus, Phlegon, Hermas, Patrobas, Hermes, and the brethren which are with them. Salute Philologus, and Julia, Nereus, and his sister, and Olympas, and all the saints which are with them. Salute one another with a holy kiss. The churches of Christ salute you.—ROMANS 16:1–16

Publisher's Preface

Charles Haddon Spurgeon
1834–1892

Ask most people today who Charles Haddon Spurgeon was, and you might be surprised at the answers. Most know he was a preacher, others remember that he was Baptist, and others go so far as to remember that he lived in England during the nineteenth century. All of this is true. Yet Charles Haddon Spurgeon was so much more.

Spurgeon was born into a family of Congregationalists in 1834, his father and grandfather both Independent preachers. This designation seems benign today, but in the mid-nineteenth century, it describes a family committed to a Nonconformist path—meaning they did not conform to the established Church of England. Spurgeon grew up in a rural village, a village virtually cut off from the Industrial Revolution rolling over most of England.

Spurgeon was born again at a Primitive Methodist meeting in 1850, at age sixteen. He soon became a Baptist (to the sorrow of his mother) and almost immediately began to preach. Considered a preaching prodigy—"a boy wonder of the fens"—Spurgeon attracted huge audiences and garnered a reputation that reached throughout the countryside and into London. As a result of his great success, Spurgeon was invited to preach at the New Park Street Chapel in London in 1854, when he was just nineteen. When he first preached at the church, they were unable to fill even two hundred seats. Within the year, Spurgeon filled the twelve-hundred-seat church to overflowing; he soon began preaching in larger and larger venues, outgrowing each, until finally in 1861, the Metropolitan Tabernacle was completed, which seated six thousand persons. This would be Spurgeon's home base for the rest of his career, until his death in 1892, at age fifty-seven.

Spurgeon married Susannah Thompson in 1856 and soon they had twin sons, Charles and Thomas, who would later follow him in his work. Spurgeon opened Pastors' College, a training school for preachers, that trained over nine hundred preachers during his lifetime. He also opened orphanages for underprivileged boys and girls, providing educations to each of the orphans. And with Susannah, he developed a program to publish and distribute Christian literature. He is said to have preached to over ten million people in his forty years of ministry. His sermons sold over twenty-five thousand copies each week, and were translated into twenty languages. He was utterly committed to spreading the gospel, through preaching and through the written word.

During Spurgeon's lifetime, the Industrial Revolution transformed England from a rural, agricultural society, to an urban, industrial society, with all the attendant difficulties and horrors of a society in major transition. The people displaced by these sweeping changes, the factory workers, the shopkeepers, these became Spurgeon's congregation. From a small village himself and transplanted to a large and inhospitable city, he was a common man, and he understood innately the spiritual needs of the common people. He was a communicator who made the gospel so relevant, who spoke so brilliantly to people's deepest needs, that listeners welcomed his message.

Keep in mind that Spurgeon preached in the days before microphones or speakers; in other words, he preached without benefit of amplifier systems. Once he preached to a crowd of over twenty-three thousand people without mechanical amplification of any sort. He himself was the electrifying presence on the platform: he did not stand and simply read a stilted sermon. Spurgeon used an outline, developing his themes extemporaneously, and speaking "in common language to common people." His sermons were filled with stories and poetry, drama and emotion. He was larger than life, always in motion, striding back and forth across the stage. He gestured broadly, acted out stories, used humor, and painted word pictures. For Spurgeon, preaching was about communicating the truth of God, and he would use any gift at his disposal to accomplish this.

Spurgeon's preaching was anchored in his spiritual life, a life rich in prayer and the study of Scripture. He was not tempted by fashion, be it theological, social, or political. Scripture was the cornerstone of Spurgeon's life and his preaching. He was an expositional preacher mostly, exploring a passage of Scripture for its meanings both within the text as well as in the lives of each member of his congregation. To Spurgeon, Scripture is alive and specifically relevant to people's lives, whatever their social status, economic situation, or time in which they live.

One has a sense that Spurgeon embraced God's revelation completely: God's revelation through Jesus Christ, through Scripture, and through his own prayer and study. For him, revelation was not a finished act: God still reveals Himself, if one made oneself available. Some recognize Spurgeon for the mystic he was, one who was willing and eager to explore the mysteries of God, able to live with those bits of truth that do not conform to a particular system of theology, perfectly comfortable with saying "This I know, and this I don't know—yet will I trust."

This collection of sermons includes Spurgeon's thoughts on a broad variety of women whose character and relationship with God made them heroes of a sort, women who responded to God's invitation, and thus experienced a profound intimacy with the Eternal One. These sermons are not a series: they were not created or intended to be sequential. Rather, they are stand-alone sermons, meant to explore specific men whose lives are part of the record of God's dealings with humankind.

Each of these sermons was preached at different times of Spurgeon's career, and each has distinct characteristics. They have not been homogenized or edited to sound as though they are all of a kind. Instead, they reflect the preacher himself, allowing the voice of this remarkable man to ring clearly as he guides the reader into a particular account, a particular event—to experience, with Spurgeon, God's particular revelation.

As you read, *listen*. These words are meant to be heard, not merely read. Listen carefully and you will hear the cadences of this remarkable preaching, the echoes of God's timeless truth traveling across the years. And above all, enjoy Spurgeon's enthusiasm, his fire, his devotion, his zeal to recognize and respond to God's timeless invitation to engage the Creator himself.

Women of the Old Testament

Hagar: Compassion for Souls

◆◆◆

Delivered on Lord's Day morning, February 5, 1871, at the Metropolitan Tabernacle, Newington. No. 974.

She went, and sat her down over against him a good way off, as it were a bowshot: for she said, "Let me not see the death of the child." And she sat over against him, and lift up her voice, and wept.—GENESIS 21:16

Briefly let us rehearse the circumstances. The child Isaac was, according to God's word, to be the heir of Abraham. Ishmael, the elder son of Abraham, by the bondwoman Hagar, resided at home with his father till he was about eighteen years of age; but when he began to mock and scoff at the younger child whom God had ordained to be the heir, it became needful that he and his mother should be sent away from Abraham's encampment. It might have seemed unkind and heartless to have sent them forth, but God, having arranged to provide for them, sent a divine command which at once rendered their expulsion necessary, and certified its success. We may rest assured that whatever God commands he will be quite certain to justify. He knew it would be no cruelty to Hagar or Ishmael to be driven into independence, and he gave a promise which secured them everything which they desired. "Also of the son of the bondwoman will I make a great nation"; and again, "I have blessed him, and will make him fruitful, and will multiply him exceedingly; twelve princes shall he beget, and I will make him a great nation." Had they both been able to go forth from Abraham's tent in faith, they might have trodden the desert with a joyous footstep, fully assured that he who bade them go, and he who promised that he would bless them, would be certain to provide all things needful for them.

Early in the morning they were sent forth on their journey, with as much provision as they could carry, and probably they intended to make their way to Egypt, from which Hagar had come. They may have lost their way; at any rate, they are spoken of as wandering. Their store of food became exhausted, the water in the skin bottle was all spent; both of them felt the fatigue of the wilderness, and the heat of the pitiless sand; they were both faint and weary, and the younger utterly failed. As long as the mother could sustain the tottering, fainting footsteps of her boy, she did so; when she could do so no longer, he swooned with weakness, and she laid him down beneath the slight shade of the desert tamarisk, that he might be as far as possible screened from the excessive heat of the sun. Looking into his face and seeing the pallor of coming death gathering upon it, knowing her inability to do anything whatever to revive him, or even to preserve his life, she could not bear to sit and gaze upon his face, but withdrew just far enough to be able still to watch with all a mother's care. She sat down in the brokenness of her spirit, her tears gushed forth in torrents, and heartrending cries of agony startled the rocks around.

It was needful that the high spirit of the mother and her son should be broken down before they received prosperity: the mother had been on a former occasion graciously humbled by being placed in much the same condition, but she had probably relapsed into a haughty spirit, and had encouraged her boy in his insolence to Sarah's son, and therefore she must be chastened yet again; and it was equally needful that the high-spirited lad should for a little bear the yoke in his youth, and that he who would grow up to be the wild man, the father of the unconquerable Arab, should feel the power of God before he received the fulfillment of the promise given to him in answer to Abraham's prayer. If I read the text right, while the mother was thus weeping, the child, almost lost to all around, was nevertheless conscious enough of his own helpless condition, and sufficiently mindful of his father's God to cry in his soul to heaven for help; and the Lord heard not so much the mother's weeping (for the feebleness of her faith, which ought to have been stronger in memory of a former deliverance, hindered her prayer), but the silent, unuttered prayers of the fainting lad went up into the ears of Elohim, and the angel of Elohim appeared, and pointed to the well. The child received the needed draft of water, was soon restored, and in him and his posterity the promise of God received and continues to receive a large fulfillment. I am not about to speak upon that narrative except as it serves me with an illustration for the subject which I would now press upon you.

Behold the compassion of a mother for her child expiring with thirst, and remember that such a compassion ought all Christians to feel toward souls that are perishing for lack of Christ, perishing eternally, perishing without hope of salvation. If the mother lifted up her voice and wept, so also should we; and if the contemplation of her dying child was all too painful for her, so may the contemplation of the wrath to come, which is to pass upon every soul that dies impenitent, become too painful for us, but yet at the same time it should stimulate us to earnest prayer and ardent effort for the salvation of our fellowmen.

I shall speak, this morning, upon *compassion for souls, the reasons which justify it, the sight it dreads, the temptation it must fight against, the paths it should pursue, the encouragement it may receive.*

I. Compassion for souls—the reasons which justify it, no, compel it.

It scarcely needs that I do more than rehearse in bare outline the reasons why we should tenderly compassionate the perishing sons of men. For first, observe, *the dreadful nature of the calamity which will overwhelm them.* Calamities occurring to our fellowmen naturally awaken in us a feeling of commiseration; but what calamity under heaven can be equal to the ruin of a soul? What misery can be equal to that of a man cast away from God, and subject to his wrath world without end! Today your hearts are moved as you hear the harrowing details of war [the Franco-Prussian War]. They have been dreadful indeed: houses burned, happy families driven as vagabonds upon the face of the earth, domestic circles and quiet households broken up, men wounded, mangled, massacred by thousands, and starved, I was about to say, by millions; but the miseries of war, if they were confined to this world alone, were nothing compared with the enormous catastrophe of tens of thousands of spirits accursed by sin, and driven by justice into the place "where their worm dieth not, and their fire is not quenched." The edge of the sword grows blunt at last, the flame of war dies out for want of fuel, but lo! I see before me a sword which is never quiet, a fire unquenchable. Alas! that the souls of men should fall beneath the infinite ire of justice.

All your hearts have been moved of late with the thought of famine, famine in a great city. The dogs of war, and this the fiercest mastiff of them all, have laid hold upon the fair throat of the beautiful city which thought to sit as a lady forever and see no sorrow; you are hastening with your gifts, if possible to remove her urgent want and to avert her starvation; but what is a famine of bread compared with that famine of the soul which our Lord describes when he represents it as pleading in vain for a drop of water to cool its tongue tormented in the flame? To be without bread for the body is terrible, but to be without the bread of life eternal, none of us can tell the weight of horror which lies there! When Robert Hall in one of the grand flights of his eloquence pictured the funeral of a lost soul, he made the sun to veil his light, and the moon her brightness; he covered the ocean with mourning and the heavens with sackcloth, and declared that if the whole fabric of nature could become animated and vocal, it would not be possible for her to utter a groan too deep, or a cry too piercing to express the magnitude and extent of the catastrophe. Time is not long enough for the sore lamentation which should attend the obsequies of a lost soul. Eternity must be charged with that boundless woe, and must utter it in weeping and wailing and gnashing of teeth. Not the tongues of prophets, nor of seraphs, could set forth all the sorrow of what it is to be condemned from the mouth of mercy, damned by the Savior who died to save, pronounced accursed by rejected love. The evil is so immense that imagination finds no place, and understanding utterly fails. Brethren, if our bowels do not yearn for men who are daily hastening toward destruction, are we men at all?

I could abundantly justify compassion for perishing men, even on the ground of *natural feelings*. A mother who did not, like Hagar, weep for her dying child—call her not "mother," call her "monster." A man who passes through the scenes of misery which even this city presents in its more squalid quarters, and yet is never disturbed by them, I venture to say he is unworthy of the name of man. Even the common sorrows of our race may well suffuse our eyes with tears, but the eternal sorrow, the infinite lake of misery—he who grieves not for this, write him down a demon, though he wear the image and semblance of a man. Do not think the less of this argument because I base it upon feelings common to all of woman born, for remember that grace does not destroy our manhood when it elevates it to a higher condition.

In this instance, what nature suggests grace enforces. The more we become what we shall be, the more will compassion rule our hearts. The Lord Jesus Christ, who is the pattern and mirror of perfect manhood, what said he concerning the sins and the woes of Jerusalem? He knew Jerusalem must perish; did he bury his pity beneath the fact of the divine decree, and steel his heart by the thought of the sovereignty or the justice that would be resplendent in the city's destruction? No, not he, but with eyes gushing like founts, he cried, "O Jerusalem, Jerusalem, how often would I have gathered thy children together as a hen gathereth her chickens under her wings! and ye would not." If you would be like Jesus, you must be tender and very pitiful. You would be as unlike him as possible if we could sit down in grim content, and, with a Stoic's philosophy, turn all the flesh within you into stone. If it be natural, then, and above all, if it be natural to the higher grace-given nature, I beseech you, let your hearts be moved with pity, do not endure to see the spiritual death of mankind. Be in agony as often as you contemplate the ruin of any soul of the seed of Adam.

Brethren, *the whole run and current, and tenor and spirit of the gospel* influences us to compassion. You are debtors, for what were you if compassion had not come to your rescue? Divine compassion, all undeserved and free, has redeemed you from your vain conversation. Surely those who receive mercy should show mercy; those who owe all they have to the pity of God should not be pitiless to their brethren. The Savior never for a moment tolerates the self-righteous isolation which would make you despise the prodigal, and cavil at his restoration, much less the Cainite spirit which cries, "Am I my brother's keeper?" No doctrine is rightly received by you if it freezes the genial current of your Christian compassion. You may know the truth of the doctrine, but you do not know the doctrine in truth if it makes you gaze on the wrath to come without emotions of pity for immortal souls. You shall find everywhere throughout the gospel that it rings of brotherly love, tender mercy, and weeping pity. If you have indeed received it in its power, the love of Christ will melt your spirit to compassion for those who are despising Christ and sealing their own destruction.

Let me beseech you to believe that it is *needful* as well as justifiable that you should feel compassion for the sons of men. You all desire to glorify Christ by becoming soul winners—I hope you do—and be it remembered that, other things being equal, he is the fittest in God's hand to win souls who pities souls most. I believe he preaches best who loves best, and in the Sunday school and in private life, each soul seeker shall have the blessing very much in proportion to his yearning for it. Paul becomes a savior of many because his heart's desire and prayer to God is that they may be saved. If you *can* live without souls being converted, you shall live without their being converted; but if your soul breaks for the longing that it has toward Christ's glory and the conversion of the ungodly, if like her of old you say, "Give me children, or I die," your insatiable hunger shall be satisfied, the craving of your spirit shall be gratified. Oh, I would to God there should come upon us a divine hunger which cannot stay itself except men yield themselves to Jesus; an intense, earnest, longing, panting desire that men should submit themselves to the gospel of Jesus. This will teach you better than the best college training how to deal with human hearts. This will give the stammering tongue the ready word; the hot heart shall burn the cords which held fast the tongue. You shall become wise to win souls, even though you never exhibit the brilliance of eloquence or the force of logic. Men shall wonder at your power—the secret shall be hidden from them, the fact being that the Holy Ghost shall overshadow you, and your heart shall teach you wisdom, God teaching your heart. Deep feeling on your part for others shall make others feel for themselves, and God shall bless you, and that right early.

But I stand not here any longer to justify what I would far rather commend and personally feel.

Did Christ o'er sinners weep,
And shall our cheeks be dry?
Let floods of consecrated grief
Stream forth from every eye.

Is God all love, and shall God's children be hard and cold? Shall heaven compassionate and shall not earth that has received hearer's mercy send back the echo of compassion? O God, make us imitators of thee in thy pity toward erring men.

II. We shall pass on to notice *the sight which true compassion dreads.*

Like Hagar, the compassionate spirit says, "Let me not see the death of the child," or as some have read it, "How can I see the death of the child?" To contemplate a soul's passing away without hope is too terrible a task! I do not wonder that ingenious persons have invented theories which aim at mitigating the terrors of the world to come to the impenitent. It is natural they should do so, for the facts are so alarming as they are truthfully given us in God's Word, that if we desire to preach comfortable doctrine and such as will quiet the consciences of idle professors, we must dilute the awful truth. The revelation of God concerning the doom of the wicked is so overwhelming as to make it penal, no, I was about to say damnable, to be indifferent and careless in the work of evangelizing the world. I do not wonder that this error in doctrine springs up just now when abounding callousness of heart needs an excuse for itself. What better pillow for idle heads than the doctrine that the finally impenitent become extinct? The logical reasoning of the sinner is, "Let us eat and drink, for tomorrow we die," and the professing Christian is not slow to feel an ease of heart from pressing responsibilities when he accepts so consolatory an opinion. Forbear this sleeping draft, I pray you, for in very deed the sharp stimulant of the truth itself is abundantly needful; even when thus stirred to duty, we are sluggish enough, and need not that these sweet but sleep-producing theories should operate upon us.

For a moment, I beseech you, contemplate that which causes horror to every tender heart; behold, I pray you, a soul lost, lost beyond all hope of restitution. Heaven's gates have shut upon the sanctified, and the myriads of the redeemed are there, but that soul is not among them, for it passed out of this world without having washed its robes in Jesus' blood. For it there are no harps of gold, no thrones of glory, no exultation with Christ; from all the bliss of heaven it is forever excluded. This punishment of loss were a heavy enough theme for contemplation. The old divines used to speak much of the *poena damni*, or the punishment of loss; there were enough in that phase of the future to make us mourn bitterly, as David did for Absalom. My child shut out of heaven! My husband absent from the seats of the blessed! My sister, my brother not in glory! When the Lord counts up his chosen, my dear companion outside the gates of pearl, outside the jeweled battlements of the New Jerusalem! O God, 'tis a heartbreaking sorrow to think of this. But then comes the punishment added to the loss. What says the Savior? "Where their worm dieth not, and the fire is not quenched." "These shall go away into everlasting punishment." And yet again, "And shall cut him asunder, and appoint him his portion with the hypocrites." And yet again, "Into outer darkness: there shall be weeping and gnashing of teeth."

"Metaphors," say you. It is true, but not meaningless metaphors. There is a meaning in each expression—and rest assured though man's metaphors sometimes exaggerate, God's never do; his symbols everywhere are true; never is there an exaggeration in the language of inspiration. Extravagances of utterance! He uses them not; his figures are substantial truth. Terrible as the scriptural emblems of punishment are, they set forth matters of undoubted fact, which if a man could look upon this day, the sight might blanch his hair and quench his eye. If we could hear the wailings of the pit for a moment, we should earnestly entreat that we might never hear them again. We have to thank God that we are not allowed to hear the dolorous cries of the lost, for if we did they would make our life bitter as gall. I cast a veil over that which I cannot paint; like Hagar I cannot bear to look at the dread reality which it breaks my heart to think upon.

How all this gathers intensity, when it comes to be our own child, our own friend! Hagar might perhaps have looked upon a dying child, but not upon her dying Ishmael. Can you bear now to think for a moment of the perdition of your own flesh and blood? Does not your spirit flinch and draw back with horror instinctively at the idea of one of your own family being lost? Yet, as a matter of stern fact, you know that some of them will be lost if they die as they are now living? At God's right hand they cannot stand unless they be made new creatures in Christ Jesus. You know that, do not try to forget it.

It will greatly add to your feeling of sorrow if you are forced to feel that the ruin of your child or of any other person may have been partly caused by your example. It must be a dreadful thing for a father to feel, "My boy learned to drink from me; my child heard the first blasphemous word from his father's lips." Or mother, if your dying daughter should say, "I was led into temptation by my mother's example," what a grief will this be! O parents, converted late in life, you cannot undo the evil which you have already done; God has forgiven you, but the mischief worked in your children's characters is indelible, unless the grace of God step in. I want you to seek after that grace with great earnestness. As you must confess that you have helped to train your child as a servant of sin, will you not long to see your evil work undone before it ends in your child's eternal destruction?

If we shall have to feel that the ruin of any of our friends or relations is partly occasioned by our own personal neglect of religion, it will cause us bitter pangs. If our example has been excellent and admirable in all respects, but that we have forgotten the Lord and his Christ, it will have been nonetheless injurious to men's souls. I sometimes think that these examples are the very worst in their effect. Immoral, ungodly men can hardly work the same measure of mischief as moral but unchristian men. I will tell you why. The ungodly quote the orderly life of the moralist as an argument that there can be goodness apart from Christianity, and this often helps men to rest satisfied apart from Christ Jesus. And what, O moralist, though you never taught your child a vice, if you taught it unbelief, and if your example helped to harm its heart in bold rebellion against God! Ah! then, how will you blame yourself when you are converted or curse yourself if both you and your child perish.

Dear friends, it makes a terrible addition to the sight of a soul being lost if we have to feel we were under responsibility concerning it, and have been in any measure unfaithful. I cannot bear the idea of any of my congregation perishing, for in addition to the compassion I hope I feel, I am influenced by a further additional consideration, for I am set as a watchman to your souls. When any die, I ask myself, "Was I faithful? Did I speak all the truth? And did I speak it from my very soul every time I preached?" John Walsh, the famous Scotch preacher, was often out of bed in the coldest night, by the hour together, in supplication; and when someone wondered that he spent so many hours upon his knees, he said, "Ah, man, I have three thousand souls to give account of in the day of judgment, and I do not know but what it is going very ill with some of them." Alas! I have more than that to give account of, and well may I cry to God that I may not see you perish. Oh, may it never be that you shall go from these pews to the lowest hell. You, too, my fellow Christian, have your own responsibilities, each one in your measure— your children, your school classes, your servants, yes, and your neighbors, for if you are not doing any good and do not assume any responsibility toward the regions in which you dwell, that responsibility rests upon you nonetheless. You cannot live in a district without being responsible to God for doing something toward the bettering of the people among whom you reside. Can you endure it then, that your neighbors should sink into hell? Do not your hearts long for their salvation?

Is it not an awful thing that a soul should perish with the gospel so near? If Ishmael had died, and the water had been within bowshot, and yet unseen till too late, it had been a dreadful reflection for the mother. Would she not have torn her hair with double sorrow? And yet many of you are being lost with the gospel ringing in your ears; you are perishing while Christ is lifted up before you; you are dying in the camp through the serpent's bite, though the brazen serpent is yonder before your eyes, and with many tears we cry to you, "Look unto Jesus Christ, and live!" Ah, woe is me, woe is me, if you perish when salvation is brought so close home to you. Some of you are very near the kingdom of God; you are very anxious, very concerned, but you have not believed in Jesus; you have much that is good, but one thing you lack. Will you perish for lack of only one thing? A thousand pities will it be if you make shipwreck in the harbor's mouth and go to hell from the gates of heaven.

We must add to all this, the remembrance that it is not one soul which is lost, but tens of thousands are going down to the pit. Mr. Beecher said in one of his sermons, "If there were a great bell hung high in heaven which the angels swung every time a soul was lost, how constantly would its solemn toll be heard!" A soul lost! The thunder would not suffice to make a knell for a lost spirit. Each time the clock ticks, a soul departs out of this world, perhaps oftener than that, and out of those who make the last journey how few mount to the skies; what multitudes descend to endless woe! O Christians, pull up the sluices of your souls and let your hearts pour out themselves in rivers of compassion.

III. In the third place, I said I would speak upon *compassion for the souls of men—the temptation it must resist.*

We must not fall into the temptation to imitate the example of Hagar too closely. She put the child under the shrubs and turned away her gaze from the all-too-mournful spectacle. She could not endure to look, but she sat where she could watch in despair. There is a temptation with each one of us to try to forget that souls are being lost. I can go home to my house along respectable streets, and naturally should choose that way, for then I need not see the poverty of the lowest quarters of the city, but am I right if I try to forget that there are Bethnal Greens and Kent Streets, and such like abodes of poverty? The close courts, the cellars, the crowded garrets, the lodging houses—am I to forget that these exist? Surely the only way for a charitable mind to sleep comfortably in London is to forget how one half of the population lives; but is it our object to live comfortably? Are we such brute beasts that comfort is all we care for; like swine in their sty? No, brethren, let us recall to our memories the sins of our great city, its sorrows and griefs, and let us remember also the sins and sorrows of the wide, wide world, and the tens of thousands of our race who are passing constantly into eternity. No, look at them! Do not close those eyes! Does the horror of the vision make your eyeballs ache? Then look until your heart aches too, and your spirit breaks forth in vehement agony before the Lord.

Look down into hell a moment; open wide the door; listen, and listen yet again. You say you cannot, it sickens your soul; let it be sickened, and in its swooning let it fall back into the arms of Christ the Savior, and breathe out a cry that he would hasten to save men from the wrath to come. Do not ignore, I pray you, what does exist. It is a matter of fact that in this congregation many are going down to hell, that in this city there are multitudes who are hastening as certainly to perdition as time is hastening to eternity. It is no dream, no fiction of a fevered brain that there is a hell. If you think so, then why dare you call yourselves Christians? Renounce your Bible, renounce your baptism, renounce your profession if one spark of honesty remains in you. Call not yourselves Christians when you deny the teaching of your Master. Since assuredly there is a dreadful hell, shut not your eyes to it, put not the souls of your fellows away among the shrubs, and sit not down in supineness. Come and look, come and look, I say, till your hearts break at the sight. Hear the cries of dying men whose consciences are awakened too late. Hear the groans of spirits who are feeling the sure consequences of sin, where sin's cure will never avail them. Let this stir you, my brethren, to action—to action immediate and intense. You tell me I preach dreadful things; yes, and they are wanted, they are wanted. Was there ever such a happy age as this? Were there ever such sleepy persons as ourselves? Take heed lest you take sad precedence of all others in the accusations of conscience, because knowing the gospel, and enjoying it, you nevertheless use so little exertion in spreading it abroad among the human race. Let us shun the temptation which Hagar's example might suggest.

IV. I will now speak upon *the path which true compassion will be sure to follow*; and what is that?

First of all, *true pity does all it can*. Before Hagar sat down and wept, she had done her utmost for her boy; she had given him the last drop from the bottle; she had supported his tottering footsteps, she had sought out the place under the shrubs where he might be a little sheltered, she had laid him down gently with soothing words, and then, but not till then, she sat herself down. Have we done all that it is possible for us to do for the unconverted around us? There are preventable causes of men's ruin. Some causes you and I cannot touch, but there are some we ought at once to remove. For instance, it is certain that many perish through ignorance. It ought never to be that a soul should perish of ignorance within a mile of where a Christian lives. I would even allot a wider area in regions where the people dwell not so thickly. It should at least be the resolve of each Christian, "Within this district where I live, so far as my ability goes, everybody shall know the gospel by some means or other. If I cannot speak to each one, I will send something for him to read; it shall not be said that a man lost his way forever because he had no Bible." The Holy Ghost alone can lead men into the truth, but it is our part to put the letter of the Word before all men's eyes.

Prejudice, too, is another preventable cause of unbelief. Some will not hear the gospel, or listen to it, because of their notions of its sternness, or of the moroseness of its professors. Such a prejudice may effectually close their hearts; be it yours to remove it. Be kind to the ungodly; be loving, be tender, be affable, be generous to them, so that you may remove all unnecessary antipathy to the gospel of Jesus. Do them all the good you can for their bodies, that they may be the more likely to believe in your love toward their souls. Let it be said by each one here, "If a soul perishes, I, at least, will have done all in my power to reclaim it."

But what next does compassion do? Having done all it can, it sits down and weeps over its own feebleness. I have not the pathos wherewith to describe to you the mother sitting there and pouring out her tears, and lifting up her plaintive voice over her child. The voice of a broken heart cannot be described, it must be heard. But ah! there is wonderful power with God in the strong crying and tears of his people. If you know how to weep before the Lord, he will yield to tears what he will not yield to anything besides. O ye saints, compassionate sinners; sigh and cry for them; be able to say, as Whitefield could to his congregation, "Sirs, if ye are lost, it is not for want of my weeping for you, for I pour out my soul day and night in petitions unto God that you may live." When Hagar's compassion had wailed itself out, she looked unto God, and God heard her. Take care that your prayers be abundant and continuous for those who are dying without hope.

And then what else does Hagar teach us? She stood there ready to do anything that was needful after the Lord had interposed. The angel opened her eyes; until then she was powerless, and sat and wept and prayed, but when he pointed to the well, did she linger for a minute? Was she unprepared with the bottle wherewith to draw water? Did she delay to put it to her child's lips? Was she slack in the blessed task? Oh no! With what alacrity did she spring to the well; with what speed did she fill the bottle; with what motherly joy did she hasten to her child and gave him the saving draft! And so I want every member here to stand ready to mark the faintest indication of grace in any soul. Watch always for the beginning of their conversion, be ready with the bottle of promise to carry a little comfort to their parched lips; watch with a mother's earnestness, watch for the opportunity of doing good to souls; yearn over them, so that when God shall work, you shall work with him *instantly*, and Jesus shall not be hindered because of your carelessness and want of faith. This is the path which the true Christian should pursue. He is earnest for souls, and therefore he lays himself out for them. If we did really know what souls are, and what it is for them to be cast away, those of us who have done very little or nothing would begin to work for Christ directly.

It is said in an old classic story, that a certain king of Lydia had a son who had been dumb from his birth, but when Lydia was captured, a soldier was about to kill the king, when the young man suddenly found a tongue, and cried out, "Soldier, would you kill the king?" He had never spoken a word before, but his astonishment and fear gave him speech. And I think if you had been dumb to that moment, if you indeed saw your own children and neighbors going down into the pit, you would cry out, "Though I never spoke before, I will speak now. Poor souls, believe in Christ, and you shall be saved." You do not know how such an utterance as that, however simple, might be blessed.

A very little child once found herself in company with an old man of eighty, a fine old man who loved little children, and who took the child upon his knee. The little one turning round to him said, "Sir, I got a grandpa just like you, and my grandpa love Jesus Christ, does you?" He said, "I was eighty-four years of age and had lived always among Christian people, but nobody ever thought it worth his while to say as much as that to me." That little child was the instrument of the old man's conversion. So have I heard the story. He knew he had not loved the Savior, and he began to seek him, and in his old age he found salvation. If as much as that is possible to a child, it is possible to you. O dear brother, if you love Jesus, burst the bonds of timidity, or it may be of supineness; snap all fetters, and from this day feel that you cannot bear to think of the ruin of a soul, and must seek its salvation if there be in earth or heaven ways and means by which you can bring a blessing to it.

V. But I must close, and the last point shall be *the encouragement which true compassion for souls will always receive*.

First take the case in hand. The mother compassionated, God compassionated too. You pity, God pities. The motions of God's Spirit in the souls of his people are the footfalls of God's eternal purposes about to be fulfilled. It is always a hopeful sign for a man that another man prays for him. There is a difficulty in getting a man to hell whom a child of God is drawing toward heaven by his intercessions. Satan is often defeated in his temptations by the intercession of the saints. Have hope then that your personal sense of compassion for souls is an indication that such souls God will bless. Ishmael, whom Hagar pitied, was a lad about whom promises had been made large and broad; he could not die; she had forgotten that, but God had not. No thirst could possibly destroy him, for God had said he would make of him a great nation. Let us hope that those for whom you and I are praying and laboring are in God's eternal purpose secured from hell, because the blood of Christ has bought them, and they must be the Lord's. Our prayers are ensigns of the will of God. The Holy Ghost leads us to pray for those whom he intends effectually to call.

Moreover, those we pray for, we may not know it, but there may be in their souls at this time a stirring of divine life. Hagar did not know that her son was praying, but God did. The lad did not speak, but God heard his heart cry. Children are often very reticent to their parents. Often and often have I talked with young lads about their souls, who have told me that they could not talk to their fathers upon such matters. I know it was so with me. When I was under concern of soul, the last persons I should have elected to speak to upon religion would have been my parents, not out of want of love to them, nor absence of love on their part; but so it was. A strange feeling of diffidence pervades a seeking soul, and drives it from its friends. Those whom you are praying for may be praying too, and you do not know it; but the time of love will come when their secret yearnings will be revealed to your earnest endeavors.

The lad was preserved after all, the well of waters was revealed, and the bottle put to his lips. It will be a great comfort to you to believe that God will hear importunate prayers. Your child will be saved, your husband will be brought in yet, good woman, only pray on. Your neighbor shall be brought to hear the truth and be converted, only be earnest about it.

I do not know how to preach this morning; the tongue cannot readily speak when the heart feels too much. I pray that we may have a great revival of religion in our midst as a church; my spirit longs and pants for it. I see a great engine of enormous strength, and a well-fashioned machine: the machine cannot work of itself, it has no power in it, but if I could get the band to unite the machine with the engine, what might be done! Behold, I see the omnipotence of God and the organization of this church. Oh, that I could get the band to bind the two together! The band is living faith. Do you possess it? Brethren, help me to pass it around the fly wheel, and oh, how God will work, and we will work through his power, and what glorious things shall be done for Christ! We must receive power from on high, and faith is the belt that shall convey that power to us. The divine strength shall be manifest through our weakness. Cease not to pray. More than you ever have done, intercede for a blessing, and the Lord will bless us: he will bless us, and all the ends of the earth shall fear him. Amen.

Sarah: And Her Daughters

❧❧❧

Delivered on Thursday evening, April 28, 1881, at the Metropolitan Tabernacle, Newington. No. 1633.

Look unto Abraham your father, and unto Sarah that bare you.—ISAIAH 51:2

*Even as Sara obeyed Abraham, calling him lord: whose daughters ye are, as
long as ye do well, and are not afraid with any amazement.*—1 PETER 3:6

I desire to thank God for having had the privilege of preaching in Exeter
Hall yesterday to a large congregation from the whole of the second verse of
Isaiah 51—"Look unto Abraham your father, and unto Sarah that bare you: for
I called him alone, and blessed him, and increased him." On that occasion I
confined my remarks to Abraham, and tried to make prominent the facts that
God called him while he was a heathen man, one man, and a lone man, and
yet he blessed him, and made him the founder of his people, multiplying his
seed as the stars and as the sand by the seashore. I devoutly beseech the Lord
to accept my testimony to his power, and to increase the faith of the many of
his servants to whom I spoke on that occasion. His Holy Spirit gave me the
word; may he cause his saints to feed upon it.

Now, I never like to do an injustice to anybody, and I feel that I did not in
that sermon speak sufficiently about Sarah, though I did not quite forget her.
Let us make up for our omissions. If we had Abraham at Exeter Hall yesterday morning, we will have Sarah at the tabernacle tonight, and maybe we shall
learn a lesson from her holy character as well as from that of her husband, and
the two lessons combined may go to the perfecting of each other. May our
great Teacher, the Holy Spirit, now instruct us.

To begin with, let us note what a happy circumstance it is when a godly,
gracious man has an equally godly and gracious wife. It is ill when there is a
difference, a radical difference, between husband and wife—when one fears
God, and the other has no regard to him. What a pain it is to a Christian
woman to be yoked with an unbelieving husband. In a case which I remember, the husband lived all his life indifferent to divine things, while the wife was
an earnest Christian woman, and saw all her children grow up in the ways of

the Lord. The father lived unregenerate, and died without giving any testimony of a change of heart.

When our sister speaks of him, it is with fearful anguish; she does not know what to say, but leaves the matter in the hands of God, often sighing, "Oh, that by a word or a look, I could have been enabled to indulge a hope that my poor husband looked to Jesus at the last." The same must be the case of a husband who has an ungodly wife. However much God may bless him in all other respects, there seems to be a great miss there, as if a part of the sun were eclipsed—that a part of life which should be all light is left in thick darkness. Oh, let those of us who have the happiness of being joined together in the Lord thank and bless God every time we remember each other. Let us pray God that, having such a privilege, so that our prayers are not hindered by irreligious partners, we may never hinder our prayers ourselves: God grant that we may give unto his name great glory because of his choice favor to us in this respect. Abraham had cause to praise God for Sarah, and Sarah was grateful for Abraham. I have not the slightest doubt that Sarah's character owed its excellence very much to Abraham: I should not wonder, however, if we discover when all things are revealed that Abraham owed as much to Sarah. They probably learned from each other; sometimes the weaker comforted the stronger, and often the stronger sustained the weaker. I should not wonder if a mutual interchange of their several graces tended to make them both rich in the things of God. Maybe Abraham had not been all that Abraham was if Sarah had not been all that Sarah was. Our first text bids us, "Look to Sarah," and we do look on her, and we thank God if we, like Abraham, are favored with holy consorts, whose amiable tempers and loving characters tend to make us better servants of God.

We notice, next, as we look to Sarah, that God does not forget the lesser lights. Abraham shines like a star of the first magnitude, and we do not at first sight observe that other star, with light so bright and pure, shining with milder radiance but with kindred luster, close at his side. The light of Mamre, which is known under the name of Abraham, resolves itself into a double star when we apply the telescope of reflection and observation. To the common eye Abraham is the sole character, and ordinary people overlook his faithful spouse, but God does not overlook. Our God never omits the good who are obscure. You may depend upon it that there is no such difference in the love of God toward different persons as should make him fix his eye only upon those that are strong, and omit those who are weak. Our eyes spy out the great things, but God's eye is such that nothing is great with him, and nothing is little. He is infinite, and therefore nothing bears any comparison to him. You remember how it is written that he who created the stars, and called them by name, also binds up the broken in heart, and heals all their wounds. He who treasures the names of his apostles notes also the women that followed in his train. He who marks the brave confessors and the bold preachers of the gospel also remembers those helpers who labor quietly in the gospel in places of retirement into which the hawk's eye of history seldom pries. Let, therefore, those here present, who count themselves to be of the tribe of Benjamin, to be little in Israel, never be discouraged on that account—for the Lord is too great to despise the little ones. You are not forgotten of God, O you who are overlooked by men. The Lord's eye is upon the creeping things innumerable in the great sea as well as upon leviathan: he will observe you. If he sends the deluging showers that make strong the cedars, which are full of sap and adorn the brow of Lebanon, so does he send to each tiny blade of grass its own drop of dew. God forgets not the less in his care for the greater. Sarah was in life covered with the shield of the Almighty as well as Abraham, her husband: in death she rested in the same tomb; in heaven she has the same joy; in the book of the Lord she has the same record.

Next notice that it would be well for us to imitate God in this: in not forgetting the lesser lights. I do not know that great men are often good examples. I am sorry when, because men have been clever and successful, they are held up to imitation, though their motives and morals have been questionable. I would sooner men were stupid and honest than clever and tricky; it is better to act rightly and fail altogether than succeed by falsehood and cunning; I would sooner bid my son imitate an honest man who has no talent, and whose life is unsuccessful, than point him to the cleverest and greatest that ever lived, whose life has become a brilliant success, but whose principles are condemnable. Learn not from the great but from the good: be not dazzled by success, but follow the safer light of truth and right. But so it is that men mainly observe that only which is written in big letters; but you know the choicest part of God's books are printed in small characters. They who would only know the rudiments may spell out the words in large type which are for babes; but those who want to be fully instructed must sit down and read the small print of God, given us in lives of saints whom most men neglect. Some of the choicest virtues are not so much seen in the great as in the quiet, obscure life. Many a Christian woman manifests a glory of character that is to be found in no public man. I am sure that many a flower that is "born to blush unseen" and, as we think, to "waste its fragrance on the desert air" [Thomas Gray] is fairer than the beauties which reign in the conservatory, and are the admiration of all. God has ways of producing very choice things on a small scale. As rare pearls and precious stones are never great masses of rock, but always lie within a narrow compass, so full often the fairest and richest virtues are to be found in the humblest individuals. A man may be too great to be good, but he cannot be too little to be gracious. Do not, therefore, always be studying Abraham, the greater character. Does not the text say, "Look unto Abraham, your father, and unto Sarah that bare you"? You have not learned the full lesson of patriarchal life until you have been in the tent with Sarah as well as among the flocks with her husband.

Furthermore, another reflection arises, namely, that faith reveals itself in various ways. Faith makes one person this, and another that. Faith in Noah makes him a shipbuilder, and the second of the world's great fathers. Faith in Abraham makes him a pilgrim and a stranger. Faith in Moses makes him plague Egypt, and feed a nation forty years in the wilderness. Faith in David makes him kill a giant, save a kingdom, and ascend a throne. Faith in Samson makes him slay a thousand Philistines, and in Rahab, it makes her save two Israelites. Faith has many ways of working, and it works according to the condition and position of the person in whom it dwells. Sarah does not become Abraham, nor does Abraham become Sarah. Faith in Isaac does not make him the same royal man as Abraham: he is always tame and gentle rather than great and noble; he comes in like a valley between the two great hills of Abraham and Jacob. Isaac is Isaac, and Isaac has such virtue as becomes him whom the Lord loved; and Jacob, too, is Jacob, and not his father; he is active and energetic and farseeing. God does not by his grace lift us out of our place. A man is made gentle, but he is not made a fool. A woman is made brave, but grace never made her masterful and domineering. Grace does not make the child so self-willed that he disobeys his father; it is something else that does that. Grace does not take away from the father his authority to command the child. It leaves us where we were, in a certain sense, as to our position, and the fruit it bears is congruous to that position.

Thus Sarah is beautified with the virtues that adorn a woman, while Abraham is adorned with all the excellences which are becoming in a godly man. According as the virtue is required, so is it produced. If the circumstances require courage, God makes his servant heroic; if the circumstances require great modesty and prudence, modesty and prudence are given. Faith is a wonderful magician's wand; it works marvels, it achieves impossibilities, it grasps the incomprehensible. Faith can be used anywhere—in the highest heaven touching the ear of God, and winning our desire of him, and in the lowest places of the earth among the poor and fallen, cheering and upraising them. Faith will quench the violence of fire, turn the edge of the sword, snatch the prey from the enemy and turn the alien to flight. There is nothing which it cannot do. It is a principle available for all times, to be used on all occasions, suitable to be used by all men for all holy ends. Those who have been taught the sacred art of believing God are the truly learned: no degree of the foremost university can equal in value that which comes with much boldness in the faith. We shall see tonight that if Abraham walks before God and is perfect—if he smites the kings that have carried Lot captive, if he does such deeds of prowess as become a man—the selfsame faith makes Sarah walk before God in her perfectness, and she performs the actions which become her womanhood, and she, too, is written among the worthies of faith who magnified the Lord.

We are led by our second text to look at the fruit of faith in Sarah. There were two fruits of faith in Sarah—she did well, and she was not afraid with any amazement. We will begin with the first.

I. It is said of her that *she did well*, "whose daughters ye are, as long as ye do well."

She did well as a wife. She was all her husband could desire, and when, at the age of 127 years, she at last fell on sleep, it is said that Abraham not only mourned for her, but the old man wept for her most true and genuine tears of sorrow. He wept for the loss of one who had been the life of his house. As a wife she did well. All the duties that were incumbent upon her as the queen of that traveling company were performed admirably, and we find no fault mentioned concerning her in that respect.

She did well as a hostess. It was her duty, as her husband was given to hospitality, to be willing to entertain his guests; and the one instance recorded is, no doubt, the representation of her common mode of procedure. Though she was truly a princess, yet she kneaded the dough and prepared the bread for her husband's guests. They came suddenly, but she had no complaint to make. She was, indeed, always ready to lay herself out to perform that which was one of the highest duties of a God-fearing household in those primitive times.

She did well also as a mother. We are sure she did, because we find that her son Isaac was so excellent a man; and you may say what you will, but in the hand of God the mother forms the boy's character. Perhaps the father unconsciously influences the girls, but the mother has evidently most influence over the sons. Any of us can bear witness that it is so in our own case. There are exceptions, of course; but, for the most part, the mother is the queen of the son, and he looks up to her with infinite respect if she be at all such as can be respected. Sarah by faith did her work with Isaac well, for from the very first, in his yielding to his father when he was to be offered up as a sacrifice, we see in him evidence of a holy obedience and faith in God which were seldom equaled, and were never surpassed.

Besides that, it is written that God said of Abraham, "I know Abraham, that he will command his children and his household after him." There is one trait in Abraham's character that, wherever he went, he set up an altar unto the Lord. His rule was a tent and an altar. Dear friends, do you always make these two things go together—a tent and an altar? Where you dwell is there sure to be family worship there? I am afraid that many families neglect it, and often it is so because husband and wife are not agreed about it, and I feel sure that there would not have been that invariable setting up of the worship of God by Abraham in his tent unless Sarah had been as godly as himself.

She did well, also, as a believer, and that is no mean point. As a believer when Abraham was called to separate himself from his kindred, Sarah went with him. She would adopt the separated life too, and the same caravan which traveled across the desert with Abraham for its master had Sarah for its mistress. She continued with him, believing in God with perseverance. Though they had no city to dwell in, she continued the roaming life with her husband, looking for "a city which hath foundations, whose builder and maker is God." She believed God's promise with all her heart, though she laughed once, because when the promise neared its realization it overwhelmed her; it was but a slip for the moment, for it is written by the apostle in Hebrews 11, "Through faith also Sarah herself received strength to conceive seed, and was delivered of a child when she was past age, because she judged him faithful who had promised." It was not by nature, but by faith, that Isaac was born, the child of another sort of laughter than that of doubt, the child according to the promise of God. She was a believing woman, then, and she lived a believing life; and so she did well.

She did well to her parents, well to her husband, well to her household, well to her guests, well before her God. Oh, that all professing Christian people had a faith that showed itself in doing well!

But never let it be forgotten that, though we preach faith, faith, faith, as the great means of salvation, yet we never say that you are saved unless there is a change worked in you, and good works are produced in you; for "faith without works is dead, being alone." Faith saves, but it is the faith which causes men to do well; and if there be a faith (and there is such a faith) which leaves a man just what he was, and permits him to indulge in sin, it is the faith of devils; perhaps not so good as that, for "the devils believe and tremble," whereas these hypocrites profess to believe, and yet dare to defy God, and seem to have no fear of him whatsoever. Sarah had this testimony from the Lord, that she did well; and her daughters you are, all of you who believe, if you do well. Be no discredit to your queenly mother. Take care that you honor your spiritual parentage, and maintain the high prestige of the elect family.

II. The point that I am to dwell upon just now is this, that she proved her faith by a second evidence: *she was "not afraid with any amazement."*

The text says, "whose daughters ye are, as long as ye do well, and are not afraid with any amazement."

She was calm and quiet, and was not put in fear by any terror. There were several occasions in which she might have been much disquieted and put about. The first was in the breaking up of her house life. You see her husband, Abraham, gets a call to go from Ur of the Chaldees. Well, it is a considerable journey, and they move to Haran. There are some women—unbelieving women—who would not have understood that. Why does he want to go away from the land in which he lives, and from all our kindred, away to Haran? That would have been her question had she not been a partaker in her husband's faith. An unbelieving woman would have said, "A call from God? Nonsense! Fanaticism! I do not believe in it," and when she saw that her husband would go she would have been afraid with great amazement. When Abraham went to Haran with his father, Terah, and Terah died in Haran, and then God called him to go farther, they had to cross the Euphrates and get right away into a land which he knew nothing of, and this must have been a sterner trial still. When they packed up their goods on the camels and on the asses, and started with their train of servants and sheep and cattle, she might very naturally have said, if she had been an unbelieving woman, "Where are you going?" "I do not know," says Abraham. "What are you going for? What are you going to get?" "I do not know," says Abraham, "God has bidden me go, but where I am going to, I do not know; and what I am going for I cannot exactly say, save that God has said, 'Get thee out from thy country and thy kindred, and I will bless thee and multiply thee, and give thee a land wherein thou shalt dwell.'" We do not read that Sarah ever asked these questions, or was ever troubled at all about them. The things were put on the camels' backs, and away she journeyed, for God had called her husband to go, and she resolved to go with him. Through floods or flames, it mattered not to her, she felt safe with her husband's God, and calmly journeyed on. She was not afraid with any amazement.

Then, though we do not hear much about her, we know that all those years she had to live in a tent. You know the man is out abroad attending to his business, and he does not know much about the discomforts of home, not even in such homes as ours. But if you were called to give up your houses and go and live in tents, well, the master might not mind it, but the mistress would. It is a very trying life for a housewife. Sarah traveled from day to day, and what with the constant moving of the tent, as the cattle had to be taken to fresh pastures, it must have been a life of terrible discomfort; yet Sarah never said a word about it.

Up tomorrow morning; every tent pin up; and all the canvas rolled away, for you must move to another station. The sun scorches like an oven, but you must ride across the plain; or if the night is cold with frost and heavy dews, still canvas is your only wall and roof. Remember, they were dwelling in tents as pilgrims and strangers, not for one day, or two, nor for a few days in a year, but for scores of years at a stretch. It was bravely done by this good woman that she was not afraid with any amazement.

Besides, they did not live in a country where they were all alone, or surrounded by friends, for the tribes around them were all of other religions and of other tastes and ways, and they would have slain Abraham and killed the whole company, if it had not been for a sort of fear that fell upon them, by which Jehovah seemed to say to them, "Touch not mine anointed, and do my prophets no harm." The patriarch and his wife dwelled in the midst of enemies, and yet they were not afraid; but if she had not been a believing woman, she must have often been afraid with great amazement.

And then there was a special time when the old man, Abraham, put on his harness and went to war. He hears that Chedorlaomer has come down with tributary kings and swept away the cities of the plain, and taken captive his nephew, Lot. Abraham says, "I will go and deliver him"; and she might have said, "My husband, you are an old man. Those gray locks should not be touched with the stains of warfare." She said nothing of the sort, but doubtless cheered him on and smiled as he invites some of his neighbors that dwelled near to go with him. She is under no distress that her husband is gone, and all the herdsmen and servants round about the tents all gone, so that she is left alone with her women servants. No; she sits at home as a queen and fears no robbers, calmly confident in her God. Abraham has gone to battle, and she fears not for him, and she needs not, for he smites the kings, and they are given like driven stubble to his bow, and he comes back laden with spoil. God was pleased with Sarah's quiet faith, because in troublous times she was not afraid with any amazement.

Then there came, a little while after, that great trial of faith which must have touched Sarah, though its full force fell on her husband. She observed the sudden disappearance of her husband and his servant. "Where is your master?

He does not come into breakfast." The servants say, "He was up a great while before day, and he has gone with the servant, and with the ass, and with Isaac." He had not told her; for Abraham had struggled enough with himself to take Isaac away to the mountain and offer him, and he could not bear to repeat the struggle in Sarah. He was gone without telling Sarah of his movements. This was a new state of things for her. He did not return all day. "Where has your master gone? I never knew him go away before without informing me. And where is Isaac?" Oh, that Isaac! How she feared for her jewel, her delight, the child of promise, the wonder of her old age. He did not come home that night, nor Abraham either; nor the next day, nor the next. Three days passed, and I can hardly picture the anxiety that would have fallen upon any one of you if you had been Sarah, unless you had enjoyed Sarah's faith, for by faith in this trying case she was not afraid with any amazement. I daresay it took three days for Abraham to come back again, so that it was a week nearly, and no Abraham and no Isaac. One would have thought she would have wandered about, crying, "Where is my husband, and where is my son?" But not so. She calmly waited, and said within herself, "If he has gone, he has gone upon some necessary errand, and he will be under God's protection; and God who promised to bless him and to bless his seed will not suffer any evil to harm him." So she rested quietly, when others would have been in dire dismay. She was not afraid with any amazement.

We hear so little said about Sarah, that I am obliged thus to picture what I feel she must have been, because human nature is so like itself, and the effect of events upon us is very like the effect which would have been produced upon the mind of Sarah.

Now, this is a point in which Christian women, and, for the matter of that, Christian men also, should seek to imitate Sarah: we should not let our hearts be troubled, but "rest in the LORD, and wait patiently for him."

What is this virtue? It is a calm, quiet trusting in God. It is freedom from fear, such as is described in another place in these words: "He shall not be afraid of evil tidings: his heart is fixed, trusting in the LORD." Or, as we read in David's words the other night, "Yea, though I walk through the valley of the shadow of death, I will fear no evil: for thou art with me; thy rod and thy staff they comfort me." It is composure of mind, freedom from anxiety, the absence of fretfulness, and clean deliverance from alarm; so that, whatever happens, trepidation does not seize upon the spirit, but the heart keeps on at its own quiet pace, delighting itself in a faithful God. This is the virtue which is worth a king's ransom, and Sarah had it. "Whose daughters ye are," if ye "are not afraid with any amazement."

When is this virtue to be exercised by us? Well, it should be exercised at all times. If we are not self-composed when we are happy, we are not likely to be calm when we are sad. I notice that if I am at all pleased with the praise of a friend, I become in that degree open to be grieved by the censure of a foe. By so much as you are elated by prosperity, by so much are you likely to be depressed when adversity comes; but if you are calm, quiet, happy—no more than that—when everything goes well, then you will be calm, quiet, happy—not less than that—when everything goes ill. To keep up an equable frame of mind is a thing to aim at, even as the gardener desires an even temperature for his choice flowers. You inquire, "Who are to exercise this virtue?" We are all to do so; but the text is specially directed to the sisterhood. I suppose women are exhorted to it, because some of them are rather excitable, a little hysterical, and apt to be fearfully depressed and utterly carried away. I am not saying that this fault is general or common among women, neither am I blaming them, but only stating the fact that some are thus afflicted, and it is a happy, happy thing if they can master it, so that they are not afraid with any amazement.

But this virtue especially serves in time of trouble, when a very serious trial threatens us. Then the Christian is not to say, "What shall I do now? I shall never endure it. I cannot live through it. Surely God has forgotten me. This trouble will crash me. I shall die of a broken heart." No. No. No. Do not talk so. My dear friend, do not talk so. If you are God's child, do not even think so. Try in patience to lift up your head, and remember Sarah, "whose daughters ye are if ye are not afraid with any amazement."

And so must it be in times of personal sickness. How many are the pains and sufferings that fall to the lot of the sisterhood! But if you have faith, you will not be afraid with any amazement. I saw one the other day who was about to suffer from the surgeon's knife. It was a serious operation, about which all stood in doubt; but I was happy to see her as composed in the prospect of it as though it had been a pleasure rather than a pain. Thus calmly resigned should a Christian be.

I went to see yesterday an aged sister—a member of this church, close upon fourscore years of age: she is dying with dropsy, and, being unable to lie down in bed, is obliged to sit up always—a posture which allows little or no rest. When I entered her room she welcomed me most heartily, which, perhaps was not wonderful, for she was greatly attached to her minister; the wonder lay in the fact that she expressed herself as being full of happiness, full of delight, full of expectancy of being with Christ. I went to comfort her; but she comforted me. What could I say? She talked of the goodness of God with an eye as full of pleasure as if she had been a maiden speaking to her young companion of her marriage day. Our sister used to sit just there, in yonder pew. I seem to see her sitting there now, but she will soon sit among the bright ones in heaven. I was charmed to see one with such evident marks of long-continued pain upon her face, but with such sweet serenity there too—yea, with more than serenity—with unspeakable joy in the Lord, such as I fear some in health and strength have not yet learned.

A Christian woman should not be afraid with any amazement either in adversity or in sickness, but her holy patience should prove her to be a true daughter of Sarah and Abraham.

Christian women in Peter's day were subject to persecution as much as their husbands. They were shut up in prison, scourged, tortured, burned, or slain with the sword. One holy woman in the early days of the church was tossed upon the horns of bulls; another was made to sit in a red-hot iron chair: thus were they tortured, not accepting deliverance. In the early days of martyrdom the women played the man as well as the men. They defied the tyrant to do his worst upon their mortal bodies, for their conquering spirits laughed at every torment. If persecuting times should come again, or if they are here already in some measure, O daughters of Sarah, do well, and be not afraid with any amazement.

And so if you should be called to some stern duty, if you should be bound to do what you feel you cannot do, recollect that anybody can do what he can do. It is the believing man who does what he cannot do. We achieve impossibilities by the power of the almighty God. Be not afraid, then, of any duty, but believe that you will be able to do it, for grace will be sufficient for you.

At last, in the prospect of death, my dear friends, may you not be afraid with any amazement! Oftentimes a deathbed is vantage ground for a Christian. Where others show their fear, and sometimes their terror, there should the believer show his peacefulness and his happy expectancy, not afraid with any amazement, whatever the form of death may be.

Now, what is the excellence of this virtue? I shall answer that question by saying it is due to God that we should not be afraid with any amazement. Such a God as we have ought to be trusted. Under the shadow of such a wing fear becomes a sin. If God were other than he is, we might be afraid; but while he is such a God it is due to him that fear be banished. Peacefulness is true worship. Quiet under alarming conditions is devotion. He worships best who is most calm in evil times.

Moreover, the excellence of this virtue is that it is most impressive to men. I do not think anything is more likely to impress the ungodly than the quiet peace of mind of a Christian in danger or near to death. If we can be happy then, our friends will ask, "What makes them so calm?" Nor is the usefulness confined to others. It is most useful to ourselves; for he who can be calm in time of trouble will be most likely to make his way through it. When you once become afraid, you cannot judge wisely as to your best course. You generally do wrong when you are frightened out of your confidence in God. When the heart begins palpitating, then the whole system is out of order for the battle of life. Be calm, and watch your opportunity. Napoleon's victories were to a large extent due to the serenity of that masterly warrior; and, depend upon it, it is so with you Christian people: you will win if you can wait. Do not be in a hurry. Consider what you should do. Do not be so alarmed as to make haste. Be patient; be quiet; wait God's time, and so wait your own time. Wait upon God to open your mouth. Ask him to guide your hand, and to do everything for you. Calmness of mind is the mother of prudence and discretion; it gives the firm foothold which is needful for the warrior when he is about to deal a victorious blow. Those who cannot be amazed by fear shall live to be amazed with mercy.

"How," says one, "can we obtain it?" That is the question. Recollect, it is an outgrowth of faith, and you will have it in proportion as you have faith. Have faith in God, and you will not be afraid with any amazement. Very early in my preaching days I had faith in God in times of thunderstorm. When I have walked out to preach, it has happened that I have been wet through with the storm, and yet I have felt no annoyance from the thunder and lightning. On one occasion I turned in by reason of the extreme severity of the rain to a little lone cottage, and I found a woman there with a child who seemed somewhat relieved when she had admitted me, but previously she had been crying bitterly with sheer alarm and terror. "Why," she said, "this is a little round lodge house, and the lightning comes in at every window. There is no place into which I can get to hide it from my eyes." I explained to her that I liked to see the lightning, for it showed me that an explosion was all over, and since I had lived to see the flash it was clear it could now do me no harm. I told her that to hear the thunder was a splendid thing, it was only God saying, "It is all over." If you live to see the lightning flash, there is nothing to be afraid of; you would have been dead, and never have seen it, if it had been sent to kill you. I tried to console her on religious grounds, and I remember well praying with her and making her happy as a bird. It was my being so calm and quiet and praying with her that cheered her up; and when I went on my way I left her in peace. You may depend upon it, my dear friends, that unless our own souls have peace we cannot communicate it to others.

In this way we must believe in God about everything. It so happened that about that matter—the thunder and lightning—I did believe in God up to the very last degree, and therefore I could not be alarmed on that score; so if you believe in God upon any other subject, whatever it is, you will have perfect peace with God about it. If you can believe God when you are in a storm at sea, that he holds the water in the hollow of his hand, you will be at peace about the tempest. It is the thing that troubles you that you must believe about; and when faith makes an application of her hand to the particular trial, then will peace of mind come to you.

This holy calm comes, also, from walking with God. No spot is so serene as the secret place of the tabernacles of the most High. Commune with God, and you will forget fear. Keep up daily fellowship with Christ in prayer, in praise, in service, in searching the word, in submitting your heart to the work of the eternal Spirit: and as you walk with God, you will find yourself calm. You know how our poet puts it:

> O for a closer walk with God,
> A calm and heavenly frame.

These go together.

If you would feed upon certain truths which will produce this calm of mind, recollect, first, that God is full of love, and therefore nothing that God sends can harm his child. Take everything from the Lord as a love token, even though it be a stroke of his rod or a cut of his knife. Everything from that dear hand must mean love, for he has said, "I have graven thee upon the palms of my hands." When you accept every affliction as a love token, then will your fear be ended.

Next, remember the faithfulness of God to his promise, and the fact that there is a promise for your particular position. The Lord is at this moment under promise to you, and that promise is registered in his Book. Search it out, and then grasp it, and say, "He must keep it; he cannot break his word." He has said, "In six troubles I will be with you." Have you got to number six? He has said, "I will never leave thee, nor forsake thee," and how can he run back from his word? If he does not leave thee nor forsake thee, what canst thou fear? Whatever is coming—poverty, sickness, shame, slander—if all the devils in hell are loosed, and they are all coming up against us at once, yet, if the Lord be with us, we will smite them hip and thigh, and send them back again to the infernal deep as quickly as the swine of old ran down a steep place into the sea and were choked in the waters. "Oh," says the devil, "I can overcome you." We say nothing to him but this—"You know your Master; you know your Master. Lie down, sir! You know your Master, and that Master is our covenant Head, our Husband, and our Lord." Neither the world, the flesh, nor the devil shall be able to overcome us, since we have the promise of a faithful God to protect us.

Many of you here tonight have gray hair or bald heads. I have always such a large proportion of aged people in my congregation that I can say to you what I might not say to the young folk. We, dear friends, ought not to be afraid, for trials are no novelties with us; we have smelled powder, and been grimed with the dust of the conflict times out of mind. We ought not to be troubled; we have been to sea before. And has not the Lord helped us? Tell it to his honor! He has been a very present help. He has borne us through such things that to doubt him would be an impudent slander upon his character. As for myself—and I suppose the language I now use would come from the lips of many here—my way has been strewn with wonders of divine mercy. Trials have abounded, and I am glad that they have: they have been opportunities for the display of divine grace. Labors have been attempted of which some said, "These are visionary schemes." But God has always been better than our faith. We have never been confounded, and I think we ought by this time to have learned that trusting in God is the most reasonable thing that we ever do. There are speculations in business, risks even in the most solid trading; but there is no speculation in believing God, no risk in trusting in him. He that hangs the world upon nothing, and yet keeps it in its place, can bring his people to have nothing, and yet to possess all things. He that makes yon arch of heaven stand secure without a buttress or a prop—a mighty arch such as no human engineer could ever contrive—he can make us stand without helpers, without friends, without riches, without strength, and stand, too, when all things else except that which God supports shall have come down in the final crash. "Trust ye in the LORD forever: for in the LORD JEHOVAH is everlasting strength." I pray for you who are most timid, that from this day you may be true daughters of Sarah, and not be afraid with any amazement. God bless you with this gracious help, and you will praise his name. Amen.

Hagar: Eyes Opened

~❦~

Delivered on Sunday morning, March 18, 1866, at the Metropolitan Tabernacle, Newington. No. 681.

And God opened her eyes, and she saw a well of water.—GENESIS 21:19
And their eyes were opened, and they knew him.—LUKE 24:31

The fall of man was most disastrous in its results to our entire being. "In
the day that thou eatest thereof thou shalt surely die" was no idle threat; for
Adam did die the moment that he transgressed the command—he died the
great spiritual death by which all his spiritual powers became then and evermore, until God should restore them, absolutely dead. I said all the spiritual
powers, and if I divide them after the analogy of the senses of the body, my
meaning will be still more clear. Through the fall the spiritual taste of man
became perverted, so that he puts bitter for sweet and sweet for bitter; he
chooses the poison of hell and loathes the bread of heaven; he licks the dust
of the serpent and rejects the food of angels. The spiritual *hearing* became
grievously injured, for man naturally no longer hears God's Word, but stops
his ears at his Maker's voice. Let the gospel minister charm never so wisely, yet
is the unconverted soul like the deaf adder which hears not the charmer's
voice. The spiritual feeling by virtue of our depravity is fearfully deadened.
That which would once have filled the man with alarm and terror no longer
excites emotion. Even the spiritual smell with which man should discern
between that which is pure and holy and that which is unsavory to the most
High has become defiled, and now man's spiritual nostril, while unrenewed,
derives no enjoyment from the sweet savor which is in Christ Jesus, but seeks
after the putrid joys of sin. As with other senses so is it with man's *sight*. He is
so spiritually blind that things most plain and clear he cannot and will not see.
The understanding, which is the soul's eye, is covered with scales of ignorance, and when these are removed by the finger of instruction, the visual orb
is still so affected that it only sees men as trees walking.

Our condition is thus most terrible, but at the same time it affords ample
room for a display of the splendors of divine grace. We are naturally so
entirely ruined, that if saved, the whole work must be of God, and the whole
glory must form the head of the triune Jehovah. There must not only be a

Christ lifted up of whom it can be said, "There is life in a look at the crucified One," but that very look itself must be given to us, or else in vain should Christ hang upon the cross; there shall be no salvation by his death to us.

I. Taking *Hagar's case* first, I shall address myself this morning to certain unconverted ones who are in a hopeful condition.

Taking Hagar's case as the model to work upon, we may see in her and in many like her a *preparedness for mercy*. In many respects she was in a fit state to become an object of mercy's help. She had a strong sense of need. The water was spent in the bottle, she herself was ready to faint, and her child lay at death's door; and this sense of need was attended by vehement desires. It is a very hard thing to bring a sinner to long after Christ: so hard, that if a sinner does really long and thirst after Jesus, the Spirit of God must have been secretly at work in his soul, begetting and fostering those desires. When the invitation is given, "Ho, every one that thirsteth," you can honestly say, "That means me." That precious gospel invitation, "Whosoever will, let him come," is evidently yours, for you do will it eagerly and vehemently. The Searcher of all hearts knows that there is no objection in your heart either to be saved or to the way of being saved; no, rather you sometimes lift your hands to heaven and say, "O God! would that I might say, 'Christ for me!'" You know that the water of life is desirable; you know more than that, you pine with an inward desire to drink of it. Your soul is now in such a state that if you do not find Jesus, you never will be happy without him. God has brought you into such a condition that you are like the magnetized needle which has been turned away from the pole by the finger of some passerby, and it cannot rest until it gets back to its place. Your constant cry is, "Give me Christ! Give me Christ, or else I die!"

This is hopeful, but let me remind you that it alone will not save you. The discovery of a leak in a vessel may be preparatory to the pumping of the ship, and to the repair of the leak; but the discovery of the leak will not of itself keep the bark afloat. The fact that you have a fever it is well for you to know; but to groan under that fever will not restore you to health. To desire after Christ is a very blessed symptom, but mere desires will not bring you to heaven. You may be hungering and thirsting after Christ, but hungering and thirsting will not save you; you must have Christ, or your salvation does not lie in your hungering and thirsting, nor in your humblings, nor in your prayings; salvation is in him who died upon the cross, and not in you.

Like Hagar, you are humbled and brought to self-despair. There was a time when you did not admit your need of a Savior; you found comfort enough in ceremonies, and in your own prayers, repentances, and so on. But now the water is spent in your bottle, and you are sitting down with Hagar, wringing your hands and weeping in despair—a blessed despair! God bring you all to it! Self-despair is next door to confidence in Christ. Rest assured, until we are empty, Jesus will never fill us; till we are stripped, he will never clothe us; until self is dead, Christ will not live in us.

It is quite certain that in Hagar's case, the will was right enough with reference to the water. It would have been preposterous indeed to say to Hagar, "If there be water, are you willing to drink?" "Willing?" she would say. "Look at my parched lips; hear my dolorous cries; look at my poor panting, dying child! How can you ask a mother if she is willing to have water while her babe is perishing for thirst?" And so with you: if I were to propose to you the question, "Are you willing to be saved?" you might look me in the face and say, "Willing! O sir, I have long passed beyond that stage. I am panting, groaning, thirsting, fainting, dying to find Christ. If he would come to me this morning, I would not only open both the gates of my heart and say, 'Come in,' but the gates are opened now before he comes, and my soul is saying, 'Oh, that I knew where I might find him, that I might even come to his seat!'" All this is hopeful, but I must again remind you that to will to be rich does not make a man rich, and that to will to be saved cannot in itself save you. Panting after health does not restore the sick man, though it may set him upon using the means, and so he may be healed; and with you your panting after salvation cannot save you, you must get beyond all this to the great Physician himself.

In the second place, *mercy was prepared* for Hagar, and is prepared for those in a like state. There was water. She thought it was a wilderness without a drop for her to drink, but there was water. Troubled conscience, there is pardon. You think it is all judgment, thunder and thunderbolt, curse and wrath, but it is not so. There is mercy. Jesus died. God is able justly to forgive sinners. God was in Christ reconciling the world unto himself, not imputing their trespasses unto them. He is a God ready to pardon, ready to forgive. There is forgiveness with him that he may be feared. There is water, there is mercy.

What is more, there is mercy for you; there is not only that general mercy which we are bound to preach to every creature, but for many of you whom I have described, I am persuaded that there is special mercy. Your names are in his book. He has chosen you from before the foundation of the world, though you do not know it. You shall be his, you are his. The hour is not far distant when, washed in the fountain and made clear, you shall cast yourselves at the Savior's feet, and be his captives in the bonds of love forever.

There is mercy for you now, if you trust Jesus. The water was not created as a new thing to supply Hagar's thirst; it was there already. If she could have seen it, she might have had it before, but she could not see it. There is mercy, there is mercy for you. All that is wanted is that you should see it, poor troubled conscience; and if you could have seen it, there would have been no necessity whatever that you should have been so long a time as you have been in despair and doubt and fear.

The water was near to Hagar; and so is Christ near to you. The mercy of God is not a thing to be sought for up yonder among the stars, nor to be discovered in the depths; it is near you, it is even in your mouth and in your heart. The Savior who walked along the streets of Jerusalem is in these aisles and in these pews; a God ready to forgive, waiting to be gracious. Do not think of my Master as though he had gone up to heaven out of your reach, and had left no mercy behind him. Let him tell you that he is as near in spirit now as he was to the disciples when he spoke to them at Emmaus. Oh, that you could see him! He is "the same yesterday, today, and forever." He is passing by; cry to him, you blind man, and you shall receive your sight! Call to him, you deaf; speak, even you whose lips are dumb, his ear can hear your soul's desires. He is near; only believe in his presence, and trust his grace, and you shall see him. It is a notion abroad that the act of faith is very mysterious. Now faith so far as it is an act of man (and an act of man it most certainly is, as well as the gift of God, for "with the heart man believeth") is one of the simplest acts of the human intellect. To trust Jesus, to lean with the soul upon him, just as with my body I am leaning on this rail; to make him all my confidence and all my rest, is what needs no learning, no previous education, needs no straining or mental effort. It is such an action that the babe and the suckling may glorify God by it; while the faith of Sir Isaac Newton, with all his learning, is not a whit more saving or less simple than the faith of the child of three years old, if brought to rest on Christ alone. The moment the dying thief looked to the Crucified and said, "Lord, remember me," he was as saved as Paul when he could say, "I have fought a good fight, I have finished my course."

I am very anxious to be understood, and therefore I am trying to speak very simply, and to talk right home to those whom I am driving at. My own case is to the point. I was for some few years, as a child, secretly seeking Jesus. If ever heart knew what the bitter anguish of sin was, I did, and when I came to understand the plan of salvation by the simple teaching of a plain, illiterate man, the next thought I had after joy that I was saved, was this: What a fool I was not to trust Jesus Christ before! I concluded that I never could have heard the gospel, but I think I was mistaken. I think I must have heard the gospel thousands of times, but did not understand it. I was like Hagar with my eyes closed. We are bound to tell you every Sabbath that trusting Jesus Christ is the way of salvation, but after you have heard that fifty thousand times, you really will not even understand what we mean by it, till the Spirit of God reveals the secret; but when you do but know it and trust in Jesus, simply as a child would trust his father's word, you will say of yourself, "How could it be? I was thirsty with the water rippling at my feet. I was famishing and perishing for hunger, and the bread was on the table. I was fretting as though there were no entrance into heaven, but there stood the door wide open right before me, if I could but have seen it." "Trust Christ, and he must save you." I will improve upon it: "Trust him, you are saved." The moment you begin to live by faith in his dear Son, there is not a sin left in God's book against you.

We pass on then in the third place to notice that although Hagar was prepared and mercy was prepared, yet *there was an impediment in the way*, for she could not see the water. There is also an impediment in your way. Hagar had a pair of bright beaming eyes, I will be bound to say, and yet she could not see the water; and men may have first-rate understandings, but not understand that simple thing, faith in the Lord Jesus Christ. You do not suffer so much from want of power to understand faith, as from a kind of haze which hovers over your eye to prevent its looking into the right place. You continue to imagine that there must be something very singular for us to feel in order to inherit eternal life. Now, this is all a mistake. Simple trust in Jesus has this difficulty in it, that it is not difficult, and therefore the human mind refuses to believe that God can intend to save us by so simple a plan. What blindness is this! So foolish and so fatal!

Is not this ignorance partly caused by legal terrors? Master Bunyan, who had a keen insight into spiritual experience, says that Christian was so troubled with that burden on his back that in running he did not look well to his steps; and therefore being much tumbled up and down in his mind, as he says, he also tumbled into the Slough of Despond. You have heard the thunder of God's law so long, that you cannot hear anything so soft and sweet as the invitation of the loving Jesus. "Come and welcome! Come and welcome!" is unheard because of the din of your sins.

The main reason I think why some do not attain early to peace is because they are looking for more than they will get, and thus their eyes are dazzled with fancies. You who dare not take Christ because you are not a full-grown Christian yet, be content to be a babe first; be satisfied to go through the seed state, and the blade state, and the ear state, and then you will get to be the full corn in the ear. Be content to begin with Christ and with Christ alone. I verily believe some of you expect that you will experience a galvanic shock, or a superhuman delirium of horror. You have an idea that to be born again is something to make the flesh creep or the bones shiver; an indescribable sensation, quite out of the compass of human feeling. Now believe me, that to be born again involves the ending of superstition and living by feeling, and brings you into the world of plain and simple truth where fools need not err. "Whosoever believeth in him is not condemned." If you can understand that and claim it as your own, you are born again; but though you should understand all human mysteries, if you are not born again, you could not truly understand that simplest of all teachings, "He that believeth and is baptized shall be saved."

Again, I am afraid some persons, with the water at their feet, do not drink it because of the bad directions that are given by ministers. When a minister closes up an address to the unconverted with this exhortation, "Now, my dear friends, go home and pray," that is a very right exhortation; but it is given to the wrong people, and in the wrong place. I do not say to you this morning, I dare not say to you, as though it were the gospel message, "Go home and pray." I hope you will pray; but there is another matter to come before prayer, namely, faith in Jesus. When Christ told his disciples to go and preach the gospel to every creature, he did not say to them, "He that prayeth shall be saved," though that would be true if he prayed aright; but "he that believeth shall be saved." Your present duty is not praying, but believing. You are to look to Jesus Christ upon the cross just as the poor serpent-bitten Israelites looked to the brazen serpent and lived. Your prayings will not do you a farthing's worth of good if you refuse to trust Jesus Christ.

When you have trusted Jesus Christ, prayer will become your breath, your native air, you will not be able to live without it; but prayer if put in the place of a childlike trust in Jesus, becomes an antichrist. It is not going to places of worship or Bible reading which saves. I am not depreciating these duties, but I am putting them in their proper position. It is depending upon the Lord Jesus Christ alone which is the true vital act by which the soul is quickened into spiritual life. If you, trusting in Christ, do not find peace and pardon, the gospel which I preach is a lie, and I will renounce it; but then that Book would be false also, for it is from that Book my message comes. This is the gospel which we have received, and which Christ has sent us to preach, that whosoever believeth in him is not condemned.

I feel certain that there are some here upon whom the Lord intends to work this morning; so we will speak, in the fourth place, upon *the divine removal of the impediment.* Hagar's blindness was removed by God. No one else could have removed it. God must open a man's eyes to understand practically what belief in Jesus Christ is. That simple verity—salvation by trust in Jesus Christ—still remains a point too hard to be seen; until the whole power of Omnipotence is made to bear upon the intellect, man does not really comprehend it. But while this was divinely removed, it was removed instrumentally. An angel spoke out of heaven to Hagar. It matters little whether it be an angel or a man, it is the Word of God which removes this difficulty. I pray that the Word of God may remove your unbelief. May you see today the light of Jesus Christ by simply trusting him! I believe there are some who are saved who still are afraid they will be lost. Many a man is looking within himself to see the evidence of grace when his anxiety, and the very light by which he looks ought to be sufficient evidence. I hope there are many of you who are just on the verge of salvation without knowing it. There has been much preparatory work in you, for you are brought to long after a Savior, you are desirous to be saved by him. There he is, take him! take him! The cup of water is put before you. Drink it! no need to wash your mouth first or to change your garments. Drink it at once. Come to Jesus as you are.

II. Oh, that the Spirit of God would give me power from on high while I try to talk to the saints from *the second case,* namely, that of the apostles in Luke 24:31.

This is no Hagar, but "Cleopas and another disciple." And yet these two suffered under the same spiritual blindness as Hagar, though not of course in the same phase of it. Carefully observe the case of these disciples, for I believe it is often our own. They ought to have known Jesus for these reasons. *They were acquainted with him;* they had been with him for years in public and in private; they had heard his voice so often that they ought to have recollected its tones. They had gazed upon that marred face so frequently that they ought to have distinguished its features. They had been admitted into his privacy, and they ought to have known his habits. That Savior walking there ought not to have been incognito to them though he was to the rest of men. So it is with us. Perhaps you have not found Jesus Christ lately. You have been to his table, and you have not met him there, and you are in a dark trouble this morning, and though he says, "It is I, be not afraid," yet you cannot see him there. Brother, we ought to know Christ, we ought to discover him at once. We know his voice, we have heard him say, "Rise up, my love, my fair one, and come away." We have looked into his face; we have understood the mystery of his grief; we have leaned our head upon his bosom. Some of us have had an experience of fifteen or twenty years, some of forty or fifty years; and yet, though Christ is near, you do not know him this morning, and you are saying, "Oh, that I knew where I might find him!"

They ought to have known him, because *he was close to them;* he was walking with them along the same road, he was not up on a mountain at a distance. Even then they ought to have known him, but he was there in the selfsame way with them; and at this hour Jesus is very near to us, sympathizing with all our griefs. He bears and endures with us still, though now exalted in glory's throne in heaven. If he be here, we ought to know him. If he be close to his people every day and in all their affliction is afflicted, we ought to perceive him. Oh, what strange blindness is this, that Christ should be near, our own well-beloved Redeemer, and yet we should not be able to detect his presence!

They ought to have seen him, because *they had the Scriptures to reflect his image,* and yet how possible it is for us to open that precious Book and turn over page after page of it, and not see Christ. They talked concerning Christ from Moses to the end of the prophets, and yet they did not see Jesus. Dear child of God, are you in that state? He feeds among the lilies of the Word, and you are among those lilies, and yet you do not see him. He is accustomed to walk through the glades of Scripture and to commune with his people, as the Father did with Adam in the cool of the day, and yet you are in the garden of Scripture but cannot see your Lord, though he is there and is never absent.

What is more, these disciples ought to have seen Jesus, for they had the Scriptures opened to them. They not only heard the Word, but they understood it. I am sure they understood it, for their hearts burned within them while he spoke with them by the way. I have known what it is, and so have you, to feel our hearts burn when we have been thinking of the precious truth of God, and yet we have said, "Oh, that I could get at him!" You have heard election, and you have wondered to yourself whether you should ever see again the face of God's first elect One. You have heard of the atonement, and the mournful story of the cross has ravished you, but you have gone from page to page of Scripture doctrine, and have received it and felt its influence, and yet that best of all enjoyments, communion with the Lord Jesus Christ, you have not comfortably possessed.

There was another reason why the disciples ought to have seen him, namely, that they had received testimonies from others about him. "But we trusted that it had been he which should have redeemed Israel: and beside all this, today is the third day since these things were done. Yea, and certain women also of our company made us astonished, which were early at the sepulcher; and when they found not his body, they came, saying, that they had also seen a vision of angels, which said that he was alive." There he was close to them. Oh! it is so strange that in the ordinances of God's house, Jesus should be there, and yet in sad intervals our hearts should get so cold and so worldly that we cannot see him. It is a blessed thing to want to see him; but oh! it is better still to see him. To those who seek him he is sweet; but to those who find him, beyond expression is he dear. In the prayer meeting you have heard some say, "If ever I loved thee, my Jesus, 'tis now," and your hearts burned within you as they thus spoke, and yet you could not say the same yourself. You have been up in the sick chamber, and you have heard the dying saint sing—

> I will love thee in life, I will love thee in death,
> And praise thee as long as thou lendest me breath;
> And say when the death dew lies cold on my brow,
> If ever I loved thee, my Jesus, 'tis now.

You have envied that dying saint, because you could not just then feel the same confident love; well this is strange, passing strange, it is wonderful—a present Savior, present with his own disciples who have long known, and who long to see, him, and yet their eyes are held so that they cannot discover him. *Why do we not see him?* I think it must be ascribed in our case to the same as in theirs, namely, our *unbelief.* They evidently did not expect to see him, and therefore they did not discover him. Brethren, to a great extent in spiritual things we shall get what we expect. The ordinary preacher of the gospel does not expect to see present conversion, and he does not see it; but there are certain brethren I have known, who have preached with the full faith that God would convert souls, and souls have been converted.

Some saints do not expect to see Christ. They read the life of Madame Guyon, and her soul-enchanting hymns, and they say, "Ah! a blessed woman this." They take down the letters of Samuel Rutherford, and when they read them through, they say, "Enchanting epistles! a strange, marvelously good man this." It does not enter into their heads that they may be Madame Guyons, and that they may have as much nearness to Christ, and as much enjoyment, as Samuel Rutherford. We have got into the habit of thinking the saints gone by stand up in elevated niches for us to stare at them with solemn awe, and fancy that we can never attain to their elevation. Brethren, they are elevated certainly, but they beckon us to follow them and point to a something beyond; they invite us to outstrip them, to get greater nearness to Christ, a clearer sense of his love, and a more ravishing enjoyment of his presence. You do not expect to see Christ, and therefore you do not see him, not because he is not there to be seen, but because your eyes are held through your unbelief.

I do not know any reason why we should not be full of joy this morning, every believing soul among us. Why hang you those harps on the willows, beloved? You have a trial, say you. Yes, but Jesus is in it. He says, "When thou passest through the rivers, I will be with thee; the floods shall not overflow thee." Why not rejoice then, since the dear Shepherd is with you? What matters it though there be clouds? They are full of rain when he is there, and they shall empty themselves upon the earth.

Now, I am sure it is the duty of every Christian, as well as his privilege, to walk in the conscious enjoyment of the love of the Lord Jesus Christ; and it may be that you came here on purpose that you might begin such a walk. The disciples had walked a long way without knowing Christ, but when they sat at his table, it was the breaking of bread that broke the evil charm, and they saw Jesus clearly at once. Do not neglect that precious ordinance of the breaking of bread. There is much more in it than some suppose. Sometimes when the preaching of the Word affords no joy, the breaking of bread might; and when reading the Word does not yield consolation, a resort to the Lord's table might be the means of comfort. There is nothing in any ordinance of itself, but there may be much sin in your neglecting it. There is nothing, for instance, in the ordinance of believers' baptism, and yet, knowing it to be a prescribed duty in God's Word, it may be that the Lord will never give you a comfortable sense of his presence till you yield to your conscience in that matter. But, waiving all that point, what you want is to see him. Faith alone can bring you to see him.

Make it your prayer this morning, "Lord, open thou mine eyes that I may see my Savior present with me, and after once seeing him may I never let him go. From this day forth may I begin like Enoch to walk with God, and may I continue walking with God till I die, that I may then dwell with him forever." I find it very easy to get near to God, compared with what it is to keep near. Enoch walked with God three hundred years; what a long walk that was! What a splendid journey through life! Why should not you begin, dear Christian, today, if you have not begun, and walk with God through the few years which remain? Oh, to get up above yon mists which dim the valley! Oh, to climb the mountain's top which laughs in the sunlight! Oh, to get away from the heavy atmosphere of worldliness and doubt, of fear, of care, of fretfulness; to soar away from the worldlings who are always earth hunting, digging into its mines and prying after its treasures, and to get up there where God dwells in the innermost circle of heavenly seclusion; where none can live but men who have been quickened from among the dead; where none can walk but men who are crucified with Christ, and who live only in him. Oh, to get up there—where no more question concerning our security can molest us; where no carking [troubling] care can disturb because all is cast upon the Lord, and rests wholly with him. Oh, to live in such an entireness of confidence and childlike faith that we will have nothing to do with anything now except with serving him and showing forth the gratitude we owe to him who has done so much for us. Christ has called you to fellowship with himself, and he is not in the grave now. He is risen! Rise you! He is ascended! Ascend with him and learn what this means: "He hath raised us up together and made us sit together in heavenly places in Christ Jesus."

Rebekah: No Compromise

Delivered on Lord's Day morning, October 7, 1888, at the Metropolitan Tabernacle, Newington. No. 2047.

And the servant said unto him, "Peradventure the woman will not be willing to follow me unto this land: must I needs bring thy son again unto the land from whence thou camest?" And Abraham said unto him, "Beware thou that thou bring not my son thither again. The LORD God of heaven, which took me from my father's house, and from the land of my kindred, and which spake unto me, and that sware unto me, saying, 'Unto thy seed will I give this land'; he shall send his angel before thee, and thou shalt take a wife unto my son from thence. And if the woman will not be willing to follow thee, then thou shalt be clear from this my oath: only bring not my son thither again."
—GENESIS 24:5–8

Genesis is both the book of beginnings and the book of dispensations. You know what use Paul makes of Sarah and Hagar, of Esau and Jacob, and the like. Genesis is, all through, a book instructing the reader in the dispensations of God toward man. Paul says, in a certain place, "which things are an allegory," by which he did not mean that they were not literal facts, but that, being literal facts, they might also be used instructively as an allegory. So may I say of this chapter. It records what actually was said and done; but at the same time, it bears within it allegorical instruction with regard to heavenly things. The true minister of Christ is like this Eleazar of Damascus; he is sent to find a wife for his Master's son. His great desire is that many shall be presented unto Christ in the day of his appearing, as the bride, the Lamb's wife.

The faithful servant of Abraham, before he started, communed with his master; and this is a lesson to us, who go on our Lord's errands. Let us, before we engage in actual service, see the Master's face, talk with him, and tell to him any difficulties which occur to our minds. Before we get to work, let us know what we are at, and on what footing we stand. Let us hear from our Lord's own mouth what he expects us to do, and how far he will help us in the doing of it. I charge you, my fellow servants, never to go forth to plead with men for God until you have first pleaded with God for men. Do not attempt to deliver a message which you have not first of all yourself received by his Holy Spirit. Come out of the chamber of fellowship with God into the pulpit of ministry among men, and there will be a freshness and a power about you which none shall be able to resist. Abraham's servant spoke and acted as one who felt bound to do exactly what his master bade him, and to say what his master told him; hence his one anxiety was to know the essence and measure of his commission.

During his converse with his master he mentioned one little point about which there might be a hitch; and his master soon removed the difficulty from his mind. It is about that hitch, which has occurred lately on a very large scale, and has upset a good many of my Master's servants, that I am going to speak this morning: may God grant that it may be to the benefit of his church at large!

I. Beginning our sermon, we will ask you, first, to *think of the servant's joyful but weighty errand.*

It was a joyful errand: the bells of marriage were ringing around him. The marriage of the heir should be a joyful event. It was an honorable thing for the servant to be entrusted with the finding of a wife for his master's son. Yet it was every way a most responsible business, by no means easy of accomplishment. Blunders might very readily occur before he was aware of it; and he needed to have all his wits about him, and something more than his wits, too, for so delicate a matter. He had to journey far, over lands without track or road; he had to seek out a family which he did not know, and to find out of that family a woman whom he did not know, who nevertheless should be the right person to be the wife of his master's son: all this was a great service.

The work this man undertook *was a business upon which his master's heart was set.* Isaac was now forty years old, and had shown no sign of marrying. He was of a quiet, gentle spirit and needed a more active spirit to urge him on. The death of Sarah had deprived him of the solace of his life, which he had found in his mother, and had, no doubt, made him desire tender companionship. Abraham himself was old and well stricken in years; and he very naturally wished to see the promise beginning to be fulfilled, that in Isaac should his seed be called. Therefore, with great anxiety, which is indicated by his making his servant swear an oath of a most solemn kind, he gave him the commission to go to the old family abode in Mesopotamia, and seek for Isaac a bride from thence. Although that family was not all that could be desired, yet it was the best he knew of; and as some heavenly light lingered there, he hoped to find in that place the best wife for his son. The business was, however, a serious one which he committed to his servant.

My brethren, this is nothing compared with the weight which hangs on the true minister of Christ. All the great Father's heart is set on giving to Christ a church which shall be his beloved forever. Jesus must not be alone: his church must be his dear companion. The Father would find a bride for the great Bridegroom, a recompense for the Redeemer, a solace for the Savior: therefore he lays it upon all whom he calls to tell out the gospel, that we should seek souls for Jesus, and never rest till hearts are wedded to the Son of God. Oh, for grace to carry out this commission!

This message was the more weighty because of the person for whom the spouse was sought. Isaac was an extraordinary personage; indeed, to the servant he was unique. He was a man born according to promise, not after the flesh, but by the power of God; and you know how in Christ, and in all that are one with Christ, the life comes by the promise and the power of God, and springs not of man. Isaac was himself the fulfillment of promise, and the heir of the promise. Infinitely glorious is our Lord Jesus as the Son of man! Who shall declare his generation? Where shall be found a helpmeet for him? A soul fit to be espoused unto him? Isaac had been sacrificed; he had been laid upon the altar, and although he did not actually die, his father's hand had unsheathed the knife wherewith to slay him. Abraham in spirit had offered up his son; and you know who he is of whom we preach, and for whom we preach, even Jesus, who has laid down his life a sacrifice for sinners. He has been presented as a whole burnt offering unto God. Oh! By the wounds, and by the bloody sweat, I ask you where shall we find a heart fit to be wedded to him? How shall we find men and women who can worthily recompense love so amazing, so divine, as that of him who died the death of the cross? Isaac had also been, in a figure, raised from the dead. To his father he was "as good as dead," as said the apostle; and he was given back to him from the dead. But our blessed Lord has actually risen from an actual death, and stands before us this day as the Conqueror of death, and the Spoiler of the grave. Who shall be joined to this Conqueror? Who is fit to dwell in glory with this glorious One? One would have thought that every heart would aspire to such happiness, and leap in prospect of such peerless honor, and that none would shrink back except through a sense of great unworthiness. Alas! it is not so, though so it ought to be.

What a weighty errand have we to fulfill to find those who shall be linked forever in holy union with the Heir of the promise, even the sacrificed and risen One! Isaac was everything to Abraham. Abraham would have said to

Isaac, "All that I have is thine." So is it true of our blessed Lord, whom he has made Heir of all things; by whom also he made the worlds, that "it pleased the Father that in him should all fullness dwell." What a dignity will be put upon any of you who are married to Christ! To what a height of eminence will you be uplifted by becoming one with Jesus! O preacher, what a work have you to do today, to find out those to whom you shall give the bracelet, and upon whose face you shall hang the jewel! To whom shall I say, "Will you give your heart to my Lord? Will you have Jesus to be your confidence, your salvation, your all in all? Are you willing to become his that he may be yours?"

Said I not truly that it was a joyful, but a weighty, errand, when you think what she must be to whom his master's son should be espoused? She must, at least, be willing and beautiful. In the day of God's power, hearts are made willing. There can be no marriage to Jesus without a heart of love. Where shall we find this willing heart? Only where the grace of God has worked it. Ah, then, I see how I may find beauty, too, among the sons of men! Marred as our nature is by sin, only the Holy Spirit can impart that beauty of holiness which will enable the Lord Jesus to see comeliness in his chosen. Alas! in our hearts there is an aversion to Christ, and an unwillingness to accept of him, and at the same time a terrible unfitness and unworthiness! The Spirit of God implants a love which is of heavenly origin, and renews the heart by a regeneration from above; and then we seek to be one with Jesus, but not till then. See, then, how our errand calls for the help of God himself.

Think what she will become who is to be married to Isaac? She is to be his delight; his loving friend and companion. She is to be partner of all his wealth; and specially is she to be a partaker in the great covenant promise, which was peculiarly entailed upon Abraham and his family. When a sinner comes to Christ, what does Christ make of him? His delight is in him: he communes with him; he hears his prayer, he accepts his praise; he works in him and with him, and glorifies himself in him. He makes the believing man joint heir with himself of all that he has, and introduces him into the covenant treasure-house, wherein the riches and glory of God are stored up for his chosen. Ah, dear friends! It is a very small business in the esteem of some to preach the gospel; and yet, if God is with us, ours is more than angels' service. In a humble way you are telling of Jesus to your boys and girls in your classes; and some will despise you as "only Sunday school teachers"; but your work has a spiritual weight about it unknown to conclaves of senators, and absent from the counsels of emperors. Upon what you say, death and hell and worlds unknown are hanging. You are working out the destinies of immortal spirits, turning souls from ruin to glory, from sin to holiness.

'Tis not a work of small import
Your loving care demands;
But what might fill an angel's heart,
And filled the Savior's hands.

In carrying out his commission, *this servant must spare no exertion*. It would be required of him to journey to a great distance, having a general indication of direction, but not knowing the way. He must have divine guidance and protection. When he reached the place, he must exercise great common sense, and at the same time a trustful dependence upon the goodness and wisdom of God. It would be a wonder of wonders if he ever met the chosen woman, and only the Lord could bring it to pass. He had all the care and the faith required. We have read the story of how he journeyed and prayed and pleaded. We should have cried, "Who is sufficient for these things?" but we see that the Lord Jehovah made him sufficient, and his mission was happily carried out.

How can we put ourselves into the right position to get at sinners and win them for Jesus? How can we learn to speak the right words? How shall we suit our teaching to the condition of their hearts? How shall we adapt ourselves to their feelings, their prejudices, their sorrows, and their temptations? Brethren, we who preach the gospel continually may well cry, "If thy presence go not with me, carry us not up hence." To seek for pearls at the bottom of the sea is child's play compared with seeking for souls in this wicked London. If God be not with us, we may look our eyes out, and wear our tongues away in vain. Only as the almighty God shall lead and guide and influence and inspire, can we perform our solemn trust; only by divine help shall we joyfully come back, bringing with us the chosen of the Lord. We are the Bridegroom's friends, and we rejoice greatly in his joy, but we sigh and cry till we have found the chosen hearts in whom he will delight, whom he shall raise to sit with him upon his throne.

II. Second, I would have you *consider the reasonable fear which is mentioned*.

Abraham's servant said, "Peradventure the woman will not be willing to follow me unto this land." This is a very serious, grave, and common difficulty. If the woman be not willing, nothing can be done; force and fraud are out of the question; there must be a true will, or there can be no marriage in this instance. Here was the difficulty: here was a will to be dealt with. Ah, my brethren! this is our difficulty still. Let me describe this difficulty in detail as it appeared to the servant, and appears to us.

She may not believe my report or be impressed by it. When I come to her and tell her that I am sent by Abraham, she may look me in the face, and say, "There be many deceivers nowadays." If I tell her that my master's son is surpassingly beautiful and rich, and that he would fain take her to himself, she may answer, "Strange tales and romances are common in these days; but the prudent do not quit their homes." Brethren, in our case this is a sad fact. The great evangelical prophet cried of old, "Who hath believed our report?" We also cry in the same words. Men care not for the report of God's great love to the rebellious sons of men. They do not believe that the infinitely glorious Lord is seeking the love of poor, insignificant man and to win it has laid down his life. Calvary, with its wealth of mercy, grief, love, and merit, is disregarded. Indeed, we tell a wonderful story, and it may well seem too good to be true; but it is sad indeed that the multitude of men go their ways after trifles, and count these grand realities to be but dreams. I am bowed down with dismay that my Lord's great love, which led him even to die for men, should hardly be thought worthy of your hearing, much less of your believing. Here is a heavenly marriage, and right royal nuptials placed within your reach; but with a sneer you turn aside, and prefer the witcheries of sin.

There was another difficulty: *she was expected to feel a love to one she had never seen.* She had only newly heard that there was such a person as Isaac, but yet she must love him enough to leave her kindred and go to a distant land. This could only be because she recognized the will of Jehovah in the matter. Ah, my dear hearers! All that we tell you is concerning things not seen as yet; and here is our difficulty. You have eyes, and you want to see everything; you have hands, and you want to handle everything; but there is one whom you cannot see as yet, who has won our love because of what we believe concerning him. We can truly say of him, "Whom having not seen, we love: in whom, though now we see him not, yet believing, we rejoice with joy unspeakable and full of glory." I know that you answer our request thus: "You demand too much of us when you ask us to love a Christ we have never seen." I can only answer, "It is even so: we do ask more of you than we expect to receive." Unless God the Holy Ghost shall work a miracle of grace upon your hearts, you will not be persuaded by us to quit your old associations, and join yourselves to our beloved Lord. And yet, if you did come to him and love him, he would more than content you; for you would find in him rest unto your souls, and a peace which passeth all understanding.

Abraham's servant may have thought: *She may refuse to make so great a change* as to quit Mesopotamia for Canaan. She had been born and bred away there in a settled country, and all her associations were with her father's house;

and to marry Isaac she must tear herself away. So, too, you cannot have Jesus, and have the world too: you must break with sin to be joined to Jesus. You must come away from the licentious world, the fashionable world, the scientific world, and from the (so-called) religious world. If you become a Christian, you must quit old habits, old motives, old ambitions, old pleasures, old boasts, old modes of thought. All things must become new. You must leave the things you have loved and seek many of those things which you have hitherto despised. There must come to you as great a change as if you had died, and were made over again. You answer, "Must I endure all this for One whom I have never seen, and for an inheritance on which I have never set my foot?" It is even so. Although I am grieved that you turn away, I am not in the least surprised, for it is not given to many to see him who is invisible, or to choose the strait and narrow way which leadeth unto life. The man or woman who will follow God's messenger to be married to so strange a Bridegroom is a rare bird.

Moreover, it might be a great difficulty to Rebekah, if she had had any difficulties at all, to think that *she must henceforth lead a pilgrim life.* She would quit house and farm for tent and gypsy life. Abraham and Isaac found no city to dwell in, but wandered from place to place, dwelling alone, sojourners with God. Their outward mode of life was typical of the way of faith, by which men live in the world, and are not of it. To all intents and purposes Abraham and Isaac were out of the world, and lived on its surface without lasting connection with it. They were the Lord's men, and the Lord was their possession. He set himself apart for them, and they were set apart for him. Rebekah might well have said, "That will never do for me. I cannot outlaw myself. I cannot quit the comforts of a settled abode to ramble over the fields wherever the flocks may require me to roam." It does not strike the most of mankind that it would be a good thing to be in the world, and yet not to be of it. They are no strangers in the world, they long to be admitted more fully into its "society." They are not aliens here with their treasures in heaven, they long to have a good round sum on earth and find their heaven in enjoying it themselves, and enriching their families. Earthworms as they are, the earth contents them. If any man becomes unworldly and makes spiritual things his one object, they despise him as a dreamy enthusiast. Many men think that the things of religion are merely meant to be read of, and to be preached about; but that to live for them would be to spend a dreamy, unpractical existence. Yet the spiritual is, after all, the only real: the material is in deepest truth the visionary and unsubstantial. Still, when people turn away because of the hardness of holy warfare, and the spirituality of the believing life, we are not astonished, for we hardly hoped it could be otherwise. Unless the Lord renews the heart, men will always prefer the bird-in-the-hand of this life to the bird-in-the-bush of the life to come.

Moreover, it might be that the woman *might not care for the covenant of promise.* If she had no regard for Jehovah and his revealed will, she was not likely to go with the man, and enter upon marriage with Isaac. He was the heir of the promises, the inheritor of the covenant privileges which the Lord by oath had promised. His chosen would become the mother of that chosen seed in whom God had ordained to bless the world throughout all the ages, even the Messiah, the seed of the woman, who should bruise the serpent's head.

Peradventure the woman might not see the value of the covenant, nor appreciate the glory of the promise. The things we have to preach of, such as life everlasting, union with Christ, resurrection from the dead, reigning with him forever and ever, seem to the dull hearts of men to be as idle tales. Tell them of a high interest for their money, of large estates to be had for a venture, or of honors to be readily gained, and inventions to be found out, they open all their eyes and their ears, for here is something worth knowing; but the things of God, eternal, immortal, boundless—these are of no importance to them. They could not be induced to go from Ur to Canaan for such trifles as eternal life, and heaven, and God.

So you see our difficulty. Many disbelieve altogether, and others cavil and object. A greater number will not even listen to our story; and of those who do listen, most are careless, and others dally with it, and postpone the serious consideration. Alas! we speak to unwilling ears.

III. In the third place, I would *enlarge upon his very natural suggestion.*

This prudent steward said, "Peradventure the woman will not be willing to follow me unto this land: must I needs bring thy son again unto the land from whence thou camest?" If she will not come to Isaac, shall Isaac go down to her?

This is the suggestion of the present hour: if the world will not come to Jesus, shall Jesus tone down his teachings to the world? In other words, if the world will not rise to the church, shall not the church go down to the world? Instead of bidding men to be converted, and come out from among sinners, and be separate from them, let us join with the ungodly world, enter into union with it, and so pervade it with our influence by allowing it to influence us. Let us have a Christian world. To this end let us revise our doctrines. Some are old-fashioned, grim, severe, unpopular; let us drop them out. Use the old phrases so as to please the obstinately orthodox, but give them new meanings so as to win philosophical infidels, who are prowling around. Pare off the edges of unpleasant truths, and moderate the dogmatic tone of infallible revelation: say that Abraham and Moses made mistakes, and that the books which have been so long had in reverence are full of errors. Undermine the old faith, and bring in the new doubt; for the times are altered, and the spirit of the age suggests the abandonment of everything that is too severely righteous, and too surely of God.

The deceitful adulteration of doctrine is attended by a falsification of experience. Men are now told that they were born good, or were made so by their infant baptism, and so that great sentence, "Ye must be born again," is deprived of its force. Repentance is ignored, faith is a drug in the market as compared with "honest doubt," and mourning for sin and communion with God are dispensed with, to make way for entertainments and socialism and politics of varying shades. A new creature in Christ Jesus is looked upon as a sour invention of bigoted Puritans. It is true, with the same breath they extol Oliver Cromwell; but then 1888 is not 1648. What was good and great three hundred years ago is mere cant today. That is what "modern thought" is telling us; and under its guidance all religion is being toned down. Spiritual religion is despised, and a fashionable morality is set up in its place. Do yourself up tidily on Sunday; behave yourself; and above all, believe everything except what you read in the Bible, and you will be all right. Be fashionable, and think with those who profess to be scientific—this is the first and great commandment of the modern school; and the second is like unto it—do not be singular, but be as worldly as your neighbors. Thus is Isaac going down into Padan-aram: thus is the church going down to the world.

Men seem to say—It is of no use going on in the old way, fetching out one here and another there from the great mass. We want a quicker way. To wait till people are born again, and become followers of Christ, is a long process: let us abolish the separation between the regenerate and unregenerate. Come into the church, all of you, converted or unconverted. You have good wishes and good resolutions; that will do: don't trouble about more. It is true you do not believe the gospel, but neither do we. You believe something or other. Come along; if you do not believe anything, no matter; your "honest doubt" is better by far than faith.

"But," say you, "nobody talks so." Possibly they do not use the same words, but this is the real meaning of the present-day religion; this is the drift of the times. I can justify the broadest statement I have made by the action or by the speech of certain ministers, who are treacherously betraying our holy religion under pretense of adapting it to this progressive age. The new plan is to assimilate the church to the world, and so include a larger area within its bounds. By semidramatic performances, they make houses of prayer to approximate to the theater; they turn their services into musical displays, and their sermons into political harangues or philosophical essays—in fact, they exchange the temple for the theater, and turn the ministers of God into actors, whose business it is to amuse men. Is it not so, that the Lord's Day is becoming more and more a day of recreation or of idleness, and the Lord's house either a joss house [Chinese temple or shrine] full of idols, or a political club, where there is more enthusiasm for a party than zeal for God? Ah me! The hedges are broken down, the walls are leveled, and to many there is henceforth no church except as a portion of the world, no God except as an unknowable force by which the laws of nature work.

This, then, is the proposal. In order to win the world, the Lord Jesus must conform himself, his people, and his Word to the world. I will not dwell any longer on so loathsome a proposal.

IV. In the fourth place, *notice his master's outspoken, believing repudiation of the proposal.*

He says, shortly and sharply, "Beware thou that thou bring not my son thither again." The Lord Jesus Christ heads that grand emigration party which has come right out from the world. Addressing his disciples, he says, "Ye are not of the world, even as I am not of the world." We are not of the world by birth, not of the world in life, not of the world in object, not of the world in spirit, not of the world in any respect whatever. Jesus, and those who are in him, constitute a new race. The proposal to go back to the world is abhorrent to our best instincts; yea, deadly to our noblest life. A voice from heaven cries, "Bring not my son thither again." Let not the people whom the Lord brought up out of Egypt return to the house of bondage; but let their children come out, and be separate, and the Lord Jehovah will be a Father unto them.

Notice how Abraham states the question. In effect, he argues it thus: *this would be to forgo the divine order.* "For," says Abraham, "the Lord God of heaven took me from my father's house, and from the land of my kindred." What, then, if he brought Abraham out, is Isaac to return? This cannot be. Hitherto the way of God with his church has been to sever a people from the world to be his elect—a people formed for himself, who shall show forth his praise. Beloved, God's plan is not altered. He will still go on calling those whom he did predestinate. Do not let us fly in the teeth of that fact, and suppose that we can save men on a more wholesale scale by ignoring the distinction between the dead in sin and the living in Zion. If God had meant to bless the family at Padan-aram by letting his chosen ones dwell among them, why did he call Abraham out at all? If Isaac may do good by dwelling there, why did Abraham leave? If there is no need of a separate church now, what have we been at throughout all these ages? Has the martyr's blood been shed out of mere folly? Have confessors and reformers been mad when contending for doctrines which, it would seem, are of no great account? Brethren, there are two seeds—the seed of the woman, and the seed of the serpent—and the difference will be maintained even to the end; neither must we ignore the distinction to please men.

For Isaac to go down to Nahor's house for a wife would be placing God second to a wife. Abraham begins at once with a reference to Jehovah, "the God of heaven"; for Jehovah was everything to him, and to Isaac also. Isaac would never renounce his walk with the living God that he might find a wife. Yet this apostasy is common enough nowadays. Men and women who profess godliness will quit what they profess to believe in order to get richer wives or husbands for themselves or their children. This mercenary conduct is without excuse. "Better society" is the cry—meaning more wealth and fashion. To the true man God is first—yea, all in all; but God is placed at the fag end [or remnant], and everything else is put before him by the base professor. In the name of God I call upon you who are faithful to God and to his truth, to stand fast, whatever you lose, and turn not aside, whatever you might gain. Count the reproach of Christ greater riches than all the treasures of Egypt. We want Abraham's spirit within us, and we shall have that when we have Abraham's faith.

Abraham felt that this would be *to renounce the covenant promise*. See how he puts it: "The God that took me from my father's house sware unto me, saying, 'Unto thy seed will I give this land.'" Are they, then, to leave the land, and go back to the place from which the Lord had called them? Brethren, we also are heirs of the promise of things not seen as yet. For the sake of this we walk by faith, and hence we become separate from those around us. We dwell among men as Abraham dwelled among the Canaanites; but we are of a distinct race: we are born with a new birth, live under different laws, and act from different motives. If we go back to the ways of worldlings and are numbered with them, we have renounced the covenant of our God, the promise is no longer ours, and the eternal heritage is in other hands. Do you not know this? The moment the church says, "I will be as the world," she has doomed herself with the world. "When the sons of God saw the daughters of men that they were fair, and took them wives of all which they chose," then the flood came and swept them all away. So will it again happen should the world take the church into its arms: then shall come some overwhelming judgment, and, it may be, a deluge of devouring fire. The covenant promise and the covenant heritage are no longer ours if we go down to the world and quit our sojourning with the Lord.

Besides, dear friends, *no good can come of trying to conform to the world.* Suppose the servant's policy could have been adopted, and Isaac had gone down to Nahor's house, what would have been the motive? To spare Rebekah the pain of separating from her friends and the trouble of traveling. If those things could have kept her back, what would she have been worth to Isaac? The test of separation was wholesome, and by no means ought it to be omitted. She is a poor wife who would not take a journey to reach her husband. And all the converts that the church will ever make by softening down its doctrine, and by becoming worldly, will not be worth one bad farthing a gross. When we get them, the next question will be, "How can we get rid of them?" They would be of no earthly use to us. It swelled the number of Israelites when they came out of Egypt that a great number of the lower order of Egyptians came out with them. Yes, but that mixed multitude became the plague of Israel in the wilderness, and we read that "the mixt multitude fell a lusting." The Israelites were bad enough, but it was the mixed multitude that always led the way in murmuring. Why is there such spiritual death today? Why is false doctrine so rampant in the churches? It is because we have ungodly people in the church and in the ministry. Eagerness for numbers, and especially eagerness to include respectable people, has adulterated many churches, and made them lax in doctrine and practice, and fond of silly amusements. These are the people who despise a prayer meeting, but rush to see "living waxworks" in their schoolrooms. God save us from converts who are made by lowering the standard, and tarnishing the spiritual glory of the church! No, no; if Isaac is to have a wife worthy of him, she will come away from Laban and the rest, and she will not mind a journey on camelback. True converts are never daunted by truth or holiness—these, in fact, are the things which charm them.

Besides, Abraham felt that *there could be no reason for taking Isaac down there,* for the Lord would assuredly find him a wife. Abraham said, "He shall send his angel before thee, and thou shalt take a wife unto my son from thence." Are you afraid that preaching the gospel will not win souls? Are you despondent as to success in God's way? Is this why you pine for clever oratory? Is this why you must have music and architecture and flowers and millinery? After all, is it by might and by power, and not by the Spirit of God? It is even so in the opinion of many. Brethren beloved, there are many things which I might allow to other worshipers which I have denied myself in conducting the worship of this congregation. I have long worked out before your very eyes the experiment of the unaided attractiveness of the gospel of Jesus. Our service is severely plain. No man ever comes hither to gratify his eye with art or his ear with music. I have set before you, these many years, nothing but Christ crucified, and the simplicity of the gospel; yet where will you find such a crowd as this gathered together this morning? Where will you find such a multitude as this meeting, Sabbath after Sabbath, for five and thirty years? I have shown you nothing but the cross, the cross without the flowers of oratory, the cross without the blue lights of superstition or excitement, the cross without diamonds of ecclesiastical rank, the cross without the buttresses of a boastful science. It is abundantly sufficient to attract men first to itself, and afterward to eternal life! In this house we have proved successfully, these many years, this great truth, that the gospel plainly preached will gain an audience, convert sinners, and build up and sustain a church. We beseech the people of God to mark that there is no need to try doubtful expedients and questionable methods. God will save by the gospel still: only let it be the gospel in its purity. This grand old sword will cleave a man's chine and split a rock in halves. How is it that it does so little of its old conquering work? I will tell you. Do you see this scabbard of artistic work, so wonderfully elaborated? Full many keep the sword in this scabbard, and therefore its edge never gets to its work. Pull off that scabbard. Fling that fine sheath to Hades, and then see how, in the Lord's hands, that glorious two-handed sword will mow down fields of men as mowers level the grass with their scythes. There is no need to go down to Egypt for help. To invite the devil to help Christ is shameful. Please God, we shall see prosperity yet, when the church of God is resolved never to seek it except in God's own way.

V. And now, fifth, observe *his righteous absolution of his servant.*

"If the woman will not be willing to follow thee, then thou shalt be clear from this my oath: only bring not my son thither again."

When we lie dying, if we have faithfully preached the gospel, our conscience will not accuse us for having kept closely to it: we shall not mourn that we did not play the fool or the politician in order to increase our congregation. Oh no! Our Master will give us full absolution, even if few be gathered in, so long as we have been true to him. "If the woman will not be willing to follow thee, then thou shalt be clear from this my oath; only bring not my son thither again." Do not try the dodges which debase religion. Keep to the simple gospel; and if the people are not converted by it, you will be clear. My dear hearers, how much I long to see you saved! But I would not belie my Lord, even to win your souls, if they could be so won. The true servant of God is responsible for diligence and faithfulness; but he is not responsible for success or nonsuccess. Results are in God's hands. If that dear child in your class is not converted, yet if you have set before him the gospel of Jesus Christ with loving, prayerful earnestness, you shall not be without your reward. If I preach from my very soul the grand truth that faith in the Lord Jesus Christ will save my hearers, and if I persuade and entreat them to believe in Jesus unto eternal life; if they will not do so, their blood will lie upon their own heads. When I go back to my Master, if I have faithfully told out his message of free grace and dying love, I shall be clear. I have often prayed that I might be able to say at the last what George Fox could so truly say: "I am clear, I am clear!" It is my highest ambition to be clear of the blood of all men. I have preached God's truth, so far as I know it, and I have not been ashamed of its peculiarities. That I might not stultify my testimony, I have cut myself clear of those who err from the faith, and even from those who associate with them. What more can I do to be honest with you? If, after all, men will not have Christ, and his gospel, and his rule, it is their own concern. If Rebekah had not come to Isaac, she would have lost her place in the holy line. My beloved hearer, will you have Jesus Christ or not? He has come into the world to save sinners, and he casts out none. Will you accept him? Will you trust him? "He that believeth and is baptized shall be saved." Will you believe him? Will you be baptized into his name? If so, salvation is yours; but if not, he himself hath said it, "He that believeth not shall be damned." Oh, do not expose yourselves to that damnation! Or, if you are set upon it, then, when the great white throne shall be seen in yonder skies, and the day of wrath has come, do me the justice to acknowledge that I bade you flee to Jesus, and that I did not amuse you with novel theories. I have brought neither flute, harp, psaltery, dulcimer, nor any other kind of music to please your ears, but I have set Christ crucified before you, and bidden you believe and live. If you refuse to accept the substitution of Christ, you have refused your own mercies. Clear me in that day of all complicity with the novel inventions of deluded men. As for my Lord, I pray of him grace to be faithful to the end, both to his truth, and to your souls. Amen.

Raḥab: The Scarlet Line in the Window

Published on Thursday, October 28, 1909; delivered at the Metropolitan Tabernacle, Newington. No. 3168.

She bound the scarlet line in the window.—Joshua 2:21

Every little incident in a remarkable conversion like that of the harlot Rahab is worthy of notice. The apostle James selected her as an illustration of the fact that faith is always attended by good works, and he asks, "Was she not justified by works when she had received the messengers?" while Paul quotes her as an instance of justification by faith, and says, "By faith the harlot Rahab perished not with them that believed not." If both these eminent apostles found an illustration of an important doctrine in her life, we surely may do the same. If the hiding of the spies under the flax had some significance, so also had the hanging out of the scarlet line.

The two spies whom Rahab had concealed made an agreement with her that she should hang out a scarlet line in the window by which she had let them down, that they might know, in the day of battle, the house in which she dwelled. She fulfilled their request and displayed the chosen emblem. In connection with that scarlet line, I observe four things.

I. First, I see here *an obedient believer.*

She was told to tie the scarlet thread in the window, and she did it; there was *exact obedience*. It was not merely *a* thread, *a* line, but the *scarlet line*. She did not substitute a blue or a green or a white line. The order was this scarlet line, not another, and she took that particular one. Obedience to God will be very much seen in small matters. Love always delights to attend to the little things, and thereby makes the little things great. I have heard of a Puritan who was charged with being too precise, but his answer was excellent, "I serve a precise God."

The Lord our God is a jealous God, and he is very jealous of his commands. It appeared a little mistake that Moses made when he struck the rock instead of speaking to it, and yet he could not enter into the promised rest because of his offense. A small action may involve a great principle, and it is for us to be very cautious and careful, searching out what the Master's will is, and then never halting or hesitating for any reason whatever, but doing his will as soon as ever we know it. Christian life should be a mosaic of minute obediences. The soldiers of Christ should be famous for their exact discipline.

I commend scrupulous obedience to all of you, and especially to those young people who have lately made a profession of their faith in Christ. Do not be as your fathers were; for the generation which is now going off the stage neither reads its Bible nor cares to know the Lord's will. If people searched the Scriptures, we should find them come together in union; but the least-read book in all the world, in proportion to its circulation, is the Word of God. It is distributed everywhere, but it is read scarcely anywhere with care and attention, and with a sincere resolve to follow its precepts at all hazards. You come and listen to us, and we give you little bits taken from it here and there, but you do not get a fair notion of it as a whole. How can you? Ministers make mistakes, and you follow them without inquiry. One elects this leader, and another that, to the creation of varieties of opinions and even of sects, which ought not to be, and would not be if all stood fast by the standard of inspired truth. If the Bible were but read, and prayed over, many errors would die a speedy death, and others would be sorely crippled. Had that inspired Book been read in the past, many errors would never have arisen. Search, then, the Book of God, I pray you; and whatever you find there, be sure to attend thereto. At all costs, keep to the Word of God.

Notice, next, that hers was *obedience in a very small matter.* She might have said, "I do not think it is essential to tie a piece of line in my window. Can I not be preserved just as well without it, seeing that I believe in the God of Israel? I have faith, and I have shown it by my works by hiding the spies; you cannot suppose for a moment that I shall perish simply because I have not complied with a regulation about a scarlet line." In this way many, nowadays, inquire whether they may not omit those duties which they consider to be nonessential to salvation. Now, this is a question which I never intend to answer for anybody else, because I never intend to ask it on my own account. Whether or not a believer will perish because some known duty or scriptural ordinance is neglected, is a question which only selfishness would raise. Are we only to do that which will procure our progress, or secure our salvation? Are we so grossly selfish as that? Does a loving child say, "If I refuse to do my father's will, shall I not still be my father's child? Shall I not still be fed and clothed by him?" Only an evil child would talk thus.

The true son inquires, "What would my father have me do? I will do it cheerfully for his sake. What does my father forbid? For what he forbids shall be hateful to me." Rise above all questions concerning essential and nonessential, and learn to obey in all things; if it be only tying a scarlet thread in the window, or washing in water, do as you are bidden, and in nothing rebel against the Word of the Lord.

Remember, too, that this small matter of obedience, as some call it, had *an important symbolical signification*. I am not sure that the spies meant by it that the scarlet thread should be the same to Rahab as the blood on the lintel and on the two side posts had been to Israel in Egypt, but it does strike me as being very probable. Those two men were so acquainted with the Passover, and the sprinkling of the blood, and the consequent preservation of all in this house, that it was very natural that they should give Rahab a sign akin to the token which God had ordained for his people Israel when his angel passed them by in the day of doom. Therefore, trifling as the color of the cord might seem, it had a deep significance; and even so, commands of God, which are little in themselves, are great in symbolic teaching. Great errors have come into the Christian church by the alteration of simple points in God's commands; and, therefore, since a little thing in the sign may involve a great thing in the substance, it becomes us to cultivate exact obedience.

"Oh!" says one, "but I fear we shall always be in error." Assuredly we shall, unless we endeavor to avoid it. Unless we give abundant attention to the Word of God, we shall fall into mistakes beyond number; errors are unavoidable if we do not study our perfect Chart, even as it is certain that a man will lose his way if he never inquires about it. At any rate, we need not rush into mistakes by omitting to use our judgment, and to inform our understanding. Ask the Lord to teach you by his Holy Spirit, and you will not be taught wrongly. Commit yourself to his instruction, and be willing to do what he teaches you, and you will not go amiss.

This woman's obedience also arose out of real faith, and was the exponent of that faith; for, when she tied the scarlet line in the window, she expressed her confidence in the fact that Jericho would be destroyed, and that she would be saved because she had received a promise to that effect. Sin would not have hidden the spies if she had not believed in their God; and after having done so, if her faith had failed her, she would not have complied with the covenant requirement to hang the scarlet line in the window. Beloved, obey in faith. The obedience of the slave is worth little; the obedience of the child is precious, for it is the fruit of love. That keeping of God's commands which comes of slavish fear lacks the very heart and bowels of obedience, for love is absent;

but, as God's dear children, resting alone in Jesus, confiding in your Father's promise, feel that *because you believe you must obey*, not because you dread hell, or expect to win heaven through any works of your own, but because you have believed in Jesus to the salvation of your soul, and therefore, it is your joy to do his bidding.

Thus I have enlarged upon the first point of the text, that, in the hanging out of the scarlet line, I discern an obedient believer.

II. Now, second, I see here *an appropriated covenant*.

These men had made a covenant with her that she should have her life spared, and the lives of her family, if she concealed their secret, and if she tied a scarlet line in the window. As she tied up that line she did, as it were, say, "I claim the covenant that you have made with me." Beloved, let us speak about this for a moment, for we want more and more to be able to appropriate covenant blessings. How do we appropriate Jesus? *By simple faith.* Faith is the hand which touches the head of the great sacrifice, and lays sin upon it, that sin may no longer lie upon the sinner. Faith grasps Jesus as the Bread of life, and makes that Bread to be our own, that we may feed upon it, and may live forever. Thus the grand thing for appropriating Christ is to obtain faith, and to gain more and more faith. Do you remember when first of all you tied a scarlet line in your window and said, "Christ is mine"? I do remember the very hour and the precise spot, but many cannot tell the moment or the occasion, nor need they agitate themselves about it if they still continue to tie that line in its place. Still, you do remember that there was such a time when you could say, "Jesus is mine." You apprehended Christ because he had apprehended you. If such an hour as that has never come to you, may it come even now! Jesus Christ can save you, but he must be appropriated, or he will be no Savior to you. Remember that God the Holy Ghost himself, though he is the Author of faith, cannot believe for you; you must believe personally for yourself.

Certain persons talk very much of repentance as the gift of the Holy Spirit, and their witness would be true if they would not exaggerate it so as to leave the impression on men's minds that the Holy Ghost repents, and that the sinner has little or nothing to do with it, for that is not true, since it is clear that the Holy Spirit has nothing to repent of, that repentance is an act of the repenting sinner's own soul, and faith a personal exercise of the heart, "for with the heart man believeth unto righteousness." If we do not ourselves repent and believe, Christ is not ours, and we are none of his, neither shall we obtain any benefit from his life and death. Tie the scarlet line in your window, for it will not be tied there for you; you must do it with your own hand. And I do pray that, even now, you may have boldness through Christ to say, "Yes, Jesus shall be mine; I dare with humble confidence to appropriate him for myself, since he is given freely to poor needy sinners, and I am such a sinner."

Faith is the first and grandest way of tying the scarlet line in the window, but let your faith follow on in *the use of the ordinances and means of grace*, for these assist her in laying hold upon Jesus. I have often found it most blessed to sit at the communion table, and feel, while I ate the bread and drank the wine, that faith was in active exercise, so that I said to myself, "Yes, as certainly as this bread is put into my mouth, and goes into my bodily system, so as to become a part of myself, so that nobody can ever take it away, even so I have by faith believed on and received into my soul the incarnate God, and in that way has he become mine, so that none can separate him from me, or me from him." The ordinance itself will not give you Christ, but often does the symbol blessedly enable the soul to realize Jesus, and contemplate him so as to partake of him. In that draft of wine, so typical of his blood, how often has our soul said, "I rest entirely upon the Redeemer's bloody sacrifice. His substitutionary pangs, griefs, and merits are all my trust before God, and I receive them as my sole reliance for the remission of sin, and take them into my very self, just as I drink of this cup, and thereby the juice of the vine courses through my veins." Continue, beloved friends, thus to appropriate Jesus Christ, and let every communion season be a tying of the scarlet line afresh in the window.

Let *your whole life* be a course of action correspondent to the belief that Christ is yours. I am afraid many believers live as though Jesus Christ did not belong to them at all, nor yet the blessings of the covenant. Do you think that we should be so desponding when we have losses in business if we really believed that all things are ours, and if we had tied the scarlet line in the window, and appropriated all things as ours in Christ? Do you think we should be so soon fluttered, and made to doubt whether we are saved or not, in times of temptation, if our faith took a firm grip of Christ, and tied the scarlet line in the window fast and firm, by claiming the covenant of grace as ours? Beloved, some of you have only appropriated a part of Christ. You believe you are pardoned, but you scarcely know that you are justified. You are justified, and covered with his righteousness, but you have not laid hold upon the sanctification which Jesus gives you. You have a measure of grace, but you have not yet believed that Christ can sanctify you wholly, spirit, soul, and body. We are stinted and stunted, lean and lethargic, because of our failure to grasp with holy confidence the infinite treasure which is stored up in our all-sufficient

Lord. He is ours, and all things are ours in him. "According to your faith be it unto you," is the rule of that great house over which Christ presides. This woman took the covenant which she had made with these men to be hers, and showed that she did so by tying up the scarlet line in the window. The covenant was made with her, and she knew it, and believed it, in like manner. O brother in Christ, by a living faith, grasp the promises of God and claim them as your own!

Here let me also say, *let us do this by displaying a corresponding restfulness.* After Rahab had tied the line in her window, we do not read that she did anything else, except bring her father, and her mother, and her brethren under her roof. She did not make preparations to defend the house against the siege; there is no notification that she appealed to the king to have a special guard to protect that part of the wall. I do not believe that she had a solitary fear or a moment's terror; the scarlet line was in the window, and she felt secure: she had appropriated the promise, and she believed it would not be broken. It is a high privilege to dwell peaceably and quietly in the finished work of Christ, and in the sure immutable promise of God, who cannot lie. Why fret you yourselves, and question you yourselves, and go about with a thousand anxieties when salvation's work was finished on the accursed tree, and Christ has gone into the glory, and has carried in his perfect work before his Father's face? Why mourn you and suspect your safety, when the Lord has raised us up together, and made us sit together in heavenly places in him? We who have believed do enter into rest; the peace of God is ours; so let us, by our resting, show that we have tied the scarlet line in our window, have claimed the finished work of Christ, and therefore rest henceforth from our own works as God did from his.

III. Third, I see here *an open declaration.*

Rahab tied the scarlet line, not in some secret part of the house, but *in the window.* It was her public declaration of faith. I do not say that everybody understood what she meant by that; only those understood it who were in the secret with her, and that sufficed. She hung out the red signal from the window, where it could be seen by those who needed to see it. It was not that she was ostentatious and wished to attract attention; but she was bound to make a public sign, and she did it. Now, some of you believe in my Lord Jesus, and yet you have never united with his people. You are resting in him, but you are mightily afraid that anybody should know it. Be not ashamed of Jesus! The wonder is that he is not ashamed of you. If he was not ashamed to take upon him your nature, and die for you, you need never blush to own his name.

Come forward, you trembling ones, tie the scarlet line in your window, and say, "We are his, and we confess it."

Let it be *a scarlet line* that you tie in the window, however, namely, an avowal of true faith in his precious blood, a declaration of confidence, in atonement by blood; for there are some who profess a sort of faith, but it is not faith in the substitution of Christ. It is unfashionable, nowadays, to believe in the old doctrine of atonement. Modern "culture" has expunged it, or altered it in such a way that no real atonement is left. There are many who are too advanced to avow the old-fashioned gospel; but, as for us, we tie forever the scarlet line in our window, and stand by the truth once delivered to the saints. Our declaration of faith is that we believe in the real and literal substitution of Christ, who died, "the Just for the unjust, that he might bring us to God." In the midst of a thousand new gospels, none of them worth the breath that utters them, we hold to that ancient gospel of the prophet Isaiah, "the chastisement of our peace was upon him; and with his stripes we are healed." Beloved believer, if the doctrine of the sacrifice of Jesus Christ, and his substitutionary atonement be indeed your hope, avow it; avow it boldly, and let there be no mistake about it in these evil times; tie the scarlet line in your window and if nobody else will see it, your brethren will mark it, and be encouraged. If nobody else will be pleased with it, your God will smile upon you, and you will be a sweet savor unto him. No man, that I know of, saw the blood upon the lintel and the two side posts, at the dead of night, in the land of Egypt, for there were none abroad to look upon it; but God saw it, and it is written, "When I see the blood, I will pass over you." When God sees our simple confidence in his dear Son, and perceives us resting upon his Word, without the admixture of human reason and opinion, then, beloved, he will accept us in the Beloved, and our house shall stand when others fall.

Every Christian ought to make his faith in the precious blood visible in many ways. It ought to be manifest in our common conversation; if we are resting in the blood of Jesus, we ought not to be able to talk a quarter of an hour without thoughtful persons perceiving that we are indeed followers of Jesus. I have heard of a man who was so entertaining and instructive in his conversation that it was said that you could not stand under an archway for five minutes with him, to get out of a shower of rain, without learning something from him. Every Christian man ought to be of this sort, in a higher style, so that you cannot be with him many minutes without perceiving him to be a man of God. Of course, in the church of Christ, the Christian man ought to hang a scarlet line out of his door at once, and let his fellow worshipers see that he is decided and resolute for the Lord his God; but he ought to do the same in his business. Customers should soon see that in your shop the common tricks of trade are detested. The scarlet line is over this door. In the house, the mistress in the management of her servants, the master as a husband and as a father, should be known to be better than others. There is a certain sect of people called "the peculiar people"; I wish we were all peculiar people in this respect, that the blood mark set us apart as not our own, but bought with a price. The Lord grant that it may be so with us!

IV. The last point is this. Here was *a dedicated house*—a house with a scarlet line in its window.

Coming here, the other afternoon, and walking down one of the back streets, I amused myself by observing how many houses were insured. I noticed the marks of the different insurance companies. There was *the sun* on one, with his bright face looking down upon us, as much as to say, "There shall be no loss here." The *globe, the star, the Phoenix*, all were there as seals of safety. Now there was only one house in Jericho that was insured, and that had for its symbol and mark of insurance a scarlet line tied in the window. What a mercy it is when houses are insured by the grace of God, and dedicated to the Lord—the very houses, and much more the inhabitants of those houses. How can you dedicate a house? I was reading, the other day, that, in Cromwell's time, you could go down Cheapside, at a certain hour in the morning, and you would see the blinds down at every house and hear the families singing, all the way along, "for," says an old divine, "in those days, a drawn blind was the scarlet line in the window." People knew, as they passed along, that there was an altar erected to God in that house. I am afraid that there are a great many streets in our towns and cities which you might traverse at any hour of the day, and not discover a solitary sign of *family prayer* going on. The practice has gone out of fashion even among many who profess to be the people of God, and farewell to any progress in godliness till we bring it back again.

I believe that, when the house and the church pull together, things are right; but when religion is made to be a thing of the church, and not of the house, when the priest is looked to instead of the father, when men cease to be priests in their own houses, then the very sinews of vital godliness have been cut. If I had to give up all weekday services, and shut up every place of worship in Christendom from Sunday to Sunday, I would prefer to do that rather than lose the morning and evening gatherings of devout households worshiping God. How much Scotland owes to her family devotions! You need not that I remind you of *The Cotter's Saturday Night*. It is the very glory of that country that they do there worship God in their houses. "There is much formality about it," cries one. Well, was there ever anything good which did not degenerate here and there? But I have witnessed, full many a time, the hearty devotion of morning and evening prayer in the north. I wonder how many houses represented by you come up to Matthew Henry's third standard. He says, "Those who pray, do well." You get up to that, I hope. "Those that read the Scriptures and pray, do better. Those that read the Scriptures and pray and sing, do best of all." I think so. This is the scarlet line with the threefold cord to it, and I would that every house hung out that scarlet line as meaning, "This house belongs to King Jesus. The devil need not trouble himself to come here, for the strong man armed keeps his goods in peace."

The beauty of it was that *all inside Rahab's house were saved.* "Come in, dear mother," said she. Who among us could bear the thought of our mother being lost? It breaks our hearts to think of such a thing. My mother lost? Oh no, that must not be! And your father lost? Oh, have you an unconverted father? I beseech you, give no slumber to your eyelids till you have done all you can to set before him the way of peace, and have pleaded for him before God with sighs and tears. And then she said, "Come in, dear brothers and sisters." I delight in Rahab for loving her household. If you have brothers and sisters who are not yet under the scarlet line, pray to God to bring them in, that all your house may be dedicated to the most High, and, without exception, all may dwell beneath the blessed bloodred token which infallibly preserves all who are sheltered beneath it.

I leave this point to notice that there are other things besides family prayer which should be like the scarlet line in the house. For instance, there should be, in every Christian house, a scarlet line put up in *the selecting of the company that is kept.* The Christian should carefully *select his friends and associates.* He should say, "He that tells lies shall not tarry in my sight." As for the drunkard and the swearer and those who use unchaste language, let them be what they may, they shall not visit within our doors, we will not tolerate them. If we are masters of our household, we try to find our children friends whom we should like to be their companions in eternity. Some parents introduce their children to young men and young women who happen to be "very respectable," as they say, but who are worldly and ungodly, and thus they do much to ruin them. It should not be so. Hang the scarlet line over the door, and if they do not love that scarlet line, religious conversation will before long make the place too hot for them. If you talk much of Jesus, the frivolous will consider that they have notice to quit.

A Christian man's house should have a scarlet line over *its reading.* I confess to great sorrow whenever I see, in a Christian man's house, commonly laid about for the use of the girls, that dreadful rubbishing yellow stuff [sensational or explicit periodicals or books] which pollutes every railway bookstall, much of it downright ungodliness, and the best of it abominable nonsense, the reading of which is a sheer waste of time. When there are thousands of good and interesting books to be read, it seems a pity that Christian people should give their time to reading which cannot profit them. Let the donkeys have their thistles, I never grudge them; and so I will not say that worldlings should not read such books; they suit them, let them have them. I have never murmured at a farmer when I have seen him going along with his great mash of all manner of garbage to give to his hogs; so long as he did not give me a basin of it for dinner, I was satisfied to let the swine have their food; and there are a great many romances and a vast mass of literature which it is vain to deny to ungodly people, for it is after their nature; but as for us, let us have none of it. I should as soon expect to see the archangel Gabriel feeding out of a hog's trough, as to see one who is a joint heir with Christ finding his pleasure in books that are half lewd and the other half absurd. Hang a scarlet line over your library door as well as everywhere else.

So let it be with *all amusements*. There are some amusements that we cannot say are absolutely bad in themselves, but they lead to evil. They go up to the edge of the precipice, and there are many who only need to get so far and they are sure to fall over. Besides, they make the Christian so like the worldling that nobody could tell which is which. Now, tie the scarlet line up. I would do so even as to what *pictures* I would hang up in my house. I am often sad to see, especially in the houses of the poor, Roman Catholic pictures exhibited on the walls, because they happen to be rather pretty and very cheap. Popish publishers have very cleverly managed to get up pictures of the Virgin, and the lying fable of her assumption to heaven, and all sorts of legends of saints and saintesses; and being brightly colored, and sold very much under price, these vile things have been introduced into thousands of houses. I have seen, to my horror, a picture of God the Father represented as an old man, a conception almost too hideous to mention, yet the picture is hung up in the cottages of England; whereas the Lord has declared that we should make no image of him, or represent him in any way, and the attempt is blasphemous. If you have a bad picture, no matter how good a work of art it is, burn it; and if you have a bad book, no matter how much it may be worth, do not sell it for somebody else to read, tear it in pieces.

Let the Christian hang up the scarlet line, and make certain that nobody shall be debauched in mind or body by anything that he tolerates in his house. I may seem to be too severe; but if my Master were to speak out of heaven, he would not rebuke that as a sin on my part; for rather would he say that we need to be much more precise and decided about evil things.

Well, you shall do what you please, you have your own liberty; but, "as for me and my house, we will serve the Lord," and the bloodred line shall be in my window. My father's father, do I not remember how, when I was a child, I used to hear his prayers for my father and for me? Well do I remember my father's conversion in answer to my grandfather's prayers. And my father, can I ever forget how he wrestled for us at the mercy seat, and God forbid it should happen that in my son's house, in years to come, there should be no altar to my God! I would sooner be without a tent for myself than without an altar for the Lord. Wherever we are, we must hang up the scarlet line. We cannot expect a blessing if we do not. Of course, I am not speaking to those who are not fathers or heads of households. If they are servants, they cannot help what is done in the house. If they are underlings who have not the power, they cannot arrange as they would; but I am speaking to those who fear the Lord and can do it. Do, beloved, dedicate your house to God from the garret to the cellar. Let there be nothing even in the cellar which you would be ashamed for Jesus Christ to see. Let there be nothing about the house but what shall be so ordered that, if your Lord should come, you could open your door, and say, "Come and welcome, Master, there is nothing here that thy servant desires to conceal."

Believe in Jesus, O ye who know him not; and ye who know him, practice what you know; and God bless you! Amen and amen.

Samson's Mother: Her Excellent Argument

~~~

Published in 1867; delivered at the Metropolitan Tabernacle, Newington. No. 1340.

And Manoah said unto his wife, "We shall surely die, because we have seen God." But his wife said unto him, "If the LORD were pleased to kill us, he would not have received a burnt offering and a meat offering at our hands, neither would he have showed us all these things, nor would as at this time have told us such things as these."—JUDGES 13:22–23

The first remark arising out of the story of Manoah and his wife is this—that oftentimes we pray for blessings which will make us tremble when we receive them. Manoah had asked that he might see the angel, and he saw him: in answer to his request the wonderful One condescended to reveal himself a second time, but the consequence was that the good man was filled with astonishment and dismay, and turning to his wife, he exclaimed, "We shall surely die, because we have seen God." Brethren, do we always know what we are asking for when we pray? We are imploring an undoubted blessing, and yet if we knew the way in which such blessing must necessarily come, we should, perhaps, hesitate before we pressed our suit. You have been entreating very much for growth in holiness. Do you know, brother, that in almost every case that means increased affliction? For we do not make much progress in the divine life except when the Lord is pleased to try us in the furnace and purge us with many fires. Do you desire the mercy on that condition? Are you willing to take it as God pleases to send it, and to say, "Lord, if spiritual growth implies trial, if it signifies a long sickness of body, if it means deep depression of soul, if it entails the loss of property, if it involves the taking away of my dearest friends, yet I make no reserve, but include in the prayer all that is needful to the good end. When I say, 'Sanctify me wholly, spirit, soul, and body,' I leave the process to thy discretion."

Suppose you really knew all that it would bring upon you, would you not pray, at any rate, with more solemn tones? I hope you would not hesitate, but, counting all the cost, would still desire to be delivered from sin; but, at any

rate, you would put up your petition with deliberation, weighing every syllable, and then when the answer came, you would not be so astonished at its
peculiar form. Often and often the blessing which we used so eagerly to
implore is the occasion of the suffering which we deplore. We do not know
God's methods.

This is the Lord's way of answering prayer for faith and grace. He comes
with rods of chastisement, and makes us smart for our follies, for thus alone
can he deliver our childish spirits from them. He comes with sharp plowshares
and tears up the soil, for thus only can we be made to yield him a harvest. He
comes with hot irons and burns us to the heart; and when we inquire, "Why
all this?" the answer comes to us, "This is what you asked for; this is the way
in which the Lord answers your requests." Perhaps, at this moment, the fainting feeling that some of you are now experiencing, which makes you fear that
you will surely die, may be accounted for by your own prayers. I should like
you to look at your present sorrows in that light, and say, "After all, I can see
that now my God has given to me exactly what I sought at his hands. I asked
to see the angel, and I have seen him, and now it is that my spirit is cast down
within me."

A second remark is this: very frequently deep prostration of spirit is the
forerunner of some remarkable blessing. It was to Manoah and to his wife the
highest conceivable joy of life, the climax of their ambition, that they should
be the parents of a son by whom the Lord should begin to deliver Israel. Joy
filled them—inexpressible joy—at the thought of it; but, at the time when the
good news was first communicated, Manoah, at least, was made so heavy in
spirit that he said, "We shall surely die, for we have seen an angel of the Lord."
Take it as a general rule that dull skies foretell a shower of mercy. Expect
sweet favor when you experience sharp affliction. Do you not remember, concerning the apostles, that they feared as they entered into the cloud on Mount
Tabor? And yet it was in that cloud that they saw their Master transfigured;
and you and I have had many a fear about the cloud we were entering,
although we were therein to see more of Christ and his glory than we had
ever beheld before. The cloud which you fear makes the external wall of that
secret chamber wherein the Lord reveals himself.

Before you can carry Samson in your arms, Manoah, you must be made
to say, "We shall surely die." Before the minister shall preach the word to thousands, he must be emptied and made to tremble under a sense of inability.
Before the Sunday school teacher shall bring her girls to Christ, she shall be
led to see how weak and insufficient she is. I do believe that whenever the
Lord is about to use us in his household, he takes us like a dish and wipes us

right out and sets us on the shelf, and then afterward he takes us down and puts thereon his own heavenly meat, with which to fill the souls of others. There must as a rule be an emptying, a turning upside down, and a putting on one side, before the very greatest blessing comes. Manoah felt that he must die, and yet die he could not, for he was to be the father of Samson, the deliverer of Israel and the terror of Philistia.

Let me offer a third remark, which is this: great faith is in many instances subject to fits. What great faith Manoah had! His wife was barren, yet when she was told by the angel that she should bear a child, he believed it, although no heavenly messenger had come to himself personally—so believed it that he did not want to see the man of God a second time to be told that it would be so, but only to be informed how to bring up the child: that was all. "Well," says old Bishop Hall, "might he be the father of strong Samson, that had such a strong faith." He had a strong faith indeed, and yet here he is saying in alarm, "We shall surely die, because we have seen God." Do not judge a man by any solitary word or act, for if you do, you will surely mistake him. Cowards are occasionally brave, and the bravest men are sometimes cowards. There are men who would be worse cowards practically if they were a little less cowardly than they are: a man may be too much a coward to confess that he is timid. Trembling Manoah was so outspoken, honest, and sincere that he expressed his feelings, which a more politic person might have concealed. Though fully believing what had been spoken from God, yet at the same time this doubt was on him, as the result of his belief in tradition: "We shall surely die, because we have seen God."

Once again, another remark is that it is a great mercy to have a Christian companion to go to for counsel and comfort whenever your soul is depressed. Manoah had married a capital wife. She was the better one of the two in sound judgment. She was the weaker vessel by nature, but she was the stronger believer, and probably that was why the angel was sent to her, for the angels are best pleased to speak with those who have faith, and if they have the pick of their company, and the wife has more faith than the husband, they will visit the wife sooner than her spouse, for they love to take God's messages to those who will receive them with confidence. She was full of faith, evidently, and so when her husband tremblingly said, "We shall surely die," she did not believe in such a mistrustful inference. Moreover, though they say that women cannot reason, yet here was a woman whose arguments were logical and overwhelming. Certain it is that women's perceptions are generally far clearer than men's reasonings; they look at once into a truth, while we are hunting for our spectacles. Their instincts are generally as safe as our reasonings, and therefore when they have in addition a clear, logical mind they make the wisest of counselors.

Well, Manoah's wife not only had clear perceptions, but she had capital reasoning faculties. She argued, according to the language of the text, that it was not possible that God should kill them after what they had seen and heard. Oh, that every man had such a prudent, gracious wife as Manoah had! Oh, that whenever a man is cast down, a Christian brother or sister stands ready to cheer him with some reminder of the Lord's past goodness, or with some gracious promise from the divine Word! It may happen to be the husband who cheers the wife, and in such a case it is equally beautiful. We have known a Christian sister to be very nervous and very often depressed and troubled: what a mercy to her to have a Christian husband whose strength of faith can encourage her to smile away her griefs, by resting in the everlasting faithfulness and goodness of the Lord.

God the Holy Spirit shall help us, we will take up the argument of Manoah's wife, and see whether it will not also comfort our hearts. She had three strings to her bow, good woman. One was—the Lord does not mean to kill us, because he has accepted our sacrifices. The second was—he does not mean to kill us, or else he would not, as at this time, have told us such things as these. So the three strings to her bow were *accepted sacrifices, gracious revelations,* and *precious promises.* Let us dwell upon each of them.

I. And, first, *accepted* sacrifices.

I will suppose that I am addressing a brother who is sadly tried, and terribly cast down, and who therefore has begun to lament:

> The Lord has forsaken me quite;
> My God will be gracious no more.

Brother, is that possible? Has not God of old accepted on your behalf the offering of his Son Jesus Christ? You have believed in Jesus, dear friend. You do not believe in him now. Lay your hand on your heart, and put the question solemnly to yourself, "Dost thou believe on the Son of God?" You are able to say, "Yes, Lord, notwithstanding all my unhappiness, I do believe in thee, and rest the stress and weight of my soul's interests on thy power to save." Well, then, you have God's own word, recorded in his own infallible Book, assuring you that Jesus Christ was accepted of God on your behalf, for he laid down his life for as many as believe in him, that they might never perish. He stood as their surety, and suffered as their substitute, is it possible that this should be unavailing, and that after all they may be cast away? The argument of

Manoah's wife was just this: "Did we not put the kid [goat] on the rock, and as we put it there was it not consumed? It was consumed instead of us; we shall not die, for the victim has been consumed. The fire will not burn us: it has spent itself upon the sacrifice. Did you not see it go up in smoke, and see the angel ascend with it? The fire is gone; it cannot fall on us to destroy us."

This being interpreted into the gospel is just this: have we not seen the Lord Jesus Christ fastened to the cross? Have we not beheld him in agonies extreme? Has not the fire of God consumed him? Have we not seen him rising, as it were, from that sacred fire in the resurrection and the ascension, to go into the glory? Because the fire of Jehovah's wrath had spent itself on him, we shall not die. He has died instead of us. It cannot be that the Lord has made him suffer, the Just for the unjust, and now will make the believer suffer too. It cannot be that Christ loved his church, and gave himself for it, and that now the church must perish also. It cannot be that the Lord has laid on him the iniquity of us all, and now will lay our iniquity on us too. It were not consistent with justice. It would make the vicarious sacrifice of Christ to be a nullity, a superfluity of cruelty which achieved nothing. The atonement cannot be made of none effect, the very supposition would be blasphemy. Oh, look, my soul, look to the redeemer's cross, and as you see how God accepts Christ, be you filled with content. Hear how the "it is finished" of Jesus on earth is echoed from the throne of God himself, as he raises up his Son from the dead, and bestows glory upon him: hear this, I say, and as you hear, attend to the power of this argument: if the Lord had been pleased to kill us, he would not have accepted his Son for us. If he meant us to die, would he have put him to death too? How can it be? The sacrifice of Jesus must effectually prevent the destruction of those for whom he offered up himself as a sacrifice. Jesus dying for sinners, and yet the sinners denied mercy! Inconceivable and impossible! My soul, whatever your inward feelings and the tumult of your thoughts, the accepted sacrifice shows that God is not pleased to kill you.

But, if you notice, in the case of Manoah, they had offered a burnt sacrifice and a meat offering too. Well, now, in addition to the great, grand sacrifice of Christ, which is our trust, we, dear brothers and sisters, have offered other sacrifices to God, and in consequence of his acceptance of such sacrifice we cannot imagine that he intends to destroy us.

First, let me conduct your thoughts back to the offering of prayer which you have presented. I will speak for myself. I recall now, running over my diary mentally, full many an instance in which I have sought the Lord in prayer, and he has most graciously heard me. I am as sure that my requests have been heard as ever Manoah could have been sure that his sacrifice was consumed upon the rock. May I not infer from this that the Lord does not mean to destroy you? You know that it had been so with you, dear brother. You are down in the dumps today, you are beginning to raise many questions about divine love; but there have been times—you know there have—when you have sought the Lord and he has heard you. You can say, "This poor man cried, and the Lord heard him, and delivered him from all his fears." Perhaps you have not jotted down the fact in a book, but your memory holds the indelible record. Your soul has made her personal boast in the Lord concerning his fidelity to his promise in helping his people in the hour of need, for you have happily proved it in your own case. Now, brother, if the Lord had been pleased to kill you, would he have heard your prayers? If he had meant to cast you out after all, would he have heard you so many times? If he had sought a quarrel against you, he might have had cause for that quarrel many years ago, and have said to you, "When you make many prayers, I will not hear." But since he has listened to your cries and tears, and many a time answered your petitions, he cannot intend to kill you.

Again, you brought to him, years ago, not only your prayers but yourself. You gave yourself over to Christ, body, soul, spirit, all your goods, all your hours, all your talents, every faculty, and every possible acquirement, and you said, "Lord, I am not my own, but I am bought with a price." Now at that time did not the Lord accept you? You have at this very moment a lively recollection of the sweet sense of acceptance you had at that time. Though you are at this time sorely troubled, yet you would not wish to withdraw from the consecration which you then made, but on the contrary you declare,

High heaven, that heard the solemn vow,
That vow renewed shall daily hear,
Till, in life's latest hour, I bow,
And bless in death a bond so dear.

Now would the Lord have accepted the offering of yourself to him if he meant to destroy you? Would he have let you say, "I am thy servant and the son of thy handmaid: thou hast loosed my bond"? Would he have permitted you to declare as you can boldly assert tonight, "I bear in my body the marks of the Lord Jesus," delighting to remember the time of your baptism into him, whereby your body washed with his pure body, was declared to be the Lord's forever? Would he enable you to feel a joy in the very mark of your consecration, as well as in the consecration itself, if he meant to slay you? Oh, surely not! He does not let a man give himself up to him and then cast him away. That cannot be.

Some of us, dear friends, can recollect how, growing out of this last sacrifice, there have been others. The Lord has accepted our offerings at other times too, for our works, faith, and labors of love have been owned of his Spirit. There are some of you, I am pleased to remember, whom God has blessed to the conversion of little children whom you brought to the Savior, and there are others on earth whom you can look upon with great joy because God was pleased to make you the instrument of their conviction and their after conversion. Some of you, I perceive, are ministers of the gospel, others of you preach at the corners of the streets, and there have been times in your lives— I am sure that you wish they were ten times as many—in which God has been pleased to succeed your efforts, so that hearts have yielded to the sway of Jesus. Now you do not put any trust in those things, nor do you claim any merit for having served your Master, but still I think they may be thrown in as a matter of consolation, and you may say, "If the Lord had meant to destroy me, would he have enabled me to preach his gospel? Would he have helped me to weep over men's souls? Would he have enabled me to gather those dear children like lambs to his bosom? Would he have granted me my longing desire to bear fruit in his vineyard, if he did not mean to bless me?"

II. Now the second argument was that they had received *gracious revelations.*

"If the Lord were pleased to kill us, he would not have showed us all these things." Now, what has the Lord shown you, my dear brother? I will mention one or two things.

First, the Lord has shown you—perhaps years ago, or possibly at this moment he is showing you for the first time—*your sin.* What a sight that was when we first had it. Some of you never saw your sins, but your sins are there all the same. In an old house, perhaps, there is a cellar into which nobody goes, and no light ever comes in. You live in the house comfortably enough, not knowing what is there; but one day you take a candle, and go down the steps, and open that moldy door, and when it is opened, dear me! What a damp, pestilential smell! How foul the floor is! All sorts of living creatures hop away from under your feet. There are growths on the very walls—a heap of roots in the corner, sending out those long yellow growths which look like the fingers of death. And there is a spider, and there are a hundred like him, of such a size as cannot be grown, except in such horrible places. You get out as quickly as ever you can. You do not like the look of it. Now the candle did not make that cellar bad; the candle did not make it filthy. No, the candle only showed what there was.

And when you [hire] in the carpenter to take down that shutter which you could not open anyhow, for it had not been opened for years, and when the daylight comes in, it seems more horrible than it did by candlelight, and you wonder, indeed, however you did go across it with all those dreadful things all around you and you cannot be satisfied to live upstairs now till that cellar downstairs has been perfectly cleansed. That is just like our heart; it is full of sin, but we do not know it. It is a den of unclean birds, a menagerie of everything that is fearful, and fierce, and furious—a little hell stocked with devils. Such is our nature; such is our heart. Now the Lord showed me mine years ago, as he did some of you, and the result of sight of one's heart is horrible. Well does Dr. Young say, "God spares all eyes but his own that fearful sight, a naked human heart." Nobody ever did see all his heart as it really is. You have only seen a part, but when seen, it is so horrible that it is enough to drive a man out of his senses to see the evil of his nature.

Now let us gather some honey out of this dead lion. Brother, if the Lord had meant to destroy us, he would not have shown us our sin, because we were happy enough previously, were we not? In our own poor way we were content enough, and if he did not mean to pardon us, it was not like the Lord to show us our sin, and so to torment us before our time, unless he meant to take it away. We were swine, but we were satisfied enough with the husks we ate; and why not let us remain swine? What was the good of letting us see our filthiness if he did not purpose to take it away? It never can be possible that God sets himself studiously to torture the human mind by making it conscious of its evil, if he never intends to supply a remedy. Oh no! A deep sense of sin will not save you, but it is a pledge that there is something begun in your soul which may lead to salvation; for that deep sense of sin does as good as say, "The Lord is laying bare the disease that he may cure it. He is letting you see the foulness of that underground cellar of your corruption, because he means to cleanse it for you."

But he has shown us more than this, for he has made us see *the hollowness and emptiness of the world.* There are some here present, who at one time, were very gratified with the pleasures and amusements of the world. The theater was a great delight to them. The ballroom afforded them supreme satisfaction. To be able to dress just after their own fancy, and to spend money on their own whims, were the very acme of delight; but there came a time when across all these the soul perceived a mysterious handwriting, which being interpreted ran thus: "Vanity of vanities; all is vanity." These very people went to the same amusements, but they seemed so dull and stupid that they came away saying, "We do not care a bit for them. The joys are all gone. What seemed gold turns out to be gilt; and what we thought marble was only white paint. The varnish is cracked, the tinsel is faded, the coloring has vanished. Mirth laughs like an idiot, and pleasure grins like madness."

We have heard the words, "Vanity of vanities; all is vanity," sounding in our hearts; and now do you think that, if the Lord had meant to kill us, he would have taught us this? Why, no; he would have said, "Let them alone, they are given unto idols. They are only going to have one world in which they can rejoice; let them enjoy it." He would have let the swine go on with their husks if he had not meant to turn them into his children, and bring them to his own bosom.

But he has taught us something better than this, namely, *the preciousness of Christ.* Unless we are awfully deceived—self-deceived, I mean—we have known what it is to lose the burden of our sin at the foot of the cross. We have known what it is to see the suitability and all-sufficiency of the merit of our dear Redeemer, and we have rejoiced in him with joy unspeakable and full of glory. If he had meant to destroy us, he would not have shown us Christ.

Sometimes also we have strong desires after God! What pinings after communion with him have we felt! What longings to be delivered from sin! What yearnings to be perfect! What aspirations to be with him in heaven, and what desires to be like him while we are here! Now these longings, cravings, desirings, yearnings, do you think the Lord would have put them into our hearts if he had meant to destroy us? What would be the good of it? Would it not be tormenting us as Tantalus was tormented? Would it not, indeed, be a superfluity of cruelty thus to make us wish for what we could never have, and pine after what we should never gain? O beloved, let us be comforted about these things. If he had meant to kill us, he would not have shown us such things as these.

III. I shall have no time to dwell upon the last source of comfort, which is what the Lord has spoken to us—*many precious promises.*

"Nor would he have told us such things as these." At almost any time when a child of God is depressed, if he goes to the Word of God and to prayer, and looks up, he will generally get a hold of some promise or other. I know I generally do. I could not tell you, dear brother, tonight, what promise would suit your case, but the Lord always knows how to apply the right word at the right time; and when a promise is applied with great power to the soul, and you are enabled to plead it at the mercy seat, you may say, "If the Lord had meant to kill us, he would not have made us such a promise as this." I have a promise that hangs up before my eyes whenever I wake every morning, and it has continued in its place for years. It is a stay to my soul. It is this: "I will not fail thee, nor forsake thee." Difficulties arise, funds run short, sickness comes; but somehow or other my text always seems to flow like a fountain: "I will not fail thee, nor forsake thee." If the Lord had meant to kill us, he would not have said that to us.

What is your promise, brother? What have you got a hold of? If you have not laid hold of any, and feel as if none belonged to you, yet there are such words as these, "This is a faithful saying and worthy of all acceptation, that Christ Jesus came into the world to save sinners," and you are one. Ah, if he had meant to destroy you, he would not have spoken a text of such a wide character on purpose to include your case. A thousand promises go down to the lowest deep into which a heart can ever descend, and if the Lord had meant to destroy a soul in the deeps, he would not have sent a gospel promise down even to that extreme.

I should like to say these two or three words to you who are unconverted, but who are troubled in your souls. You think that God means to destroy you. Now, dear friend, I take it that if the Lord had meant to kill you, he would not have sent the gospel to you. If there had been a purpose and a decree to destroy you, he would not have brought you here. Now you are sitting to hear that Jesus has died to save such as you are. You are sitting where you are bidden to trust him and be saved. If the Lord had meant to slay you, I do not think he would have sent me on such a fruitless errand as to tell you of a Christ who could not save you. Some of you have had your lives spared very remarkably. You have been in accidents on land or on sea, perhaps in battle and shipwreck. You have been raised from a sickbed. If the Lord had meant to destroy you, surely he would have let you die then; but he has spared you, and you are getting on in years; surely it is time that you yielded to his mercy and gave yourself up into the hands of grace. If the Lord had meant to destroy you, surely, he would not have brought you here, for, possibly, I am addressing one who has come here, wondering why. All the time that he has been sitting here, he has been saying to himself, "I do not know how I got into this place, but here I am." God means to bless you tonight, I trust, and he will, if you breathe this prayer to heaven, "Father, forgive me! I have sinned against heaven and before thee, but for Christ's sake forgive me! I put my trust in thy Son." You shall find eternal life, rejoicing in the sacrifice which God has accepted. You shall one of these days rejoice in the revelations of his love, and in the promises which he gives you, and say as we say tonight, "If the Lord were pleased to kill us, he would not have showed us all these things."

Ruth: Deciding for God

❧

Intended for reading on Lord's Day, June 24, 1900; delivered on Thursday evening, April 21, 1881, at the Metropolitan Tabernacle, Newington. No. 2680.

And Ruth said, "Entreat me not to leave thee, or to return from following after thee: for whither thou goest, I will go; and where thou lodgest, I will lodge: thy people shall be my people, and thy God my God."—RUTH 1:16

This was a very brave, outspoken confession of faith. Please to notice that it was made by a woman, a young woman, a poor woman, a widow woman, and a foreigner. Remembering all that, I should think there is no condition of gentleness or of obscurity or of poverty or of sorrow, which should prevent anybody from making an open confession of allegiance to God when faith in the Lord Jesus Christ has been exercised. If that is your experience, my dear friend, then whoever you may be, you will find an opportunity, somewhere or other, of declaring that you are on the Lord's side. I am glad that all candidates for membership in our church make their confession of faith at our church meetings. I have been told that such an ordeal must keep a great many from joining us; yet I notice that, where there is no such ordeal, they often have very few members, but here are we with five thousand six hundred, or thereabouts, in church fellowship, and very seldom, if ever, finding anybody kept back by having to make an open confession of faith in Christ. It does the man, the woman, the boy, or the girl, whoever it is, so much good for once, at least, to say right out straight, "I am a believer in the Lord Jesus Christ, and I am not ashamed of it," that I do not think we shall ever deviate from our custom.

I have also noticed that, when people have once confessed Christ before men, they are very apt to do it again somewhere else; and they thus acquire a kind of boldness and outspokenness upon religious matters, and a holy courage as followers of Christ, which more than make up for any self-denial and trembling which the effort may have cost them.

I think Naomi was quite right to drive Ruth, as it were, to take this brave stand, in which it became an absolute necessity for her to speak right straight out, and say, in the words of our text, "Intreat me not to leave thee, or to return from following after thee: for whither thou goest, I will go; and where thou lodgest, I will lodge: thy people shall be my people, and thy God my

God." What is there for any of us to be ashamed of in acknowledging that we belong to the Lord Jesus Christ? What can there be that should cause us to be ashamed of Jesus, or make us blush to own his name?

> Ashamed of Jesus! that dear Friend
> On whom my hopes of heaven depend!
> No: when I blush, be this my shame,
> That I no more revere his name.

We ought to be ashamed of being ashamed of Jesus; we ought to be afraid of being afraid to own him; we ought to tremble at trembling to confess him, and to resolve that we will take all suitable opportunities that we can find of saying, first to relatives, and then to all others with whom we come into contact, "We serve the Lord Christ."

I should think that Naomi was—certainly she ought to have been—greatly cheered by hearing this declaration from Ruth, especially the last part of it: "Thy people shall be my people, and thy God my God." Naomi had suffered great temporal loss; she had lost her husband and her two sons; but now she had found the soul of her daughter-in-law; and I believe that, according to the scales of true judgment, there ought to have been more joy in her heart at the conversion of Ruth's soul than grief over the death of her husband and her sons. Our Lord Jesus has told us that "there is joy in the presence of the angels of God over one sinner that repenteth"; and I always understand, by that expression, that there is joy in the heart of God himself over every sinner's repentance. Well, then, if Naomi's husband and sons were true believers—if they had been walking aright before the Lord—as, let us hope, they had done, she need not have felt such sorrow for them as could at all compare with the joy of her daughter-in-law being saved.

Perhaps, some of you, dear friends, have had bereavements in your homes; but if the death—the temporal death—of one should be the means of the spiritual life of another, there is a clear gain, I am sure there is; and though you may have gone weeping to the grave, yet, if you have evidence that, with those tears, there were also tears of repentance on the part of others of your family, and with that sad glance into the grave there was also a believing look at the dying, risen, and living Savior, you are decidedly a gainer, and you need not say, with Naomi, "I went out full, and the Lord hath brought me home again empty." Really Naomi, with her converted daughter-in-law at her side, if she had only been able to look into the future, might have been a happier woman than when she went away with her husband and her boys, for now she had with her one who was to be in the direct line of the progenitors of

Christ—a right royal woman; for I count that the line of Christ is the true imperial line, and that they were the most highly honored among men and women who were in any way associated with the birth of the Savior into this world; and Ruth, though a Moabitess, was one of those who were elected to share in this high privilege. So I beg you, if you have been sorrowful because of any deaths in your family circle, to pray God to outweigh that sorrow with a greater measure of joy because, by his grace, he has brought other members of your family to trust in Jesus.

Another thought strikes me here; that is, that it was when Naomi returned to the land which she ought never to have left, it was when she came out from the idolatrous Moabites among whom she had, as you see, relatives, and friends, and acquaintances—it was when she said, "I will go back to my own country, and people, and God"—that then the Lord gave her the soul of this young woman who was so closely related to her. It may be that some of you professedly Christian people have been living at a distance from God. You have not led the separated life; you have tried to be friendly with the world as well as with Christ, and your children are not growing up as you wish they would. You say that your sons are not turning out well, and that your girls are dressy, and flighty, and worldly. Do you wonder that it is so? "Oh!" you say, "I have gone a good way to try to please them, thinking that, perhaps, by so doing, I might win them for Christ." Ah! you will never win any soul to the right by a compromise with the wrong. It is decision for Christ and his truth that has the greatest power in the family, and the greatest power in the world, too. If a soldier in the barracks is converted, and he says, "I mean to be a Christian; but, at the same time, I will join with the other men as much as I can; I will sometimes step into the public house with them," and so forth, he will do no good. But the moment he boldly takes his stand for his new Captain, and is known to be a Christian, his comrades may begin to scoff at him, but they will also begin to be impressed; and if he bravely maintains that stand, and never gives way in the least degree, but is faithful to his Lord and Master, then he will be likely to see conversions among his fellow soldiers.

It was while Naomi was on her way back to her own land that she heard the good news that her dear daughter-in-law had decided to be a follower of Jehovah, and to say, "Thy people shall be my people, and thy God my God." This gave her great joy; but how must some of you Christian people feel when you find out that others have been caused to stumble through your living at a distance from Christ? What pangs of remorse will seize you when you discover that your arm has been paralyzed for good, that you have been unable to lead others to the Savior, because you yourself were living so far off from him that it was a serious question whether you were not growing to be a worshiper of the Moabite idols, and giving up altogether your profession of being a follower of the one true God! Now, with this as a preface, I come distinctly to the subject of the text. Here is a young woman who says to a follower of Jehovah, "Thy people shall be my people, and thy God my God."

I. My first observation is, that *affection for the godly should influence us to godliness.*

It did so in this case. Affection for their godly mother-in-law influenced both Orpah and Ruth for a time, "and they said unto her, 'Surely we will return with thee unto thy people.'" They were both drawn part of the way toward Canaan; but alas! natural affection has not sufficient power in itself to draw anybody to decision for God. It may be helpful to that end; it may be one of the "cords of a man" and "bands of love" which God, in his infinite mercy, often uses in drawing sinners to himself; but there has to be something more than that mere human affection. Still, it ought to be of some service in leading to decision; and it is a very dreadful thing when those who have godly parents seem to be the worse rather than the better for that fact, or when men, who have Christian wives, rebel against the light, and become all the more wicked because God has blessed their homes with godly women who speak to them, lovingly and tenderly, concerning the claims of the religion of Jesus. That is a terrible state of affairs, for it ought always to be the case that our affection for godly people should help to draw us toward godliness. In Ruth's case, by the grace of God, it was the means of leading her to the decision expressed in our text, "Thy people shall be my people, and thy God my God."

Many forces may be combined to bring others to this decision. First, *there is the influence of companionship.* Nobody doubts that evil company tends to make a man bad, and it is equally sure that good companionship has a tendency to influence men toward that which is good. It is a happy thing to have side by side with you one whose heart is full of love to God. It is a great blessing to have as a mother a true saint, or to have as a brother or a sister one who fears the Lord; and it is a special privilege to be linked for life, in the closest bonds, with one whose prayers may rise with ours, and whose praises may also mingle with ours. There is something about Christian companionship which must tell in the right direction unless the heart be resolutely bent on mischief.

There is something more than this, however, and that is, *the influence of admiration.* There can be no doubt whatever that Ruth looked with loving reverence and admiration upon Naomi, for she saw in her a character which won her heart's esteem and affection. The few glimpses which we have of that godly woman, in this book of Ruth, show us that she was a most disinterested and unselfish person, not one who, because of her own great sorrow, would burden others with it, and pull them down to her own level in order that they might in some way assist her. She was one who considered the interests of others rather than her own; and all such persons are sure to win admiration and esteem. When a Christian man so lives that others see something about him which they do not perceive in themselves, that is one way in which they are often attracted toward the Christian life. When the sick Christian is patient, when the poor Christian is cheerful, when the believer in Christ is forgiving, generous, tenderhearted, sympathetic, honest, upright, then it is that observers say, "Here is something worth looking at; whence came all this excellence?" And they take knowledge of them that they have been with Jesus, and that they have learned these things of him; and in that way they are themselves inclined to become his followers.

Nor is it only by companionship and admiration that people are won to the Savior; there is also *the influence of instruction*. I have no doubt that Naomi gave her daughter-in-law much helpful teaching. Ruth would want to know about Naomi's God, and Naomi would be only too glad to tell her all she knew. When the Spaniards went over to South America, they treated the poor natives so badly that the Indians did not wish to know anything about the Spaniards' god, for they thought, from the cruelties they had suffered, that he must be a devil; and there are certain sorts of professors who are so unkind, they have such an absence of everything gentle and generous about them, that one does not want to know anything about their god, for if they are like him, probably he is the devil.

But, dear friends, it ought not to be so with us. We should make people want to know what our religion really is, and then be ready to tell them. I have no doubt that, many a time, in the land of Moab, when her daughters-in-law ran in to see her, Naomi would begin telling them about the deliverance at the Red Sea, and how the Lord brought his people through the wilderness, and how the goodly land, which flowed with milk and honey, had been given to them by the hand of Joshua. Then she would tell them about the tabernacle and its worship, and talk to them about the lamb, and the red heifer, and the bullock, and the sin offering, and so on; and it was thus, probably, that Ruth's heart had been won to Jehovah the God of Israel. And, perhaps, for that reason—because of Naomi's instruction—Ruth said to her, "'Thy people shall be my people.' I know so much about them, that I want to be numbered with them. 'And thy God shall be my God.' You have told me about him, what wonders he has worked, and I have resolved to trust myself under the shadow of his wings." Well, beloved, it ought to be thus with us also. We should take care that the influence of our companionship, the influence of our lives, in which there should be something for observers to admire, and the influence of our conversation, which should be full of gracious instruction, should lead those who come under our influence in the right way.

Besides that, I have no doubt that some persons are drawn toward good things by *a desire to cheer the godly persons whom they love;* and, though I do not put this forward as one of the highest and strongest motives, yet I do feel at liberty to suggest to some young people here that their sins are a great grief to their loving fathers and mothers, and that, if their hearts were given to Christ, it would fill the whole house with holy joy. It was a great joy to me when my sons were born, but it was an infinitely surpassing joy as, one after the other, they told me that they had sought and found the Savior. To pray with them, to point them yet more fully to Christ, to hear the story of their spiritual troubles, and to help them out of their spiritual difficulties, was an intense satisfaction to my soul. Ah! my young friends, you do not know how much those who love you would be cheered if you were converted—especially any of you who have not lived as you should have done—who have, perhaps, even gone away from home, and acted in a way that might well bring your father's gray hairs in sorrow to the grave. I think that he would almost dance with delight if he could only hear that you were truly converted to God.

I know a minister who took out of his pocket an old letter that was nearly worn to pieces; he made a journey from the country to bring it up for me to see. It was not really old, it was worn out because he had so constantly taken it out to read. It was somewhat to this effect. His son had been such a scapegrace, and such a disgrace to his family, that he was helped to go abroad, and he came to London to join the ship. As he had heard his father speak of me, he thought that he would spend his last Thursday night, before starting on the Friday morning, in hearing me in this tabernacle; and here God met with him, for I was moved by the Holy Spirit to say, "Here you are, Jack; going away from home, from your father's house. Oh, that the great Father in heaven would take you to himself!" It happened that his name was Jack, so it was the very word for him, and the Lord blessed it to him there and then. He went to America. He did not write to his father to tell him about his conversion till he had had time to prove the reality of it; but when he had been baptized, and had joined the church, and walked consistently for six months, he sent the good news home. The old man said, "I thought he might have been lost at sea, but the Lord had saved him through your preaching. God bless you, sir!" I had a thousand blessings heaped upon my head by that grateful father. It was only a simple sermon that I had preached on a Thursday night, but it was the means of that son's conversion, and it was the source of great joy to that father; he did not mind about his son being in America, or what he was doing, so long as he had become a true believer in the Lord Jesus Christ. What a mercy it would be if this sermon should be blessed as that one was!

I think, too, that there was another thing which had great influence over Ruth, as it has had over a great many other people. That is, *the fear of separation.* "Ah!" said one to me, only last week, "it used to trouble me greatly when my wife went downstairs to the communion, and I had to go home or to remain with the spectators in the gallery. I did not like to be separated from her even here; and then, sir, the thought stole over me, 'What if I have to be divided from her forever and ever?'" I think that a similar reflection ought, with the blessing of God, to impress a good many. Young man, if you live and die impenitent, you will see your mother no more, except it be from an awful distance, with a great gulf fixed between her and you, so that she cannot cross over to you, or you go over to her. There will come a day when one shall be taken and another left; and before the great separation takes place, at the judgment seat of Christ, when there shall be a sundering made between the goats and the sheep, and between the tares and the wheat, I do implore you to let the influence of the godly whom you love help to draw you toward decision for God and his Christ.

II. My time would fail me if I dwelled longer on this point, though it is a very interesting one, so I must pass on to my second observation, which is, that *resolves to godliness will be tested.*

Ruth speaks very positively: "Thy people shall be my people, and thy God my God." This was her resolve, but it was a resolve which had already been put to the test, and had in great measure satisfactorily passed through it.

First, *it had been tested by the poverty and the sorrow of her mother-in-law.* Naomi said, "The Almighty hath dealt very bitterly with me"; yet Ruth says, "Thy God shall be my God." I like that brave resolution of the young Moabitess. Some people say, "We should like to be converted, for we want to be happy." Yes, but suppose you knew that you would not be happy after conversion, you ought still to wish to have this God to be your God. Naomi has lost her husband, she has lost her sons, she has lost everything; she is going back penniless to Bethlehem, and yet her daughter-in-law says to her, "Thy God shall be my God." O dear friends, if you can share the lot of Christians when they are in trouble, if you can take God and affliction, if you can accept Christ and a cross, then your decision to be his follower is true and real. It has been tested by the afflictions and the trials which you know belong to the people of God, yet you are content to suffer with them in taking their God to be your God too.

Next, Ruth's decision had been tested when *she was bidden to count the cost.* Naomi had put the whole case before her. She had told her daughter-in-law that there was no hope that she should ever bear a son who could become a husband to Ruth, and that she had better stay and find a husband in her own land. She set before her the dark side of the case—possibly too earnestly. She seemed as if she wanted to persuade her to go back, though I do not think that, in her heart, she could really have wished her to do so. But, my young friend, before you say to any Christian, "Thy people shall be my people, and thy God my God," count the cost. Recollect, if you are following an evil trade, you will have to give it up; if you have formed bad habits, you will have to forsake them; and if you have had bad companions, you will have to leave them. There are a great many things which have afforded you pleasure, which must become painful to you, and must be renounced. Are you prepared to follow Christ through the mire and the slough, as well as along the high road, and down in the valley as well as up upon the hills? Are you ready to carry his cross as you hope, afterward, to share his crown? If you can stand the test in detail— such a test as Christ set before those who wanted to be his followers on earth, then is your decision a right one, but not else.

Ruth had been tried, too, by the apparent coldness of one in whom she trusted, and whom she had a right to trust, for Naomi did not at all encourage her; indeed, she seemed to discourage her. I am not sure that Naomi is to be blamed for that, and I am not certain that she is to be much praised. You know, it is quite possible for you to encourage people too much. I have known some encouraged in their doubts and fears till they never could get out of them. At the same time, you can certainly very easily chill inquirers and seekers. And though Naomi showed her love to Ruth, yet she did not seem to have any very great desire to bring her to follow Jehovah. This is a test that many young people find to be very trying; but this young woman said to her mother-in-law, "Intreat me not to leave thee, or to return from following after thee: for whither thou goest, I will go; and where thou lodgest, I will lodge: thy people shall be my people, and thy God my God."

Another trial for Ruth was the drawing back of her sister-in-law. Orpah kissed Naomi, and left her; and you know the influence of one young person upon another when they are of the same age, or when they are related as these two were. You went to the revival meeting with a friend, and she was as much impressed as you were. She has gone back to the world, and the temptation is for you to do the same. Can you stand out against it? You two young men went to hear the same preacher, and you both felt the force of the Word; but your companion has gone back to where he used to be. Can you hold out now, and say, "I will follow Christ alone if I cannot find a companion to go with me"? If so, it is well with you.

Can ye cleave to your Lord?
Can ye cleave to your Lord,
When the many turn aside?
Can ye witness he hath the living Word,
And none upon earth beside?
And can ye endure with the virgin band,
The lowly and pure in heart,
Who, whithersoever the Lamb doth lead,
From his footsteps ne'er depart?

Do ye answer, "We can"? Do ye answer, "We can,
Through his love's constraining power"?
But, ah! remember the flesh is weak,
And will shrink in the trial-hour.
Yet yield to his love, who round you now,
The bands of a man would cast;
The cords of his love, who was given for you,
To the altar binding you fast.

But one of the worst trials that Ruth had was *the silence of Naomi*. I think that is what is meant, for after she had solemnly declared that she would follow the Lord, we read, "When she saw that she was steadfastly minded to go with her, then she left speaking unto her." She left off stating the black side of the case, but she does not appear to have talked to her about the bright side. "She left speaking unto her." The good woman was so sorrowful that she could not talk, her heartbreak was so great that she could not converse, but such silence must have been very trying to Ruth; and when a young person has just joined the people of God, it is a severe test to be brought face to face with a very mournful Christian, and not to get one encouraging word. Sometimes, brethren and sisters, we must swallow our own bitter pills as fast as ever we can, that we may not discourage others by making a wry face over them. It is sometimes the very best thing a sorrowful person can do to say, "I must not be sad; here is young So-and-So coming in. I must be cheerful now, for here comes one who might be discouraged by my grief." You remember how the psalmist, when he was in a very mournful state of mind, said, "If I say, I will speak thus; behold, I should offend against the generation of thy children. When I thought to know this, it was too painful for me." Let it be too painful for us to give any cause for stumbling or disquietude to those who have just come to the Savior, but let us cheer and encourage them all we can.

Still, Naomi's silence did not discourage Ruth; she was evidently a strong-minded though gentle young woman, and she gave herself up to God and his people without any reserve. Even though she might not be helped much by the older believer, and might even be discouraged by her, and still more by the departure of her sister-in-law, Orpah, yet still she pressed on in the course she had chosen. Well, you do the same, Mary; and you, Jane and John and Thomas. Will you be like Mr. Pliable, and go back to the City of Destruction? Or will you, like Christian, pursue your way, and steadfastly hold on through the Slough of Despond, or whatever else may be in your pathway, to the Celestial City?

III. Now, third, and very briefly, *true godliness must mainly lie in the choice of God.*

That is the very pith of the text: "Thy God shall be my God."

First, dear friends, *God is the believer's choicest possession;* indeed, it is the distinguishing mark of a Christian that he owns a God. Naomi had not much else—no husband, no son, no lands, no gold, no silver, no pleasure even; but she had a God. Come, now, my friend, are you determined that, henceforth, and forever, the Lord shall be your chief possession? Can you say, "God shall be mine; my faith shall grasp him now, and hold him fast?"

Next, *God was, henceforth, to Ruth, as he had been to Naomi, her Ruler and Lawgiver.* When anyone truthfully says, "God shall be my God," there is some practical meaning about that declaration; it means, "He shall influence me; he shall direct me; he shall lead me; he shall govern me; he shall be my King. I will yield to him and obey him in everything. I will endeavor to do all things according to his will. God shall be my God." You must not want to take God to be your helper, in the sense of making him to be your servant; but to be your Master, and so to help you. Dear friends, does the Holy Spirit lead you to make this blessed choice, and to declare, "This God shall be mine, my Law-giver and Ruler from this time forth"?

Well, then, *he must also be your Instructor.* At the present day, I am afraid that nine people out of ten do not believe in the God who is revealed to us in the Bible. "What?" you say. It is so, I grieve to say. I can point you to newspapers, to magazines, to periodicals, and also to pulpits by the score, in which there is a new god set up to be worshiped; not the God of the Old Testament, he is said to be too strict, too severe, too stern for our modern teachers. They do not believe in him. The God of Abraham is dethroned by many nowadays; and in his place they have a Moloch [idol god of Moab], like those of whom Moses spoke, "new gods that came newly up, whom your fathers feared not." They shudder at the very mention of the God of the Puritans. If Jonathan Edwards were to rise from the dead, they would not listen to him for a minute, they would say that they had quite a new god since his day; but, brethren, I believe in the God of Abraham and of Isaac and of Jacob; this God is my God—aye, the God that drowned Pharaoh and his host at the Red Sea, and moved his people to sing "hallelujah" as he did it; the God that caused the earth to open, and swallow up Korah, Dathan, and Abiram, and all their company—a terrible God is the God whom I adore—he is the God and Father of our Lord and Savior Jesus Christ, full of mercy, compassion, and grace, tender and gentle, yet just and dreadful in his holiness, and terrible out of his holy places. This is the God whom we worship, and he who comes to him in Christ, and trusts in him, will take him to be his Instructor, and so shall he learn aright all that he needs to know. But woe unto the men of this day, who have made unto themselves a calf of their own devising, which has no power to bless or to save them! "Thy God" says Ruth to Naomi—not another god—not Chemosh or Molech, but Jehovah—"shall be my God"; and so she took him to be her Instructor, as we also must do.

Then, let us take him to be *our entire trust and stay.* O my beloved friends, the happiest thing in life is to trust God—first to trust him with your soul through Jesus Christ the Savior, and then to trust him with everything, and in everything. I am speaking what I do know. The life of sense is death, but the life of faith is life indeed. Trust God about temporals—no, I do not know any division between temporals and spirituals—trust God about everything, about your daily livelihood, about your health, about your wife, about your children; live a life of faith in God, and you will truly live, and all things will be right about you. It is because we get partly trusting God and partly trusting ourselves that we are often so unhappy. But when, by simple faith, you just cast yourselves on God, then you find the highest joy and bliss that is possible on earth, and a whole series of wonders is spread out before you; your life becomes like a miracle, or a succession of miracles, God hearing your prayers, and answering you out of heaven, delivering you in the time of trial, supplying your every need, and leading you ever onward by a matchless way which you know not, which every moment shall cause you greater astonishment and delight as you see the unfoldings of the character of God. Oh, that each one of you would say, "This God shall be my God; I will trust him; by his grace, I will trust him now."

IV. The last thing is, that *this decision should lead us to cast in our lot with God's people as well as with himself,* for Ruth said, "Thy people shall be my people."

She might have said, "You are not well spoken of, you Jews, you Israelites; the Moabites, among whom I have lived, hate you." But, in effect, she said, "I am no Moabitess now. I am going to belong to Israel, and to be spoken against too. They have all manner of bad things to say in Moab about Bethlehem-Judah; but I do not mind that, for I am going to be henceforth an inhabitant of Bethlehem, and to be reckoned in the number of the Bethlehemites, for no longer am I of Moab and the Moabites."

Now, dear friend, will you thus cast in your lot with God's people; and though they are spoken against, will you be willing to be spoken against too? I daresay that the Bethlehemites were not all that Ruth could have wished them to be. Even Naomi was not; she was too sad and sorrowful; but, still, I expect that Ruth thought that her mother-in-law was a better woman than she was herself. I have heard people find fault with the members of our churches, and say that they cannot join with them, for they are such an inferior sort of people. Well, I know a great many different sorts of people; and, after all, I shall be quite content to be numbered with God's people, as I see them even in his visible church, rather than to be numbered with any other persons in the whole world. I count the despised people of God the best company I have ever met with; and I often say of this tabernacle, as I hope members of other churches can say of their own places of worship—

> Here my best friends, my kindred dwell,
> Here God my Savior reigns.

"Oh!" says one, "I will join the church when I can find a perfect one." Then you will never join any. "Ah!" you say, "but perhaps I may." Well, but it will not be a perfect church the moment after you have joined it, for it will cease to be perfect as soon as it receives you into its membership. I think that, if a church is such as Christ can love, it is such as I can love; and if it is such that Christ counts it as his church, I may well be thankful to be a member of it. Christ "loved the church, and gave himself for it"; then may I not think it an honor to be allowed to give myself to it?

Ruth was not joining a people out of whom she expected to get much. Shame on those who think to join the church for what they can get! Yet the loaves and fishes are always a bait for some people. But there was Ruth, going with Naomi to Bethlehem, and all that the townsfolk would do would be to turn out and stare at them, and say, "Is this Naomi? And pray who is this young woman that has come with her? This Naomi—dear me! How altered she is! How worn she looks! Quite the old woman to what she was when she left us." Not much sympathy was given to them, as far as I gather from that remark; yet Ruth seemed to say, "I do not care how they treat me; they are God's people, even if they have a great many faults and imperfections, and I am going to join them." And I invite all of you who can say to us, "your God is our God," to join with the people of God, openly, visibly, manifestly, decidedly, without any hesitancy, even though you may gain nothing by it. Perhaps you will not; but, on the other hand, you will bring a good deal to it, for that is the true spirit of Christ. "It is more blessed to give than to receive." Yet, in any case, cast in your lot with the people of God, and share and share alike with them.

I conclude by saying that, whatever the other Bethlehemites might be, there was among them one notable being, and it was worthwhile to join the nation for the sake of union with him. Ruth found it all out by degrees. There was a near kinsman among those people, and his name was Boaz. She went to glean in his field; and, by and by, she was married to him. Ah! that was the reason why I cast in my lot with the people of God, for I said to myself, "There is One among them who, whatever faults they may have, is so fair and lovely that he more than makes up for all their imperfections. My Lord Jesus Christ, in the midst of his people, makes them all fair in his fairness; and makes me feel that, to be poor with the poorest and most illiterate of the church of Christ, meeting in a village barn, is an unspeakable honor, since he is among them." Our Lord Jesus Christ himself is always present wherever two or three are gathered together in his name. If his name is in the list, there may be a number of odds and ends put down with him—members of different denominations, some weird persons, some very old people; but as long as his name is in the list, I do not mind about what others are there, put my name down. Oh, that I might have the eternal honor of having it written even at the bottom of the page beneath the name of Jesus, my Lord, the Lamb!

As Boaz was there, it was enough for Ruth; and as Christ is here, that is quite enough for me. So I hope I have said sufficient to persuade you, who say that our God is your God, to come and join with us, or with some other part of Christ's church, and so to make his people to be your people. And mind you do it at once, and in the scriptural fashion, and God bless you in the doing of it, for Christ's sake! Amen.

Ruth: Her Reward

⚫

Delivered on Lord's Day evening, June 29, 1885, at the Metropolitan Tabernacle, Newington. No. 1851.

The LORD recompense thy work, and a full reward be given thee of the LORD God of Israel, under whose wings thou art come to trust.—RUTH 2:12

This was the language of Boaz, a man of substance and of note in Bethlehem, to a poor stranger of whom he had heard that she had left her kindred, and the idols of her nation, that she might become a worshiper of the living and true God. He acted a noble part when he cheered her, and bade her be of good courage, now that she was casting in her lot with Naomi and the chosen nation. Observe that he saluted her with words of tender encouragement; for this is precisely what I want all the elder Christians among you to do to those who are the counterparts of Ruth. You who have long been believers in the Lord Jesus, who have grown rich in experience, who know the love and faithfulness of our covenant God, and who are strong in the Lord, and in the power of his might; I want you to make a point of looking out for the young converts, and speaking to them goodly words, and comfortable words, whereby they may be cheered and strengthened. There is a text, a very short one, which I would like often to preach from in reference to those who are newly saved, and I would invite you continually to be practicing it: that text is, *"Encourage him."* So many will throw cold water upon the aspirant after holiness, that I would urge others of you heartily to cheer him. Where spiritual life is weak, it should be nurtured with affectionate care. We desire to cherish, not to censure. That the lambs may grow they must be shepherded. That the tender babes in the household may become strong members of the divine family, they must be nursed and fed. If Ruth is to be happy in the land of Israel, a Boaz must look after her, and be her true friend. Let her nearest kinsmen be speedy in fulfilling this duty.

I have no doubt that much sorrow might be prevented if words of encouragement were more frequently spoken fitly and in season; and therefore to withhold them is sin. I am afraid that many poor souls have remained in darkness, shut in within themselves, when two or three minutes' brotherly cheer might have taken down the shutters, and let in the light of day. Many matters are real difficulties to young believers, which are no difficulties to us who have been longer in the way. You and I could clear up in ten minutes' conversation questions and doubts which cause our uninstructed friends months of misery. Why are we so reticent when a word would send our weaker brethren on their way rejoicing? Therefore, I do entreat all of you whom God has greatly blessed, to look after those that are of low estate in spiritual things, and try to cheer and encourage them. As you do this, God will bless you in return; but, if you neglect this tender duty, it may be that you yourselves will grow despondent and be yourselves in need of friendly succor. Encouragement is due to young converts: every Ruth ought to be comforted when she casts in her lot with the people of God.

I think I can say for every Christian here, that the young converts among us have our very best wishes. We desire for them every good and spiritual gift. It will be our wisdom to turn our kindly wishes into prayers. Wishes are lame, but prayer has legs, aye, wings, with which it runs, and even flies, toward God. Wishes are baskets, but prayer fills them with bread. Wishes are clouds, but prayer is the rain. See how Boaz, wishing well as he did to the humble maiden from Moab, spoke with her, and then spoke with God in prayer for her. I take it that my test is a prayer as well as a benediction: "Jehovah recompense thy work, and a full reward be given thee of Jehovah, God of Israel, under whose wings thou art come to trust." Let us pray more than ever for the feeble-minded and the young. Think of them whenever the king grants you an audience. Search them out with kindly care, as a shepherd looks for his young lambs; and then lay them in the bosom of your love, and carry them over rough places.

We should, in all probability, see a much more rapid growth in grace among our young converts if they were better nursed and watched over. Some of us owed much to old-experienced Christians in our younger days. I know I did. I shall forever respect the memory of a humble servant in the school wherein I was usher, at New Market; an old woman, who talked with me concerning the things of the kingdom and taught me the way of the Lord more perfectly. She knew the doctrines of grace better than many a doctor of divinity; and she held them with the tenacious grasp of one who found her life in them. It was my great privilege to help her in her old age; and but a little while ago she passed away to heaven. Many things did I learn of her, which today I delight to preach. Let it be said of us, when we, too, grow old, that those who were children when we were young were helped by us to become useful in their riper years. They will not forget us if we have been to them what Aquila and Priscilla were to Apollos, or Ananias to Paul, or Paul to Timothy. They will pray for us, and God will bless us in answer to their prayers when the grass-hopper to us becomes a burden [Eccles. 12:5], and our infirmities are multiplied.

Having thus introduced the text, let us notice in this model word of encouragement, *what the convert has done* that we should encourage him; second, *what full reward that is which he will receive*; and, third, following out the historical connection of the text, I should like to conclude by noticing *what figure sets forth this full reward*—a reward which we desire for every Ruth who has left those who were outside of the covenant in Moab to come and join herself with the Israel of God, and the God of Israel.

I. First, then, *what has the young convert done?* We illustrate the subject by the instance of Ruth.

Many young converts deserve encouragement because *they have left all their old associates.* Ruth, no doubt, had many friends in her native country, but she tore herself away to cling to Naomi and her God. Perhaps she parted from a mother and a father; if they were alive she certainly left them to go to the Israelites' country. Possibly she bade adieu to brothers and sisters, certainly she quitted old friends and neighbors; for she resolved to go with Naomi and share her lot. She said, "Entreat me not to leave thee, or to return from following after thee: for whither thou goest, I will go: and where thou lodgest, I will lodge: thy people shall be my people, and thy God my God: where thou diest, will I die, and there will I be buried: the LORD do so to me, and more also, if ought but death part thee and me."

The young convert is an emigrant from the world and has become, for Christ's sake, an alien. Possibly he had many companions, friends who made him merry after their fashion, men of fascinating manners, who could easily provoke his laughter, and make the hours dance by; but, because he found in them no savor of Christ, he has forsaken them, and for Christ's sake they have forsaken him. Among his old associates he has become as a speckled bird, and they are all against him. You may, perhaps, have seen a canary which has flown from its home, where it enjoyed the fondness of its mistress: you have seen it out among the sparrows. They pursue it as though they would tear it into pieces, and they give it no rest anywhere. Just so the young convert, being no longer of the same feather as his comrades, is the subject of their persecution. He endures trials of cruel mockings, and these are as hot irons to the soul. He is now to them a hypocrite, and a fanatic; they honor him with ridiculous names by which they express their scorn. In their hearts they crown him with a fool's cap, and write him down as both idiot and knave. He will need to exhibit years of holy living before they will be forced into respect for him; and all this because he is quitting their Moab to join with Israel. Why should he leave them? Has he grown better than they? Does he pretend to be a saint? Can he not drink with them as he once did? He is a protest against their excesses, and men don't care for such protests. Can he not sing a jolly song as they do? Indeed, he has turned saint; and what is a saint but a hypocrite? He is a deal too precise and puritanical and is not to be endured in their free society.

According to the grade in life, this opposition takes one form or another, but in no case does Moab admire the Ruth who deserts her idols to worship the God of Israel. It is not natural that the prince of darkness should care to lose his subjects, or that the men of the world should love those who shame them.

Is it not most appropriate that you older Christian people, who have long been separated from the world, and are hardened against its jeers, should step in and defend the newcomers? Should you not say, "Come you with us, and we will do you good: we will be better friends to you than those you have left. We will accompany you on a better road than that from which you have turned; and we will find you better joys than worldlings can ever know"? When our great King is represented as saying to his spouse, "Forget also thine own people, and thy father's house," he adds, "so shall the king greatly desire thy beauty: for he is thy Lord"; thus he gives her new company to supply the place of that which she gives up. Let us gather a hint from this and make society for those whom the world casts out. Perhaps there has come into this house at this time a man or woman who has just rushed out of the City of Destruction, only too glad to be outside its walls. The poor soul does not know which way to run, only he knows that he must run away from his former evil place, for he finds that the city is to be destroyed. O brothers, while such fugitives are wondering which way to go, and their evil companions are inviting them to return, step in, and show them the true place of shelter. Run with them to the clefts of the Rock. Uplift them if they stumble; guide them if they miss their way. Keep off their former tempters; form a bodyguard around them; escort them till they are out of immediate danger; charm them with your loving conversation till they forget their false friends. When Ruth had quit her former connections, it was wise and kind for Boaz to address her in the words of comfort which I will again quote to you: "The LORD recompense thy work, and a full reward be given thee of the LORD God of Israel, under whose wings thou art come to trust."

Next, Ruth, having left her old companions, *had come among strangers*. She was not yet at home in the land of Israel, but confessed herself "a stranger." She knew Naomi, but in the whole town of Bethlehem she knew no one else.

When she came into the harvest field the neighbors were there gleaning, but they were no neighbors of hers: no glance of sympathy fell upon her from them; perhaps they looked at her with cold curiosity. They may have thought, "What business has this Moabitess to come here to take away a part of the gleaning which belongs to the poor of Israel?" I know that such feelings do arise among country people when a stranger from another parish comes gleaning in the field. Ruth was a foreigner, and, of course, in their eyes an intruder. She felt herself to be alone, though under the wings of Israel's God. Boaz very properly felt that she should not think that courtesy and kindness had died out of Israel; and he made a point, though he was by far her superior in station, to go to her and speak a word of encouragement to her. Should not certain of you follow the same practice? May I not call you to do so at once? There will come into our assemblies those that have been lately impressed with a sense of their guilt, or have newly sought and found the Savior: should they be suffered to remain strangers among us long? Should not recognition, companionship, and hospitality be extended to them to make them feel at home with us?

I would sincerely assure any that have come to this tabernacle for a time, and are still unnoticed, that they are singularly unfortunate; for, as a rule, a stranger is looked after and in every case he will be welcomed. If you have been overlooked, you must have been sitting in rather an odd part of the building, for certain of our friends give themselves to the work of hunting up newcomers, and conversing with them; so much so that now and then I get complaints of their supposed intrusion, which complaints much delight me, for they show that earnestness still survives among us. Be prudent, gentle, and courteous, of course; but do be on the watch for any who are seeking the Lord, and are desirous to unite with his people. I have occasionally to hear a friend say, "Sir, I attended your ministry for months, but those who sat with me in the pew never took the slightest notice of me. I often wished they would, for I was really desirous to be led by the hand to the Savior." I do not like to hear that accusation. I would infinitely rather that people should complain that you spoke too much of religion to them than that you never said a word. Your supposed intrusion might be greatly to your credit, but your silent indifference must be to your dishonor. Do let us try with all our hearts so to look every man upon the things of others that no single seeking soul shall feel itself deserted. Seekers should be spared the agony of crying, "No man careth for my soul." Are you a believer? Then you are my brother. We are no more strangers and foreigners, but fellow citizens with the saints, and of the household of God. We would lay ourselves out to bring our fellowmen to Jesus, and to aid new converts in finding perfect peace at his feet.

Let us learn the art of personal address. Do not let us be so bashful and retiring that we leave others in sorrow because we cannot screw up our courage to say a kind and tender word in the name of the Lord Jesus. Come, let us pluck up courage, and encourage every Ruth when she is timid among strangers. Let us help her to feel at home in Emmanuel's land.

The new convert is like Ruth in another respect: he is *very low in his own eyes*. Ruth said to Boaz, "Why have I found grace in thine eyes, that thou shouldest take knowledge of me, seeing I am a stranger?" She said again, "Let me find favor in thy sight, my lord; for that thou hast comforted me, and for that thou hast spoken friendly unto thine handmaid, though I be not like unto one of thine handmaidens." She had little self-esteem, and therefore she won the esteem of others. She felt herself to be a very inconsiderable person, to whom any kindness was a great favor; and so do young converts, if they are real and true. We meet with a certain class of them who are rather pert and forward, as the fashion of the day is in certain quarters; and then we do not think so much of *them* as they do of themselves; but the genuine ones, who are truly renewed, and who really hold out, and continue to the end, are always humble, and frequently very trembling, timid, and diffident. They feel that they are not worthy to be put among the children, and they come to the Lord's table with holy wonder.

I remember when I first went to the house of God as a Christian youth, who had lately come to know the Lord, that I looked with veneration on every officer and member of the church. I thought them all, if not quite angels, yet very nearly as good; at any rate, I had no disposition to criticize *them*, for I felt myself to be so undeserving. I do not think that I have quite so high an idea of all professed Christians as I had then, for I am afraid that I could not truthfully entertain it; but, for all that, I think far better of them than many are apt to do. I believe that young people, when first brought to Christ, have so deep a sense of their own imperfection and know so little of the infirmities of others, that they look up to the members of the church with a very high esteem, and this fixes upon such members, officers, and pastors a great responsibility. Since these converts are lowly in their own eyes, it is proper and safe to encourage them; moreover, it is kind and needful to do so. Never be critical and severe with them, but deal tenderly with their budding graces; a frosty sentence may nip them; a genial word will develop them.

Our Lord bids you feed the lambs; act the shepherd toward them, and never overdrive them, lest they faint by the way. It is a lovely sight to see a matronly Christian cheering on her class of girls, bearing with their way-wardness and folly, and fostering everything that is hopeful in them. These are the mothers in Israel, to whom shall be honor. I love to see the advanced man of God giving a hearty grip to a youth, loving him, and advising him, yes, and adding a word of praise when it can be judiciously applied. With unequal footsteps, the raw recruits are trying to keep step with the better-trained soldiers. Let their comrades smile upon them, and see in them the warriors of the future, who shall rally to the standard when our warfare is ended.

Once more, the young convert is like Ruth because he has *come to trust under the wings of Jehovah, the God of Israel*. Herein is a beautiful metaphor. You know that the wing of a strong bird especially, and of any bird relatively, is strong. It makes a kind of arch, and from the outer side you have the architectural idea of strength. Under the wings, even of so feeble a creature as a hen, there is a complete and perfect refuge for her little chicks, judging from without. And then the inside of the wing is lined with soft feathers for the comfort of the young. The interior of the wing is arranged as though it would prevent any friction from the strength of the wing to the weakness of the little bird. I do not know of a more snug place than under the wing feathers of the hen. Have you never thought of this? Would not the Lord have us in time of trouble come and cower down under the great wing of his omnipotent love, just as the chicks do under the mother?

Here is the Scripture: "He shall cover thee with his feathers, and under his wings shalt thou trust: his truth shall be thy shield and buckler." What a warm defense! When I have seen the little birds put their heads out from under the feathers of their mother's breast, it has looked like the perfection of happiness; and when they have chirped their little notes, they have seemed to tell how warm and safe they were, though there may have been a rough wind blowing around the hen. They could not be happier than they are. If they run a little way, they are soon back again to the wing, for it is house and home to them; it is their shield and succor, defense and delight.

This is what our young converts have done: they have come, not to trust themselves, but to trust in Jesus. They have come to find a righteousness in Christ—yes, to find everything in him, and so they are trusting, trusting under the wings of God. Is not this what you are doing? You full-grown saints—is not this your condition? I know it is. Very well then; encourage the younger sort to do what you delight to do: say to them, "There is no place like this: let us joyously abide together under the wing of God." There is no rest, no peace, no calm, no perfect quiet, like that of giving up all care, because you cast your care on God; renouncing all fear, because your only fear is a fear of offending God. Oh, the bliss of knowing that sooner may the universe be dissolved than the great heart that beats above you cease to be full of tenderness and love to all those that shelter beneath it. Faith, however little, is a precious plot of the Lord's right hand planting; do not trample on it, but tend it with care, and water it with love.

II. But now I must come closer to the text. Having shown you what these converts have done to need encouragement, I want in the second place, to answer the question, *what is the full reward of those who come to trust under the wings of God?*

I would answer that a full reward will come to us in that day when we lay down these bodies of flesh and blood, that they may sleep in Jesus, while our unclothed spirits are absent from the body but present with the Lord. In the disembodied state, we shall enjoy perfect happiness of spirit; but a fuller reward will be ours when the Lord shall come a second time, and our bodies shall rise from the grave to share in the glorious reign of the descended King. Then in our perfect manhood we shall behold the face of him we love, and shall be like him. Then shall come the adoption, to wit, the redemption of our body; and we, as body, soul, and spirit, a trinity in unity, shall be forever with Father, Son, and Holy Ghost, our triune God. This unspeakable bliss is the full reward of trusting beneath the wings of Jehovah.

But there is a present reward, and to that Boaz referred. There is in this world a present recompense for the godly, notwithstanding the fact that many are true afflictions of the righteous. Years ago a brother minister printed a book, *How to Make the Best of Both Worlds,* which contained much wisdom; but at the same time many of us objected to the title, as dividing the pursuit of the believer, and putting the two worlds too much on a level. Assuredly, it would be wrong for any godly man to make it his object in life to make the best of both worlds in the way which the title is likely to suggest. This present world must be subordinate to the world to come and is to be cheerfully sacrificed to it, if need be. Yet, be it never forgotten, if any man will live unto God, he will make the best of both worlds, for godliness has the promise of the life that now is as well as of that which is to come. Even in losing the present life for Christ's sake, we are saving it, and self-denial and taking up the cross are but forms of blessedness. If we seek first the kingdom of God and his righteousness, all other things shall be added to us.

Do you ask me, "How shall we be rewarded for trusting in the Lord?" I answer, first, by the *deep peace of conscience* which he will grant you. Can any reward be better than this? When a man can say, "I have sinned, but I am forgiven," is not that forgiveness an unspeakable boon? My sins were laid on Jesus, and he took them away as my scapegoat, so that they are gone forever, and I am consciously absolved. Is not this a glorious assurance? Is it not worth worlds? A calm settles down upon the heart which is under the power of the blood of sprinkling; a voice within proclaims the peace of God, and the Holy Spirit seals that peace by his own witness; and thus all is rest. If you were to offer all that you have to buy this peace, you could not purchase it; but were it purchasable it were worthwhile to forgo the dowry of a myriad worlds to win it. If you had all riches and power and honor, you could not reach the price of the pearl of peace. The revenues of kingdoms could not purchase so much as a glance at this jewel. A guilty conscience is the undying worm of hell; the torture of remorse is the fire that never can be quenched: he that hath that worm gnawing at his heart and that fire burning in his bosom is lost already. On the other hand, he that trusts in God through Christ Jesus is delivered from inward hell pangs: the burning fever of unrest is cured. He may well sing for joy of soul, for heaven is born within him and lies in his heart like the Christ in the manger. O harps of glory, you ring out no sweeter note than that of transgression put away by the atoning sacrifice!

That, however, is only the beginning of the believer's reward. He that has come to trust in God shall be "quiet from fear of evil." What a blessing that must be! "He shall not be afraid of evil tidings; his heart is fixed, trusting in the LORD." When a man is at his very highest as to this world's joy, he hears the whisper of a dark spirit saying, "Will it last?" He peers into the morrow with apprehension, for he knows not what may be lurking in his path. But when a man is no longer afraid, but is prepared to welcome whatever comes, because he sees in it the appointment of a loving Father, why, then he is in a happy state. Suppose one went home tonight and found, as Job did, that all his estate had been burned or stolen, and that his family had all died on a sudden, what a splendid condition must he be in if he could say amid his natural agony, "The LORD gave, and the LORD hath taken away; blessed be the name of the LORD"! Such possession of the soul in patience is one of the full rewards of faith. He that has it wears a nobler decoration within his breast than all the stars that royalty could bestow. Deliverance from the pangs of conscience and freedom from the griefs of fear make up a choice favor such as only God can give.

More than this: the man who trusts in God rests in him with respect to all the supplies he now needs, or shall ever need. What happy music gladdens the green pastures of that Twenty-third Psalm! I am half inclined to ask you to rise and sing it, for my heart is leaping for joy while I rehearse the first stanza of it:

The Lord my Shepherd is:
I shall be well supplied.
Since he is mine and I am his,
What can I want beside?

Usually man is made up of wants—and he must have reached the land of abounding wealth who boldly asks, "What can I want beside?" We are never quite content; it always needs a little more to fill the cup to the brim; but only think of singing, "What can I want beside?" Is not this sweet content a full reward from the Lord in whom we trust? Human nature has swallowed a horse leech, and henceforth it cries night and day, "Give, give, give": who but the Lord can stay this craving? The vortex of dissatisfaction threatens to suck in the main ocean and still to remain unfilled; but the Lord rewards faith by satisfying its mouth with good things, and making it sing:

What want shall not our God supply
From his redundant stores?
What streams of mercy from on high
An arm almighty pours!

I cannot imagine a fuller present reward than complete rest from all anxiety, and calm confidence in a Providence which can never fail.

Another part of the believer's great gain lies in *the consciousness that all things are working together for his good*. Nothing is, after all, able to injure us. Neither pains of body, nor sufferings of mind, nor losses in business, nor cruel blows of death, can work us real ill. The thefts of robbers, the mutterings of slanderers, the changes of trade, the rage of the elements, shall all be overruled for good. These many drugs and poisons, compounded in the mortar of the unerring Chemist, shall produce a healthy potion for our souls: "we know that all things work together for good to them that love God, to them who are the called according to his purpose." It is a great joy to know this to be an unquestionable fact, and to watch with expectation to see it repeated in our own case. It takes the sting at once out of all these wasps that otherwise would have worried us, and it transforms them into bees, each one gathering honey for us. Is not this a reward for which a man may well forgo the flatteries of sin? O faith, you enrich and ennoble all who entertain you!

Then, let me tell you, they that trust in God and follow him have another full reward, and that is, *the bliss of doing good*. Can any happiness excel this? This joy is a diamond of the first water [highest quality]. Match me, if you can, the joy of helping the widow and the fatherless! Find me the equal of the delight of saving a soul from death and covering a multitude of sins. It were worth worlds to have faith in God even if we lived here forever, if our sojourn could be filled up with doing good to the poor and needy, and rescuing the erring and fallen. If you desire to taste the purest joy that ever flowed from the fonts of paradise, drink of the unselfish bliss of saving a lost soul. When faith in God teaches you to forgo self, and live wholly to glorify God and benefit your fellowmen, it puts you on the track of the Lord of angels, and by following it, you will come to reign with him.

There has lately passed away from our midst on this side of the river one who in his earlier days knew the curse of drunkenness, but was led by hearing the gospel in the street to seek and find a Savior, and so to escape from the bondage of an evil habit. He became a Christian temperance man, devoting himself, I was about to say, every day in the week, to the cause, for I think he did so; all his spare time was spent for that sacred purpose. He has lately passed away, but not without having enjoyed a reward from his God. When I used to look into the face of our friend Mr. Thorniloe, I felt that he had received a full return for casting himself upon the Lord; for the joy of his heart shone in his countenance, and delight in his work caused it to be his recreation. O drunkard, if you could become such as he was, total abstinence would be no trial, but a pleasure! O idle professor, if you would be as diligent in serving your Lord as he was, life would be music to you. He who has himself fallen into a sin should find his chief joy in seeking to reclaim others from the like condemnation, and in doing so he will light upon clouds of felicities and flocks of joys. As a shepherd rejoices most when he has found his straying sheep, so will you who trust in the Lord if you will in future lay yourselves out to pluck men from eternal ruin.

Brothers and sisters, there remains the singular and refined joy which comes of a humble *perception of personal growth*. Children rejoice when they find that they are growing more like their parents and may soon hope to be strong and full grown. Most of us recollect our childish mirth when we began to wear garments which we thought would make us look like men. When I first wore boots and walked through the stubble with my big uncle, I felt that I was somebody. That, of course, was childish pride; but it has its commendable analogy in the pleasure of gathering spiritual strength and becoming equal to higher labors and deeper experiences. When you find that you do not lose your temper under provocation, as you did a year ago, you are humbly thankful. When an evil lust is driven away, and no longer haunts you, you are quietly joyful, rejoicing with trembling. When you have sustained a trial which once would have crushed you, the victory is exceedingly sweet. Every advance in holiness is an advance in secret happiness. To be a little more meet for heaven is to have a little more of heaven in the heart. As we mellow for the celestial garner, we are conscious of a more pervading sweetness, which in itself is no mean reward of virtue.

Let me tell you another splendid part of this full reward, and that is to have *prevalence with God in prayer*. Somebody called me, in print, a hypocrite, because I said that God had heard my prayers. This was evidently malicious: a man might be called fanatical for such a statement, but I cannot see the justice of imputing hypocrisy on that account. If by hypocrisy be meant a sincere conviction that the great God answers prayer, I will be more and more hypocritical as long as I live. I will glory in the name of God—the God that hears my prayer. If that writer had claimed that *he* prayed and had been heard, it is possible that he would have been guilty of hypocrisy: of that matter he is personally the best informed, and I leave the question with himself; but he has no right to measure my corn with his bushel. Certainly, I shall not use his bushel to measure my corn, but I shall speak what I know and am persuaded of. In deep sincerity I can bear testimony that the Lord hears prayer, and that it is his desire so to do. Many a saint of God has but to ask and have. When such men wrestle with God in prayer, they always prevail, like Israel of old at Jabbok when he grasped the angel, and would not let him go without a blessing. If you have got this power to the full, you will often say to yourself, "If I had nothing else but power at the throne of grace, I have more than enough to recompense me for every self-denial." What are the jests and jeers of an ungodly and ignorant world in comparison with the honor of being favored of the Lord to ask what we will, and receive the utmost of our desires?

Many other items make up the full of the reward; but perhaps the chief of all is *communion with God*—to be permitted to speak with him as a man speaks with his friend—to be led by the divine Bridegroom to sit down in the banqueting house while his banner over us is love. Those who dwell outside the palace of love know nothing about our secret ecstasies and raptures. We cannot tell them much about our spiritual delights, for they would only turn again and rend us. The delights of heavenly fellowship are too sacred to be commonly displayed. There is a joy, the clearest foretaste of heaven below, when the soul becomes as the chariot of Amminadib by the energy of the Holy Spirit. I believe, brethren, that our lot, even when we are poor and sorrowful and cast down, is infinitely to be preferred to that of the loftiest emperor who does not know the Savior. Oh, poor kings, poor princes, poor peers, poor gentry, that do not know Christ! But happy paupers that know him! Happy slaves that love him! Happy dying men and women that rejoice in him! Those have solid joy and lasting pleasure who have God to be their all in all. Come, then, and put your trust under the wings of God, and you shall be blessed in your body and in your soul, blessed in your house and in your family, blessed in your basket and in your store, blessed in your sickness and in your health, blessed in time and in eternity; for the righteous are blessed of the Lord, and their offspring with them. My prayer for every young convert is the benediction of Boaz, "The LORD recompense thy work, and a full reward be given thee of the LORD God of Israel, under whose wings thou art come to trust." May this benediction rest on each one of you forever.

III. Finally, *what figure sets forth this full reward?*

What was the full reward that Ruth obtained? I do not think that Boaz knew the full meaning of what he said. He could not foresee all that was appointed of the Lord. In the light of Ruth's history, we will read the good man's blessing. This poor stranger, Ruth, in coming to put her trust in the God of Israel was giving up everything: yes, but she was also gaining everything. If she could have looked behind the veil which hides the future, she could not have conducted herself more to her own advantage than she did. She had no prospect of gain; she followed Naomi, expecting poverty and obscurity; but in doing that which was right, she found the blessing which makes rich. She lost her Moabite kindred, but she found a noble kinsman in Israel. She quit the home of her fathers in the other land to find a heritage among the chosen tribes, a heritage redeemed by one who loved her. Ah! when you come to trust in Christ, you find in the Lord Jesus Christ one who is next of kin to you, who redeems your heritage, and unites you to himself. You thought that he was a stranger; you were afraid to approach him; but he comes near to you, and you find yourself near to his heart, and one with him forever.

Yes, this is a fair picture of each convert's reward. Ruth found what she did not look for, she found a husband. It was exactly what was for her comfort and her joy, for she found rest in the house of her husband, and she became possessed of his large estate by virtue of her marriage union with him. When a poor sinner trusts in God, he does not expect so great a boon, but to his surprise, his heart finds a husband and a home and an inheritance priceless beyond all conception; and all this is found in Christ Jesus our Lord. Then is the soul brought into loving, living, lasting, indissoluble union with the Well Beloved, the unrivaled Lord of love. We are one with Jesus. What a glorious mystery is this!

Ruth obtained an inheritance among the chosen people of Jehovah. She could not have obtained it except through Boaz, who redeemed it for her; but thus she came into indisputable possession of it. When a poor soul comes to God, he thinks that he is flying to him only for a refuge, but, indeed, he is coming for much more; he is coming for a heritage undefiled, and that fades not away. He becomes an heir of God, a joint heir with Jesus Christ.

As I conclude I bear this my personal testimony to the benefit of godliness for this life. Apart from the glories of heaven I would wish to live trusting in my God, and resting in him for this present life; since I need his present aid for every day as truly as I shall need it at the last day. Men speak of *secularism* as attending to the things which concern our present life, and I am bold to assert that the purest and best secularism is that which trusts itself with God for things immediately around us. We shall be wise to make secular things sacred by trusting them with God. Faith is not for eternity alone, but for this fleeting hour also: it is good for the shop and for the marketplace, for the field and for the domestic hearth. For the cares of the moment, as well as for all else, we take refuge under the wings of God. There shall we be blessed for Christ's sake. Amen.

Ruth: Mealtime in the Cornfields

⁓ᴰᶜ⁓

Delivered on Sunday morning, August 2, 1863, at the Metropolitan Tabernacle, Newington. No. 522.

And Boaz said unto her, "At mealtime come thou hither, and eat of the bread, and dip thy morsel in the vinegar." And she sat beside the reapers: and he reached her parched corn, and she did eat, and was sufficed, and left.
—RUTH 2:14

If we lived in the country, it would not be necessary for me to remind you that the time of harvest has again happily come upon us. I saw, one day last week, a fine sample of the new wheat, part of a considerable quantity which had just been sold; and in many places I have observed the fields yielding their sheaves to the reapers' sickle. Loud let us lift our praise to God for the abundance which loads the land. An unusually heavy crop has been given in many quarters, and scarcely anywhere is there any deficiency. While there is so much of distress abroad—while the great manufacture of our country is standing still—we should be grateful that God is pleased to alleviate the sufferings of the poor, by an unusually bountiful harvest. And we must not forget to pray, that during the next few weeks, the Lord would be pleased to give suitable weather, that so the corn may be safely gathered into the garner; that there may be abundance of bread, and no complaining in our streets. I always feel it necessary, just at this season, to give these hints, because God's natural remembrances cannot reach us: we hear not the lark teaching us how to praise, nor do the green fields of grass, and the yellow ears of corn, preach to us of the Lord's bounty. Little is there to be learned from these long corridors of dreary cells, which we call streets and houses. Dull brown or dirty white bricks everywhere I see; enough to make one earthly, however much we may pant for heavenly things. We see neither the green blade nor the full corn in the ear, and we are so apt to forget that we all depend upon the labor of the field. Let us unite with the peasant and his master, in blessing and praising the God of providence, who first covered the fields with grass for the cattle, and now with herb for the food of man.

This morning we are going to the cornfields, as we did last year, not however, so much to glean, as to rest with the reapers and the gleaners, when under some widespreading oak, they sit down to take refreshment. We hope there will be found some timid gleaner here, who will accept our invitation to come and eat with us, and who will find confidence enough to dip her morsel in the vinegar. May they have courage to feast to the full on their own account, and then to carry home a portion to their needy friends at home.

I. Our first point this morning is this: *that God's reapers have their mealtimes.*

Those who work for God will find him a good master. He cares for oxen, and has commanded his Israel, "Thou shalt not muzzle the ox when he treadeth out the corn." Much more does he care for his servants who serve him. "He hath given meat unto them that fear him: he will ever be mindful of his covenant." The reapers in Jesus' fields shall not only receive a blessed reward at the last, but they shall have plenteous comforts by the way. He is pleased to pay his servants twice: first in the labor itself, and a second time in the labor's sweet results. He gives them such joy and consolation in the service of their Master, that it is a sweet employ, and they cry, "We delight to do thy will, O Lord." As heaven is made up of serving God day and night, so to true workers, their constantly serving God on earth brings with it a rich foretaste of heaven.

God has ordained certain mealtimes for his reapers; and he has appointed that one of these shall be *when they come together to listen to the Word preached.* If God be with our ministers, they act as the disciples did of old, for they received the barley loaves and fishes from Christ as he multiplied them, and handed them to the people. We, of ourselves, cannot feed one soul, much less thousands; but when the Lord is with us, we can keep as good a table as Solomon himself, with all his fine flour and fat oxen and roebucks and fallow deer. When the Lord blesses the provisions of his house, no matter how many thousands there may be, all his poor shall be filled with bread. I hope, beloved, you know what it is to sit under the shadow of the Word with great delight, and find the fruit thereof sweet unto your taste. Where the doctrines of grace are boldly and plainly delivered to you in connection with the other truths of revelation; where Jesus Christ upon his cross is *ever* lifted up; where the work of the Spirit is not forgotten; where the glorious purpose of the Father is never despised, there is sure to be food for the children of God. We have learned not to feed upon oratorical flourishes, or philosophical refinings; we leave these fine things, these twelfth-cake ornaments, to be eaten by those little children who can find delight in such unhealthy dainties: we prefer to hear truth, even when roughly spoken, to the fine garnishings of eloquence without the truth. We care little about how the table is served, or of what ware the dishes are made, so long as the covenant bread and water, and the promised oil and wine, are given us. Certain grumblers among the Lord's reapers do not feed under the preached Word, because they do not intend to feed; they come to the House of Bread on purpose to find fault, and therefore they go away empty. My verdict is, "It serves them right." Little care I to please such hearers. I would as soon feed bears and jackals, as attempt to supply the wants of grumbling professors. How much mischief is done by observations made upon the preacher! How often do we censure where our God approves.

We have heard of a high doctrinal deacon, who said to a young minister who was supplying the pulpit on probation, "I should have enjoyed your sermon very much, sir, if it had not been for that last appeal to the sinner. I do not think that dead sinners should be exhorted to believe in Jesus." When that deacon reached home, he found his own daughter in tears. She became converted to God, and united with the church of which that young man ultimately became the minister. How was she converted, think you? By that address at the close of the sermon, which her father did not like. Take heed of railing at that by which the Holy Ghost saves souls. There may be much in the sermon which may not suit you or me, but then we are not the only persons to be considered. There is a wide variety of characters, and all our hearers must have "their portion of meat in due season." Is it not a selfishness very unlike the spirit of a Christian, which would make me find fault with the provisions, because I cannot eat them all? There should be the unadulterated milk for the babe in grace, as well as the strong substantial meat for the full-grown believer. Beloved, I know that however murmurers may call our manna "light bread," yet our gracious God does "in this mountain make unto all people a feast of fat things, a feast of wines on the lees, of fat things full of marrow, of wines on the lees well refined."

Often, too, our gracious Lord appoints us mealtimes *in our private readings and meditations.* Here it is that his "paths drop fatness." Nothing can be more fattening to the soul of the believer than feeding upon the Word, and digesting it by frequent meditations. No wonder that some grow so little, when they meditate so little. Cattle must chew the cud; it is not what they crop with their teeth, but that which is masticated, and afterward digested by rumination, that nourishes them. We must take the truth, and roll it over and over again in the inward parts of our spirit, and so we shall extract divine nourishment therefrom. Have you not, my brethren, frequently found a Benjamin's mess prepared for you in a choice promise of your God? Is not meditation the land of Goshen to you? If men once said, "There is corn in Egypt," may they not always say, that the finest of the wheat is to be found in secret prayer? Private devotion is a land which flows with milk and honey; a paradise yielding all manner of fruits; a banqueting house of choice wines. Ahasuerus might make a great feast, but all his 120 provinces could not furnish such dainties as the closet offers to the spiritual mind. Where can we feed and lie down in green pastures in so sweet a sense as we do in our musings on the Word? Meditation distills the quintessence from the Scriptures, and gladdens our mouth with a sweetness which exceeds the virgin honey dropping from the honeycomb. Your retired seasons and occasions of prayer should be to you regal entertainments, or at least refreshing seasons, in which, like the reapers at noonday, you sit with Boaz and eat of your Master's generous provisions.

The Shepherd of Salisbury Plain—you who have read that excellent book will remember—was wont to say, "That when he was lonely, and when his wallet was empty, his Bible was to him meat, and drink, and company too." He is not the only man who has found a fullness in the Word when there is want without.

During the battle of Waterloo, a godly soldier mortally wounded was carried by his comrade into the rear, and being placed with his back propped up against a tree, he besought his friend to open his knapsack, and take out the Bible which he had carried in it. "Read to me," he said, "one verse, before I close my eyes in death." His comrade read him that verse: "Peace I leave with you, my peace I give unto you: not as the world giveth give I unto you"; and there, fresh from the whistling of the bullets, and the roll of the drum, and the tempest of human conflict, that believing spirit enjoyed such holy calm, that before he fell asleep in the arms of Jesus, he said, "Yes, I have a peace with God which passeth all understanding, which keeps my heart and mind through Jesus Christ." Saints most surely have their mealtimes when they are alone in meditation.

Let us not forget, that there is one specially ordained mealtime which ought to occur oftener, but which, even monthly, is very refreshing to us—I mean the Supper of the Lord. There you have literally, as well as spiritually, a meal. The table is richly spread; it has upon it both meat and drink; there is the bread and the wine, and looking at what these symbolize, we have before us a table richer than that which kings could furnish. There we have the flesh and the blood of our Lord Jesus Christ, whereof if a man eat, he shall never hunger and never thirst, for that bread shall be unto him everlasting life. Oh, the sweet seasons we have known at the Lord's Supper. If some of you really did understand the enjoyment of feeding upon Christ in that ordinance, you would chide yourselves for not having united with the church in fellowship. In

keeping the Master's commandments there is a "great reward," and consequently in neglecting them there is a great loss of reward. Christ is not so tied
to the sacramental table as to be always found of those who partake there, but
still it is in the way that we may expect the Lord to meet with us. "If ye love
me, keep my commandments" is a sentence of touching power. "And his commandments are not grievous" is the confession of all obedient sons. Sitting at
this table, our soul has mounted up from the emblem to the reality; we have
eaten bread in the kingdom of God, and have leaned our head upon Jesus'
bosom. "He brought me to the banqueting house, and his banner over me was
love." On these occasions we may compare ourselves to poor Mephibosheth,
who though lame and despicable in his own esteem, yet was made to sit at
King David's table; or we may liken ourselves to the little ewe lamb in the
parable, which did eat of its Master's bread, and drink from his cup, and slept
in his bosom. The prodigal, who once fed upon husks, sits down to eat the
bread of children. We, who were worthy to be esteemed as dogs, are here permitted to take the place of adopted sons and daughters.

Besides these regular mealtimes, there are others which God gives us, at
seasons when perhaps we little expect them. You have been walking the street,
and suddenly you have felt a holy flowing out of your soul toward God; or in
the middle of business, your heart has been melted with love and made to leap
for joy even as the brooks which have been bound with winter's ice leap to feel
the touch of spring. You have been groaning, dull and earthbound; but the
sweet love of Jesus has embraced you when you scarcely thought of it, and
your spirit, all free, and all on fire, has rejoiced to dance before the Lord with
timbrels and high-sounding cymbals, like Miriam of old. I have had times
occasionally in preaching, when I would fain have kept on far beyond the
appointed hour, for my happy soul was like a vessel wanting vent. Seasons
too you have had on your sickbeds, when you would have been content to be
sick always, if you could have your bed so well made, and your head so softly
pillowed.

> These are the joys he lets us know
> In fields and villages below:
> Gives us a relish of his love,
> But keeps his noblest feast above.

Our blessed Redeemer comes to us in the morning, and wakes us up with
such sweet thoughts upon our soul, we know not how they came; as if, when
the dew was visiting the flowers, a few drops of heaven's dew had fallen upon
us. In the cool eventide too, as we have gone to our beds, our meditation of

him has been sweet. No, in the night watches, when we tossed to and fro, and could not sleep, he has been pleased to become our song in the night.

He is the spring of all my joys,
The life of my delights;
The glory of my brightest days,
And comfort of my nights.

God's reapers find it hard work to reap; but they find a blessed solace when they sit down and eat of their Master's rich provisions; then, with renewed strength, they go with sharpened sickle, to reap again in the noontide heat.

Let me observe, that while these mealtimes come, we know not exactly when, there are certain seasons when we may expect them. The Eastern reapers generally sit down under the shelter of a tree, or a booth, to take refreshment during the heat of the day. And certain I am, that when trouble, affliction, persecution, and bereavement become the most painful to us, it is then that the Lord hands out to us the sweetest comforts. As we said last Thursday night, some promises are written in sympathetic ink, and can only have their meaning brought out by holding them before the fire of affliction. Some verses of Scripture must be held to the fire till they are scorched, before the glorious meaning will stand forth in clear letters before our eyes. We must work till the hot sun forces the sweat from our face; we must bear the burden and heat of the day before we can expect to be invited to those choice meals which the Lord prepares for those who are diligent in his work. When your day of trouble is the hottest, then the love of Jesus shall be sweetest; when your night of trial is the darkest, then will his candle shine most brightly about you; when your head aches most heavily—when your heart palpitates most terribly—when heart and flesh fail you, then he will be the strength of your life, and your portion forever.

Again, these mealtimes frequently occur before a trial. Elijah must be entertained beneath a juniper tree, for he is to go a forty days' journey in the strength of that meat. You may suspect some danger near when your delights are overflowing. If you see a ship taking in great quantities of provision, it is bound for a distant port. And when God gives you extraordinary seasons of communion with Jesus, you may look for long leagues of tempestuous sea. Sweet cordials prepare for stern conflicts. Times of refreshing also occur after trouble or arduous service. Christ was tempted of the devil, and afterward angels came and ministered unto him. Jacob wrestled with God, and then afterward, at Mahanaim, hosts of angels met him. Abraham wars with the kings, and returns from their slaughter; then is it that Melchizedek refreshes him with bread and wine. After conflict, content; after battle, banquet. When you have waited on your Lord, then you shall sit down, and your Master will gird himself and wait upon you. Yes, let the worldling say what he will about the hardness of religion, we do not find it so. We do confess that reaping is no child's play; that toiling for Christ has its difficulties and its troubles; but still the bread which we eat is very sweet, and the wine which we drink is crushed from celestial clusters—

I would not change my blessed estate
For all the world calls good or great.
And while my faith can keep her hold,
I envy not the sinner's gold.

II. Follow me while we turn to a second point. *To these meals the gleaner is affectionately invited.*

That is to say, the poor, trembling stranger who has not strength enough to reap; who has no right to be in the field, except the right of charity—the poor, trembling sinner, conscious of his own demerit, and feeling but little hope and little joy. To the meals of the strong-handed, fully assured reaper, the *gleaner* is invited.

The gleaner is invited, in the text, to *come.* "At mealtime come thou hither." We have known some who felt ashamed to come to the house of God; but we trust you will none of you be kept away from the place of feasting by any shame on account of your dress, or your personal character, or your poverty; no, nor even on account of your physical infirmities. "At mealtime come thou hither." I have heard of a deaf woman who could never hear a sound, and yet she was always in the house of God, and when asked why, her reply was, because a friend found her the text, and then God was pleased to give her many a sweet thought upon the text while she sat in his house; besides, she said she felt that as a believer, she ought to honor God by her *presence* in his courts, and recognizing her union with his people; and, better still, she always liked to be in the best of company, and as the presence of God was there, and the holy angels, and the saints of the most High, whether she could hear or no, she would go.

There is a brother whose face I seldom miss from this house, who, I believe, has never in his life heard a sound, and cannot make an articulate utterance, yet he is a joyful believer, and loves the place where God's honor dwells. Well, now, I think if such persons find pleasure in coming, we who can hear, though we feel our unworthiness, though we are conscious that we are not fit to come, should be desirous to be laid in the house of God, as the sick were at the pool of Bethesda, hoping that the waters may be stirred, and that we may step in and be healed. Trembling soul, never let the temptations of the devil keep you from God's house. "At mealtime come thou hither."

Moreover, she was bidden not only to come, but to eat. Now, whatever there is sweet and comfortable in the Word of God, you that are of a broken and contrite spirit, are invited to partake of it. "Jesus Christ came into the world to save sinners"—sinners such as you are. "In due time Christ died for the ungodly"—for such ungodly ones as you feel yourselves to be. You are desiring this morning to be Christ's. Well, you may be Christ's. You are saying in your heart, "Oh, that I could eat the children's bread!" You may eat it. You say, "I have no right." But he gives you the invitation! Come without any other right than the right of his invitation. I know you will say how unworthy you are.

> Let not conscience make you linger,
> Nor of fitness fondly dream.

But since he bids you "come," take him at his word; and if there be a promise, believe it; if there be rich consolation, drink it; if there be an encouraging word, accept it, and let the sweetness of it be yours.

Note further, that she was not only invited to eat the bread, but to dip her morsel in the vinegar. We must not look upon this as being some sour stuff. No doubt there are crabbed souls in the Church, who always dip their morsel in the sourest imaginable vinegar, and with a grim liberality invite others to share a little comfortable misery with them; but the vinegar in my text is altogether another thing. This was either a compound of various sweets expressed from fruits, or else it was that weak kind of wine mingled with water which is still commonly used in the harvest fields of Italy, and the warmer parts of the world—a drink not exceedingly strong, but excellently cooling, and good enough to impart a relish to the reapers' food. It was, to use the only word which will give the meaning, a sauce, which the Orientals used with their bread. As we use butter, or as they on other occasions used oil, so in the harvest field, believing it to have cooling properties, they used what is here called vinegar.

Beloved, the Lord's reapers have sauce with their bread; they have sweet consolations; they have not merely doctrines, but the holy unction which is the essence of doctrines; they have not merely truths, but a hallowed and ravishing delight accompanies the truths. Take, for instance, the doctrine of election, which is like the bread; there is a sauce to dip that in. When I can say, "He loved me before the foundations of the world," the personal application, the personal enjoyment of my interest in the truth becomes a sauce into which I dip my morsel. And you, poor gleaner, are invited to dip your morsel in it too. I used to hear people sing that hymn of Toplady's, which begins—

A debtor to mercy alone,
Of covenant mercy I sing;
Nor fear with thy righteousness on,
My person and offerings to bring.

And rises to its climax—

Yes, I to the end shall endure,
As sure as the earnest is given;
More happy, but not more secure,
The glorified spirits in heaven.

And I used to think I could never sing that hymn. It was the sauce, you know. I might manage to eat some of the plain bread, but I could not dip it in that sauce. It was too high doctrine, too sweet, too consoling. But I thank God I have since ventured to dip my morsel in it, and now I hardly like my bread without it. I would have every trembling sinner be prepared to take the *comfortable* parts of God's Word, even those called "*high.*" I hope, brethren, you will never grow as some Christians do, who like all sauce, and no bread. There are some high-flying brethren, who must have nothing but the vinegar; and very sour it turns upon their stomachs too. I hope you will love the bread. A little of the vinegar, a little of the spice, and much savor; but let us keep to the bread as well; let us love all revealed truth; and if there be a trembling gleaner here, let me invite and persuade her to come hither, to eat the bread, and to dip her morsel in the sauce.

Now I think I see her, and she is half prepared to come, for she is very hungry, and she has brought nothing with her this morning; but she begins to say, "I have no right to come, for I am not a reaper; I do nothing for Christ; I did not even come here this morning to honor him; I came here, as gleaners go into a cornfield, from a selfish motive, to pick up what I could for myself; and all the religion that I have lies in this—the hope that *I* may be saved; I do not glorify God; I do no good to other people; I am only a selfish gleaner; I am not a reaper." Ah! but you are *invited* to come. Make no questions about it. Boaz bids you. Take his invitation and enter at once. But, you say, "I am such a *poor* gleaner; though it is all for myself, yet it is little I get at it; I get a few thoughts while the sermon is being preached, but I lose them before I reach home." I know you do, poor weak-handed woman. But still, Jesus invites you. Come! Take you the sweet promise as he presents it to you, and let no bashfulness of yours send you home hungry. "But," you say, "I am a stranger; you do not know my sins, my sinfulness, and the waywardness of my heart." But Jesus does; and yet Jesus invites you! He knows you are but a Moabitess, a stranger from the commonwealth of Israel; but he bids you. Is not that enough? "Eat the bread, and dip thy morsel in the vinegar." "But," you say, "I owe so much to him already; it is so good of him to spare my forfeited life, and so tender of him to let me hear the gospel preached at all; I cannot have the presumption to be an intruder, and sit with the reapers." Oh! but he *bids* you. There is more presumption in your doubting than there *could* be in your believing. He bids you. Will you refuse Boaz? Shall Jesus' lips give the invitation, and will you say no? Come, now, come. Remember that the little which Ruth could eat did not make Boaz any the poorer; and all that you want will make Christ nonetheless glorious, or full of grace. What! are your necessities large? Yes, but his supplies are larger. Do you require great mercy? He is a great Savior. I tell you, that his mercy is no more to be exhausted than the sea is to be drained; or than the sun is to be rendered dim by the excess of the light which he pours forth today. Come. There is enough for you, and Boaz will not be hurt thereby. Moreover, let me tell you a secret—Jesus *loves* you; therefore it is that he would have you feed at his table. If you are now a longing, trembling sinner, willing to be saved, but conscious that you deserve it not, Jesus loves you, sinner, and he will take more delight in seeing you eat than you will take in the eating. Let the sweet love he feels in his soul toward you draw you to him. And what is more—but this is a great secret, and must only be whispered in your ear—*he intends to be married to you*; and when you are married to him, why, the fields will be yours; for, of course, if you are the spouse, you are joint proprietor with him. Is it not so? Does not the wife share with the husband? All those promises which are "yea and amen in Christ" shall be yours; no, they all are yours now, for "the man is next of kin unto you," and before long he will spread his skirt over you, and take you unto himself forever, espousing you in faithfulness, and truth, and righteousness. Will you not eat of your own? "Oh! but," says one, "how can it be? I am a stranger." Yes, a stranger: but Jesus Christ loves the stranger. "A publican, a sinner"; but he is "the friend of publicans and sinners." "An outcast"; but he "gathereth together the outcasts of Israel." "A stray sheep"; but the Shepherd "leaves the ninety and nine," to seek it. "A lost piece of money"; but he "sweeps the house" to find you. "A prodigal son"; but he sets the bells aringing when he knows that you will return. Come, Ruth! Come, trembling gleaner! Jesus invites you: accept the invitation. "At mealtime come thou hither, and eat of the bread, and dip thy morsel in the vinegar."

III. Now, third—and here is a very sweet point in the narrative. *Boaz reached her the parched corn.*

"She did come and eat." Where did she sit? You notice, she "sat beside the reapers." She did not feel that she was one of them—she "sat beside" them. Just as some of you do, who do not come down here this evening to the Lord's Supper, but sit in the gallery. You are sitting "beside the reapers." You are sitting this morning as if you were not one of us—had no right to be among the people of God; still you will sit beside us. If there is a good thing to be had, and you cannot get it, you will get as near as you can to those who *do*; you think there is some comfort even in looking on at the gracious feast. "She sat beside the reapers." And while she was sitting there, what happened? Did she stretch forth her hand and get the food herself? No, it is written, "He reached her parched corn." Ah! that is it. I give the invitation, brother, today; give it earnestly, affectionately, sincerely; but I know very well, that while I give it, no trembling heart will accept it, unless the King himself comes near, and feasts his saints today. He must reach the parched corn; *he* must give you to drink of "the juice of the spiced wine of his pomegranate." How does he do this? By his gracious spirit, he first of all *inspires your faith*. You are afraid to think it can be true, that such a sinner as you are accepted in the beloved; he breathes upon you, and your faint hope becomes an expectancy, and that expectation buds and blossoms into an appropriating faith, which says, "Yes, my beloved is *mine*, and his desire is toward *me*." Having done this, the Savior does more; *he sheds abroad the love of God in your heart.* The love of Christ is like sweet perfume in a box. Now, he who put the perfume in the box is the only person that knows how to take the lid off. He, with his own skillful hand, takes the lid from the box; then it is "shed abroad" like "ointment poured forth." You know it may be there, and yet not be shed abroad. As you walk in a wood, there may be a dove or a partridge there, and yet you may never see it; but when you startle it, and it flies or runs before you, then you perceive it. And there may be the love of God in your heart, not in exercise, but still there; and at last you may have the privilege of seeing it—seeing your love mount with wings to heaven, and your faith running without weariness. Christ *must* shed abroad that love; his spirit must put your graces into exercise.

But Jesus does more than this; he reaches the parched corn with his own hand, when *he gives us close communion with him.* Do not think that this is a dream; I tell you there is such a thing as talking with Christ today. As certainly as I can talk with my dearest friend, or find solace in the company of my beloved wife, so surely may I speak with Jesus, and find intense delight in the company of Emmanuel. It is not a fiction. We do not worship a far-off Savior; he is a God near at hand. We do not adore him as one who is gone away to heaven, and who never can be approached; but he is near us, in our mouth and in our heart, and we do today walk with him as the elect did of old, and commune with him as his apostles did on earth; not after the flesh, it is true, but spiritual men value spiritual communion better than any carnal fellowship.

Yet once more let me add, the Lord Jesus is pleased to reach the parched corn, in the best sense, when the Spirit gives us the infallible witness within, that we are "born of God." A man may know that he is a Christian infallibly. Philip de Morny, who lived in the time of Prince Henry of Navarre, was wont to say that the Holy Spirit had made his own salvation to him as clear a point as ever a problem proved to a demonstration in Euclid could be. You know with what mathematical precision the scholar of Euclid solves a problem or proves a proposition, and just the same, with as absolute a precision, as certainly as twice two are four, we may "know that we have passed from death unto life." The sun in the heavens is not more clear to the eye than his own salvation to an assured believer; such a man would as soon doubt his own existence, as suspect his interest in eternal life.

Now let the prayer be breathed by poor Ruth, who is trembling yonder. Lord, reach me the parched corn! "Draw me, we will run after thee." Lord, send thy love into my heart!

> *Come, Holy Spirit, heavenly Dove,*
> *With all thy quickening powers,*
> *Come, shed abroad a Savior's love,*
> *And that shall kindle ours.*

There is no getting at Christ, except by Christ revealing himself to us.

IV. And now the last point. After Boaz had reached the parched corn, we are told that *"She did eat, and was sufficed, and left."*

So shall it be with every Ruth. Sooner or later every penitent shall become a believer. There may be a space of deep conviction, and a period of much hesitation; but there shall come a season, when the soul decides for the Lord. "If I perish, I perish." I will go as I am to Jesus. I will not play the fool any longer with my *buts* and *ifs,* but since he bids me believe that he died for me, I will believe it, and will trust his cross for my salvation. And oh! whenever you shall be privileged to do this, you shall be "satisfied."

She did eat, and was satisfied. Your head shall be satisfied with the precious truth which Christ reveals; your heart shall be content with Jesus, as the altogether lovely object of affection; your hope shall be satisfied, for whom have you in heaven but Christ? Your desire shall be satiated, for what can even the hunger of your desire wish for more than "to know Christ, and to be found in him." You shall find Jesus fill your conscience, till it is at perfect peace; he shall fill your judgment, till you know the certainty of his teachings; he shall fill your memory with recollections of what he did, and fill your imagination with the prospects of what he is yet to do. You shall be "satisfied."

Still, still it shall be true, that you shall leave something. She was satisfied, and she "left." Some of us have had deep drafts; we have thought that we could take in all of Christ; but when we have done our best, we have had to leave a vast remainder. We have sat down with a ravenous appetite at the table of the Lord's love, and said, "Now, nothing but the infinite can ever satisfy me; I am such a great sinner that I must have infinite merit to wash my sin away"; but we have had our sin removed, and found that there was merit to spare; we have had our hunger relieved, and found that there was a redundance for others who were in a similar case. There are certain sweet things in the Word of God which you and I have not enjoyed yet, and which we cannot enjoy yet; we are obliged to leave them for a while. "I have yet many things to say unto you, but ye cannot bear them now." There is a knowledge to which we have not attained—a place of fellowship nearer yet to Christ. There are heights of communion which as yet our feet have not climbed—virgin snows upon the mountain untrodden by the foot of man. There is a yet beyond, and there will be forever.

But please to notice: it is not in the text, but it is recorded a verse or two further on, what she did with her leavings. It is a very bad habit, I believe, at feasts, to carry anything home with you; but she did, for that which was left she took home; and when she reached Naomi, and showed her the quantity of wheat in her apron, after she had asked, "Where hast thou gleaned today?" and had received the answer, she gave to Naomi a portion of that which she had reserved after she was sufficed. So it shall be even with you, poor tremblers, who think you have no right to any for yourselves; you shall be able to eat and be quite satisfied, and what is more, you shall have a morsel to carry to others in a like condition.

I am always pleased to find the young believer beginning to pocket something for other people. When you hear a sermon, you think, "Well, poor mother cannot get out today, I will tell her something about it. There now, that point will just suit her; I will take that, if I forget anything else; I will tell her that by the bedside. There is my brother William, who will not come with me to chapel; I wish he would; but, now, there was something which struck me in the sermon, and when I get close to him, I will tell him that, and I will say, 'Will you not come this evening?' I will tell him those portions which interested me; perhaps they will interest him." There are your children in the Sunday school class. You say, "That illustration will do for them." I think sometimes, when I see you putting down my metaphors on little scraps of paper, that you may recollect to tell somebody else; I would fain give more where they are so well used; I would let fall an extra handful, on purpose that there may be enough for you, and for your friends. There is an abominable spirit of self among some professors, prompting them to eat their morsel alone. They get the honey; it is a wood full of honey, like Jonathan's wood; and yet they are afraid—afraid, lest they should eat it all up; so they try to maintain a monopoly.

I do know some congregations which seem to me to be a sort of spiritual protectionists; they are afraid heaven will be too full, that there will not be room enough for them. When an invitation is given to a sinner, they do not like it—it is too open, too general; and when there is a melting heart and a tearful eye for the conversion of other people, they feel quite out of their element; they never know what it is to take home that which is left, and give to others. Cultivate an unselfish spirit. Seek to love as you have been loved. Remember that "the law and the prophets" lie in this, to "love the Lord your God with all your heart, and your neighbor as yourself." How can you love him as yourself, if you do not love his soul? You have loved your own soul; through grace you have been led to lay hold on Jesus. Love your neighbor's soul and never be satisfied till you see him in the enjoyment of those things which are the charm of your life and the joy of your spirit. I do not know how to give my invitation in a more comfortable way; but as we are sitting down to feed at his table in the evening of this day, I pray the Master to reach a large handful of parched corn to some trembling sinner, and enable him to eat and be satisfied.

Hannah: A Woman of Sorrowful Spirit

⟵⟶

Delivered at the Metropolitan Tabernacle, Newington, in 1880. No. 1515.

Hannah answered and said, "No, my lord, I am a woman of a sorrowful spirit."—1 SAMUEL 1:15

The special cause of Hannah's sorrow arose from the institution of polygamy, which, although it was tolerated under the old law, is always exhibited to us in practical action as a most fruitful source of sorrow and sin. In no one recorded instance in Holy Scripture is it set forth as admirable; and in most cases the proofs of its evil effects lie open to the sun. We ought to be grateful that under the Christian religion that abomination has been wiped away; for even with such husbands as Abraham, Jacob, David, and Solomon it did not work toward happiness or righteousness. The husband found the system a heavy burden, grievous to be borne, for he soon found out the truth of the wise man's advice to the Sultan, "First learn to live with two tigresses, and then expect to live happily with two wives." The wife must in nearly every case have felt the wretchedness of sharing a love which ought to be all her own. What miseries Eastern women have suffered in the harem none can tell or perhaps imagine.

In the case before us, Elkanah had trouble enough through wearing the double chain, but still the heaviest burden fell upon his beloved Hannah, the better of his two wives. The worse the woman, the better she could get on with the system of many wives, but the good woman, the true woman, was sure to smart under it. Though dearly loved by her husband, the jealousy of the rival wife embittered Hannah's life, and made her "a woman of a sorrowful spirit." We thank God that no longer is the altar of God covered with tears, with weeping, and with crying out, of those wives of youth who find their husbands' hearts estranged and divided by other wives. Because of the hardness of their hearts, the evil was tolerated for a while, but the many evils which sprang of it should suffice to put a ban upon it among all who seek the welfare of our race. In the beginning the Lord made for man but one wife. And wherefore one? For he had the residue of the spirit, and could have breathed into as many as he pleased. Malachi answers, "That he might seek a godly seed." As if it was quite clear that the children of polygamy would be ungodly, and only in the house of one man and one wife would godliness be found. This witness is of the Lord and is true.

But enough sources of grief remain; more than enough; and there is not in any household, I suppose, however joyous, the utter absence of the cross. The worldling says, "There is a skeleton in every house." I know little about such dead things, but I know that a cross of some sort or other must be borne by every child of God. All the trueborn heirs of heaven must pass under the rod of the covenant. What son is there whom the Father chastens not? The smoking furnace is part of the insignia of the heavenly family, without which a man may well question whether he stands in covenant relationship to God at all. Probably some Hannah is now before me, smarting under the chastening hand of God, some child of light walking in darkness, some daughter of Abraham bowed down by Satan, and it may not be amiss to remind her that she is not the first of her kind, but that in years gone by there stood at the door of God's house one like to her, who said of herself, "No, my lord, I am a woman of a sorrowful spirit." May the ever blessed Comforter, whose work lies mainly with the sorrowful, fill our meditation with consolation at this time.

I. In speaking of this "woman of a sorrowful spirit," we shall make this first remark—*that much that is precious may be connected with a sorrowful spirit.*

In itself, a sorrowful spirit is not to be desired. Give us the bright eye, the cheerful smile, the vivacious manner, the genial tone. If we do not desire mirth and merriment, yet give us at least that calm peace, that quiet composure, that restful happiness which makes home happy wherever it pervades the atmosphere. There are wives, mothers, and daughters who should exhibit more of these cheerful graces than they now do, and they are very blamable for being petulant, unkind, and irritable; but there are others, I doubt not, who labor to their utmost to be all that is delightful, and yet fail in the attempt, because, like Hannah, they are of a sorrowful spirit, and cannot shake off the grief which burdens their heart. Now, it is idle to tell the night that it should be brilliant as the day, or bid the winter put on the flowers of summer; and equally vain is it to chide the broken heart. The bird of night cannot sing at heaven's gate, nor can the crushed worm leap like a hart up on the mountains. It is of little use exhorting the willow whose branches weep by the river to lift up its head like the palm, or spread its branches like the cedar: everything must act according to its kind; each nature has its own appropriate ways, nor can it escape the bonds of its fashioning. There are circumstances of constitution, education, and surroundings which render it difficult for some very excellent persons to be cheerful: they are predestined to be known by such a name as this: "a woman of a sorrowful spirit."

Note well the precious things which went in Hannah's case with a sorrowful spirit. The first was true godliness; she was *a godly woman*. As we read the chapter, we are thoroughly certified that her heart was right with God. We cannot raise any question about the sincerity of her prayer or the prevalence of it. We do not doubt for a moment the truthfulness of her consecration. She was one that feared God above many, an eminently gracious woman, and yet "a woman of a sorrowful spirit." Never draw the inference from sorrow that the subject of it is not beloved of God. You might more safely reason in the opposite way, though it would not be always safe to do so, for outward circumstances are poor tests of a man's spiritual state. Certainly Dives, in his scarlet and fine linen, was not beloved of God, while Lazarus, with the dogs licking his sores, was a favorite of heaven; and yet it is not every rich man that is cast away, or every beggar that will be borne aloft by angels. Outward condition can lead us to no determination one way or another. Hearts must be judged, conduct and action must be weighed, and a verdict given otherwise than by the outward appearance. Many persons feel very happy, but they must not therefore infer that God loves them; while certain others are sadly depressed, it would be most cruel to suggest to them that God is angry with them. It is never said, "whom the Lord loveth he enricheth," but it is said, "whom the Lord loveth he chasteneth."

Affliction and suffering are not proofs of sonship, for "many sorrows shall be to the wicked"; and yet, where there are great tribulations, it often happens that there are great manifestations of the divine favor. There is a sorrow of the world that "worketh death"—a sorrow which springs from self-will and is nurtured in rebellion, and is therefore an evil thing, because it is opposed to the divine will. There is a sorrow which eats "as doth a canker," and breeds yet greater sorrows, so that such mourners descend with their sorrowful spirits down to the place where sorrow reigns supreme, and hope shall never come. Think of this, but never doubt the fact that a sorrowful spirit is in perfect consistency with the love of God and the possession of true godliness. It is freely admitted that godliness ought to cheer many a sorrowful spirit more than it does. It is also admitted that much of the experience of Christians is no Christ-ian experience, but a mournful departure from what true believers ought to be and feel.

There is very much that Christians experience which they never ought to experience. Half the troubles of life are homemade and utterly unnecessary. We afflict ourselves perhaps, ten times more than God afflicts us. We add many thongs to God's whip: when there would be but one, we must needs make nine. God sends one cloud by his providence, and we raise a score by our unbelief. But taking all that off, and making the still further abatement that the gospel commands us to rejoice in the Lord always, and that it would never bid us do so if there were not abundant causes and arguments for it, yet, for all that, a sorrowful spirit may be possessed by one who most truly and deeply fears the Lord. Never judge those whom you see sad, and write them down as under the divine anger, for you might err most grievously and most cruelly in making so rash a judgment. Fools despise the afflicted, but wise men prize them. Many of the sweetest flowers in the garden of grace grow in the shade, and flourish in the drip. I am persuaded that he "who feedeth among the lilies" has rare plants in his flora, fair and fragrant, choice and comely, which are more at home in the damps of mourning than in the glaring sun of joy. I have known such, who have been a living lesson to us all, from their brokenhearted penitence, their solemn earnestness, their jealous watchfulness, their sweet humility, and their gentle love. These are lilies of the valley, bearing a wealth of beauty pleasant even to the King himself. Feeble as to assurance, and to be pitied for their timidity, yet have they been lovely in their despondencies and graceful in their holy anxieties. Hannah, then, possessed godliness despite her sorrow.

In connection with this sorrowful spirit of hers, Hannah was *a lovable woman*. Her husband greatly delighted in her. That she had no children was to him no depreciation of her value. He said, "Am I not better to thee than ten sons?" He evidently felt that he would do anything in his power to uplift the gloom from her spirit. This fact is worth noting, for it does so happen that many sorrowful people are far from being lovable people. In too many instances their griefs have soured them. Their affliction has generated acid in their hearts, and with that acrid acid they bite into everything they touch; their temper has more of the oil of vitriol in it than of the oil of brotherly love. Nobody ever had any trouble except themselves; they brook no rival in the realm of suffering, but persecute their fellow sufferers with a kind of jealousy, as if they alone were the brides of suffering, and others were mere intruders. Every other person's sorrow is a mere fancy, or make-believe, compared with theirs. They sit alone, and keep silence; or when they speak, their silence would have been preferable.

It is a pity it should be so, and yet so it is that men and women of a sorrowful spirit are frequently to be met with those who are unloving and unlovable. The more heartily, therefore, do I admire in true Christian people the grace which sweetens them so that the more they suffer themselves the more gentle and patient they become with other sufferers, and the more ready to bear whatever trouble may be involved in the necessities of compassion. Beloved, if you are much tried and troubled, and if you are much depressed in spirit, entreat the Lord to prevent your becoming a killjoy to others. Remember your Master's rule, "And thou, when thou fastest, anoint thy head, and wash thy face, that thou appear not unto men to fast." I say not that our Lord spoke the word with the exact meaning I am now giving to it, but it is a kindred sense. Be cheerful even when your heart is sad. It is not necessary that every heart should be heavy because I am burdened; of what use would that be to me or to anyone else? No, let us try to be cheerful that we may be lovable, even if we still remain of a sorrowful spirit. Self and our own personal woes must not be our life-psalm nor our daily discourse. Others must be thought of, and in their joys we must try to sympathize.

In Hannah's case, too, the woman of a sorrowful spirit was *a very gentle woman*. Peninnah with her harsh and haughty and arrogant speech vexed her sorely to make her fret, but we do not find that she answered her. At the annual festival, when Peninnah had provoked her most, she stole away to the sanctuary to weep alone, for she was very tender and submissive. When Eli said, "How long wilt thou be drunken? Put away thy wine from thee," she did not answer him tartly, as she might well have done. Her answer to the aged priest is a model of well have done. Her answer to the aged priest is a model of gentleness. She most effectually cleared herself, and plainly refuted the harsh imputation, but she made no retort, and murmured no charge of injustice. She did not tell him that he was ungenerous in having thought so harshly, nor was there anger in her grief. She excused his mistake. He was an old man. It was his duty to see that worship was fitly conducted, and, if he judged her to be in a wrong state, it was but faithfulness on his part to make the remark; and she took it, therefore, in the spirit in which she thought he offered it. At any rate, she bore the rebuke without resentment or repining.

Now some sad people are very tart, very sharp, very severe, and, if you misjudge them at all, they inveigh against your cruelty with the utmost bitterness. You are the unkindest of men if you think them less than perfect. With what an air and tone of injured innocence will they vindicate themselves! You have committed worse than blasphemy if you have ventured to hint a fault. I am not about to blame them, for we might be as ungentle as they if we were to be too severe in our criticism on the sharpness which springs of sorrow; but it is very beautiful when the afflicted are full of sweetness and light, and like the sycamore figs are ripened by their bruising. When their own bleeding wound makes them tender of wounding others, and their own hurt makes them more ready to bear what of hurt may come through the mistakes of others, then have we a lovely proof that "sweet are the uses of adversity." Look at your Lord. Oh, that we all would look at him, who when he was reviled, reviled not again, and who, when they mocked him, had not a word of upbraiding, but answered by his prayers, saying, "Father, forgive them, for they know not what they do." See you not that much that is precious may go with a sorrowful spirit?

There was more, however, than I have shown you, for Hannah was *a thoughtful woman*, for her sorrow drove her first within herself, and next into much communion with her God. That she was a highly thoughtful woman appears in everything she says. She does not pour out that which first comes to hand. The product of her mind is evidently that which only a cultivated soil could yield. I will not just now speak of her son, further than to say that for loftiness of majesty and fullness of true poetry, it is equal to anything from the pen of that sweet psalmist of Israel, David himself. The virgin Mary evidently followed in the wake of this great poetess, this mistress of the lyric art.

Remember, also, that though she was a woman of a sorrowful spirit, she was *a blessed woman*. I might fitly say of her, "Hail, thou that art highly favored! The Lord is with thee. Blessed art thou among women." The daughters of Belial could laugh and make merry, and regard her as the dust beneath their feet, but yet had she with her sorrowful spirit found grace in the sight of the Lord. There was Peninnah, with her quiver full of children, exulting over the barren mourner, yet was not Peninnah blessed, while Hannah, with all her griefs, was dear unto the Lord. She seems to be somewhat like him of another age, of whom we read that Jabez was more honorable than his brethren because his mother bare him with sorrow. Sorrow brings a wealth of blessing with it when the Lord consecrates it; and if one had to take his position with the merry, or with the mournful, he would do well to take counsel of Solomon, who said, "It is better to go to the house of mourning than to the house of feasting." A present flash is seen in the mirth of the world, but there is vastly more true light to be found in the griefs of Christians. When you see how the Lord sustains and sanctifies his people by their afflictions, the darkness glows into noonday.

II. We come now to a second remark, which is that *much that is precious may come out of a sorrowful spirit*: it is not only to be found with it, but may even grow out of it.

Observe, first, that through her sorrowful spirit Hannah *had learned to pray*. I will not say but what she prayed before this great sorrow struck her, but this I know, she prayed with more intensity than before when she heard her rival talk so exceedingly proudly, and saw herself to be utterly despised. O brothers and sisters, if you have a secret grief, learn where to carry it, and delay not to take it there. Learn from Hannah. Her appeal was to the Lord. She poured not out the secret of her soul into mortal ear, but spread her grief before God in his own house, and in his own appointed manner. She was in bitterness of soul, and prayed to the Lord. Bitterness of soul should always be thus sweetened. Many are in bitterness of soul, but they do not pray, and therefore the taste of the wormwood remains: Oh, that they were wise and looked upon their sorrows as the divine call for prayer, the cloud which brings a shower of supplication! Our troubles should be steeds upon which we ride to God; rough winds which hurry our bark into the haven of all prayer. When the heart is merry we may sing psalms, but concerning the afflicted it is written, "Let him pray." Thus bitterness of spirit may be an index of our need of prayer, and an incentive to that holy exercise.

O daughter of sorrow, if in your darkened chamber you shall learn the art of prevailing with the Well Beloved, your bright-eyed maidens, down whose cheeks no tears have ever rushed, may well envy you, for to be proficient in the art and mystery of prayer is to be as a prince with God. May God grant that if we are of a sorrowful spirit, we may in the same proportion be of a prayerful spirit; and we need scarcely desire a change.

In the next place, Hannah *had learned self-denial*. This is clear, since the very prayer by which she hoped to escape out of her great grief was a self-denying one. She desired a son, that her reproach might be removed; but if her eyes might be blessed with such a sight, she would cheerfully resign her darling to be the Lord's as long as he lived. Mothers wish to keep their children about them. It is natural that they should wish to see them often. But Hannah, when most eager for a man-child, asking but for one, and that one as the special gift of God, yet does not seek him for herself, but for her God. She has it on her heart, that as soon as she has weaned him, she will take him up to the house of God and leave him there, as a dedicated child whom she can only see at certain festivals. Read her own words: "O LORD of hosts, if thou wilt indeed look on the affliction of thine handmaid, and remember me, and not forget thine handmaid, but wilt give unto thine handmaid a man-child, then I will give him unto the LORD all the days of his life, and there shall no razor come upon his head." Her heart longs not to see her boy at home, his father's daily pride, and her own hourly solace, but to see him serving as a Levite in the house of the Lord. She thus proved that she had learned self-denial.

Brethren and sisters, this is one of our hardest lessons: to learn to give up what we most prize at the command of God, and to do so cheerfully. This is real self-denial, when we ourselves make the proposition, and offer the sacrifice freely, as she did. To desire a blessing that we may have the opportunity of parting with it, this is self-conquest: have we reached it? O you of a sorrowful spirit, if you have learned to crucify the flesh, if you have learned to keep under the body, if you have learned to cast all your desires and wills at his feet, you have gained what a thousand times repays you for all the losses and crosses you have suffered. Personally, I bless God for joy, I think I could sometimes do with a little more of it; but I fear, when I take stock of my whole life, that I have very seldom made any real growth in grace except as the result of being digged about and dunged by the stern husbandry of pain. My leaf is greenest in showery weather: my fruit is sweetest when it has been frosted by a winter's night.

Another precious thing had come to this woman, and that was, *she had learned faith*. She had become proficient in believing promises. It is very beautiful to note how at one moment she was in bitterness, but as soon as Eli had said, "Go in peace: and the God of Israel grant thee thy petition that thou hast asked of him," "the woman went her way and did eat, and her countenance was no more sad." She had not yet obtained the blessing, but she was persuaded of the promise, and embraced it, after that Christly fashion which our Lord taught us when he said, "Believe that ye have the petitions which ye have asked, and ye shall have them"; she wiped her tears, and smoothed the wrinkles from her brow, knowing that she was heard. By faith she held a man-child in her arms, and presented it to the Lord. This is no small virtue to attain. When a sorrowful spirit has learned to believe God, to roll its burden upon him, and bravely to expect succor and help from him, it has learned by its losses how to make its best gains, by its griefs how to unfold its richest joys. Hannah is one of the honored band who through faith "received promises;" therefore, O you who are of a sorrowful spirit, there is no reason why you should not also be of a believing spirit, even as she was.

Still more of preciousness this woman of a sorrowful spirit found growing out of her sorrow, but with one invaluable item I shall close the list: she had evidently *learned much of God*. Driven from common family joys, she had been drawn near to God, and in that heavenly fellowship she had remained a humble waiter and watcher. In seasons of sacred nearness to the Lord, she had made many heavenly discoveries of his name and nature, as her son makes us perceive.

First, she now knew that the heart's truest joy is not in children, nor even in mercies given in answer to prayer, for she began to sing, "My heart rejoiceth in the LORD"—not "in Samuel," but in Jehovah her chief delight was found. "Mine horn is exalted in the LORD"—not "in that little one whom I have so gladly brought up to the sanctuary." No. She says in the first verse, "I rejoice in thy salvation," and it was even so. God was her exceeding joy, and his salvation her delight. Oh! it is a great thing to be taught to put earthly things in their proper places, and when they make you glad yet to feel, "My gladness is in God; not in corn and wine and oil, but in the Lord himself; all my fresh springs are in him."

Next, she had also discovered the Lord's glorious *holiness,* for she sang, "There is none holy as the LORD." The wholeness of his perfect character charmed and impressed her, and she sang of him as far above all others in his goodness.

She had perceived his *all-sufficiency,* she saw that he is all in all, for she sang, "There is none beside thee; neither is there any rock like our God."

She had found out God's *method in providence,* for how sweetly she sings, "The bows of the mighty men are broken, and they that stumbled are girded with strength." She knew that this was always God's way—to overturn those who are strong in self, and to set up those who are weak. It is God's way to unite the strong with weakness, and to bless the weak with strength. It is God's peculiar way, and he abides by it. The full he empties, and the empty he fills. Those who boast of the power to live he slays; and those who faint before him as dead, he makes alive.

She had also been taught *the way and method of his grace* as well as of his providence, for never did a woman show more acquaintance with the wonders of divine grace than she did when she sang, "He raiseth up the poor out of the dust, and lifteth up the beggar from the dunghill, to set them among princes, and to make them inherit the throne of glory." This, too, is another of those ways of the Lord which are only understood by his people.

She had also seen the *Lord's faithfulness* to his people. Some Christians, even in these gospel days, do not believe in the doctrine of the final perseverance of the saints, but she did. She sang, "He will keep the feet of his saints"; and, beloved, so he will, or none of them will ever stand.

She had foreseen also somewhat of *his kingdom,* and of the glory of it. Her prophetic eye, made brighter and clearer by her holy tears, enabled her to look into the future, and looking, her joyful heart made her sing, "He shall give strength unto his king, and exalt the horn of his anointed."

III. And now, last, *much that is precious will yet be given to those who are truly the Lord's, even though they have a sorrowful spirit.*

For, first, Hannah had *her prayers answered.* Ah! little could she have imagined when Eli was rebuking her for drunkenness, that within a short time she should be there, and the same priest should look at her with deep respect and delight because the Lord had favored her. And you, my dear friend of a sorrowful spirit, would not weep so much tonight if you knew what is in store for you. You would not weep at all if you guessed how soon all will change, and like Sarah you will laugh for very joy. You are very poor; you scarcely know where you will place your head tonight; but if you knew in how short a time you will be among the angels, your penury would not cause you much distress. You are sickening and pining away, and will soon go to your long home. You would not be so depressed if you remembered how bright around your head will shine the starry diadem, and how sweetly your tongue shall pour forth heavenly sonnets such as none can sing but those who, like you, have tasted of the bitter waters of grief. It is better on before! It is better on before! Let these things cheer you if you are of a sorrowful spirit. There shall be a fulfillment of the things which God has promised to you. Eye hath not seen, nor ear heard, the things he hath laid up for you, but his Spirit reveals them to you at this hour.

Not only did there come to Hannah after her sorrow an answered prayer, but *grace to use that answer.* I do not think that Hannah would have been a fit mother for Samuel if she had not first of all been of a sorrowful spirit. It is not everybody that can be trusted to educate a young prophet. Many a fool of a woman has made a fool of her child. He was so much her "duck" that he grew up to be a goose. It needs a wise woman to train up a wise son, and therefore I regard Samuel's eminent character and career as largely the fruit of his mother's sorrow, and as a reward for her griefs. Hannah was a thoughtful mother, which was something, and her thought induced diligence. She had slender space in which to educate her boy, for he left her early to wear the little coat, and minister before the Lord; but in that space her work was effectually done, for the child Samuel worshiped the very day she took him up to the temple. In many of our homes we have a well-drawn picture of a child at prayer, and such I doubt not was the very image of the youthful Samuel. I like to think of him with that little coat on that linen ephod—coming forth in solemn style, as a child-servant of God, to help in the services of the temple.

Hannah had acquired another blessing, and that was *the power to magnify the Lord.* Those sweet songs of hers, especially that precious one which we have been reading—where did she get it from? I will tell you. You have picked up a shell, have you not, by the seaside, and you have put it to your ear, and heard it sing of the wild waves? Where did it learn this music? In the deeps. It had been tossed to and fro in the rough sea until it learned to talk with a deep, soft meaning of mysterious things, which only the salt sea caves can communicate. Hannah's poesy was born of her sorrow; and if everyone here that is of a sorrowful spirit can but learn to tune his harp as sweetly as she tuned hers, he may be right glad to have passed through such griefs as she endured.

Moreover, her sorrow *prepared her to receive further blessings,* for after the birth of Samuel she had three more sons and two daughters, God thus giving her five for the one that she had dedicated to him. This was grand interest for her loan: 500 percent. Parting with Samuel was the necessary preface to the reception of other little ones. God cannot bless some of us till first of all he has tried us. Many of us are not fit to receive a great blessing till we have gone through the fire. Half the men that have been ruined by popularity have been so ruined because they did not undergo a preparatory course of opprobrium and shame. Half the men who perish by riches do so because they had not toiled to earn them, but made a lucky hit, and became wealthy in an hour. Passing through the fire anneals the weapon which afterward is to be used in the conflict; and Hannah gained grace to be greatly favored by being greatly sorrowing. Her name stands among the highly favored women because she was deeply sorrowing.

Last of all, it was by suffering in patience that she became so brave a witness for the Lord, and could so sweetly sing, "There is none holy as the LORD, neither is there any rock like our God." We cannot bear testimony unless we test the promise, and therefore happy is the man whom the Lord tests and qualifies to heave [raise] a testimony to the world that God is true. To that witness I would set my own personal seal.

The Queen of Sheba: Consulting with Jesus

Published 1902; delivered at New Park Street Chapels, Southwark. No. 2778.

And when the queen of Sheba heard of the fame of Solomon concerning the name of the LORD, *she came to prove him with hard questions. . . . And Solomon told her all her questions: there was not any thing hid from the king, which he told her not.*—1 KINGS 10:1, 3

As our Lord has given the queen of Sheba for a sign [Matt. 12:42], it would be unbecoming if we did not try to learn all that we can from that sign. She came "to hear the wisdom of Solomon"; but Christ is "greater than Solomon" in every respect. He is greater in wisdom; for, though Solomon was wise, he was not Wisdom itself, and that Jesus is. In the book of Proverbs he is referred to under the name of Wisdom, and the apostle Paul tells us that he is made of God unto us wisdom. They who really know him know something of how wise he is, and how truly he may be called Wisdom. Because he is with the Father, and knows the Father, he has such wisdom as no one else can have. "No man knoweth the Son, but the Father; neither knoweth any man the Father, save the Son, and he to whomsoever the Son will reveal him." He knows the deep things of God, for he came down from heaven bringing his Father's greatest secrets in his heart. To him, therefore, men ought to come if they wish to be wise, and ought we not to wish for wisdom? To whom else can we go if we go not to him "in whom are hid all the treasures of wisdom and knowledge"?

I. First, then I call upon you to *admire this queen's mode of procedure when she came to Solomon.*

We are told, in the text, that "she came to prove him with hard questions." She wanted to prove whether he was as wise as she had been led to believe, and her mode of proving it was by endeavoring to learn from him. She put difficult questions to him in order that she might be instructed by his wisdom; and if you want to ascertain what the wisdom of Christ is, the way to know it is to come and sit at his feet, and learn of him. I know of no other method; it is a very sure one, and it will be a very profitable and blessed one if you adopt it. He has himself said, "Take my yoke upon you, and learn of me; for I am meek and lowly in heart: and ye shall find rest unto your souls."

Jesus came forth from God to be "the faithful Witness" to the truth, and therefore we are bound to believe what he says; and, certainly, we shall never fully appreciate his wisdom unless we are willing to receive his testimony. The psalmist says, "O taste and see that the LORD is good"; but, in this case, we must test and prove that the Lord is wise. There are some who despise the wisdom of Christ; and if you probe them, you will discover that they were never willing to learn of him. His own words are, "Except ye be converted, and become as little children, ye shall not enter into the kingdom of heaven." The wisdom of Christ cannot be known by those who refuse to be disciples, that is, learners. We must learn of him before we are competent to judge whether Christ is wise, or not; and never did a disciple sit humbly at his feet, never did one, in the spirit of a little child, sit with Mary at the feet of the great Teacher, without saying, as he listened to the gracious words that proceeded out of his mouth, "The half was not told me. O the depth of the riches both of the wisdom and the knowledge that are to be found in him!"

The queen of Sheba is also to be admired in that, wishing to learn from Solomon, *she asked him many questions*—not simply one or two, but many. Some people say, though I do not know how true it is, that curiosity is largely developed in women. I think I have known some men who have had a tolerably large share of it also. In this case, however, the woman's curiosity was wise and right; it was a wise thing, on her part, when she was in the presence of such a man of wisdom, to try to learn all that she could from him; and therefore she questioned him about all sorts of things. Very likely she brought before him the difficulties connected with her government, various schemes relating to trade, the modes of war, or the arts of peace; possibly she talked to him concerning the beasts of the field and the fish of the sea and the fowls of the air; but I am persuaded that she also talked about higher things—the things of God; and I am led to that conclusion by the expression in the first verse of my text, "When the queen of Sheba heard of the fame of Solomon concerning the name of the LORD, she came to prove him with hard questions." The report that came to her had to do with Jehovah, the God of Israel, as well as with Solomon; so we may rest assured that she put to him many difficult questions concerning the state of her heart, her character, her present position before God, and her future relationship to Israel's God. Questions on those points are not easy to answer, but she took care to ask them so that, when she reached her home, she might not have to say, "I wish I had asked Solomon about that matter; then I should no longer be in doubt."

Now, beloved, if you want to know the wisdom of Christ, you must ask him many questions. Come and inquire of him about anything you please. There is nothing which he does not know of earth, of heaven, and of hell. He knows the past, the present, the future; the things of every day, and the things of that last great day of days. He knows the things of God as nobody else knows them, for he is one with the Father, and with the Spirit, and he can tell us all that we need to know. Come to him, then, with every question that has ever puzzled you, and with every doubt that has ever staggered you. Resort not so much to your own thoughts, or to the counsels and arguments of your fellow creatures; but consult with him who spoke as never man spoke, and whose wisdom, like Alexander's sword, can cut each Gordian knot, and end in a moment all the difficulties that trouble your spirit.

But the main point, for which I admire the queen of Sheba, is that *she proved Solomon "with hard questions."* Was she not wise? If she had asked Solomon questions which a schoolboy could reply to, it would have been almost an insult to him. No, if Solomon's wisdom is to be tested, let him be proved with "hard questions." If a man is really wise, he likes to have inquiries put to him which a man with less wisdom could not answer. If the queen's questions had been such as she could herself answer, why need she have gone all that long way to ask Solomon to reply to them? Or if she had somebody at her home, wherever it was, who could have replied to her questions, why need she have gone to Jerusalem? It was because she had no one else to help her that she brought her questions to the one who, because of his superlative wisdom, would be able to answer them. This would relieve her mind, and send her home satisfied upon many points that had previously troubled her; so she did well to bring her "hard questions" to Solomon.

But I have known some—I think I know some still—who seem as if they could not ask Christ a hard question. For instance, they feel that they are great sinners; and they think that, if they had not sinned so much, he might be better able to forgive them, so they do not like to bring their hard questions to King Jesus. Others have a hard struggle to conquer some fierce passion or some reigning lust, and they think they must overcome that evil themselves. Then do you think that my Master is only a little Savior? He is the great Physician; will you only bring to him a cut finger or an aching tooth to cure? Oh, he is such a Savior that you may bring to him the worst, the most abject and depraved of men, for they are those who can best prove his power to save! When you feel yourselves most lost, then come to him; when you are at your worst state, when you think you are almost damned, and wonder that you are not altogether so, then come to him. If yours is a hard case, bring it to the almighty Savior. Do you think he only came into the world to save those who are decent and good? You know what he himself said, "They that are whole have no need of the physician, but they that are sick: I came not to call the righteous, but sinners to repentance."

And, beloved, hearken yet again. Are you in some very sharp trial? Is your spirit terribly depressed, and have you, because of that, kept away from Christ? Have you felt that you could go to him with your everyday burdens, but not with that special load? But why not take that also to him? Prove him with hard questions; the harder, the better. Do you not remember the Indian nurse, who said to the invalid lady who seemed as if she did not like to lean too heavily upon her, "If you love me, lean hard." That is what your Lord says to you, "If you love me, lean hard upon me." The more of your weight you rest upon him, the better pleased will he be. The more you trust him, the more you prove your confidence in him, the closer will be the union between you. Christ is the Bearer of a world's iniquities; so he may readily enough be the Bearer of your most extraordinary griefs. Prove the Lord Jesus in every possible way, for he loves so to be proved. The more needy the outcast, the louder does the gospel trumpet blow that they, who are ready to perish, may come and be saved.

II. Now, second, *let us imitate her example, in reference to Christ, who is "greater than Solomon."*

Let us prove him with hard questions. Let us bring to him some nuts to be cracked, some diamonds to be cut, some difficulties to be solved. I do not know what hard question may be resting upon the mind of any of you, but I will briefly mention ten hard questions which Jesus answers. They are only ten out of ten thousand that might be put to him, for there is no hard question which he cannot answer.

Here is the first hard question. *How can a man be just with God?* It stands in the book of Job, and it seems to stand there unanswered: "How should man be just with God?" There is nobody, on the face of the earth, who could have answered that question if it had not been made possible by our Lord Jesus Christ. There is no way of being just in the sight of God except through him. But if we come to him, he will tell us that we ourselves must stand in the place of condemnation, and confess that, for our sin, we deserve the wrath of God. We must always admit that no merits of ours can ever win his favor; that, in fact, we have no merits of our own, but are undeserving, ill-deserving, hell-deserving sinners; and when we occupy that position, then, of his own abounding grace and mercy, God will reckon us as just through Christ Jesus.

Our Lord Jesus also tells us how a man can be just with God as he reminds us that he is the covenant Head of his believing people; that, as in Adam, the first head, all men fell, so those who are in him who is the second Adam, the Lord from heaven, all rise again. "As by one man's disobedience many were made righteous." Righteousness in the sight of God comes, through the headship of Christ, to all who are in him. Christ has honored the law of God, he has obeyed every jot and tittle of it; and his obedience is reckoned as the obedience of all who are in him. The question, "How can a man be just with God?" is, therefore, answered thus. Jesus says, "I have stood in the place of the guilty, and have rendered to God's law a perfect obedience. This is imputed to all who believe, and God regards them as just through my righteousness." Oh, glorious doctrine of imputation! Happy are all they who believe it, and rejoice in it.

Here is another hard question. *How can God be just, and yet the Justifier of the ungodly?* If he be just, surely he must condemn the ungodly; yet we know, of a certainty, many who have been ungodly, whom God has been pleased to meet with, and to justify so completely that they have been heard to say, "Who shall lay anything to the charge of God's elect? It is God that justifieth." How can this be? Only Jesus can answer the question, and he answers it thus: "I have borne the penalty that was due to sin; I have stood in the sinner's place, and suffered that which has fully satisfied the claims of divine justice on his behalf; I have paid the sinner's debt, so the law may well let him go free." "He was wounded for our transgressions, he was bruised for our iniquities: the chastisement of our peace was upon him; and with his stripes we are healed. All we like sheep have gone astray; we have turned every one to his own way; and the LORD hath laid on him the iniquity of us all." The great Sin-Bearer has suffered in the sinner's stead; the sword of divine justice smote him, for he stood in the sinner's place, willingly bearing the sinner's penalty; and, now that sin has been punished upon him, God can be just, and yet be the Justifier of all who believe in his dear Son.

The next question is one which has puzzled many. *How can a man be saved by faith alone without works, and yet no man can be saved by a faith that is without works?* If you are puzzled by this question, our Lord Jesus Christ will tell you, in this Book, through which he still speaks to us, that we are to believe in him for salvation, and not to bring any works of our own as the ground of our trust; not even our own faith, so far as it is a work, for a man is saved by grace, that is, by God's free favor, not by works of righteousness which he has himself done. "For by grace are ye saved through faith; and that not of yourselves; it is the gift of God; not of works, lest any man should boast." That truth is as clearly taught in Scripture as it can possibly be; but then it is equally true that no man may claim that he is saved unless the faith, which he professes to have, is an active, living faith, which makes him love God, and, consequently, do that which is well pleasing in his sight. If I say that I believe in God, yet continue to live in sin willfully and knowingly, then I have not so good a faith as the devils have, for they "believe and tremble." There are some men who profess to believe in God, yet who do not tremble before him, but are impudent and presumptuous. That is not the kind of faith that saves the soul; saving faith is that which produces good works, which leads to repentance, or is accompanied by it, and leads to love of God, and to holiness, and to a desire to be made like unto the Savior. Good works are not the root of faith, but they are its fruit. A house does not rest upon the slates on its roof, yet it would not be fit to live in if it had not a roof; and, in like manner, our faith does not rest upon our good works, yet it would be a poor and useless faith if it had not some of the fruit of the Spirit to prove that it had come from God. Jesus Christ can tell us how a man can aim at being as holy as God is holy, and yet never talk about his holiness, or dream of trusting in it. We would live as if we were to be saved by our own works, yet place no reliance whatever upon them, but count them as dross, that we may win Christ, and be found in him, not having our own righteousness, which is of the law, but that which is through the faith of Christ, the righteousness which is God by faith.

Here is another hard question, which once greatly puzzled a ruler of the Jews. You know his name, Nicodemus: "the same came to Jesus by night." This was his hard question: *"How can a man be born when he is old?"* At first sight, it seems as if that were unanswerable; but Jesus Christ has said, "Behold, I make all things new." Even under the old dispensation, God's promise to his people was "A new heart also will I give you, and a new spirit will I put within you: and I will take away the stony heart out of your flesh, and I will give you a heart of flesh." All this is impossible with man, but it is possible with God. The Holy Spirit regenerates a man, causes him to be born again, so that, though his bodily frame remains the same, yet his inner spirit becomes like that of a little child, and as a newborn babe, he desires the unadulterated milk of the Word that he may grow thereby. Yes, there is a total change worked in men when they believe in Jesus Christ. He said to Nicodemus, "Except a man be born again, he cannot see the kingdom of God"; but men, who are old, can be born again, "by the Word of God, which liveth and abideth forever." Graybeard, you can be born again; leaning on your staff for very age, though you have outnumbered three score years and ten, you can be born again; and if you were a hundred years of age, yet if you should believe in Jesus, by the power of the eternal Spirit, you would at once be made a new creature in Christ Jesus.

Here is another hard question. *How can God, who sees all things, no longer see any sin in believers?* That is a puzzle which many cannot understand. God is everywhere, and everything is present to his all-seeing eye, yet he says, through the prophet Jeremiah, "'In those days, and in that time,' saith the LORD, 'the iniquity of Israel shall be sought for, and there shall be none.'" I venture to say that even God himself cannot see that which no longer exists; even his eye rests not on a thing that is not; and thus is it with the sin of those who have believed in Jesus; it has ceased to be. God himself has declared, "I will remember their sin no more." But can God forget? Of course he can, as he says that he will. The work of the Messiah was described to Daniel in these remarkable words, "to finish the transgression, and to make an end of sins, and to make reconciliation for iniquity, and to bring in everlasting righteousness." To make an end of sins? Well, then, there is an end of them, according to that other gracious, divine declaration, "I have blotted out, as a thick cloud, thy transgressions, and, as a cloud, thy sins." Oh, what blessed words! Hence, they are gone, they have ceased to be, Christ has obliterated them; and, therefore, God no longer sees them. Oh, the splendor of the pardon which God has bestowed upon all believers, making a clean sweep of all their sins forever!

Here is another hard question. *How can a man see the invisible God?* Yet Christ said, "Blessed are the pure in heart: for they shall see God"; and the angel said to John: "His servants shall serve him, and they shall see his face." This hard question is putting in another form the difficulty which Philip brought to Jesus: "Lord, shew us the Father, and it sufficeth us." Jesus answered him, "Have I been so long time with you, and yet hast thou not known me, Philip? He that hath seen me hath seen the Father." In the person of his dear Son, God the Father has displayed himself before the eyes of men, as John says, "The Word was made flesh, and dwelt among us (and we beheld his glory, the glory as of the only begotten of the Father), full of grace and truth." Jesus himself said, "I and my Father are one"; so that we can see the invisible Father in the person of Jesus Christ his Son.

Moving upward in Christian experience, here is another hard question. *How can it be true that "whosoever is born of God sinneth not," yet men who are born of God do sin?* Ah! that is a question which has puzzled man; but we must remember that every man of God is two men in one. That new part of him, which is born of God, that new nature which was implanted in regeneration, cannot sin because it is born of God. It is the incorruptible seed, which lives and abides forever; but, as far as the man is still in the flesh, it is true that "the carnal mind is enmity against God: for it is not subject to the law of God, neither indeed can be." The old nature sins through the force of nature; but the new nature sins not, because it is born of God.

This helps also to answer another hard question. *How can a man be a new man, and yet be constantly sighing because he finds in himself so much of the old man?* The Holy Spirit guided the apostle Paul to instruct us upon this matter. There is the new man within us, which leaps for joy because of the heavenly life; but alas! there is also the old man. Paul calls it "the body of this death." There it is, and you know that it is the older of the two, and that it will not go out if it can help it. It says to the new nature, "What right have you here?" "I have the right of grace," answers the new nature; "God put me here, and here I mean to stay." "Not if I can prevent it," cries the old nature; "I will stamp you out, or I will smother you with doubts, or puff you up with pride, or kill you with the poison of unbelief; but out you shall go somehow." "No," replies the new nature; "out I never will go, for I have come to stay here. I came in the name and under the authority of Jesus; and where Jesus comes, he comes to reign, and I mean to reign over you." He deals some heavy blows at the old nature, and smites him to the dust; but it is not easy to keep him under. That old nature is such a horrible companion for the new nature, that it often makes him cry, "O wretched man that I am! who shall deliver me from the body of this death?" But even while he is thus crying out, he is not afraid of the ultimate issue; he feels sure of victory. The new nature sits and sings; even, as it were, within the ribs of death, with the stench of corruption in its nostrils, it still sits and sings, "I thank God through Jesus Christ our Lord," and triumphs still in him. We are not going to be overcome, beloved. "Sin shall not have dominion over you: for you are not under the law, but under grace." But, my brethren, it is a tremendous struggle; and if our Lord had not instructed his servant Paul to tell us about his own experience, some of us would have been obliged to cry, "If it be so, why am I thus?" Christ knows all about the inner life of his people, and his Word explains what may appear mysterious to you; so when next you feel this conflict raging within your spirit, you will understand it, and say, "It is not because I am dead in sin; for, if I were dead, I should not have this fighting. It is because I have been quickened that this battle is going on."

Here is one more of these hard questions. *How can a man be sorrowful, yet always rejoicing?* That is one of the apostle Paul's riddles, of which he gives us a great number, such as these. How can a man be poor, yet make many rich? How can a man be cast down, yet not destroyed; persecuted, yet not forsaken? How can a man be less than nothing, and yet possess all things? The explanation is that, while we are in this body, we must suffer and smart and pine; but thanks be to God! He has taught us to glory in tribulation also, and to expect the great reward that awaits us by and by; so that if we are full of sorrow, we accept the sorrow joyfully; if we are made to smart, we bow beneath the rod and look for the after blessed results from it. So we can sigh, yet at the same time sing.

I have one more hard question. *How can a man's life be in heaven while he still lives on earth?* May you all understand this riddle by learning what Paul means when he says, "For ye are dead, and your life is hid with Christ in God"; who "hath raised us up together, and made us sit together in heavenly places in Christ Jesus"! Even now, the heavenly life may be enjoyed by us, although we still live upon earth; and, sometimes, we are half inclined to say, with the apostle, "Whether in the body, or out of the body, I cannot tell: God knoweth." Yet we soon discover that we are in the body, for we have physical wants, temptations, and trials; and then we cry, "Woe is me, that I sojourn in Mesech, that I dwell in the tents of Kedar!" Yet, perhaps, the next moment, we say, "My treasure is all packed up and gone on before me; and I stand on tiptoe, waiting to be called away; for, where my treasure is, there my heart is also, and they are both above the skies with my dear Lord and Savior."

III. Now in closing, let us *answer certain questions of a practical character.*

Answer, first, this question: How can we come to Christ? He is in heaven, so we cannot climb up to him there. Yes, but he has graciously said, "Lo, I am with you always, even unto the end of the world." And though we see him not, and hear him not, yet in spirit he is among us at this moment. You need not stir even a step in order to get to him. If Jesus were again upon earth, he could not, in his bodily presence, be in all places at once. Suppose he were in London, what would they do who live in Australia, and wanted to get to him? They might die on the voyage. Or if he were at Jerusalem, how many poor people would never be able to get to Palestine! It is much better that he is not on earth; it is more expedient for us, because his Spirit is everywhere; and, desiring to think about him, wishing to know him, seeking him, and, above all, trusting him, we have come to him.

"Well," says one, "supposing that is done, *how can we ask Christ hard questions?*" You may ask anything of him just the same as if you could see him. You need not even speak the question; if you think it, he hears it. Pray to him, for he hears prayer. Wherever there is the praying lip of a sinner, there is the hearing ear of the Savior.

"But," you say, *"if I ask of him, how will he answer me?"* Do not expect that he will answer you in a dream, or by any vocal sound. He has spoken all you need to know in this Book. Read it, study it, that you may learn what he has revealed. We who preach are not worth hearing unless what we say is taken out of the Bible. Listen to us when we do so preach, because, oftentimes, the words of the Book may seem cold to you; but, if we translate them into warm lip language, they will go home to your heart. You will understand them better, and feel them better, as coming from one who loves you, and who is a man of flesh and blood like yourselves. "Yes," says one, "I would fain come to Christ with my doubts and difficulties, and here is one question that I want him to answer now. *How is it that I read, in the Word of God, that he hath limited a day, and yet you bid me come to him now?"* Yes, I do bid you come to him now; and what is more, I tell you that his own word is "him that cometh to me I will in no wise cast out." "But is it not also true that he limiteth a day?" Yes, he does; but shall I tell you how he limits it? "Again, he limiteth a certain day, saying in David, 'Today,' after so long a time, as it is said, 'Today if ye will hear his voice, harden not your hearts.'" Blessed be his holy name, if he has limited you, he has limited you to today; and if I live to see your face tomorrow, I will still say the same to you. The limit is a very gracious one; it is "today." If ever a soul does come to Christ, when he does come, it is today; and if you come this day, you will be within the limit, for he has said, "Today if ye will hear his voice, harden not your hearts." Today then, dear soul, is within the boundary; this night, ere you go to your home, you are just within the limit. "Today if ye will hear his voice, harden not your hearts." Accept him now; trust him now; come to him with your hard questions now; come to him with your hard doubts, come with your hard infidelity, come with your hard obstinacy; come just as you are, and cast yourself at those dear pierced feet of his, for there is not a question that he will not answer, not a difficulty that he will not overcome, nor a sin that he will not pardon, and send you away rejoicing.

I think I hear someone say, "What is all this about? Are there really any people in the world who want God in this fashion?" Yes, there are; and we are grieved if you are not one of them; for, believe me, friend, all who are living as if there were no God are missing everything that truly makes up life. I heard a young man say, "I should like to see a little life." Yes, I hope you will, and a great deal of life too; but there is no life in the purlieus of vice; that is death, rottenness, stench, corruption, like the valley of Hinnom and the burning of Tophet. Flee from it. But life is to be found by coming to God; and by trusting

Jesus you get to God, and so become the possessor of eternal life. Then, getting to know God, you help to make the world all alive. The very times and season seem to have changed to you, for things are not what they once were. The wilderness and the solitary places rejoice, and the desert blooms as the rose. If I could live ten thousand years on earth without my God, and perpetually swim in a sea of sensual delights, I would beg to be annihilated sooner than have to undergo such a doom. But let God send or withhold whatever he pleases of temporal favors, if he will but give me to know that he is mine, and that I am his, it shall be all I will ask of him. I mean what I say, and I believe that every child of God, who has once enjoyed the full light of his countenance, will say the same.

The Queen of Sheba: Heart-Communing

꧖

Published in 1902; delivered at New Park Street Chapels, Southwark. No. 2779.

She communed with him of all that was in her heart.—1 KINGS 10:2

It appears that the queen of Sheba, when she had once obtained an interview with the great and wise king of Israel, was not content with merely putting to him various difficult questions. For she unbosomed herself to him, told out all that lay concealed in her heart; and Solomon listened attentively to her, and, no doubt, so spoke to her that he sent her away rejoicing.

It is not generally a wise thing to tell all that is in your heart. Solomon himself said, "A fool uttereth all his mind; but a wise man keepeth it in till afterwards." There are many things which you had better not tell to anybody. Make no one your confidant completely. If you do, you run great risks of making an Ahithophel or a Judas for yourself. David said, in his haste, that all men were liars. That was not quite true; probably, what he meant was that, if we trust all men, we shall soon find ourselves deceived; but if we could meet with a Solomon—one who had been divinely endowed with wisdom, as he was, it might be safe for us to bring all our questions and tell all our troubles to him. At any rate, we know of One, who is "greater than Solomon," to whom it is most safe and blessed to tell out all that is in our heart. He is willing to listen to us, and to commune with us; and the more frank and open we are with him, the better will he be pleased, and the better will it be for us. That is to be our subject, heart-communing with Jesus, spiritualizing the action of the queen of Sheba, when she came to Solomon, and "communed with him of all that was in her heart."

I. We will begin by saying that *we ought to commune with Jesus of all that is in our heart.*

I do not mean all of you who are present; I mean all those who have been redeemed from among men by his most precious blood, all those who are believing in him, and who call him their Savior, their Master, their Lord. You are bound to tell him all that is in your heart, and to have no secrets hidden away from him within your soul.

Tell Jesus all that is in your heart, for neglect of intercourse with Christ, of the most intimate kind is ungenerous toward him. Are there any professing Christians here, who have lived for a month without conscious communion with Christ? If I were to speak of a longer period, and to ask, "Are there not some professing Christians here, who have lived for three months without conscious communion with Christ," I am afraid there are some who, if they were honest and truthful, would have to reply, "That is the case with us." If so, think what that means; you profess to belong to Jesus, and to be his disciple, yet you confess that you have lived all this while without real, intimate communication with him who is your Master and Lord. What is more, you profess to be not only one of his disciples, but one of his friends. "Is this thy kindness to thy Friend?" I may go further than that, for you believe yourself to be married to Christ, for that is the union which exists between himself and his people. That would be a strange kind of marriage union in which the wife should be in the presence of her husband, and not even speak to him by the week, by the month, by the three months, by the six months together. For them to have no fellowship with one another, no mutual interchange of love, no communications with each other, would be regarded as unnatural, and would be rightly condemned; but do we not, sometimes, act toward our heavenly Bridegroom in just that manner? Are we not, too often, like the men of the world who do not know him? Do we not live as if we did not know him, or as if he were no longer present with us? It ought not to be thus; unless we would act contrary to all the dictates of our higher nature, we must be continually holding intimate intercourse with our Lord Jesus Christ.

And we must tell him all that is in our heart, because *to conceal anything from so true a Friend betrays the sad fact that there is something wrong to be concealed.* Is there anything that you do that you could not tell to Jesus? Is there anything you love that you could not ask him to bless? Is there any plan now before you that you could not ask him to sanction? Is there anything in your heart which you would wish to hide from him? Then it is a wrong thing; be you sure of that. The thing must be evil, or else you would not wish to conceal it from him whom, I trust, you do really love. O my Lord, wherefore should I desire to hide anything from you? If I do want to hide it, then, surely, it must be because it is something of which I have cause to be ashamed; so help me to get rid of it. O Christian brothers and sisters, I beseech you to live just as you would do if Christ Jesus were in your room, in your bedchamber, in your shop, or walking along the street with you, for his spiritual presence is there! May there never be anything about you which you wish to conceal from him!

If we cannot tell Jesus all that is in our heart, *it shows a want of confidence in his love, or his sympathy, or his wisdom, or his power.* When there is something that the wife cannot tell to her husband, or there begin to be some secret things on the part of one of them, that cannot be revealed to the other, there will soon be an end of mutual love and peace and joy. Things cannot go on well in the home while there has to be concealment. O beloved, I beseech you to love Christ too much to keep anything back from him! Love him so much that you can trust him even with the little frivolous things which so often worry and vex you. Love him so much that you can tell him all that is in your heart, nor ever for a moment wish to keep back anything from him.

If we do not tell it all to Jesus, it looks as if we had not confidence in his love, and therefore thought that he would not bear with us; or else that we had not confidence in his sympathy, and fancied that he would not take any notice of us; or else that we had not confidence in his wisdom, and thought that our trouble was too perplexing to bring to him; or else that we had not confidence in his power, and dreamed that he could not help us in such an emergency. Let this never be the case with any of you; but, every day, unburden your heart to Christ, and never let him think that you even begin to distrust him. So shall you keep up a frank and open and blessed fellowship between Christ and your own soul.

I am quite certain that if you will carry out the plan I am commending to you, it *will bring you great ease of mind*; whereas, if you do not, you will continue to have much uneasiness. Is there anything that I have not told to Jesus— anything in which I could not have fellowship with him? Then there is something wrong with me. Are you keeping your trouble to yourself and trying to manage without consulting with Jesus? Well, then, if anything goes wrong, you will have the responsibility of it; but if you take it all to him, and leave it with him, it cannot go wrong whatever happens; and even if it should seem to do so, you would not have the responsibility of it.

I believe that our trials usually come out of the things that we do not take to the Lord; and, moreover, I am sure that we make greater blunders in what we consider to be simple matters, which we need not take to the Lord, than we do in far more difficult matters which we take to him. The men of Israel were deceived by the Gibeonites because they had on old shoes and clouted, and had moldy bread in their wallets, and the Israelites said, "It is perfectly clear that these men must have come from a long distance; look at their old boots and their ragged garments"; so they made a covenant with them, and inquired not the will of the Lord. If it had not appeared to them to be quite so clear a case, they would have asked the Lord for direction, and then they would have been rightly guided. It is when you think you can see your way that you go wrong; when you cannot see your way, but trust to God to lead you by a way that you know not, you will go perfectly right. I am persuaded that it is so that the simplest and plainest matter kept away from Christ will turn out to be a maze, while the most intricate labyrinth, under the guidance of Christ, will prove to have in it straight road for the feet of all those who trust in the infallible wisdom of their Lord and Savior.

On the other hand, if you do not come to Jesus, and commune with him of all that is in your heart, *you will lose his counsel and help, and the comfort that comes from them.* I do not suppose anybody here knows what he has lost in this way, and I can hardly imagine how you are to calculate what you have lost of spiritual good that you might have had. There is many a child of God, who might be rich in all the intents of bliss, who continues to be as poor as Lazarus the beggar; he has hardly a crumb of comfort to feed upon, and is full of doubts and fears, when he might have had full assurance long ago. There is many an heir of heaven who is living upon the mere husks of gospel food when he might be eating the rich fare of which Moses speaks: "Butter of kine, and milk of sheep, with fat of lambs, and rams of the breed of Bashan, and goats, with the fat of kidneys of wheat." Very often, beloved, you have not because you ask not; or because you believe not, or because you do not confide in Jesus, and commune with him. How strong the weakling might be if he would go to Jesus more frequently! How rich the poor soul might be if it would draw continually from Christ's inexhaustible treasury! Oh, what might we not be if we would but live up to our privileges! Might we not live in the suburbs of heaven, and often, as it were, be close to the pearly gates, if we would but go and tell all to Jesus, and commune with him concerning all that is in our hearts?

Sometimes, our naughty habit of *reticence toward Jesus is aggravated by our eagerness to tell our troubles to others.* In the time of trial, we often imitate King Asa, who, when he was sick, "sought not to the Lord, but to the physicians." It was not wrong to go to the physicians, but he should have gone to the Lord first. It is the same with many of you as it was with Asa, away you go to your neighbor over the fence, or you call in a friend, and have a talk with him in your own drawing room, or you go to some great one, and tell him all your trouble; yet how much have you gained by doing so? Have you not often found that you would have been wiser if you had followed Solomon's advice,

"Go not into thy brother's house in the day of thy calamity"? Have you not also frequently discovered that, when you have talked over your griefs with your friends, they still remain?

You say that you want a friend; yet he who is the Friend that sticketh closer than a brother is neglected by you. Suppose the Lord Jesus Christ were to meet some of you, and you were to say to him, "Good Master, we are in trouble"; and suppose he should say to you, "Where have you been with your trouble? You have not been to me"; and you were to reply, "No, Lord, we have been consulting with flesh and blood; we have been asking our friends to help us"; and suppose he were to say to you, "And have they disappointed you?" and you had to reply, "Yea, Lord, they have"; suppose he looked at you severely, and said, "Where you have already gone, you had better go again. You went to your friends first; are you coming to me last? Am I to play the lackey to you, and do you only come to me after having tried all the others?" Ah! if he did talk like that, what could you reply? Why, I think your only answer could be, and I trust your answer now will be, "Jesus, Master, I have too much forgotten thee. I have not regarded thee as a real present friend. I have gone to my neighbors because I could see them, and speak with them, and hear what they had to say to me; but I have thought of thee as if thou wert a myth, or, perhaps, I have not thought of thee at all. Forgive me, Lord, for I do believe that thou art, and that thy Word is true, which declares that thou are ever with thy people, and help me, henceforth, by thy grace, always to come to thee."

II. Second, *we need not cease communing with Christ for want of topics.*

The queen of Sheba and Solomon came at last to an end of their talk; they could not go on speaking to one another forever. But with regard to ourselves and our Lord, there need never be any end to our communion with him, for the subjects upon which we can have fellowship with him are almost innumerable. Let me mention just a few of them.

There are, first, *your sorrows.* Are you very grieved? Are you smitten of God, and afflicted? Then, brother, sister, you may well go to Jesus with your sorrows, for he is the "man of sorrows, and acquainted with grief." He knows all about you, and all about your sorrows too. There is not a pang that you have ever felt but he has felt the like. If you will only talk with him, you will find an open ear, and a sympathetic heart, and a ready hand, all placed at your disposal. "What do you mean, sir? Do you mean that I am to sit down in my room, and tell Jesus all about my troubles?" Yes, I do mean just that; and as you would do if you could see him sitting in the chair on the other side of the fire, sit down, and tell it all to him. If you have a quiet and secluded chamber, speak aloud if that will help you; but, anyhow, tell it all to him, pour into his ear and heart the story which you cannot disclose to anyone else. "But it seems so fanciful to imagine that I can really speak to Jesus." Try it, beloved; if you have faith in God, you will discover that it is not a matter of fancy, but the most blessed reality in the world. If you can only see what your eye perceives, it is no use for you to do as I say; in fact, you cannot do it. But if you have the inner eyes that have been enlightened by the Holy Spirit, and if your heart discerns the invisible presence of the once-crucified but now glorified Savior, tell him the whole story of your grief. Oftentimes, after you have done, you will find that it will cease to grieve you anymore.

Then, also, tell him *your joys,* for he can have as much true fellowship with the joyous as with the sad. Go, young sister, young brother, in the gladness of your first youthful joy, and tell it all to Jesus. He rejoiced in spirit when he was upon the earth; and, now, he has the joy that was set before him when he endured the cross and despised the shame. If you tell him your joys, he will sober them—not sour them. He will take away from them their earthly effervescence, and impart to them a spiritual flavor, and an abiding sweetness, so that, even in common things, your joy shall not become idolatrous and sinful. You who are bereft of creature comforts should pray that you may find all things in God; but you who have such comforts, and are full of joy, should pray this prayer—that you may find God in all things. They are both good prayers. That latter petition you joyous souls may well pray to Jesus, and he will answer it, and you shall find that the marriage feast is all the better for Jesus being there to turn the water into wine, and that to all earthly joys he adds a bliss which they could not otherwise possess.

Some people say that we Christians get into ecstasies and raptures, and then we hardly know our head from our heels, and we are so excited that we are not fair witnesses as to matters of fact. I do not think that the church has often had too much excitement, the fault has usually been something quite in the opposite direction; but my own conviction is that we do not see the glory of Christ when we are excited, or when we are in an ecstasy, one half so well as we do in our cool, calm, reflective moments. I know a great many Christian people who are by no means fools; if you try to do business with them, you will find that they are as shrewd and wide-awake as any men. I should like to appeal to them about this matter. I believe that I have myself a certain degree of common sense, and I venture to say that Christ never appears to me so glorious as when I am perfectly cool and collected, just as I should be if I were sitting down to write out some statistics, or to work out a mathematical problem, or to make up an account and strike a balance.

Whenever, in the very calmest and quietest manner, I begin to think of my Lord and Master, he then most of all strikes me as glorious. Our religion does not require the excitements and stimulants upon which some seem to live; but when we are in the most serene state of mind and heart, then we can best see the glories of Christ. O sirs, my Master would have you sit down, and count the cost of being his servants! He would make you arithmeticians, that, after you have counted the cost, you may see that he is worth ten thousand times more than he could ever cost you. He would have you survey him, and look upon him from all points of view—look at his person, his work, his offices, his promises, his achievements—that in all things you may see how glorious he is. I ask you calmly to see what kind of Lord and Master he is, and what sort of glory it is that surrounds him; and if you will do so—that is, if your hearts have really been changed by his grace—you will say, "Oh yes! tell it, the wide world over, that it is simple common sense to believe in Christ, that it is irrational to reject him, that the best use of your reason is to lay it at his feet, and that the truest wisdom is to count yourself but a fool in comparison with him, and to sit with Mary, and listen to his wondrous words."

You may, also, go to Jesus, and tell him all about *your service.* You have begun to work for the Lord, and you are very pleased with the opportunity of doing something for him; but you do not find it to be all sweetness. Perhaps you are like Martha who was "cumbered" with her service for Christ. When she was preparing a dinner for him, she was greatly worried over it. The servants would burn the meat, or she was afraid that one very special delicacy would be spoiled altogether. Besides, somebody had broken the best dish, and the tablecloth did not look as white as she liked to see it. Martha was also troubled because Mary did not help her, so she went to the Master about it, which was the most sensible thing she could do. I can speak very sympathetically about this matter, for I get worrying concerning it sometimes. I want to see Christ served with the best that I have, and with the best that all his people have; and if things go a little awry, and will not work quite rightly, I am apt to become fidgety; but this will not do, either for me or for you. We must go and tell the Master about it. He will set it all right, and make us see that it is all right. Suppose any of you have not been treated kindly by your fellow members even when you were trying to do good, suppose that the girls in your class have grieved you, suppose that you have been rapped over the knuckles when you really meant to be serving your Lord, what are you to do? Again I say, "Tell it all to Jesus, comfort or complaint." Do not come and tell me. If I could help you, I would; but there is One who is far better than any pastor on earth to go to, even the great Shepherd and Bishop of souls, our Lord Jesus Christ.

Then, next, go and tell Jesus all *your plans*. You think you will do something for him, do you not? Do not begin till you have told him all about what you mean to do. He had great plans for the redemption of his people, but he communicated them all to his Father; no, I would rather say that he drew them out of his Father's eternal decrees. Go and tell him what you are planning for the glory of God, and the good of men, and you may, perhaps, discover that some of it would be a mistake.

When you have any successes, go and tell him. The seventy disciples returned to Jesus with joy, saying, "Lord, even the devils are subject unto us through thy name." If you have the high honor of winning a soul, tell Jesus, and be sure to give God all the glory of it. Sing *"Non nobis, Domine"*—"Not unto us, O Lord, not unto us, but unto thy name give glory, for thy mercy, and for thy truth's sake."

And when you have any failures—when your hopes are disappointed—go and tell it all to Jesus. I do not know whether I make myself clearly understood upon all these points; but I feel that working side by side with Christ is the only style of working at which a man can keep on year after year. If you get alone away from your Master—if you have sorrows or joys which are all your own, and which you do not tell to him, you will get into a sad state; but if you feel, "He is near me, he is with me," and if you act upon that belief by constantly communicating with him concerning what you feel, and what you believe, and what you do, you will lead a holy and blessed and useful and happy life.

I have not time to complete the long list of topics on which we are to commune with Jesus; but, in brief, let me urge you to tell him all your desires. If you desire anything that you ought to desire, and may desire, let him know it. Tell him also all your fears. Tell him that you are sometimes afraid to die. Tell him every fear that distresses you; for, as a nurse is tender with her child, so is Christ with his people.

Tell him all your loves. Bring before him, in prayer, all upon whom your love is set. Tell him especially all you can about your love to himself; and ask him to make it firmer, stronger, more abiding, more potent over the whole of your life. Often sing a song to Jesus, your Best Beloved, and say, "Now will I sing to my Well Beloved a song touching my Beloved." Sing and speak often to him; and whenever you have any mysteries which you cannot explain or tell to anyone else, go and ask him to read the inscription that is engraved upon your heart, and to decipher the strange hieroglyphics which no one else can read.

III. Now I will close when I have briefly shown you, in the third place, that *we shall never cease communing with Christ for want of reasons*.

I am not speaking now to those who have never communed with my Lord. I have often communed with him, I do still commune with him, and so do many of you; and I say that, we shall never cease communing with him for lack of reasons.

For, first, *it is most ennobling to have fellowship with the Son of God*; "and truly our fellowship is with the Father, and with his Son Jesus Christ." I have heard it said of some men, that to know them is a liberal education. If you are only slightly acquainted with them, you are sure to learn much from them; but to know Christ is to know everything that is worth knowing, and he is our All in All.

It is also *highly beneficial to commune with Christ*. I know of nothing that can lift you up so much above the evil influences of an ungodly world as constantly abiding in close fellowship with Christ, and telling out to him all that you feel in your heart of hearts.

How *consoling* it is to do this! You forget your griefs while you commune with him. How sanctifying it is! A man cannot take delight in sin while he walks with Christ. Communion with him will make a man leave off sinning, or else sinning will make him leave off communing. You will not be perfect while you are in this world, but the nearest way to perfection lies along the pathway where Jesus walks. How delightful it is, too, to commune with Jesus! There is no other joy that is at all comparable with it, and it prepares us for the higher joys above. When those who walk with Christ on earth come to live with him above, there will certainly be a change in some respects, but it will be no new experience to them. Did he not love his saints, and seek their fellowship while they were here below? Then they shall have that fellowship continued above. Did they not walk with God here? They shall walk with Jesus up there.

Are there any of Christ's followers who seldom commune with him? Beloved, shall I not chide you if that is true of you? My Master is looking down upon you at this moment. Does he need to speak to you? He did not speak to Peter when the boastful apostle had denied his Lord. Jesus turned, and looked upon Peter; and I trust he will look upon you; that those dear eyes, which wept for you, will gaze right down into your soul; and that his blessed heart, that bled for you, will look out of those eyes of his upon you. He seems to say, "Do you indeed love me, as you never wish for my company? Can you love me?"

And then, I think that my Master looks upon some here who have never had any communion with him at all, and he says, "Is it nothing to you that I loved mankind, and came to earth, and died to save sinners? Is it nothing to you that I bid you trust me, and that I promise to save you if you do so? Will you still refuse to trust me? Will you turn upon your heel away from me? Oh, why will you die? Why will you die?"

Esther: And Providence

❦

Delivered on Lord's Day morning, November 1, 1874, at the Metropolitan Tabernacle, Newington. No. 1201.

Though it was turned to the contrary, that the Jews had rule over them that hated them.—ESTHER 9:1

You are probably aware that some persons have denied the inspiration of the book of Esther because the name of God does not occur in it. They might with equal justice deny the inspiration of a great number of chapters in the Bible, and of a far greater number of verses. Although the name of God does not occur in the book of Esther, the Lord himself is there most conspicuously in every incident which it relates. I have seen portraits bearing the names of persons for whom they were intended, and they certainly needed them, but we have all seen others which required no name, because they were such striking likenesses that the moment you looked upon them you knew them. In the book of Esther, as much as in any other part of the Word of God, and I had almost committed myself by saying—more than anywhere else, the hand of Providence is manifestly to be seen.

To condense the whole of the story of the book of Esther into one sermon would be impossible, and therefore I must rely upon your previous acquaintance with it; I must also ask your patience if there should be more of history in the sermon than is usual with me. All Scripture is given by inspiration, and is profitable, whether it be history or doctrine. God never meant the book of Esther to lie dumb, and whatever it seemed good to him to teach us by it, it ought to be our earnest endeavor to learn.

The Lord intended by the narrative of Esther's history to set before us a wonderful instance of his providence, that when we had viewed it with interest and pleasure, we might praise his name, and then go on to acquire the habit of observing his hand in other histories, and especially in our own lives. Well does Flavel say, that he who observes Providence will never be long without a Providence to observe. The man who can walk through the world and see no God is said upon inspired authority to be a fool; but the wise man's eyes are in his head, he sees with an inner sight, and discovers God everywhere at work. It is his joy to perceive that the Lord is working according to his will in heaven and earth and in all deep places.

It has pleased God at different times in history to startle the heathen world into a conviction of his presence. He had a chosen people, to whom he committed the true light, and to these he revealed himself continually. The rest of the world was left in darkness, but every now and then the divine glory flamed through the gloom, as the lightning pierces the blackness of tempest. Some by that sudden light were led to seek after God, and found him; others were rendered uneasy and without excuse, though they continued in their blind idolatry. The wonderful destruction of Pharaoh and his armies at the Red Sea was a burst of light, which startled the midnight of the world by giving proof to mankind that the Lord lived, and could accomplish his purposes by suspending the laws of nature and working miracles. The marvelous drama enacted at Shushan, the capital of Persia, was intended to be another manifestation of the being and glory of God, working not as formerly, by a miracle, but in the usual methods of his providence, and yet accomplishing all his designs. It has been well said that the book of Esther is a record of wonders without a miracle, and therefore, though equally revealing the glory of the Lord, it sets it forth in another fashion from that which is displayed in the overthrow of Pharaoh by miraculous power.

Let us come now to the story. There were two races, one of which God had blessed and promised to preserve, and another of which he had said that he would utterly put out the remembrance of it from under heaven. Israel was to be blessed and made a blessing, but of Amalek the Lord had sworn that "The LORD will have war with Amalek from generation to generation." These two peoples were therefore in deadly hostility, like the seed of the woman and the seed of the serpent, between whom the Lord himself has put an enmity. Many years had rolled away; the chosen people were in great distress, and at this far-off time there still existed upon the face of the earth some relics of the race of Amalek. Among them was one descended of the royal line of Agag, whose name was Haman, and he was in supreme power at the court of Ahasuerus, the Persian monarch.

Now it was God's intent that a last conflict should take place between Israel and Amalek; the conflict which began with Joshua in the desert was to be finished by Mordecai in the king's palace. This last struggle began with great disadvantage to God's people. Haman was prime minister of the far-extending empire of Persia, the favorite of a despotic monarch, who was pliant to his will. Mordecai, a Jew in the employment of the king, sat in the king's gate; and when he saw proud Haman go to and fro, he refused to pay to him the homage which others rendered obsequiously. He would not bow his head or bend his knee to him, and this galled Haman exceedingly. It came into his mind that this Mordecai was of the seed of the Jews, and with the remembrance came the high ambition to avenge the quarrel of his race. He thought it scorn to touch only one man, and resolved that in himself he would incarnate all the hate of generations, and at one blow sweep the accursed Jews, as he thought them, from off the face of the earth.

He went in to the king, with whom his word was power, and told him that there was a singular people scattered up and down the Persian Empire, different from all others, and opposed to the king's laws, and that it was not for the king's profit to suffer them. He asked that they might all be destroyed, and he would pay into the king's treasury an enormous sum of money to compensate for any loss of revenue by their destruction. He intended that the spoil which would be taken from the Jews should tempt their neighbors to kill them, and that the part allotted to himself should repay the amount which he advanced, thus he would make the Jews pay for their own murder. He had no sooner asked for this horrible grant than the monarch conceded it; taking his signet ring from off his finger, he bade him do with the Jews as seemed good to him. Thus the chosen seed are in the hands of the Agagite, who thirsts to annihilate them. Only one thing stands in the way. The Lord has said, "No weapon that is formed against thee shall prosper, and every tongue that riseth against thee in judgment thou shalt condemn." We shall see what happens, and learn from it.

I. First, we shall learn from the narrative that *God places his agents in fitting places for doing his work.*

The Lord was not taken by surprise by this plot of Haman; he had foreseen it and forestalled it. It was needful, in order to match this cunning, malicious design of Haman, that someone of the Jewish race should possess great influence with the king. How was this to be effected? Should a Jewish girl become queen of Persia, the power she would possess would be useful in counteracting the enemy's design. This had been all arranged years before Haman had concocted in his wicked heart the scheme of murdering the Jews. Esther, whose sweet name signifies myrtle, had been elevated to the position of queen of Persia by a singular course of events. It happened that Ahasuerus, at a certain drinking bout, was so far gone with wine as to forget all the proprieties of Eastern life, and sent for his queen, Vashti, to exhibit herself to the people and the princes. No one dreamed in those days of disobeying the tyrant's word, and therefore all stood aghast when Vashti, evidently a woman of right royal spirit, refused to degrade herself by being made a spectacle before that ribald rout of drinking princes, and refused to come. For her courage Vashti was divorced, and a new queen was sought for.

We cannot commend Mordecai for putting his adopted daughter in competition for the monarch's choice; it was contrary to the law of God, and dangerous to her soul in the highest degree. It would have been better for Esther to have been the wife of the poorest man of the house of Israel than to have gone into the den of the Persian despot. The Scripture does not excuse, much less commend, the wrongdoing of Esther and Mordecai in thus acting, but simply tells us how divine wisdom brought good out of evil, even as the chemist distills healing drugs from poisonous plants. The high position of Esther, though gained contrary to the wisest of laws, was overruled for the best interests of her people. Esther in the king's house was the means of defeating the malicious adversary. But Esther alone would not suffice; she is shut up in the harem, surrounded by her chamberlains and her maids of honor, but quite secluded from the outside world. A watchman was needed outside the palace to guard the people of the Lord, and to urge Esther to action when help is wanted.

Mordecai, her cousin and foster father, obtained an office which placed him at the palace gate. Where could he be better posted? He is where much of the royal business will come under his eye, and he is quick, courageous, and unflinching. Never had Israel a better sentinel than Mordecai, the son of Kish, a Benjamite—a very different man from that other son of Kish, who had suffered Amalek to escape in former times. His relationship to the queen allowed him to communicate with her through Hatach, her chamberlain, and, when Haman's evil decree was published, it was not long before intelligence of it reached her ear, and she felt the danger to which Mordecai and all her people were exposed. By singular providences did the Lord place those two most efficient instruments in their places. Mordecai would have been of little use without Esther, and Esther could have rendered no aid had it not been for Mordecai. Meanwhile, there is a conspiracy hatched against the king, which Mordecai discovers, and communicates to the highest authority, and so puts the king under obligation to him, which was a needful part of the Lord's plan.

Now, brethren, whatever mischief may be brewing against the cause of God and truth, and I daresay there is very much going on at this moment, for neither the devil nor the Jesuits nor the atheists are long quiet, this we are sure of, the Lord knows all about it, and he has his Esther and his Mordecai ready at their posts to frustrate their designs. The Lord has his men well placed, and his ambushes hidden in their coverts, to surprise his foes. We need never be afraid but what the Lord has forestalled his enemies and provided against their mischief.

Every child of God is where God has placed him for some purpose, and the practical use of this first point is to lead you to inquire for what practical purpose has God placed each one of you where you now are. You have been wishing for another position where you could do something for Jesus; do not wish anything of the kind, but serve him where you are. If you are sitting at the king's gate, there is something for you to do there, and if you were on the queen's throne, there would be something for you to do there; do not ask either to be gatekeeper or queen, but whichever you are, serve God therein. Brother, are you rich? God has made you a steward, take care that you are a good steward. Brother, are you poor? God has thrown you into a position where you will be the better able to give a word of sympathy to poor saints. Are you doing your allotted work? Do you live in a godly family? God has a motive for placing you in so happy a position. Are you in an ungodly house? You are a lamp hung up in a dark place; mind you shine there. Esther did well, because she acted as an Esther should, and Mordecai did well, because he acted as a Mordecai should. I like to think, as I look over you all—God has put each one of them in the right place, even as a good captain well arranges the different parts of his army, and though we do not know his plan of battle, it will be seen during the conflict that he has placed each soldier where he should be. Our wisdom is not to desire another place, nor to judge those who are in another position, but each one being redeemed with the precious blood of Jesus, should consecrate himself fully to the Lord, and say, "Lord, what would you have me to do, for here I am, and by thy grace I am ready to do it." Forget not then the fact that God in his providence places his servants in positions where he can make use of them.

II. Second, the Lord not only arranges his servants, but *he restrains his enemies.*

I would call your attention particularly to the fact that Haman, having gained a decree for the destruction of all the Jews upon a certain day, was very anxious to have his cruel work done thoroughly, and therefore, being very superstitious and believing in astrology, he bade his magicians cast lots that he might find a lucky day for his great undertaking. The lots were cast for the various months, but not a single fortunate day could be found till hard by the close of the year, and then the chosen day was the thirteenth of the twelfth month. On that day the magicians told their dupe that the heavens would be propitious, and the star of Haman would be in the ascendant. Truly the lot was cast into the lap, but the disposal of it was of the Lord. See ye not that there were eleven clear months left before the Jews would be put to death, and that would give Mordecai and Esther time to turn round, and if anything could be done to reverse the cruel decree they had space to do it in. Suppose that the lot had fallen on the second or third month, the swift dromedaries and camels and messengers would scarcely have been able to reach the extremity of the Persian dominions, certainly a second set of messengers to counteract the decree could not have done so, and, humanly speaking, the Jews must have been destroyed; but oh, in that secret council chamber where sit the sorcerers and the man who asks counsel at the hands of the infernal powers, the Lord himself is present, frustrating the tokens of the liars and making diviners mad. Vain were their enchantments and the multitude of their sorceries; the astrologers, the star gazers, and the monthly prognosticators were all fools together, and led the superstitious Haman to destruction. "Surely there is no enchantment against Jacob, nor divination against Israel." Trust ye in the Lord, ye righteous, and in patience possess your souls. Leave your adversaries in the hands of God, for he can make them fall into the snare which they have privately laid for you.

Notice attentively that Haman selected a mode of destroying the Jews which was wonderfully overruled for their preservation. They were to be slain by any of the people among whom they lived who chose to do so, and their plunder was to reward their slayers. Now, this was a very cunning device, for greed would naturally incite the baser sort of men to murder the thrifty Jews, and no doubt there were debtors who would also be glad to see their creditors disposed of. But see the loophole for escape which this afforded! If the decree had enacted that the Jews should be slain by the soldiery of the Persian Empire it must have been done, and it is not easy to see how they could have escaped, but, the matter being left in private hands, the subsequent decree that they might defend themselves was a sufficient counteraction of the first edict. Thus the Lord arranged that the wisdom of Haman should turn out to be folly after all.

In another point, also, we mark the restraining hand of God, namely, that Mordecai, though he had provoked Haman to the utmost, was not put to death at once. Haman "refrained himself." Why did he do so? Proud men are usually in a mighty tiff if they consider themselves insulted, and are ready at once to take revenge; but Haman "refrained himself"; until that day in which his anger burned furiously, and he set up the gallows, he smothered his passion. I marvel at this; it shows how God makes the wrath of man to praise him, and the remainder he doth restrain. Mordecai must not die a violent death by Haman's hand. The enemies of the church of God and of his people can never do more than the Lord permits; they cannot go a hair's breadth beyond the divine license, and when they are permitted to do their worst, there is always some weak point about all that they do, some extreme folly which renders their fury vain. The wicked carry about them the weapons of their own destruction, and when they rage most against the most High, the Lord of all brings out of it good for his people and glory to himself. Judge not providence in little pieces, it is a grand mosaic, and must be seen as a whole. Say not of any one hour, "this is dark"—it may be so, but that darkness will minister to the light, even as the ebony gloom of midnight makes the stars appear the more effulgent. Trust in the Lord forever, for in the Lord Jehovah there is everlasting strength. His wisdom will undermine the mines of cunning, his skill will overtop the climbings of craft; "he taketh the wise in their own craftiness, and the counsel of the froward is carried headlong."

III. Next we will notice that *God in his providence tries his people.*

You must not suppose that those who are God's servants will be screened from trial; that is no part of the design of providence. "If ye be without chastisement," says the apostle, "then are ye bastards and not sons." God's intent is to educate his people by affliction, and we must not therefore dream that an event is not providential because it is grievous; no, you may count it to be all the more so, for "the LORD trieth the righteous." Observe that God tried Mordecai. He was a quiet old man, I have no doubt, and it must have been a daily trial to him to stand erect, or to sit in his place when that proud peer of the realm went strutting by. His fellow servants told him that the king had commanded all men to pay homage to Haman, but he held his own, not, however, without knowing what it might cost him to be so sternly independent. Haman was an Amalekite, and the Jew would not bow before him. But what a trouble it must have been to the heart of Mordecai, when he saw the proclamation that all the Jews must die. The good man must have bitterly lamented his unhappy fate in being the innocent cause of the destruction of his nation. "Perhaps," he thought within himself, "I have been too obstinate. Woe is me; my whole house, and my whole people are to be slain because of what I have done." He put on sackcloth and cast ashes on his head, and was full of sorrow, a sorrow which we can hardly realize; for even if you know you have done right, yet if you bring down trouble, and especially destruction, upon the heads of others it cuts you to the quick. You could bear martyrdom for yourself, but it is sad to see others suffer through your firmness.

Esther also had to be tried. Amid the glitter of the Persian court, she might have grown forgetful of her God, but the sad news comes to her, "Your cousin and your nation are to be destroyed." Sorrow and dread filled her heart. There was no hope for her people, unless she would go in unto the king—that despot from whom one angry look would be death; she must risk all, and go unbidden into his presence, and plead for her nation. Do you wonder that she trembled? Do you marvel that she asked the prayers of the faithful? Are you surprised to see both herself and her maids of honor fasting and lamenting before God? Do not think, my prosperous friend, that the Lord has given you a high place that you may escape the trials which belong to all his people; yours is no position of ease, but one of the hottest parts of the battle. Neither the lowest and most quiet position, nor the most public and exposed condition will enable you to escape the "much tribulation" through which the church militant must fight its way to glory. Why should we wish it? Should not the gold be tested in the crucible? Should not the strong pillar sustain great weights? When the Menai bridge was first flung across the straits, the engineer did not stipulate that his tube should never be tried with great weights; on the contrary, I can imagine his saying, "Bring up your heaviest trains and load the bridge as much as ever you will, for it will bear every strain." The Lord tries the righteous because he has made them of metal which will endure the test, and he knows that by the sustaining power of his Holy Spirit they will be held up and made more than conquerors; therefore is it a part of the operation of Providence to try the saints. Let that comfort those of you who are in trouble at this time.

IV. But we must pass on to note, fourth, that *the Lord's wisdom is seen in arranging the smallest events so as to produce great results.*

We frequently hear persons say of a pleasant or a great event, "What a providence!" while they are silent as to anything which appears less important, or has an unpleasant savor. But, my brethren, the place of the gorse [evergreen] upon the heath is as fixed as the station of a king, and the dust which is raised by a chariot wheel is as surely steered by Providence as the planet in its orbit. There is as much providence in the creeping of an aphid upon a rose leaf as in the marching of an army to ravage a continent. Everything, the most minute as well as the most magnificent, is ordered by the Lord who has prepared his throne in the heavens, whose kingdom rules over all. The history before us furnishes proof of this.

We have reached the point where Esther is to go in unto the king and plead for her people. Strengthened by prayer, but doubtless trembling still,

Esther entered the inner court, and the king's affection led him instantly to stretch out the golden scepter. Being told to ask what she pleases, she invites the king to come to a banquet and bring Haman with him. He comes and for the second time invites her to ask what she wills to the half of his kingdom. Why, when the king was in so kind a spirit, did not Esther speak? He was charmed with her beauty, and his royal word was given to deny her nothing, why not speak out? But no, she merely asks that he and Haman will come to another banquet of wine tomorrow. O daughter of Abraham, what an opportunity have you lost! Wherefore did you not plead for your people? Their very existence hangs upon your entreaty, and the king has said, "What wilt thou?" and yet you are backward! Was it timidity? It is possible. Did she think that Haman stood too high in the king's favor for her to prevail? It would be hard to say. Some of us are very unaccountable, but on that woman's unaccountable silence far more was hanging than appears at first sight. Doubtless she longed to bring out her secret, but the words came not. God was in it; it was not the right time to speak, and therefore she was led to put off her disclosure. I daresay she regretted it, and wondered when she should be able to come to the point, but the Lord knew best.

After that banquet Haman went out joyfully at the palace gate, but being mortified beyond measure by Mordecai's unbending posture, he called for his wife and his friends, and told them that his riches and honors availed him nothing so long as Mordecai, the Jew, sat in the king's gate. They might have told him, "You will destroy Mordecai and all his people in a few months, and the man is already fretting himself over the decree; let him live, and be you content to watch his miseries and gloat over his despair!" But no, they counsel speedy revenge. Let Mordecai be hanged on a gibbet on the top of the house, and let the gallows be set up at once, and let Haman early in the morning ask for the Jew's life, and let his insolence be punished. Go, call the workmen, and let the gallows be set up at a great height that very night. It seemed a small matter that Haman should be so enraged just at that hour, but it was a very important item in the whole transaction, for had he not been so hasty, he would not have gone so early in the morning to the palace, and would not have been at hand when the king said, "Who is in the court?"

But what has happened? Why, that very night, when Haman was devising to hang up Mordecai, the king could not sleep. What caused the monarch's restlessness? Why happened it on that night of all others? Ahasuerus is master of 127 provinces, but not master of ten minutes' sleep. What shall he do? Shall he call for soothing instruments of music, or beguile the hours with a tale that is told, or with a merry ballad of the minstrel? No, he calls for a book. Who would have thought that this luxurious prince must listen to a reader at dead of night? "Bring a book!" What book? A volume perfumed with roses, musical with songs, sweet as the notes of the nightingale? "No, bring the chronicles of the empire." Dull reading, that! But there are 127 provinces—which volume shall the page bring from the recorder's shelves? He chose the record of Shushan the royal city. That is the center of the empire, and its record is lengthy. In which section shall the reader make a beginning? He may begin where he pleases, but before he closes the book the story of the discovery of a conspiracy by Mordecai has been read in the king's hearing. Was not this a singular accident? Singular if you like, but no accident. Out of ten thousand other records the reader pitches upon that one of all others. The Jews tell us that he began at another place, but that the book closed and fell open at the chapter upon Mordecai. Be that as it may, this is certain, that the Lord knew where the record was, and guided the reader to the right page. Speaking after the manner of men, there were a million chances against one that the king of Persia should, in the dead of the night, be reading the chronicle of his own kingdom, and that he should light upon this particular part of it. But that was not all, The king is interested. He had desired to go to sleep, but that wish is gone, and he is in haste to act. He says, "This man Mordecai has done me good service. Has he been rewarded?" "No." Then cries the impulsive monarch, "He shall be rewarded at once. Who is in the court?" It was the most unlikely thing in the world for the luxurious Ahasuerus to be in haste to do justice, for he had done injustice thousands of times without remorse, and chiefly on that day when he wantonly signed the death warrant of that very Mordecai and his people. For once, the king is intent on being just, and at the door stands Haman—but you know the rest of the story, and how he had to lead Mordecai in state through the streets. It seems a very small matter whether you or I shall sleep tonight or toss restlessly on our beds, but God will be in our rest or in our wakefulness; we know not what his purpose may be, but his hand will be in it. Neither does any man sleep or wake but according to the decree of the Lord.

Observe well how this matter prepared the way for the queen at the next banquet; for when she unfolded her sorrow and told of the threatened destruction of the Jews, and pointed to that wicked Haman, the king must have been the more interested and ready to grant her request, from the fact that the man who had saved his life was a Jew, and that he had already awarded the highest honors to a man in every way fitted to supersede his worthless favorite. All was well, the plotter was unmasked, the gibbet ready, and he who ordered it was made to try his own arrangements.

V. Our next remark is *the Lord in his providence calls his own servants to be active.*

This business was done, and well done, by divine providence, but those concerned had to pray about it. Mordecai and all the Jews outside in Shushan fasted, and cried unto the Lord. Unbelievers inquire, "What difference could prayer make?" My brethren, prayer is an essential part of the providence of God, so essential, that you will always find that when God delivers his people, his people have been praying for that deliverance. They tell us that prayer does not affect the most High and cannot alter his purposes. We never thought it did; but prayer is a part of the purpose and plan and a most effective wheel in the machinery of Providence. The Lord sets his people praying, and then he blesses them. Moreover, Mordecai was quite sure the Lord would deliver his people, and he expressed that confidence, but he did not therefore sit still; he stirred up Esther, and when she seemed a little slack, he put it very strongly, "If thou altogether holdest thy peace at this time, then enlargement and deliverance will arise from another place, but thou and thy father's house shall be destroyed."

Nerved by this message, Esther braced herself to the effort. She did not sit still and say, "The Lord will arrange this business; there is nothing for me to do," but she both pleaded with God and ventured her life and her all for her people's sake, and then acted very wisely and discreetly in her interviews with the king. So, my brethren, we rest confidently in Providence, but we are not idle. We believe that God has an elect people, and therefore do we preach in the hope that we may be the means, in the hands of his Spirit, of bringing this elect people to Christ. We believe that God has appointed for his people both holiness here and heaven hereafter; therefore do we strive against sin, and press forward to the rest which remains for the people of God. Faith in God's providence, instead of repressing our energies, excites us to diligence. We labor as if all depended upon us, and then fall back upon the Lord with the calm faith which knows that all depends upon him.

VI. Now must we close our historical review with the remark that in the end *the Lord achieves the total defeat of his foes and the safety of his people.*

Never was a man so utterly defeated as Haman. Never was a project so altogether turned aside. He was taken in his own trap, and he and his sons were hanged up on the gibbet set up for Mordecai. As for the Jews, they were in this special danger, that they were to be destroyed on a certain day, and though Esther pleaded with the king for their lives, he was not able to alter his decree, though willing to do so, for it was a rule of the constitution that the law of the Medes and Persians altered not. The king might determine what he pleased, but when he had once decreed it he could not change it, the people feeling it better to submit to the worst established law than to be left utterly to every capricious whim of their master. Now, what was to be done? The decree was given that the Jews might be slain, and it could not be reversed. Here was the door of escape—another decree was issued giving the Jews permission to defend themselves, and take the property of any who dared to attack them; thus one decree effectually neutralized the other. With great haste this mandate was sent all over the kingdom, and on the appointed day the Jews stood up for themselves and slew their foes. According to their tradition, nobody attempted to attack them except the Amalekites, and consequently only Amalekites were slain, and the race of Amalek was on that day swept from off the face of the earth. God thus gave to the Jews a high position in the empire, and we are told that many became Jews, or were proselytes to the God of Abraham, because they saw what God had done.

As I commenced by saying that God sometimes darted flashes of light through the thick darkness, you will now see what a flash this must have been. All the people were perplexed when they found that the Hebrews might be put to death, but they must have been far more astonished when the decree came that they might defend themselves. All the world inquired, "Why is this?," and the answer was, "The living God, whom the Jews worship, has displayed his wisdom and rescued his people." All nations were compelled to feel that there was a God in Israel, and thus the divine purpose was fully accomplished, his people were secured, and his name was glorified to the world's end.

From the whole we learn the following lessons.

First, it is clear that *the divine will is accomplished, and yet men are perfectly free agents*. Haman acted according to his own will; Ahasuerus did whatever he pleased; Mordecai behaved as his heart moved him, and so did Esther. We see no interference with them, no force or coercion; hence the entire sin and responsibility rest with each guilty one, yet, acting with perfect freedom, none of them acts otherwise than divine providence had foreseen. "I cannot understand it," says one. My dear friend, I am compelled to say the same—I do not understand it either. I have known many who think they comprehend all things, but I fancy they had a higher opinion of themselves than truth would endorse. Certain of my brethren deny free agency, and so get out of the difficulty; others assert that there is no predestination, and so cut the knot. As I do not wish to get out of the difficulty, and have no wish to shut my eyes to any part of the truth, I believe both free agency and predestination to be facts. How they can be made to agree I do not know, or care to know; I am satisfied to know anything which God chooses to reveal to me, and equally content not to know what he does not reveal. There it is. Man is a free agent in what he does, responsible for his actions, and verily guilty when he does wrong, and he will be justly punished too. And if he be lost, the blame will rest with himself alone. But yet there is One who rules over all, who, without complicity in their sin, makes even the actions of wicked men to subserve his holy and righteous purposes. Believe these two truths, and you will see them in practical agreement in daily life, though you will not be able to devise a theory for harmonizing them on paper.

Next, we learn *what wonders can be worked without miracles.* When God does a wonderful thing by suspending the laws of nature, men are greatly astonished and say, "This is the finger of God"; but nowadays they say to us, "Where is your God? He never suspends his laws now!" Now, I see God in the history of Pharaoh, but I must confess I see him quite as clearly in the history of Haman, and I think I see him in even a grander light; for (I say it with reverence to his holy name) it is a somewhat rough method of accomplishing a purpose to stop the wheel of nature and reverse wise and admirable laws; certainly it reveals his power, but it does not so clearly display his immutability. When, however, the Lord allows everything to go on in the usual way, and gives mind and thought, ambition, and passion their full liberty, and yet achieves his purpose, it is doubly wonderful. In the miracles of Pharaoh we see the finger of God, but in the wonders of Providence, without miracle, we see the hand of God. Today, whatever the event may be, the attentive eye will as clearly see the Lord as if by miraculous power the hills had leaped from their places, or the floods had stood upright as a heap. I am sure that God is in the world, yes, and is at my own fireside, and in my chamber, and manages my affairs, and orders all things for me, and for each one of his children. We want no miracles to convince us of his working, the wonders of his providence are as great marvels as miracles themselves.

Next we learn *how safe the church of God is.* At one time the people of God seemed to be altogether in Haman's power. Nero once said that he wished his enemies had but one neck that he might destroy them all at a blow, and Haman seemed to have realized just such power. Yet the chosen nation was delivered, the Jewish people lived on until the Messiah came, and does exist, and will exist till they shall enjoy the bright future which is decreed for them. So is it with the church of God today. The foes of truth can never put out the candle which God has lit, never crush the living seed which the Lord Jesus has sown in his own blood-bought people. Brethren, be not afraid, but establish your hearts in God.

Again, we see that the wicked will surely come to an ill end. They may be very powerful, but God will bring them down. They may be very crafty, and may plot and plan, and may think that even God himself is their accomplice, because everything goes as they desire; but they may be sure their sin will find them out. They may dig deep as hell, but God will undermine them, and they may climb as high as the stars, but God will be above them to hurl them down. Wicked man, I charge you if you be wise, turn you from your career of opposition to the most High; you cannot stand against him, neither can you outwit him. Cease, I beseech you, from this idle opposition, and hear the voice of his gospel which says, "Confess your sin and forsake it. Believe in Jesus, the Son of God, the great atoning sacrifice, and even you shall yet be saved." If you do not so, upon your own head shall your iniquities fall.

Last of all, let each child of God rejoice that we have a Guardian so near the throne. Every Jew in Shushan must have felt hope when he remembered that the queen was a Jewish girl. Today let us be glad that Jesus is exalted.

> He is at the Father's side,
> The Man of love, the crucified.

How safe are all his people, for "if any man sin, we have an advocate with the Father, Jesus Christ the righteous." There is one that lies in the bosom of God who will plead for all those who put their trust in him. Therefore be ye not dismayed, but let your souls rest in God, and wait patiently for him, for sooner shall heaven and earth pass away than those who trust the Lord shall perish. "They shall not be ashamed nor confounded, world without end." Amen.

The Good Shepherdess

Delivered on Lord's Day morning, June 1, 1873, at the Metropolitan Tabernacle, Newington. No. 1115.

Tell me, O thou whom my soul loveth, where thou feedest, where thou makest thy flock to rest at noon: for why should I be as one that turneth aside by the flocks of thy companions? If thou know not, O thou fairest among women, go thy way forth by the footsteps of the flock, and feed thy kids beside the shepherds' tents.—SONG OF SOLOMON 1:7–8

The bride was most unhappy and ashamed because her personal beauty had been sorely marred by the heat of the sun. The fairest among women had become swarthy as a sunburned slave. Spiritually it is so with a chosen soul full often. The Lord's grace has made her fair to look upon, even as the lily; but she has been so busy about earthly things that the sun of worldliness has injured her beauty. The bride with holy shamefacedness exclaims, "Look not upon me, for I am black, because the sun hath looked upon me." She dreads alike the curiosity, the admiration, the pity, and the scorn of men, and turns herself alone to her Beloved, whose gaze she knows to be so full of love that her swarthiness will not cause her pain when most beneath his eye. This is one index of a gracious soul—that whereas the ungodly rush to and fro, and know not where to look for consolation, the believing heart naturally flies to its well-beloved Savior, knowing that in him is its only rest.

It would appear from the preceding verse that the bride was also in trouble about a certain charge which had been given to her, which burdened her, and in the discharge of which she had become negligent of herself. She says, "They made me the keeper of the vineyards," and she would wish to have kept them well, but she felt she had not done so, and that, moreover, she had failed in a more immediate duty—"Mine own vineyard have I not kept." Under this sense of double unworthiness and failure, feeling her omissions and her commissions to be weighing her down, she turned around to her Beloved and asked instruction at his hands. This was well. Had she not loved her Lord she would have shunned him when her comeliness was faded, but the instincts of her affectionate heart suggested to her that he would not discard her because of her imperfections. She was, moreover, wise thus to appeal to her Lord against herself.

Beloved, never let sin part you from Jesus. Under a sense of sin, do not fly from him; that were foolishness. Sin may drive you *from* Sinai; it ought to draw you *to* Calvary. To the fountain we should fly with all the greater alacrity when we feel that we are foul; and to the dear wounds of Jesus, whence all our life and healing must come, we should resort with the greater earnestness when we feel our soul to be sick, even though we fear that sickness to be unto death. The bride, in the present case, takes to Jesus her troubles, her distress about herself, and her confession concerning her work. She brings before him her double charge, the keeping of her own vineyard, and the keeping of the vineyards of others. I know that I shall be speaking to many this morning who are busy in serving their Lord; and it may be that they feel great anxiety because they cannot keep their own hearts near to Jesus: they do not feel themselves warm and lively in the divine service; they plod on, but they are very much in the condition of those who are described as "faint, yet pursuing." When Jesus is present, labor for him is joy, but in his absence his servants feel like workers underground, bereft of the light of the sun. They cannot give up working for Jesus; they love him too well for that, but they pine to have his company while they are working for him, and like the young prophets who went to the wood to cut down every man a beam for their new house, they say to their master, "Be content, we pray thee, and go with thy servants." Our most earnest desire is that we may enjoy sweet communion with Jesus while we are actively engaged in his cause. Indeed, beloved, this is most important to all of us. I do not know of any point which Christian workers need more often to think upon than the subject of keeping their work and themselves near to the Master's hand.

Our text will help us to this, under three heads. We have here, first, *a question asked*—"Tell me, O thou whom my soul loveth, where thou feedest, where thou makest thy flock to rest at noon?" Second, *an argument used*—"Why should I be as one that turneth aside by the flocks of thy companions?" And, third, we have *an answer obtained*—"If thou know not, O thou fairest among women, go thy way forth by the footsteps of the flock, and feed thy kids beside the shepherds' tents."

I. Here is *a question asked*.

Every word of the inquiry is worthy of our careful meditation. You will observe, first, concerning it, that it is *asked in love*. She calls him to whom she speaks by the endearing title "O thou whom my soul loveth." Whatever she may feel herself to be, she knows that she loves him. She is black [from the sun], and ashamed to have her face gazed upon, but still she loves her Bridegroom. She has not kept her own vineyard as she ought to have done, but still she loves him; that she is sure of, and therefore boldly declares it. She loves him as she loves none other in all the world. He only can be called "him whom my soul loveth." She knows none at all worthy to be compared with him, none who can rival him. He is her bosom's Lord, sole prince and monarch of all her affections. She feels also that she loves him intensely—from her inmost *soul* she loves him. The life of her existence is bound up with him: if there be any force and power and vitality in her, it is but as fuel to the great flame of her love, which burns alone for him.

Mark well that it is not "O thou whom my soul believes in." That would be true, but she has passed further. It is not "O thou whom my soul honors." That is true too, but she has passed beyond that stage. Nor is it merely "O thou whom my soul trusts and obeys." She is doing that, but she has reached something warmer, more tender, more full of fire and enthusiasm, and it is "O thou whom my soul loveth." Now, beloved, I trust many of us can speak so to Jesus. He is to us the Well Beloved, "the chief amongst a myriad"; "his mouth is every sweetness, yea, all of him is loveliness," and our soul is wrapped up in him, our heart is altogether taken up with him. We shall never serve him aright unless it be so. Before our Lord said to Peter, "Feed my lambs," and "Feed my sheep," he put the question, "Simon, son of Jonas, lovest thou me?" and this he repeated three times; for until that question is settled, we are unfit for his service. So the bride here, having both herself and her little flock to care for, avows that she loves the spouse as if she felt that she would not dare to have a part of his flock to look after if she did not love him; as if she saw that her right to be a shepherdess at all depended upon her love of the great Shepherd. She could not expect his help in her work, much less his fellowship in the work, unless there was first in her that all-essential fitness of love to his person. The question therefore becomes instructive to us, because it is addressed to Christ under a most endearing title; and I ask every worker here to take care that he always does his work in a spirit of love, and always regards the Lord Jesus not as a taskmaster, not as one who has given us work to do from which we would fain escape, but as our dear Lord, whom to serve is bliss, and for whom to die is gain. "O thou whom my soul loveth" is the right name by which a worker for Jesus should address his Lord.

Now note that the question, as it is asked in love, is also asked of him. "Tell me, O thou whom my soul loveth, where thou feedest." She asked him to tell her, as if she feared that none but himself would give her the correct answer; others might be mistaken, but he could not be. She asked of him because she was quite sure that he would give her the kindest answer. Others might be indifferent, and might scarcely take the trouble to reply: but if Jesus would tell her himself, with his own lips, he would mingle love with every word, and so console as well as instruct her. Perhaps she felt that nobody else could tell her as he could, for others speak to the ear, but he speaks to the heart: others speak with lower degrees of influence, we hear their speech but are not moved thereby; but Jesus speaks, and the Spirit goes with every word he utters, and therefore we hear to profit when he converses with us. I do not know how it may be with you, my brethren, but I feel this morning that if I could get half a word from Christ it would satisfy my soul for many a day. I love to hear the gospel, and to read it, and to preach it; but to hear it fresh from himself, applied by the energy of the Holy Spirit! Oh, this were refreshment! This were energy and power! Therefore, Savior, when your workers desire to know where you feed, tell them yourself, speak to their hearts by your own Spirit, and let them feel as though it were a new revelation to their inmost nature. "Tell me, O thou whom my soul loveth." It is asked in love: it is asked of him.

Now, observe what the question is. She wishes to know how Jesus does his work, and where he does it. It appears, from the eighth verse, that she herself has a flock of kids to tend. She is a shepherdess, and would fain feed her flock; hence her question, "Tell me where thou feedest?" She desires those little ones of hers to obtain rest as well as food, and she is troubled about them; therefore she says, "Tell me where thou makest thy flock to rest," for if she can see how Jesus does his work, and where he does it, and in what way, then she will be satisfied that she is doing it in the right way, if she closely imitates him and abides in fellowship with him. The question seems to be just this: "Lord, tell me what are the truths with which you do feed your people's souls; tell me what are the doctrines which make the strong ones weak and the sad ones glad; tell me what is that precious meat which you are wont to give to hungry and fainting spirits, to revive them and keep them alive; for if you tell me, then I will give my flock the same food; tell me where the pasture is wherein you do feed your sheep, and straightaway I will lead mine to the selfsame happy fields. Then tell me how you make your people to rest. What are those promises which you do apply to the consolation of their spirit, so that their cares and doubts and fears and agitations all subside? You have sweet meadows where you make your beloved flock to lie calmly down and slumber; tell me where those meadows are that I may go and fetch the flock committed to my charge, the mourners whom I ought to comfort, the distressed ones whom I am bound to relieve, the desponding whom I have endeavored to encourage; tell me, Lord, where you make your flock to lie down, for then, under your help, I will go and make my flock to lie down too. It is for myself, but yet far more for others, that I ask the question, 'Tell me where thou feedest, where thou makest them to rest at noon.'" I have no doubt that the spouse did desire information for herself and for her own good, and I believe Dr. Watts had caught some of the spirit of the passage when he sang—

> Fain would I feed among thy sheep,
> Among them rest, among them sleep.

But it does not strike me that this is all the meaning of the passage by a very long way. The bride says, "Tell me where thou feedest thy flock," as if she would wish to feed with the flock; "where thou makest thy flock to rest," as if she wanted to rest there too: but it strikes me the very gist of the thing is this, that she wished to bring her flock to feed where Christ's flock feeds, and to lead her kids to lie down where Christ's little lambs were reposing; she desired, in fact, to do her work in his company; she wanted to mix up her flock with the Lord's flock, her work with his work, and to feel that what she was doing she was doing for him, yes, and with him and through him. She had evidently met with a great many difficulties in what she had tried to do. She wished to feed her flock of kids, but could not find them pasture. Perhaps when she began her work as a shepherdess, she thought herself quite equal to the task, but now the same sun which had bronzed her face had dried up the pasture, and so she says, "O thou that knowest all the pastures, tell me where thou feedest, for I cannot find grass for my flock," and suffering herself from the noontide heat, she finds her little flock suffering too; and she inquires, "Where dost thou make thy flock to rest at noon? Where are cool shadows of great rocks which screen off the sultry rays when the sun is in its zenith and pours down torrents of heat? For I cannot shade my poor flock and give them comfort in their many trials and troubles. I wish I could. O Lord, tell me the secret art of consolation; then will I try to console my own charge by the self-same means." We would know the groves of promise and the cool streams of peace, that we may lead others into rest. If we can follow Jesus, we can guide others, and so both we and they will find comfort and peace. That is the meaning of the request before us.

Note well that she said most particularly, "Tell *me*." "O Master, do not merely tell your sheep where you feed, though they want to know; but tell me where you feed, for I would fain instruct others." She would fain know many things, but chiefly she says, "Tell me *where thou feedest*," for she wished to feed others. We want practical knowledge, for our desire is to be helped to bring others into rest, to be the means of speaking peace to the consciences of others, as the Lord has spoken peace to ours. Therefore the prayer is "tell me." "Thou art my model, O great Shepherd; thou art my wisdom. If I be a shepherd to thy sheep, yet am I also a sheep beneath thy shepherdry, therefore teach thou me, that I may teach others."

I do not know whether I make myself plain to you, but I wish to put it very simply. I am preaching to myself perhaps a great deal more than to you. I am preaching to my own heart. I feel I have to come, Sabbath after Sabbath, and weekday after weekday, and tell you a great many precious things about Christ, and sometimes I enjoy them myself; and if nobody else gets blessed by them, I do, and I go home and praise the Lord for it; but my daily fear is lest I should be a handler of texts for you, and a preacher of good things for others, and yet remain unprofited in my own heart. My prayer is that the Lord Jesus will show me where he feeds his people, and let me feed with them, that then I may conduct you to the pastures where he is, and be with him myself at the same time that I bring you to him. You Sunday school teachers and evangelists, and others, my dear, earnest comrades, for whom I thank God at every remembrance, I feel that the main point you have to watch about is that you do not lose your own spirituality while trying to make others spiritual. The great point is to live near to God. It would be a dreadful thing for you to be very busy about other men's souls and neglect your own. Appeal to the Well Beloved, and entreat him to let you feed your flock where he is feeding his people, that he would let you sit at his feet, like Mary, even while you are working in the house, like Martha. Do not do less, but rather more; but ask to do it in such communion with him that your work shall be melted into his work, and what you are doing shall be really only his working in you, and you rejoicing to pour out to others what he pours into your own soul. God grant it may be so with you all, my brethren.

II. Second, here is *an argument used.*

The bride says, "Why should I be as one that turneth aside by the flocks of thy companions?" If she should lead her flock into distant meadows, far away from the place where Jesus is feeding his flock, it would not be well. As a shepherdess would naturally be rather dependent, and would need to associate herself for protection with others, suppose she should turn aside with other shepherds, and leave her Bridegroom, would it be right? She speaks of it as a thing most abhorrent to her mind, and well might it be. For, first, would it not look very unseemly that the bride should be associating with others than the Bridegroom? They have each a flock: there is he with his great flock, and here is she with her little one. Shall they seek pastures far off from one another? Will there not be talk about this? Will not onlookers say, "This is not seemly: there must be some lack of love here, or else these two would not be so divided"? Stress may be put, if you like, upon that little word *I*. Why should I, thy blood-bought spouse; I, betrothed unto thee, or ever the earth was; I, whom thou hast loved—why should I turn after others and forget you? Beloved, you had better put the emphasis in your own reading of it just there. Why should I, whom the Lord has pardoned, whom the Lord has loved, whom the Lord has favored so much—I, who have enjoyed fellowship with him for many years—I, who know that his love is better than wine—I, who have aforetime been inebriated with his sweetness—Why should I turn aside? Let others do so if they will, but it would be uncomely and unseemly for me.

I pray you, brother and sister, try to feel that—that for you to work apart from Christ would have a bad look about it; that for your work to take you away from fellowship with Jesus would have a very ugly appearance: it would not be among the things that are honest and of good repute. For the bride to feed her flock in other company would look like unfaithfulness to her husband. What, shall the bride of Christ forsake her Beloved? Shall she be unchaste toward her Lord? Yet it would seem so if she makes companions of others and forgets her Beloved. Our hearts may grow unchaste to Christ even while they are zealous in Christian work. I dread very much the tendency to do Christ's work in a cold, mechanical spirit; but above even that I tremble lest I should be able to have warmth for Christ's work and yet should be cold toward the Lord himself. I fear that such a condition of heart is possible—that we may burn great bonfires in the streets for public display, and scarcely keep a live coal upon our hearth for Jesus to warm his hands at. When we meet in the great assembly, the good company helps to warm our hearts, and when we are working for the Lord with others they stimulate us and cause us to put forth all our energy and strength, and then we think, "Surely my heart is in a healthy condition toward God." But, beloved, such excitement may be a poor index of our real state. I love that quiet, holy fire which will glow in the closet and flame forth in the chamber when I am alone, and that is the point I am more fearful about than anything else, both for myself and for you, lest we should be doing Christ's work without Christ; having much to do but not thinking much of him; cumbered about much serving and forgetting him. Why, that would soon grow into making a Christ out of our own service, an antichrist out of our own labors. Beware of that! Love your work, but love your

Master better; love your flock, but love the great Shepherd better still, and ever keep close to him, for it will be a token of unfaithfulness if you do not.

And mark again, "Why should I be as one that turneth aside by the flocks of thy companions?" We may read this as meaning, "Why should I be so unhappy as to have to work for thee, and yet be out of communion with thee?" It is a very unhappy thing to lose fellowship with Jesus, and yet to have to go on with religious exercises. If the wheels are taken off your chariot, it is no great matter if nobody wants to ride, but how if you are called upon to drive on? When a man's foot is lamed, he may not so much regret it if he can sit still, but if he be bound to run a race he is greatly to be pitied. It made the spouse doubly unhappy even to suppose that she, with her flock to feed and herself needing feeding too, should have to turn aside by the flocks of others and miss the presence of her Lord. In fact the question seems to be put in this shape: "What reason is there why I should leave my Lord? What apology could I make, what excuse could I offer for so doing? Is there any reason why I should not abide in constant fellowship with him? Why should I be as one that turns aside? Perhaps it may be said that others turn aside, but why should I be as one of them? There may be excuses for such an act in others, but there can be none for me: your rich love, your free love, your undeserved love, your special love to me, has bound me hand and foot: how can I turn aside? There may be some professors who owe you little, but I, once the chief of sinners, owe you so much, how can I turn aside? There may be some with whom you have dealt hardly who may turn aside, but you have been so tender, so kind to me, how can I forget you? There may be some who know but little of you, whose experience of you is so slender that their turning aside is not to be wondered at; but how can I turn aside when you have shown me your love, and revealed your heart to me? Oh, by the banqueting house where I have feasted with you, by the Hermonites and the hill Mizar, where you have manifested your love, by the place where deep called to deep, and then mercy called to mercy; by those mighty storms and sweeping hurricanes in which you were the shelter of my head, by ten thousand thousand mercies past which have been my blessed portion, why should I be as one that turns aside by the flocks of your companions?"

Let me address the members of this church, and say to you, if all the churches in Christendom were to go aside from the gospel, why should you? If in every other place the gospel should be neglected, and an uncertain sound should be given forth; if ritualism should swallow up half the churches and rationalism the rest, yet why should you turn aside? You have been peculiarly a people of prayer; you have also followed the Lord fully in doctrine and an ordinance; and consequently you have enjoyed the divine presence, and have prospered beyond measure. We have cast ourselves upon the Holy Ghost for strength, and have not relied upon human eloquence, music, or beauties of color or architecture. Our only weapon has been the simple, plain, full gospel, and why should we turn aside? Have we not been favored for these many years with unexampled success? Has not the Lord added unto our numbers so abundantly that we have not had room enough to receive them? Has he not multiplied the people and increased the joy? Hold fast to your first love, and let no man take your crown. I thank God there are churches still, a few in England and yet more in Scotland, which hold fast the doctrines of the gospel and will not let them go. To them I would say, why should you turn aside? Should not your history, both in its troublous and its joyous chapters, teach you to hold fast the form of sound words?

Above all, should we not try to live as a church, and individually, also, in abiding fellowship with Jesus; for if we turn aside from him, we shall rob the truth of its aroma, yes, of its essential fragrance. If we lose fellowship with Jesus, we shall have the standard, but where will be the Standard-bearer? We may retain the candlestick, but where shall be the Light? We shall be shorn of our strength, our joy, our comfort, our all, if we miss fellowship with him. God grant, therefore, that we may never be as those who turn aside.

III. Third, we have here *an answer given* **by the Bridegroom to his beloved.**

She asked him where he fed, where he made his flock to rest, and he answered her. Observe carefully that this answer is given in tenderness to her infirmity; not ignoring her ignorance, but dealing very gently with it. "If thou know not"—a hint that she ought to have known, but such a hint as kind lovers give when they would fain forbear to chide. Our Lord is very tender to our ignorance. There are many things which we do not know, but ought to have known. We are children when we should be men and have to be spoken to as unto carnal—unto babes in Christ, when we should have become fathers. Is there one among us who can say, "I am not faulty in my knowledge"? I am afraid the most of us must confess that if we had done the Lord's will better, we should have known his doctrine better; if we had lived more closely to him, we should have known more of him. Still, how very gentle the rebuke is. The Lord forgives our ignorance and condescends to instruct it.

Note next that the answer is given in great love. He says, "O thou fairest among women." That is a blessed cordial for her distress. She said, "I am black"; but he says, "O thou fairest among women." I would rather trust

Christ's eyes than mine. If my eyes tell me I am black, I will weep, but if he assures me I am fair, I will believe him and rejoice. Some saints are more apt to remember their sinfulness, and grieve over it, than to believe in their righteousness in Christ, and triumph in it. Remember, beloved, it is quite as true today that you are all fair and without spot as that you are black, because the sun has looked upon you. It must be true, because Jesus says so. Let me give you one of the sayings of the Bridegroom to his bride: "Thou art all fair, my love; there is no spot in thee." "Ah, that is a figure," say you. Well, I will give you one that is not a figure. The Lord Jesus, after he had washed his disciples' feet, said, "He that is washed needeth not except to wash his feet for he is clean every whit"; and then he added, "And ye are clean." If you desire an apostolic word to the same effect, let me give you this: "Who shall lay anything to the charge of God's elect?"—anything—any little thing or any great thing either. Jesus has washed his people so clean that there is no spot, no wrinkle, nor any such thing upon them in the matter of justification before God.

> In thy surety thou art free,
> His dear hands were pierced for thee;
> With his spotless vesture on,
> Holy as the Holy One.

How glorious is this. Jesus does not exaggerate when he thus commends his church. He speaks plain, sober truth. "O thou fairest among women," says he. My soul, do you not feel love to Christ when you remember that he thinks you beautiful? I cannot see anything in myself to love, but he does, and calls me "all fair." I think it must be that he looks into our eyes and sees himself, or else this, that he knows what we are going to be, and judges us on that scale. As the artist, looking on the block of marble, sees in the stone the statue which he means to fetch out of it with matchless skill, so the Lord Jesus sees the perfect image of himself in us, from which he means to chip away the imperfections and the sins until it stands out in all its splendor. But still it is gracious condescension which makes him say, "Thou art fairest among women," to one who mourned her own sunburned countenance.

The answer contains much sacred wisdom. The bride is directed where to go that she may find her beloved and lead her flock to him. "Go thy way forth by the footprints of the flock." If you will find Jesus, you will find him in the way the holy prophets went, in the way of the patriarchs and the way of the apostles. And if your next desire be to find your flock, and to make them lie down, very well, go and feed them as other shepherds have done—Christ's own shepherds whom he has sent in other days to feed his chosen.

I feel very glad, in speaking from this text, that the Lord does not give to his bride in answer to her question some singular directions of great difficulty, some novel prescriptions singular and remarkable. Just as the gospel itself is simple and homely, so is this exhortation and direction for the renewal of communion. It is easy, it is plain. You want to get to Jesus, and you want to bring those under your charge to him. Very well, then, do not seek out a new road, but simply go the way which all other saints have gone. If you want to walk with Jesus, walk where other saints have walked; and if you want to lead others into communion with him, lead them by your example where others have gone. What is that? If you want to be with Jesus, go where Abraham went in the path of separation. See how he lived as a pilgrim and a sojourner with his God. If you would see Jesus, "Come ye out from among them, be ye separate, touch not the unclean thing." You shall find Jesus when you have left the world. If you would walk with Jesus, follow the path of obedience. Saints have never had fellowship with Jesus when they have disobeyed him. Keep his statutes and observe his testimonies, be jealous over your conduct and character; for the path of obedience is the path of communion. Be sure that you follow the ancient ways with regard to the Christian ordinances: do not alter them, but keep to the good old paths. Stand and inquire what apostles did, and do the same. Jesus will not bless you in using fanciful ceremonies of human invention. Keep to those which he commands, which his Spirit sanctions, which his apostles practiced. Above all, if you would walk with Jesus, continue in the way of holiness; persevere in the way of grace. Make the Lord Jesus your model and example; and by treading where the footprints of the flock are to be seen, you will both save yourself and them that hear you; you shall find Jesus, and they shall find Jesus too.

We might have supposed that the Lord would have said, "If you want to lead your flock aright, array yourself in sumptuous apparel, or go get your music and fine anthems; by these fair things you will fascinate the Savior into your sanctuaries"; but it is not so. The incense which will please the Lord Jesus is that of holy prayer and praise, and the only rituals which are acceptable to him are these: to visit the fatherless and the widow, and to keep oneself unspotted from the world. This is all he wants. Follow that, and you shall both go right and lead others right.

Then the Spouse added, "Feed thy kids beside the shepherds' tents." Now, who are these shepherds? There be many in these days who set up for shepherds, who feed their sheep in poisonous pastures. Keep away from them; but there are others whom it is safe to follow. Let me take you to the twelve principal shepherds who came after the great Shepherd of all. You want to bless your children, to save their souls, and have fellowship with Christ in the doing of it; then teach them the truths which the apostles taught. And what were they? Take Paul as an example. "I determined not to know anything among you save Jesus Christ, and him crucified." That is feeding the kids beside the shepherds' tents, when you teach your children Christ, much of Christ, all of Christ, and nothing else but Christ. Mind you stick to that blessed subject. And when you are teaching them Christ, teach them all about his life, his death, his resurrection; teach them his Godhead and his manhood. You will never enjoy Christ's company if you doubt his divinity. Take care that you feed your flock upon the doctrine of the atonement. Christ will have no fellowship with a worker unless he represents him fairly, and you cannot represent Christ truthfully unless you see the ruddy hue of his atoning blood as well as the lily purity of his life. "Feed thy kids beside the shepherds' tents," then will you teach them the atoning sacrifice, and justification by faith, and imputed righteousness, and union with the risen Head, and the coming of the great One, wherein we shall receive the adoption, to wit, the redemption of the body from the grave.

I speak the truth and lie not when I say that if we want to teach a congregation so as to bless them, and keep in fellowship with Christ at the same time ourselves, we must be very particular to teach nothing but the truth—not a part of it, but all of it. Preach that blessed doctrine of election. Oh, the depths of divine love which are contained in that blessed truth! Do not shirk it or keep it in the background. You cannot expect Christ's presence if you do. Teach the doctrine of man's depravity. Lay the sinner low. God will not bless a ministry which exalts men. Preach the doctrine of the Holy Spirit's effectual calling, for if we do not magnify the Spirit of God, we cannot expect that he will make our work to stand. Preach regeneration. Let it be seen how thorough the change is, that we may glorify God's work. Preach the final perseverance of the saints. Teach that the Lord is not changeable—casting away his people, loving them today and hating them tomorrow. Preach, in fact, the doctrines of grace as you find them in the Book. Feed them beside the shepherds' tents.

Yes, and feed the kids there—the little children. I begin to feel more and more that it is a mistake to divide the children from the congregation. I believe in special services for children, but I would also have them worship with us. If our preaching does not teach children, it lacks some element which it ought to possess. The kind of preaching which is best of all for grown-up people is that in which children also will take delight. I like to see the congregation made up not all of the young, nor all of the old, not all of the mature, nor all of the inexperienced, but some of all sorts gathered together. If we are teaching children salvation by works, and grown-up people salvation by grace, we are pulling down in the schoolroom what we build up in the church, and that will never do. Feed the kids with the same gospel as the grown-up sheep, though not exactly in the same terms; let your language be appropriate to them, but let it be the same truth. God forbid that we should have our Sunday schools the hotbeds of Arminianism, while our churches are gardens of Calvinism. We shall soon have a division in the camp if that be so. The same truth for all; and you cannot expect Christ to be with you in feeding your little flocks unless you feed them where Christ feeds us.

Where does he feed us but where the truth grows? Oh, when I read some sermons, they remind me of a piece of common by the roadside, after a hungry horde of sheep have devoured every green thing; but when I read a solid gospel sermon of the Puritans, it reminds me of a field kept for hay, which a farmer is at last obliged to give up to the sheep. The grass has grown almost as high as themselves, and so they lie down in it, eating and resting too. Give me the doctrines of grace, and I am in clover. If you have to feed others, take them there. Do not conduct them to the starved pastures of modern thought and culture. Preachers are starving God's people nowadays. Oh, but they set out such beautiful china plates, such wonderful knives and forks, such marvelous vases and damask tablecloths! But as for food, the plates look as if they had been smeared with a feather, there is so little on them. The real gospel teaching is little enough. They give us nothing to learn, nothing to digest, nothing to feed upon; it is all slops and nothing substantial. Oh, for the good old corn of the kingdom; we want that, and I am persuaded that when the churches get back to the old food again, when they begin to feed their flocks beside the shepherds' tents, and when in practical living Christians, the saints, get back to the old puritanic method, and follow once again the tracks of the sheep, and the sheep follow the tracks of Christ, then we shall get the church into fellowship with Jesus, and Jesus will do wonders in our midst. But to get that, each individual must aim at winning it for himself, and if the Lord shall grant it to each one of us, then it will be granted to the whole, and the good times which we desire will certainly have come.

My beloved, do you desire to work with Christ? Do you want to feel that Jesus is at your right hand? Then go and work in his way. Teach what he would have you teach, not what you would like to teach. Go and work for him, as he would have you work, not as your prejudices might prescribe to you. Be obedient. Follow the footsteps of the flock. Be diligent also to keep hard by the shepherds' tents, and the Lord bless you more and more, you and your children, and his shall be the glory.

I have spoken only to God's people. I would there had been time to speak to the unconverted too, but to them I can only say this: may God grant you grace to know the beauties of Jesus, for then you will love him too. May he also show you the deformities of yourselves, for then you will desire to be cleansed and made lovely in Christ.

And remember, if any one of you wants Christ, he wants you; and if you long for him, he longs for you. If you seek him, he is seeking you. If you will now cry to him, he is already crying after you. "Whosoever will, let him come and take of the water of life freely." The Lord save you for his name's sake. Amen.

The Bride: Heavenly Lovesickness!

Delivered on Sunday morning, November 8, 1863, at the Metropolitan Tabernacle, Newington. No. 539.

I charge you, O daughters of Jerusalem, if ye find my beloved, that ye tell him, that I am sick of love.—SONG OF SOLOMON 5:8

Sick! that is a sad thing; it moves your pity. Sick of love—lovesick! that stirs up other emotions which we shall presently attempt to explain. No doubt certain sicknesses are peculiar to the saints: the ungodly are never visited with them. Strange to say, these sicknesses, to which the refined sensibilities of the children of God render them peculiarly liable, are signs of vigorous health. Who but the beloved of the Lord ever experience that *sin-sickness* in which the soul loathes the very name of transgression, is unmoved by the enchantments of the tempter, finds no sweetness in its besetting sins, but turns with detestation and abhorrence from the very thought of iniquity? Not less is it for these, and these alone, to feel that *self-sickness* whereby the heart revolts from all creature confidence and strength, having been made sick of self, self-seeking, self-exalting, self-reliance, and self of every sort. The Lord afflicts us more and more with such self-sickness till we are dead to self, its puny conceits, its lofty aims, and its unsanctified desires.

Then there is a *twofold lovesickness*. Of the one kind is that lovesickness which comes upon the Christian when he is transported with the full enjoyment of Jesus, even as the bride elated by the favor, melted by the tenderness of her Lord, says in the Song 2:5: "Stay me with flagons, comfort me with apples: for I am sick of love." The soul overjoyed with the divine communications of happiness and bliss which came from Christ, the body scarcely able to bear the excessive delirium of delight which the soul possessed, she was so glad to be in the embraces of her Lord, that she needed to be stayed under her overpowering weight of joy.

Another kind of lovesickness widely different from the first, is that in which the soul is sick, not because it has too much of Christ's love, but because it has not enough present consciousness of it; sick, not of the enjoyment, but of the longing for it; sick, not because of excess of delight, but because of sorrow for an absent lover. It is to this sickness we call your attention this morning. Their lovesickness breaks out in two ways, and may be viewed in two lights. It is, first of all, the soul *longing for a view of Jesus Christ in grace*; and then again, it is the same soul *possessing the view of grace, and longing for a sight of Jesus Christ in glory*. In both these senses we, as accurately as the spouse, may adopt the languishing words, "If ye find my beloved, tell him that I am sick of love."

I. First, then, let us consider our text as the language of a soul *longing for the view of Jesus Christ in grace.*

Do you ask me concerning the sickness itself: What is it? It is the sickness of a soul panting after communion with Christ. The man is a believer; he is not longing after salvation as a penitent sinner under conviction, for he is saved. Moreover, he has love to Christ, and knows it; he does not doubt his evidence as to the reality of his affection for his Lord, for you see the word used is "my beloved," which would not be applicable if the person speaking had any doubt about her interest; nor did she doubt her love, for she calls the spouse, "my beloved." It is the longing of a soul, then, not for salvation, and not even for the certainty of salvation, but for the enjoyment of present fellowship with him who is her soul's life, her soul's all. The heart is panting to be brought once more under the apple tree; to feel once again his "left hand under her head, while his right hand doth embrace her." She has known, in days past, what it is to be brought into his banqueting house, and to see the banner of love waved over her, and she therefore cries to have love visits renewed. It is a panting after communion.

Gracious hours, my dear friends, are never perfectly at ease except they are in a state of nearness to Christ; for mark you, when they are not near to Christ, they lose their peace. The nearer to Jesus, the nearer to the perfect calm of heaven; and the further from Jesus, the nearer to that troubled sea which images the continual unrest of the wicked. There is no peace to the man who doth not dwell constantly under the shadow of the cross; for Jesus is our peace, and if he be absent, our peace is absent too. I know that being justified, we have peace with God, but it is "through our Lord Jesus Christ." So that the justified man himself cannot reap the fruit of justification, except by abiding in Christ Jesus, who is the Lord and Giver of peace. The Christian without fellowship with Christ loses all his life and energy; he is like a dead thing. Though saved, he lies like a lumpish log—

His soul can neither fly nor go
To reach eternal joys.

He is without vivacity, yes, more, he is without animation till Jesus comes; but when the Lord sensibly sheds abroad his love in our hearts, then *his* love kindles ours; then our blood leaps in our veins for joy, like the Baptist in the womb of Elizabeth. The heart when near to Jesus has strong pulsations, for since Jesus is in that heart, it is full of life, of vigor, and of strength. Peace, liveliness, vigor—all depend upon the constant enjoyment of communion with Christ Jesus. The soul of a Christian never knows what *joy* means in its true solidity, except when she sits like Mary at Jesus' feet. Beloved, all the joys of life are nothing to us; we have melted them all down in our crucible, and found them to be dross. You and I have tried earth's vanities, and they cannot satisfy us; no, they do not give a morsel of meat to satiate our hunger. Being in a state of dissatisfaction with all mortal things, we have learned through divine grace, that none but Jesus, none but Jesus can make our souls glad. "Philosophers are happy without music" said one of old. So Christians are happy without the world's good. Christians, with the world's good, are sure to bemoan themselves as naked, poor, and miserable, unless their Savior be with them. You that have ever tasted communion with Christ will soon know why it is that a soul longs after him. What the sun is to the day, what the moon is to the night, what the dew is to the flower, such is Jesus Christ to us. What bread is to the hungry, clothes to the naked, the shadow of a great rock to the traveler in a weary land, such is Jesus Christ to us. What the turtle is to her mate, what the husband is to his spouse, what the head is to the body, such is Jesus Christ to us; and therefore, if we have him not, no, if we are not conscious of having him; if we are not one with him, no, if we are not consciously one with him, little marvel if our spirit cries in the words of the Song, "I charge you, O ye daughters of Jerusalem, if ye find my beloved, tell him that I am sick of love."

Such is the character of this lovesickness. We may say of it, however, before we leave that point, that it is *a sickness which has a blessing attending it*: "Blessed are they that do hunger and thirst after righteousness"; and therefore, supremely blessed are they who thirst after the righteous One—after him, who in the highest perfection embodies pure, immaculate, spotless righteousness. Blessed is that hunger, for it comes from God. It bears a blessing within it; for if I may not have the blessedness in full bloom of being filled, the next best thing is the same blessedness in sweet bud of being empty till I am filled with Christ. If I may not feed on Jesus, it shall be next door to heaven to be allowed to hunger and thirst after him. There is a hallowedness about that hunger, since it sparkles among the beatitudes of our Lord. Yet it is a sickness, dear friends, which, despite the blessing, *causes much pain*. The man who is sick after Jesus will be dissatisfied with everything else; he will find that dainties have lost their sweetness and music its melody and light its brightness, and life itself will be darkened with the shadow of death to him, till he finds his Lord, and can rejoice in him. Beloved, you shall find that this thirsting, this sickness, if it ever gets hold upon you, is *attended with great vehemence*. The desire is vehement, as coals of juniper. You have heard of hunger that it breaks through stone walls: but stone walls are no prison to a soul that desires Christ. Stone walls—no, the strongest natural barriers—cannot keep a lovesick heart from Jesus. I will venture to say that the temptation of heaven itself, if it could be offered to the believer without his Christ, would be as less than nothing; and the pains of hell, if they could be endured, would be gladly ventured upon by a lovesick soul, if he might but find Christ. As lovers sometimes talk of doing impossibilities for their fair ones, so certainly a spirit that is set on Christ will laugh at impossibility, and say, "It shall be done." It will venture upon the hardest task, go cheerfully to prison and joyfully to death, if it may but find its beloved, and have its lovesickness satisfied with his presence. Perhaps this may suffice for a description of the sickness here intended.

You may inquire concerning the cause of this lovesickness. What makes a man's soul so sick after Christ? Understand that it is the *absence* of Christ which makes this sickness in a mind that really understands the preciousness of his presence. The spouse had been very willful and wayward, she had taken off her garments, had gone to her rest, her sluggish slothful rest, when her beloved knocked at the door. He said "Open to me, my beloved; for my head is filled with dew, and my locks with the drops of the night." She was too slothful to wake up to let him in. She urged excuses—"I have put off my coat; how shall I put it on? I have washed my feet; how shall I defile them?" The beloved stood waiting, but since she opened not he put in his hand by the hole of the lock, and then her bowels were moved toward him. She went to the door to open it, and to her surprise, her hands dropped with myrrh, and her fingers with sweet smelling myrrh upon the handles of the lock. There was the token that he had been there, but he was gone. Now she began to bestir herself, and seek after him. She sought him through the city, but she found him not. Her soul failed her; she called after him, but he gave her no answer, and the watchman, who ought to have helped her in the search, smote her, and took away her veil from her. Therefore it is that now she is seeking, because she has lost her beloved. She should have held him fast and not have permitted him to go. He is absent, and she is sick till she finds him. Mingled with the sense of absence is *a consciousness of wrongdoing*. Something in her seemed to say, "How could you drive him away? That heavenly Bridegroom who knocked and pleaded hard, how could you keep him longer there amid the cold dews of night? O unkind heart! what if your feet had been made to bleed by your rising? What if all your body had been chilled by the cold wind, when you were treading the floor? What had it been compared with his love to you?" And so she is sick to see him, that she may weep out her love and tell him how vexed she is with herself that she should have held to him so loosely, and permitted him so readily to depart.

So, too, mixed with this, was *great wretchedness* because he was gone. She had been for a little time easy in his absence. That downy bed, that warm coverlet, had given her a peace, a false, cruel, and a wicked peace, but she has risen now, the watchmen have smitten her, her veil is gone, and, without a friend, the princess, deserted in the midst of Jerusalem's streets, has her soul melted for heaviness, and she pours out her heart within her as she pines after her Lord. "No love but my love, no lord but my lord," says she, with sobbing tongue and weeping eyes; for none else can gratify her heart or appease her anxiety.

Beloved, have you never been in such a state, when your faith has begun to droop, and your heart and spirits have fled from you? Even then it was your soul was sick for him. You could do without him when Mr. Carnal-Security was in the house and feasted you, but when he and his house have both been burned with fire, the old lovesickness came back, and you wanted Christ, nor could you be satisfied till you found him once again. There was *true love* in all this, and this is the very pith of all lovesickness. Had not she loved, absence would not have made her sick, nor would her repentance have made her grieve. Had she not loved, there would have been no pain because of absence, and no sinking of spirits, but she did love, thence all this sickness. It is a delightful thing to be able to know when we have lost Christ's company, that we do love him—"'Yea, Lord, thou knowest all things; thou knowest that I love thee.' I did deny thee, yea, in the moment of thy sorrow, I said, 'I know not the man.' I did curse and swear that men might think I was no follower of thine, but still thou knowest all things; thou knowest that I love thee." When you can feel this, dear friends, the consciousness that you love will soon work in you a *heart-burning*, so that your soul will not be satisfied till you can tell out that love in the Master's presence, and he shall say unto you, as a token of forgiveness, "Feed my sheep."

I do not doubt that in this sickness there had been *some degree of fear*. Sorrowful woman! She was half afraid she might never find him again. She had been about the city—where could he be? She had sought him on the walls and on the ramparts, but he was not there. In every ordinance, in every means of grace, in secret and in public prayer, in the Lord's Supper, and in the reading of the Word, she had looked after him, but he was not there; and now she was half afraid that though he might give his presence to others, yet never to her, and when she speaks, you notice there is half a fear in it. She would not have asked others to tell him if she had any assuring hope that she should meet him herself—"If ye find him," she seems to say, "O ye true converts, you that are the real grace-born daughters of Jerusalem; if he reveals himself to you, though he never may to me, do me this kindness, tell him that I am sick of love."

There is half a fear here, and yet there is *some hope*. She feels that he must love her still, or else why send a message at all? She would surely never send this sweet message to a flinty, adamantine heart, "Tell him I am sick of love"; but she remembered when the glancings of her eyes had ravished him; she remembered when a motion from her hand had made his heart melt, and when one tear of her eyes had opened all his wounds afresh. She thinks, "Perhaps, he loves me still as he loved me then, and my moanings will enchain him; my groans will constrain him and lead him to my help." So she sends the message to him—"Tell him, tell him I am sick of love."

To gather up the causes of this lovesickness in a few words, does not the whole matter spring from *relationship?* She is his spouse; can the spouse be happy without her beloved lord? It springs from union; she is part of himself. Can the hand be happy and healthy if the life-floods stream not from the heart and from the head? Fondly realizing her *dependence*, she feels that she owes all to him, and gets her all from him. If then the fountain be cut off, if the streams be dried, if the great source of all be taken from her, how can she but be sick? And there is besides this, *a life and a nature* in her which makes her sick. There is a life like the life of Christ, nay, her life is in Christ, it is hid with Christ in God; her nature is a part of the divine nature; she is a partaker of the divine nature. Moreover she is in *union* with Jesus, and this piece divided, as it were, from the body, wriggles, like a worm cut asunder, and pants to get back to where it came from. These are the causes of it. You will not understand my sermon this morning but think me raving, unless you are spiritual men. "But the spiritual judgeth all things, yet he himself is judged of no man."

What endeavors such lovesick souls will put forth. Those who are sick for Christ will first send their *desires* to him. Men use pigeons sometimes to send their messages. Why, what sort of carrier pigeons do they use? The pigeon is of no use to send anywhere but to the place from which it came, and my desires after Christ came from him, and so they will always go back to the place from which they came; they know the way to their own dovecote, so I will send him my sighs and my groans, my tears and my moans. Go, go, sweet doves, with swift and clipping wings, and tell him I am sick of love. Then she would send her *prayers*. Ah! I think she would say of her desires, "They will never reach him; they know the way but their wings are broken, and they will fall to the ground and never reach him." Yet she will send them whether they reach him or not. As for her prayers, they are like arrows.

Sometimes messages have been sent into besieged towns bound to an arrow, so she binds her desires upon the arrow of her prayers, and then shoots them forth from the bow of her faith. She is afraid they will never reach him, for her bow is slack, and she knows not how to draw it with her feeble hands which hang down.

So what does she? She has traversed the streets; she has used *the means*; she has done everything; she has sighed her heart out, and emptied her soul out in prayers. She is all wounds till he heals her; she is all a hungry mouth till he fills her; she is all an empty brook till he replenishes her once again, and so now she *goes to her companions*, and she says, "If ye find my beloved, tell him I am sick of love." This is using the intercession of the saints. It is unbelief that makes her use it, and yet there is a little faith mixed in her unbelief. It was an unbelief but not a misbelief. There is efficacy in the intercession of saints. Not of dead saints—they have enough to do to be singing God's praises in heaven without praying for us—but saints on earth can take up our case. The king has his favorites; he has his cupbearers; he has some that are admitted into great familiarity with him: give me a share in a good man's prayers. I attribute under God the success the Lord has given me, to the number of souls in every quarter of the earth who pray for me—not you alone, but in every land there are some that forget me not when they draw near in their supplications. Oh! we are so rich when we have the prayers of saints. When it is well with thee, speak for me to the Captain of the host, and if he should say to thee, "What was his message?" I have no other message but that of the spouse, "Tell him I am sick of love." Any of you who have close familiarity with Jesus, be the messengers, be the heavenly talebearers between lovesick souls and their divine Lord. Tell him, tell him we are sick of love. And you that cannot thus go to him, do seek the help and aid of others.

But after all, as I have said this is unbelief though it is not misbelief, for how much better it would have been for her to *tell him herself*. "But," you say, "she could not find him." No, but if she had had faith, she would have known that her prayers could; for our prayers know where Christ is when we do not know, or rather, Christ knows where our prayers are, and when we cannot see him they reach him nevertheless. A man who fires a cannon is not expected to see all the way which the shot goes. If he has his cannon rightly sighted and fires it, there may come on a thick fog, but the shot will reach the place; and if you have your hearts sighted by divine grace after Christ, you may depend upon it, however thick the fog, the hot shot of your prayer will reach the gates of heaven though you cannot tell how or where. Be satisfied to go to Christ yourself. If your brethren will go, well and good, but I think their proper answer to your question would be in the language of the women in the sixth chapter, the first verse: "Whither is thy beloved gone, O thou fairest among women? whither is thy beloved turned aside? that we may seek him with thee." They will not seek him *for* us they say, but they can seek him *with* us. Sometimes when there are six pair of eyes, they will see better than one; and so, if five or six Christians seek the Lord in company, in the prayer meeting, or at his table, they are more likely to find him. "We will seek him with thee."

Blessed lovesickness! We have seen its character and its cause, and the endeavors of the soul under it; let us just notice *the comforts which belong to such a state as this*. Briefly they are these—*you shall be filled*. It is impossible for Christ to set you longing after him without intending to give himself to you. It is as when a great man does make a feast. He first puts plates upon the table, and then afterward there comes the meat. Your longings and desirings are the empty plates to hold the meat. Is it likely that he means to mock you? Would he have put the dishes there if he did not intend to fill them with his oxen and with his fatlings? He makes you long: he will certainly satisfy your longings.

Remember, again, that he will give you himself all the sooner for the bitterness of your longings. The more pained your heart is at his absence, the shorter will the absence be. If you have a grain of contentment without Christ, that will keep you longer tarrying; but when your soul is sick till your heart is ready to break, till you cry, "Why tarries he? Why are his chariots so long in coming?" when your soul faints until your Beloved speaks unto you, and you are ready to die from your youth up, then in no long space he will lift the veil from his dear face, and your sun shall rise with healing beneath his wings. Let that console you.

Then, again, when he does come, as come he will, oh, how sweet it will be! I think I have the flavor in my mouth now, and the fullness of the feast is yet to come. There is such a delight about the very thought that he will come, that the thought itself is the prelude, the foretaste of the happy greeting. What! Will he once again speak comfortably to me? Shall I again walk the bed of spices with him? Shall I ramble with him among the groves while the flowers give forth their sweet perfume? I shall! I shall! and even now my spirit feels his presence by anticipation: "Or ever I was aware, my soul made me like the chariots of Amminadib." You know how sweet it was in the past. Beloved, what times we have had, some of us. Oh, whether in the body or out of the body, we cannot tell—God knows. What mountings! Talk of eagles' wings—they are earthly pinions and may not be compared with the wings with which he carried us up from earth. Speak of mounting beyond clouds and stars!—they were left far, far behind. We entered into the unseen, beheld the invisible, lived in the immortal, drank in the ineffable, and were blessed with the fullness of God in Christ Jesus, being made to sit together in heavenly places in him. Well, all this is to come again: "I will see you again, and your heart shall rejoice." "A little while, and ye shall not see me: and again, a little while, and ye shall see me." "'In a little wrath I hid my face from thee for a moment; but with everlasting kindness will I have mercy on thee,' saith the LORD thy Redeemer." Think of this. Why, we have comfort even in this sickness of love. Our heart, though sick, is still whole, while we are panting and pining after the Lord Jesus.

> O love divine, how sweet thou art!
> When shall I find my willing heart
> All taken up with thee?
> I thirst, I faint, I die to prove
> The fullness of redeeming love—
> The love of Christ to me.

II. And now, second, with as great brevity as we can. This love-sickness may be seen in a soul longing for a view of Jesus in his glory.

And here we will consider the complaint itself for a moment. This ailment is not merely a longing after communion with Christ on earth—that has been enjoyed, and generally this sickness follows that—

> When I have tasted of the grapes,
> I sometimes long to go
> Where my dear Lord the vineyard keeps
> And all the clusters grow.

It is the enjoyment of Eshcol's firstfruits which makes us desire to sit under our own vine and our own fig tree before the throne of God in the blessed land.

Beloved, this sickness is characterized by certain marked symptoms; I will tell you what they are. There is a loving and a longing, a loathing and a languishing. Happy soul that understands these things by experience. There is a loving in which the heart cleaves to Jesus—

> *Do not I love thee from my soul?*
> *Then let me nothing love:*
> *Dead be my heart to every joy*
> *When Jesus cannot move.*

A sense of his beauty! an admiration of his charms! a consciousness of his infinite perfection! Yea; greatness, goodness, and loveliness, in one resplendent ray combine to enchant the soul till it is so ravished after him that it cries with the spouse, "Yea, he is altogether lovely. This is my beloved, and this is my friend, O ye daughters of Jerusalem." Sweet loving this—a love which binds the heart with chains of more than silken softness, and yet than adamant more firm.

Then there is *a longing*. She loves him so that she cannot endure to be absent from him; she pants and pines. You know it has been so with saints in all ages; whenever they have begun to love they have always begun to long after Christ. John, the most loving of spirits, is the author of those words which he so frequently uses—"Come quickly, even so, come quickly." "Come quickly" is sure to be the fruit of earnest love. See how the spouse puts it—"O that thou wert as my brother, that sucked the breasts of my mother! when I should find thee without, I would kiss thee; yea, I should not be despised." She longs to get hold of him; she cannot conclude her song without saying, "Make haste, my beloved, and be thou like to a roe or to a young hart upon the mountains of spices." There is a longing to be with Christ. I would not give much for your religion if you do not long to be with the object of your heart's affections.

Then comes *a loathing*. When a man is sick with the first lovesickness, then he does not loathe—it is, "Stay me with flagons, comfort me with apples." When a man has Christ, he can enjoy other things; but when a man is longing after Christ and seeking after Christ, he loathes everything else—he cannot bear anything besides. Here is my message to Jesus: "Tell him—" what? Do I want crowns and diadems? Crowns and diadems are naught to me. Do I want wealth and health and strength? They are all very well in their way. No—"Tell him, tell the Beloved of my soul that I grieve after himself—his gifts are good—I ought to be more grateful for them than I am, but let me see his face; let me hear his voice. I am sick of love, and nothing but that can satisfy me, everything else is distasteful to me."

And then there is a languishing. Since she cannot get the society of Christ, cannot as yet behold him on his throne nor worship him face to face, she is sick until she can. For a heart so set on Christ will walk about traversing highway and byway, resting nowhere till it finds him. As the needle once magnetized will never be easy until it finds the pole, so the heart once Christianized never will be satisfied until it rests on Christ—rests on him, too, in the fullness of the beatific vision before the throne. This is the character of the lovesickness.

As to its object—what is that? "Tell him that I am sick of love"; but what is the sickness for? Brethren, when you and I want to go to heaven, I hope it is the true lovesickness. I catch myself sometimes wanting to die and be in heaven for the sake of rest; but is not that a lazy desire? There is a sluggish wish that makes me long for rest. Perhaps we long for the happiness of heaven—the harps and crowns. There is a little selfishness in that, is there not? Allowable, I grant you; but is not there a little like selfishness? Perhaps, we long to see dear children, beloved friends that have gone before; but there is a little of the earthy there. The soul may be as sick as it will, without rebuke, when it is sick to be with Jesus. You may indulge this, carry it to its utmost extent without either sin or folly. What am I sick with love for? For the pearly gates?—no; but for the pearls that are in his wounds. What am I sick for? For the streets of gold?—no; but for his head which is as much fine gold. For the melody of the harps and angelic songs?—no; but for the melodious notes that come from his dear mouth. What am I sick for? For the nectar that angels drink?—no; but for the kisses of his lips. For the manna on which heavenly souls do feed?—no; but for himself, who is the meat and drink of his saints himself; himself—my soul pines to see him. Oh, what a heaven to gaze upon! What bliss to talk with the man, the God, crucified for me; to weep my heart out before him; to tell him how I love him, for he loved me and gave himself for me; to read my name written on his hands and on his side—yes, and to let him see that his name is written on my heart in indelible lines; to embrace him. Oh! what an embrace when the creature shall embrace his God—to be forever so close to him, that not a doubt, nor a fear, nor a wandering thought can come between my soul and him forever—

> *Forever to behold him shine,*
> *Forevermore to call him mine,*
> *And see him still before me;*
> *Forever on his face to gaze,*

And meet his full assembled rays,
While all the Father he displays
To all the saints in glory.

What else can there be that our spirit longs for? This seems an empty thing to worldlings, but to the Christian this is heaven summed up in a word— "To be with Christ, which is far better" than all the joys of earth. This is the object, then, of this lovesickness.

Ask you yet again what are the excitements of this sickness? What is it makes the Christian long to be at home with Jesus? There are many things. There are sometimes some very little things that set a Christian longing to be at home. You know the old story of Swiss soldiers, that when they have enlisted into foreign service, they never will permit the band to play the "Ranz des Vaches"—the "Song of the Cows," because as soon as ever the Swiss hears the "Song of the Cows," he thinks of his own dear Alps, and the bells upon the cows' necks, and the strange calls of the herd boys, as they sing to one another from the mountains' peaks; and he grows sick and ill with homesickness. So if you were banished, if you were taken prisoner or a slave, why, to hear some note of one of old England's songs would set your spirit to pining for home, and I do confess, when I hear you sing sometimes—

Jerusalem! my happy home!
Name ever dear to me;
When shall my labors have an end,
In joy, and peace, and thee?

it makes me say, "Ye daughters of Jerusalem, if ye find my beloved, tell him, that I am sick of love." It is the home song that brings the homesickness. When we remember what he used to be to us, what sweet visits we have had from him, then we get sick to be always with him, and, best of all, when we are in his presence, when our soul is overjoyed with his delights, when the great deep sea of his love has rolled over the masthead of our highest thoughts, and the ship of our spirit has gone right down, foundering at sea in the midst of an ocean of delights, ah, then its highest, its deepest thought is, "Oh, that I may always be with him, in him, where he is, that I might behold his glory—the glory which his Father gave him, and which he has given me, that I may be one with him, world without end." I do believe, brethren, that all the bitters and all the sweets make a Christian, when he is in a healthy state, sick after Christ: the sweets make his mouth water for more sweets, and the bitters make him pant for the time when the last dregs of bitterness shall be over. Wearying temptations, as well as rapt enjoyments, all set the spirit on the wing after Jesus.

Well now, friends, what is the cure of this lovesickness? Is it a sickness for which there is any specific remedy? There is only one cure that I know of, but there are some palliatives. A man that is sick after Christ longs to be with him, and pants for the better land, singing as we did just now—

> Father, I long, I faint to see
> The place of thine abode.

He must have the desire realized, before the thirst of his fever will be assuaged. There are some palliatives, and I will recommend them to you. Such for example is a strong faith that realizes the day of the Lord and the presence of Christ, as Moses beheld the promised land and the goodly heritage, when he stood on the top of Pisgah. If you do not get heaven when you want it, you may attain to that which is next door to heaven, and this may bear you up for a little season. If you cannot get to behold Christ face to face, it is a blessed makeshift for the time to see him in the Scriptures, and to look at him through the glass of the Word. These are palliatives, but I warn you, I warn you of them. I do not mean to keep you from them, use them as much as ever you can, but I warn you from expecting that it will cure that lovesickness. It will give you ease but it will make you more sick still, for he that lives on Christ gets more hungry after Christ. As for a man being satisfied and wanting no more when he gets Christ—why he wants nothing but Christ it is true, in that sense he will never thirst; but he wants more and more and more and more of Christ. To live on Christ is like drinking seawater, the more you drink the more thirsty you grow. There is something very satisfying in Christ's flesh; you will never hunger except for that, but the more you eat of it, the more you may; and he that is the heartiest feaster, and has eaten the most, has the best appetite for more. Oh, strange is this, but so it is; that which we would think would remove the lovesickness, and is the best stay to the soul under it, is just that which brings it on more and more. But there is a cure, there is a cure, and you shall have it soon—a black draft, and in it a pearl: a black draft called death. You shall drink it, but you shall not know it is bitter, for you shall swallow it up in victory. There is a pearl, too, in it—melted in it. Jesus died as well as you, and as you drink it, that pearl shall take away all ill effect from the tremendous draft. You shall say, "O death, where is thy sting? O grave, where is thy victory?" When you have once drunk that black draft, you are secure against that lovesickness forever. For where are you? No pilgrimage, no weary flight through cold ether, you are with him in paradise. Do you hear that, soul? You are with him in paradise, never to be separated, not for an instant; never to have a wandering thought, not one; never to find your love waning or growing cold again; never to doubt his love to you any more; never more to be vexed and tempted by sighing after what you cannot view. You shall be with him, where he is—

> *Far from a world of grief and sin,*
> *With God eternally shut in.*

Till then, beloved, let us strive to live near the cross. Those two mountains, Calvary and Zion, stand right opposite one another. The eye of faith can sometimes almost span the interval. And the loving heart, by some deep mystery of which we can offer you no solution, will often have its sweetest rapture of joy in the fellowship of his griefs. So have I found a satisfaction in the wounds of a crucified Jesus, which can only be excelled by the satisfaction I have yet to find in the sparkling eyes of the same Jesus glorified. Yes; the same Jesus! Well spoke the angels on Mount Olivet: "This same Jesus, which is taken up from you into heaven, shall so come in like manner as ye have seen him go into heaven." This same Jesus! My soul dotes on the words; my lips are fond of repeating them. This same Jesus!

> *If in my soul such joy abounds,*
> *While weeping faith explores his wounds,*
> *How glorious will those scars appear,*
> *When perfect bliss forbids a tear!*
> *Think, O my soul, if 'tis so sweet*
> *On earth to sit at Jesus' feet,*
> *What must it be to wear a crown*
> *And sit with him upon his throne?*

Would to God you all had this lovesickness! I am afraid many of you have it not. May he give it to you. But oh! if there be a soul here that wants Jesus, he is welcome. If there is one heart here that says, "Give me Christ," you shall have your desire. Trust Jesus Christ, and he is yours; rely upon him, you are his. God save you and make you sick *of* vanities, sick *after* verities; pining even unto sickness for Jesus Christ, the beloved of my soul, the sum of all my hope, the sinners' only refuge, and the praise of all his saints; to whom be everlasting glory. Amen.

Women of the New Testament

The Mother of Jesus: Mary's Song

⟞⟨⟩⟝

Delivered on Sunday morning, December 25, 1864, at the Metropolitan Tabernacle, Newington. No. 606.

And Mary said, "My soul doth magnify the Lord, and my spirit hath rejoiced in God my Savior."—LUKE 1:46–47

Mary was on a visit when she expressed her joy in the language of this noble song. It were well if all our social intercourse were as useful to our hearts as this visit was to Mary. "Iron sharpeneth iron; so a man sharpeneth the countenance of his friend"; Mary, full of faith, goes to see Elizabeth, who is also full of holy confidence, and the two are not long together before their faith mounts to full assurance, and their full assurance bursts forth in a torrent of sacred praise. This praise aroused their slumbering powers, and instead of two ordinary village women, we see before us two prophetesses and poetesses, upon whom the Spirit of God abundantly rested. When we meet with our kinsfolk and acquaintance, let it be our prayer to God that our communion may be not only pleasant, but profitable; that we may not merely pass away time and spend a pleasant hour, but may advance a day's march nearer heaven, and acquire greater fitness for our eternal rest.

Observe, this morning, the sacred joy of Mary that you may imitate it. This is a season when all men expect us to be joyous. We compliment each other with the desire that we may have a "Merry Christmas." Some Christians who are a little squeamish, do not like the word *merry*. It is a right good old Saxon word, having the joy of childhood and the mirth of manhood in it, it brings before one's mind the old song of the waits, and the midnight peal of bells, the holly and the blazing log. I love it for its place in that most tender of all parables, where it is written, that, when the long-lost prodigal returned to his father safe and sound, "They began to be merry." This is the season when we are expected to be happy; and my heart's desire is that, in the highest and best sense, you who are believers may be "merry." Mary's heart was merry within her; but here was the mark of her joy, it was all holy merriment, it was every drop of it sacred mirth. It was not such merriment as worldlings will revel in today and tomorrow, but such merriment as the angels have around the throne, where they sing, "Glory to God in the highest," while we sing, "On earth peace, goodwill toward men." Such merry hearts have a continual feast. I want you, children of the bride chamber, to possess today and tomorrow, yes, all your days, the high and consecrated bliss of Mary, that you may not only read her words, but use them for yourselves, ever experiencing their meaning: "My soul doth magnify the Lord, and my spirit hath rejoiced in God my Savior."

Observe, first, that she sings; second, she sings sweetly; third, shall she sing alone?

I. First observe, that Mary sings.

Her subject is a Savior; she hails the incarnate God. The long-expected Messiah is about to appear. He for whom prophets and princes waited long is now about to come, to be born of the Virgin of Nazareth. Truly there was never a subject of sweeter song than this—the stooping down of Godhead to the feebleness of manhood. When God manifested his power in the works of his hands, the morning stars sang together, and the sons of God shouted for joy; but when God manifests himself, what music shall suffice for the grand psalm of adoring wonder? When wisdom and power are seen, these are but attributes; but in the incarnation it is the divine person which is revealed wrapped in a veil of our inferior clay: well might Mary sing, when earth and heaven even now are wondering at the condescending grace.

Worthy of peerless music is the fact that "the Word was made flesh and dwelt among us." There is no longer a great gulf fixed between God and his people; the humanity of Christ has bridged it over. We can no more think that God sits on high, indifferent to the wants and woes of men, for God has visited us and come down to the lowliness of our estate. No longer need we bemoan that we can never participate in the moral glory and purity of God, for if God in glory can come down to his sinful creature, it is certainly less difficult to bear that creature, blood washed and purified, up that starry way, that the redeemed one may sit down forever on his throne. Let us dream no longer in somber sadness that we cannot draw near to God so that he will really hear our prayer and pity our necessities, seeing that Jesus has become bone of our bone and flesh of our flesh, born a babe as we are born, living a man as we must live, bearing the same infirmities and sorrows, and bowing his head to the same death. Oh, can we not come with boldness by this new and living way, and have access to the throne of the heavenly grace, when Jesus meets us as Emmanuel, God with us? Angels sang, they scarcely knew why. Could they understand why God had become man? They must have known that herein was a mystery of condescension; but all the loving consequences which the incarnation involved even their acute minds could scarcely have guessed; but we see the whole, and comprehend the grand design most fully. The manger of Bethlehem was big with glory; in the incarnation was wrapped up all the blessedness by which a soul, snatched from the depths of sin, is lifted up to the heights of glory. Shall not our clearer knowledge lead us to heights of song which angelic guesses could not reach? Shall the lips of cherubs move to flaming sonnets, and shall we who are redeemed by the blood of the incarnate God be treacherously and ungratefully silent!

> Did archangels sing thy coming?
> Did the shepherds learn their lays?
> Shame would cover me, ungrateful,
> Should my tongue refuse to praise.

This, however, was not the full subject of her holy hymn. Her peculiar delight was not that there was a Savior to be born, but that *he was to be born of her*. Blessed among women was she, and highly favored of the Lord; but we can enjoy the same favor; no, we must enjoy it, or the coming of a Savior will be of no avail to us. Christ on Calvary, I know, takes away the sin of his people; but none have ever known the virtue of Christ upon the cross, unless they have the Lord Jesus formed in them as the hope of glory. The stress of the Virgin's canticle is laid upon God's special grace to her. Those little words, the personal pronouns, tell us that it was truly a personal affair with her. "My soul doth magnify the Lord, and my spirit hath rejoiced in God my Savior." The Savior was peculiarly, and in a special sense, hers. She sang no "Christ for all"; but *"Christ for me"* was her glad subject. Beloved, is Christ Jesus in your heart? Once you looked at him from a distance, and that look cured you of all spiritual diseases, but are you now living upon him, receiving him into your very vitals as your spiritual meat and drink? In holy fellowship you have oftentimes fed upon his flesh and been made to drink of his blood; you have been buried with him in baptism unto death; you have yielded yourselves a sacrifice to him, and you have taken him to be a sacrifice for you; you can sing of him as the spouse did, "His left hand is under my head, and his right hand doth embrace me. . . . My beloved is mine, and I am his: he feedeth among the lilies." This is a happy style of living, and all short of this poor slavish work. Oh! you can never know the joy of Mary unless Christ becomes truly and really yours; but oh! when he is yours, yours within, reigning in your heart, yours controlling all your passions, yours changing your nature, subduing your corruptions, inspiring you with hallowed emotions; yours within, a joy unspeakable and full of glory—oh! then you *can* sing, you *must* sing, who can restrain your tongue? If all the scoffers and mockers upon earth should bid you hold your peace, you must sing; for your spirit must rejoice in God your Savior.

We should miss much instruction if we overlooked the fact that the choice poem before us is *a hymn of faith*. As yet there was no Savior born, nor, as far we can judge, had the Virgin any evidence such as carnal sense requires to make her believe that a Savior would be born of her. "How can this thing be?" was a question which might very naturally have suspended her song until it received an answer convincing to flesh and blood; but no such answer had been given. She knew that with God all things are possible, she had his promise delivered by an angel, and this was enough for her: on the strength of the Word which came forth from God, her heart leaped with pleasure and her tongue glorified his name. When I consider what it is which she believed, and how unhesitatingly she received the Word, I am ready to give her, as a woman, a place almost as high as that which Abraham occupied as a man; and if I dare not call her the mother of the faithful, at least let her have due honor as one of the most excellent of the mothers in Israel. The benediction of Elizabeth, Mary right well deserved, "Blessed is she that believeth." To her, the "substance of things hoped for" was her faith, and that was also her "evidence of things not seen"; she knew, by the revelation of God, that she was to bear the promised Seed who should bruise the serpent's head; but other proof she had none.

This day there are those among us who have little or no conscious enjoyment of the Savior's presence; they walk in darkness and see no light; they are groaning over inbred sin, and mourning because corruptions prevail; let them now trust in the Lord, and remember that if they believe on the Son of God, Christ Jesus is within them; and by faith they may right gloriously chant the hallelujah of adoring love. What—though the sun gleam not forth today, the clouds and mists have not quenched his light; and though the Sun of righteousness shine not on you at this instant, yet he keeps his place in yonder skies, and knows no variableness, neither shadow of a turning. If with all your digging, the well spring not up, yet there abides a constant fullness in that deep, which crouches beneath in the heart and purpose of a God of love. What—if like David, you are much cast down, yet like him do you say unto your soul, "Hope thou in God, for I shall yet praise him for the help of his countenance." Be glad then with Mary's joy: it is the joy of a Savior completely hers, but evidenced to be so, not by sense, but by faith. Faith has its music as well as sense, but it is of a diviner sort: if the viands on the table make men sing and dance, feastings of a more refined and ethereal nature can fill believers with a hallowed plenitude of delight.

Still listening to the favored Virgin's canticle, let me observe that her low-liness does not make her stay her song; no, it imports a sweeter note into it. "For he hath regarded the low estate of his handmaiden." Beloved friend, you are feeling more intensely than ever the depth of your natural depravity, you are humbled under a sense of your many failings, you are so dead and earth-bound even in this house of prayer, that you cannot rise to God; you are heavy and sad, while our Christmas carols have been ringing in your ears; you feel yourself to be today so useless to the church of God, so insignificant, so ut-terly unworthy, that your unbelief whispers, "Surely, surely, you have nothing to sing for." Come, my brother, come my sister, imitate this blessed Virgin of Nazareth, and turn that very lowliness and meanness which you so painfully feel, into another reason for unceasing praise; daughters of Zion, sweetly say in your hymns of love, "He hath regarded the low estate of his handmaiden." The less worthy I am of his favors, the more sweetly will I sing of his grace. What if I be the most insignificant of all his chosen; then will I praise him who with eyes of love has sought me out, and set his love upon me. "I thank thee, O Father, Lord of heaven and earth, that while thou hast hid these things from the wise and prudent, thou hast revealed them unto babes: even so, Father; for so it seemed good in thy sight." I am sure, dear friends, the remembrance that there is a Savior, and that this Savior is yours, must make you sing; and if you set side by side with it the thought that you were once sinful, unclean, vile, hateful, and an enemy to God, then your notes will take yet a loftier flight, and mount to the third heaven, to teach the golden harps the praise of God.

It is right well worthy of notice, that *the greatness of the promised blessing* did not give the sweet songstress an argument for suspending her thankful strain. When I meditate upon the great goodness of God in loving his people before the earth was, in laying down his life for us, in pleading our cause before the eternal throne, in providing a paradise of rest for us forever, the black thought has troubled me, "Surely this is too high a privilege for such an insect of a day as this poor creature, man." Mary did not look at this matter unbelievingly; although she appreciated the greatness of the favor, she did but rejoice the more heartily on that account. "For he that is mighty hath done to me great things." Come, soul, it is a great thing to be a child of God, but your God does great wonders, therefore be not staggered through unbelief, but tri-umph in your adoption, great mercy though it be. Oh! it is a mighty mercy, higher than the mountains, to be chosen of God from all eternity, but it is true that even so are his redeemed chosen, and therefore you sing of it. It is a deep and unspeakable blessing to be redeemed with the precious blood of Christ, but you are so redeemed beyond all question. Therefore doubt not, but shout aloud for gladness of heart. It is a rapturous thought, that you shall dwell above, and wear the crown, and wave the palm branch forever; let no mistrust interrupt the melody of your psalm of expectation, but—

> *Loud to the praise of love divine,*
> *Bid every string awake.*

What a fullness of truth is there in these few words: "He that is mighty hath done to me great things." It is a text from which a glorified spirit in heaven might preach an endless sermon. I pray you, lay hold upon the thoughts which I have in this poor way suggested to you, and try to reach where Mary stood in holy exultation. The grace is great, but so is its Giver; the love is infinite, but so is the heart from which it wells up; the blessedness is unspeakable, but so is the divine wisdom which planned it from of old. Let our hearts take up the Virgin's Magnificat, and praise the Lord right joyously at this hour.

Still further, for we have not exhausted the strain, *the holiness of God has sometimes damped the ardor of the believer's joy*; but not so in Mary's case. She exults in it: "And holy is his name." She weaves even that bright attribute into her song. Holy Lord! when I forget my Savior, the thought of thy purity makes me shudder; standing where Moses stood upon the holy mountain of thy law, I do exceedingly fear and quake. To me, conscious of my guilt, no thunder could be more dreadful than the seraph's hymn of "Holy! holy! holy! Lord God of Sabaoth." What is thy holiness but a consuming fire which must utterly destroy me—a sinner? If the heavens are not pure in thy sight and thou chargeth thine angels with folly, how much less then can thou bear with vain, rebellious man, that is born of woman? How can man be pure, and how can thine eyes look upon him without consuming him quickly in thine anger? But, O thou holy One of Israel, when my spirit can stand on Calvary and see thy holiness vindicate itself in the wounds of the man who was born at Bethlehem, then my spirit rejoices in that glorious holiness which was once her terror. Did the thrice holy God stoop down to man and take man's flesh? Then is there hope indeed! Did a holy God bear the sentence which his own law pronounced on man? Does that holy God incarnate now spread his wounded hands and plead for me? Then, my soul, the holiness of God shall be a consolation to thee. Living waters from this sacred well I draw; and I will add to all my notes of joy this one, "and holy is his name." He hath sworn by his holiness, and he will not lie; he will keep his covenant with his anointed and his seed forever.

When we take to ourselves the wings of eagles, and mount toward heaven in holy praise, the prospect widens beneath us; even so as Mary poises herself upon the poetic wing, she looks down the long aisles of the past, and beholds the mighty acts of Jehovah in the ages long back. Mark how her strain gathers majesty; it is rather the sustained flight of the eagle-winged Ezekiel, than the flutter of the timid dove of Nazareth. She sings, "His mercy is on them that fear him from generation to generation." She looks beyond the captivity, to the days of the kings, to Solomon, to David, along through the Judges into the wilderness, across the Red Sea to Jacob, to Isaac, to Abraham, and onward, till, pausing at the gate of Eden, she hears the sound of the promise, "The seed of the woman shall bruise the serpent's head." How magnificently she sums up the book of the wars of the Lord, and rehearses the triumphs of Jehovah, "He hath shewed strength with his arm; he hath scattered the proud in the imagination of their hearts." How delightfully is mercy intermingled with judgment in the next canto of her psalm: "He hath put down the mighty from their seats, and exalted them of low degree. He hath filled the hungry with good things; and the rich he hath sent empty away."

My brethren and sisters, let us, too, sing of the past, glorious in faithfulness, fearful in judgment, teeming with wonders. Our own lives shall furnish us with a hymn of adoration. Let us speak of the things which we have made touching the King. We were hungry, and he filled us with good things; we crouched upon the dunghill with the beggar, and he has enthroned us among princes; we have been tossed with tempest, but with the eternal Pilot at the helm, we have known no fear of shipwreck; we have been cast into the burning fiery furnace, but the presence of the Son of man has quenched the violence of the flames. Tell out, O daughters of music, the long tale of the mercy of the Lord to his people in the generations long departed. Many waters could not quench his love, neither could the floods drown it; persecution, famine, nakedness, peril, sword—none of these have separated the saints from the love of God which is in Christ our Lord. The saints beneath the wing of the most High have been ever safe; when most molested by the enemy, they have dwelled in perfect peace: "God is their refuge and strength, a very present help in trouble." Plowing at times the bloodred wave, the ship of the church has never swerved from her predestined path of progress. Every tempest has favored her: the hurricane which sought her ruin has been made to bear her the more swiftly onward. Her flag has braved these eighteen hundred years the battle and the breeze, and she fears not what may yet be before her. But lo! she nears the haven; the day is dawning when she shall bid farewell to storms; the waves already grow calm beneath her; the long-promised rest is near at hand; her Jesus himself meets her, walking upon the waters; she shall enter into her eternal haven, and all who are on board shall, with their Captain, sing of joy, and triumph, and victory through him who hath loved her and been her deliverer.

When Mary thus tuned her heart to glory in her God for his wonders in the past, she particularly dwelled upon the note of election. The highest note in the scale of my praise is reached when my soul sings, "I love him because he first loved me." Well does Kent put it—

> *A monument of grace,*
> *A sinner saved by blood;*
> *The streams of love I trace,*
> *Up to the fountain, God;*
> *And in his mighty breast I see,*
> *Eternal thoughts of love to me.*

We can scarcely fly higher than the source of love in the mount of God. Mary has the doctrine of election in her song: "He hath put down the mighty from their seats, and exalted them of low degree. He hath filled the hungry with good things; and the rich he hath sent empty away." Here is distinguishing grace, discriminating regard; here are some suffered to perish; here are others, the least deserving and the most obscure, made the special objects of divine affection. Do not be afraid to dwell upon this high doctrine, beloved in the Lord. Let me assure you that when your mind is most heavy and depressed, you will find this to be a bottle of richest cordial. Those who doubt these doctrines, or who cast them into the cold shade, miss the richest clusters of Eshcol; they lose the "wines on the lees well refined"; "the fat things full of marrow"; but you who by reason of years have had your senses exercised to discern between good and evil, you know that there is no honey like this, no sweetness comparable to it. If the honey in Jonathan's wood, when but touched enlightened the eyes to see, this is honey that will enlighten your heart to love and learn the mysteries of the kingdom of God. Eat, and fear not a surfeit; live upon this choice dainty, and fear not that you shall grow weary of it, for the more you know, the more you will want to know; the more your soul is filled, the more you will desire to have your mind enlarged, that you may comprehend more and more the eternal, everlasting, discriminating love of God.

But one more remark upon this point. You perceive she does not finish her song till she has reached the covenant. When you mount as high as election, tarry on its sister mount, the covenant of grace. In the last verse of her song, she sings, "As he spake to our fathers, to Abraham, and to his seed forever." To her, that was the covenant; to us who have clearer light, the ancient

covenant made in the council chamber of eternity is the subject of the greatest delight. The covenant with Abraham was in its best sense only a minor
copy of that gracious covenant made with Jesus, the everlasting Father of the
faithful, before the blue heavens were stretched abroad. Covenant engagements are the softest pillows for an aching head; covenant engagements with
the surety, Christ Jesus, are the best props for a trembling spirit.

> His oath, his covenant, his blood,
> Support me in the raging flood;
> When every earthly prop gives way,
> This still is all my strength and stay.

If Christ did swear to bring me to glory, and if the Father swore that he
would give me to the Son to be a part of the infinite reward for the travail of
his soul; then, my soul, till God himself shall be unfaithful, till Christ shall
cease to be the truth, till God's eternal council shall become a lie, and the red
roll of his election shall be consumed with fire, you are safe. Rest you, then,
in perfect peace, come what will; take your harp from the willows, and never
let your fingers cease to sweep it to strains of richest harmony. Oh, for grace
from first to last to join the Virgin in her song.

II. Second, *she sings sweetly.*

She praises her God right *heartily.* Observe how she plunges into the midst
of the subject. There is no preface, but "My soul doth magnify the Lord, and
my spirit hath rejoiced in God my Savior." When some people sing, they
appear to be afraid of being heard. Our poet puts it—

> With all my powers of heart and tongue
> I'll praise my Maker in my song;
> Angels shall hear the notes I raise,
> Approve the song, and join the praise.

I am afraid angels frequently do not hear those poor, feeble, dying whis-
perings, which often drop from our lips merely by force of custom. Mary is all
heart; evidently her soul is on fire; while she muses, the fire burns; then she
speaks with her tongue. May we, too, call home our wandering thoughts, and
wake up our slumbering powers to praise redeeming love. It is a noble word
that she uses here: "My soul doth magnify the Lord." I suppose it means, "My
soul doth endeavor to make God great by praising him." He is as great as he
can be in his being; my goodness cannot extend to him; but yet my soul would
make God greater in the thoughts of others, and greater in my own heart. I

would give the train of his glory wider sweep; the light which he has given me I would reflect; I would make his enemies his friends; I would turn hard thoughts of God into thoughts of love. "My soul would magnify the Lord." Old Trapp says, "My soul would make greater room for him." It is as if she wanted to get more of God into her, like Rutherford, when he says, "Oh, that my heart were as big as heaven, that I might hold Christ in it"; and then he stops himself—"But heaven and earth cannot contain him. Oh, that I had a heart as big as seven heavens, that I might hold the whole of Christ within it." Truly this is a larger desire than we can ever hope to have gratified; yet still our lips shall sing, "My soul doth magnify the Lord." Oh, if I could crown him; if I could lift him higher! If my burning at the stake would but add a spark more light to his glory, happy should I be to suffer. If my being crushed would lift Jesus an inch higher, happy were the destruction which should add to his glory! Such is the hearty spirit of Mary's song. Again, her praise is very joyful: "My spirit hath rejoiced in God my Savior." The word in the Greek is a remarkable one. I believe it is the same word which is used in the passage, "Rejoice ye in that day and leap for joy." We used to have an old word in English which described a certain exulting dance, a "galliard." That word is supposed to have come from the Greek word here used. It was a sort of leaping dance; the old commentators call it a levalto. Mary in effect declares, "My spirit shall dance like David before the ark, shall leap, shall spring, shall bound, shall rejoice in God my Savior." When we praise God, it ought not to be with dolorous and doleful notes. Some of my brethren praise God always on the minor key or in the deep, deep bass: they cannot feel holy till they have the horrors. Why cannot some men worship God except with a long face? I know them by their very walk as they come to worship: what a dreary pace it is! how solemnly proper and funereal indeed! They do not understand David's psalm:

> Up to her courts with joys unknown,
> The sacred tribes repair.

No, they come up to their Father's house as if they were going to jail, and worship God on Sunday as if it were the most doleful day in the week. It is said of a certain Highlander, when the Highlanders were very pious, that he once went to Edinburgh, and when he came back again he said he had seen a dreadful sight on Sabbath, he had seen people at Edinburgh going to church with happy faces. He thought it wicked to look happy on Sunday; and that same notion exists in the minds of certain good people hereabouts; they fancy that when the saints get together, they should sit down and have a little comfortable misery, and but little delight. In truth, moaning and pining is not the appointed way for worshiping God. We should take Mary as a pattern. All the year round I recommend her as an example to fainthearted and troubled ones. "My spirit hath rejoiced in God my Savior." Cease from rejoicing in sensual things, and with sinful pleasures have no fellowship, for all such rejoicing is evil. But you cannot rejoice too much in the Lord. I believe that the fault with our public worship is that we are too sober, too cold, too formal. I do not exactly admire the ravings of our Primitive Methodist friends when they grow wild; but I should have no objection to hear a hearty "hallelujah!" now and then. An enthusiastic burst of exultation might warm our hearts; the shout of "glory!" might fire our spirits. This I know, I never feel more ready for true worship than when I am preaching in Wales, when the whole sermon throughout, the preacher is aided rather than interrupted by shouts of "glory to God!" and "bless his name!" Why then one's blood begins to glow, and one's soul is stirred up, and this is the true way of serving God with joy. "Rejoice in the Lord alway; and again I say, Rejoice." "My spirit hath rejoiced in God my Savior."

She sings sweetly, in the third place, because she sings confidently. She does not pause while she questions herself, "Have I any right to sing?" but no, "My soul doth magnify the Lord, and my spirit hath rejoiced in God my Savior. For he hath regarded the low estate of his handmaiden." "If" is a sad enemy to all Christian happiness; "but," "peradventure," "doubt," "surmise," "suspicion," these are a race of highwaymen who waylay poor timid pilgrims and steal their spending money. Harps soon get out of tune, and when the wind blows from the doubting quarter, the strings snap by wholesale. If the angels of heaven could have a doubt, it would turn heaven into hell. "If thou be the Son of God" was the dastardly weapon wielded by the old enemy against our Lord in the wilderness. Our great foe knows well what weapon is the most dangerous. Christian, put up the shield of faith whenever you see that poisoned dagger about to be used against you. I fear that some of you foster your doubts and fears. You might as well hatch young vipers, and foster the cockatrice. You think that it is a sign of grace to have doubts, whereas it is a sign of infirmity. It does not prove that you have no grace when you doubt God's promise, but it does prove that you want more; for if you had more grace, you would take God's Word as he gives it, and it would be said of you as of Abraham, that "he staggered not at the promise of God, through unbelief, being fully persuaded that what he had promised he was able also to perform." God help you to shake off your doubts. Oh! these are devilish things. Is that too hard a word? I wish I could find a harder. These are felons; these are rebels, who seek to rob Christ of his glory; these are traitors who cast mire upon the escutcheon of my Lord. Oh! these are vile traitors; hang them on a gallows, high as Haman's; cast them to the earth, and let them rot like carrion, or bury them with the burial of an ass. Abhorred of God are doubts; abhorred of men let them be. They are cruel enemies to your souls; they injure your usefulness; they despoil you in every way. Smite them with "the sword of the Lord and of Gideon"! By faith in the promise, seek to drive out these Canaanites and possess the land. O you men of God, speak with confidence, and sing with sacred joy.

There is something more than confidence in her song. She sings with great familiarity, "My soul doth magnify the Lord, and my spirit hath rejoiced in God my Savior. For he that is mighty hath done to me great things; and holy is his name." It is the song of one who draws very near to her God in loving intimacy. I always have an idea when I listen to the reading of the liturgy, that it is a slave's worship. I do not find fault with its words or sentences; perhaps of all human compositions, the liturgical service of the Church of England is, with some exceptions, the noblest, but it is only fit for slaves or at the best for subjects. The whole service through, one feels that there is a boundary set round about the mountain, just as at Sinai. Its litany is the wail of a sinner, and not the happy triumph of a saint. The service genders unto bondage and has nothing in it of the confident spirit of adoption. It views the Lord far off, as one to be feared rather than loved, and to be dreaded rather than delighted in. I have no doubt it suits those whose experience leads them to put the Ten Commandments near the communion table, for they hereby evidence that their dealings with God are still on the terms of servants and not of sons. For my own part I want a form of worship in which I may draw near to my God, and come even to his feet, spreading my case before him and ordering my cause with arguments; talking with him as a friend talks with his friend or a child with its father; otherwise the worship is little worth to me. Our Episcopalian friends, when they come here, are naturally struck with our service, as being irreverent, because it is so much more familiar and bold than theirs. Let us carefully guard against really deserving such a criticism, and then we need not fear it; for a renewed soul yearns after that very intercourse which the formalist calls irreverent. To talk with God as my Father, to deal with him as with one whose promises are true to me, and to whom I, a sinner washed in blood, and clothed in the perfect righteousness of Christ, may come with boldness, not standing far off; I say this is a thing which the outer-court worshiper cannot understand. There are some of our hymns which speak of Christ with such familiarity that the cold critic says, "I do not like such expressions, I could not sing them." I quite agree with you, Sir Critic, that the language would not befit you, a stranger; but a child may say a thousand things which a servant must not. I remember a minister altering one of our hymns—

> Let those refuse to sing
> Who never knew our God;
> But favorites of the heavenly King
> May speak their joys abroad.

He gave it out: "But subjects of the heavenly King." Yes; and when he gave it out, I thought, "That is right; you are singing what you feel; you know nothing of discriminating grace and special manifestations, and therefore you keep to your native level, 'subjects of the heavenly King.'" But oh, my heart wants a worship in which I can feel, and express the feeling that, I am a favorite of the heavenly King, and therefore can sing his special love, his manifested favor, his sweet relationship, his mysterious union with my soul. You never get right till you ask the question, "Lord, how is it that thou will manifest thyself unto us, and not unto the world?" There is a secret which is revealed to us, and not to the outside world; an understanding which the sheep receive and not the goats. I appeal to any of you who during the week are in an official position; a judge, for instance. You have a seat on the bench, and you wear no small dignity when you are there. When you get home there is a little fellow who has very little fear of your judgeship, but much love for your person, who climbs your knee, who kisses your cheek, and says a thousand things to you which are meet and right enough as they come from him, but which you would not tolerate in court from any man living. The parable needs no interpretation.

When I read some of the prayers of Martin Luther they shock me, but I argue with myself thus: "It is true I cannot talk to God in the same way as Martin, but then perhaps Martin Luther felt and realized his adoption more than I do, and therefore was not less humble because he was more bold. It may be that he used expressions which would be out of place in the mouth of any man who had not known the Lord as he had done." O my friends, sing this day of our Lord Jesus as one near to us. Get close to Christ, read his wounds, thrust your hand into his side, put your finger into the print of the nails, and then your song shall win a sacred softness and melody not to be gained elsewhere.

I must close by observing that while her song was all this, yet how very humble it was, and how full of gratitude. The papist calls her "mother of God," but she never whispers such a thing in her song. No, it is "God my Savior"; just such words as the sinner who is speaking to you might use, and such expressions as you sinners who are hearing me can use too. She wants a Savior, she feels it; her soul rejoices because there is a Savior for her. She does not talk as though she could commend herself to him, but she hopes to stand accepted in the Beloved. Let us then take care that our familiarity has always blended with it the lowliest prostration of spirit, when we remember that he is God over all, blessed forever, and we are nothing but dust and ashes; he fills all things, and we are less than nothing and vanity.

III. The last thing was to be—*shall she sing alone?*

Yes, she must, if the only music we can bring is that of carnal delights and worldly pleasures. There will be much music tomorrow which would not chime in with hers. There will be much mirth tomorrow, and much laughter, but I am afraid the most of it would not accord with Mary's song. It will not be, "My soul doth magnify the Lord, and my spirit hath rejoiced in God my Savior." We would not stop the play of the animal spirits in young or old; we would not abate one jot of your relish of the mercies of God, so long as you break not his command by wantonness or drunkenness or excess: but still, when you have had the most of this bodily exercise, it profits little, it is only the joy of the fleeting hour, and not the happiness of the spirit which abides; and therefore Mary must sing alone, as far as you are concerned. The joy of the table is too low for Mary; the joy of the feast and the family grovels when compared with hers.

But shall she sing alone? Certainly not, if this day any of us by simple trust in Jesus can take Christ to be our own. Does the Spirit of God this day lead you to say, "I trust my soul on Jesus?" My dear friend, then you have conceived Christ: after the mystical and best sense of that word, Christ Jesus is conceived in your soul. Do you understand him as the Sin-bearer, taking away transgression? Can you see him bleeding as the substitute for men? Do you accept him as such? Does your faith put all her dependence upon what he did, upon what he is, upon what he does? Then Christ is conceived in you, and you may go your way with all the joy that Mary knew; and I was half ready to say, with something more; for the natural conception of the Savior's holy body was not one tenth so meet a theme for congratulation as the spiritual conception of the holy Jesus within your heart when he shall be in you the hope of glory. My dear friend, if Christ be yours, there is no song on earth too high, too holy for you to sing; no, there is no song which thrills from angelic lips, no note which thrills archangel's tongue in which you may not join. Even this day, the holiest, the happiest, the most glorious of words and thoughts and emotions belong to you. Use them! God help you to enjoy them; and his be the praise, while yours is the comfort evermore. Amen.

Peter's Mother-in-Law: A Lift for the Prostrate

Published on Thursday, March 22, 1906; delivered on Lord's Day evening, September 19, 1875, at the Metropolitan Tabernacle, Newington. No. 2980.

And he [Jesus] came and took her by the hand, and lifted her up; and immediately the fever left her, and she ministered unto them.—MARK 1:31

Peter's wife's mother was sick of a very terrible fever. It was no ordinary one, such as, we are told, is common in the district when she lived; but "Luke, the beloved physician," as Paul calls the Evangelist, tells us that "Simon's wife's mother was taken with a great fever." You know that it is the nature of fever to leave the patient prostrate even when the disease itself departs; but Jesus Christ not only intended to heal Peter's wife's mother, and to heal her at once, but he also meant that she should be so completely cured that she should have no lingering prostration. Christ's cures are always perfect cures, not partial ones. He does not cause the fever to go and permit the prostration to remain, but he takes away both the fever and the prostration.

It is possible that the poor patient had almost given up all hope of recovery; and, probably, those who were round about her would also have despaired if they had not had faith in the great Physician, the Lord Jesus Christ. It was, therefore, for her encouragement, and for theirs also, that our Lord bent over the bed whereon the fevered woman lay, took her by the hand, thus cheering her by showing that he was not afraid to come into contact with her, and then gently lifted her up; and she, yielding to the kindly pressure rose, and sat up—no, not merely sat up, but left the bed, being so perfectly restored that she began at once to minister to them as the housewife whose duty it was to care for their comfort.

I hope that there are many in this congregation whom Jesus Christ means to bless; but they are, at present, in a state of utter prostration; they are so despondent that their spirits sink almost to the point of despair. They cannot believe that there is mercy for them; they have relinquished all hope of that. They did, at one time, have some measure of hope, but it is all gone now. They are in the prostrate condition of Peter's mother-in-law, and they need Christ to do for them the two things which he did for her. First, *he came into contact with her;* and, second, *he gently lifted her up, and completely restored her.* May he do the like for you!

I. Our first concern, in looking after prostrate souls, is to tell them that *Jesus Christ comes into contact with them.*

You think, my poor distressed friend, that Jesus Christ will have nothing to do with you. You have read and heard about him, but he seems to you to be a long way off, and you cannot reach him; neither does it seem at all probable to you that he will ever come your way and look in pity upon you. Now listen.

In the first place, *Jesus Christ has come into contact with you,* for you are a member of the human race, of which Jesus Christ also became a member by his incarnation. Never forget that, while it is perfectly true that Christ "is over all, God blessed forever," yet it is equally true that he deigned to be born into this world, as the infant of an earthly mother, and that he condescended to live here under the same conditions as the rest of us, suffering the same weakness, and sickness, and sorrow, and death as we do, for our sakes. Never think of Jesus, I pray you, as though he were only a spirit, at whose presence you have cause to be alarmed; but think of him, as a man like yourselves, eating and drinking as others did—not a recluse, shutting himself away from sinners, but living as a man among men, the perfect specimen of manhood, the man Christ Jesus, for thus he has come near to you. You would not be afraid to speak to one of your fellowmen; then, do not be afraid to speak to Jesus. Tell him all the details of your case, for he was never a man of a proud and haughty spirit. He was not one who said, "Stand by, for I am holier than thou"; but he was a man with a great heart of love. He was so full of attractiveness that even children came and clustered around his feet, and when his disciples would have driven them away, he said, "Suffer the little children to come unto me, and forbid them not: for of such is the kingdom of God." He never repelled even the very worst of mankind when they approached him; but he longed to gather them to himself. He wept over the guilty city of Jerusalem, and said, "How often would I have gathered thy children together, even as a hen gathereth her chickens under her wings, and ye would not!" Come, then, distressed spirit, and see, in the very fact that Jesus is Emmanuel, God with us, that he has come near to you, and laid his hand upon you.

"Ah!" you say, "I can comprehend that he has come near to men; but then, I am not merely a man, but a sinful man." Yes, and *Jesus has come near to sinful men,* and his name is called Jesus because he is the Savior from sin. His work in this world was not to seek saints, but "to seek and to save that which was lost." My Master's errand was not to the good, the excellent, the righteous, but to the evil, the unholy, the unrighteous. He said, "They that are whole have no need of the physician, but they that are sick: I came not to call the righteous, but sinners to repentance." If he did not come to save sinners, why did he come as a sacrifice?

Sacrifice is only required where there is sin—an atonement is only needed where there is guilt. Christ comes to you, a guilty sinner, and he lays his hand upon you, even as he laid it upon Peter's wife's mother when she was sick with that great fever.

Do I hear you say, as in a whisper, as if you were afraid that anyone else should hear you, that you are not only a sinner, but a great sinner—that you have sinned beyond the ordinary guilt of the common mass of mankind, that there are some points in which the crimson of your guilt is of a deeper dye than that of any other man? My friend, let me assure you that *Jesus Christ came to save the chief of sinners.* Do you see him, on the cross, enduring those indescribable pangs of death? Can you hear his death cries and that soul-piercing shriek, "My God, my God, why hast thou forsaken me?" and still think that such a death as that was on behalf of little sinners' trifling offenses, mere peccadilloes or mistakes? Ah no! the Son of God came to give his life a ransom for many great sins and many great sinners. The grandeur of the atonement of Christ is a proof that its object was the removal of sin, however great that sin may be. The Son of God is himself the Savior of sinners; there must, therefore, be a colossal greatness about sin to need the Son of God to remove it, and to need that the Son of God should die before the more than Herculean labor of putting sin away could be performed; but, having put away sin by the sacrifice of himself, he is now able to save even the greatest of sinners.

That Jesus has come into contact with great sinners is very clear; or, as you read the record of his life, you see that *his preaching was constantly aimed at just such characters.* If you take a survey of his usual congregations, you will discover that they were largely made up of such characters. The Pharisees said, with contempt, but no doubt with truth, "This man receiveth sinners, and eateth with them." Just at that very time, we have the record, "Then drew near unto him all the publicans and sinners for to hear him." His preaching evidently attracted them, and he never seems to have been surprised that it did, nor to have expressed his disgust that he should have drawn around him such a low and degraded class of hearers. No; but, on the contrary, he said that he was sent to seek lost sheep till he found them, and to welcome the wandering prodigal when he came back to his Father's house. Our Lord Jesus

Christ, from the character of his congregation and the tone of his preaching, evidently came to this world on purpose to come into contact with the very worst of sinners. I want you to realize, dear friend, that my Lord Jesus Christ is a man, and that he is not a man who has come to look for congenial companions who might be worthy to be numbered among his acquaintances; but he has come to look after uncongenial men and women to whom he may bring the blessings of salvation. He has come, not to be ministered unto, but to minister; not to receive, but to bestow boons; his object in being here, in this world, is not to pick out, here and there, a noble and notable character; but to seek after souls that need his grace, and to come to them and bless and save them. So he has, in this respect, come near to you. Remember that commission of his, which he gave to his disciples a little while before he went back to heaven: "Go ye into all the world, and preach the gospel to every creature." On another occasion, after his resurrection, he reminded them "that repentance and remission of sins should be preached in his nation among all nations, beginning at Jerusalem"; that is, beginning at the very place where the people lived who had crucified him. Begin where they live who have stained their hands with my blood. Begin with them, and then go to every other creature in the whole world, and say to sinners in every part of the globe, "Whosoever believeth on the Son of God hath everlasting life." In giving that commission, our Lord Jesus Christ reached his hand across the centuries that he might touch you, and I have come here to obey his commission by preaching the gospel to you, for you are included in the term *every creature*. So Jesus Christ comes into contact with you through the preaching of his word at this very moment.

There is one solemn thought that I should like you to think of; it is this: having entered this house of prayer, and having heard the gospel, as you will have done before this service is over, *the Lord Jesus Christ has so come into contact with you that you will never lose the impress of that contact, whether you are lost or saved.* If you are lost, you will have the additional guilt of having rejected him; neither can you ever clear yourself of that guilt, do what you may. Your ears have heard the Word, so that, if you do not receive it, you will be numbered among those to whom the gospel came, but who judged themselves unworthy of everlasting life, like some of those to whom the apostle Paul preached; and, therefore, it shall condemn you. For, to everybody who hears the gospel, there is a savor in it; to some, it is a savor of death unto death, and to others a savor of life unto life. There is not a man, woman, or child who has understanding enough to know what we mean by preaching the gospel, who will be able to go out of this house of prayer without receiving some token of contact with the Lord Jesus Christ. Either his blood will be upon you to save you, or else there will be realized in you that dreadful curse which the Jews invoked upon themselves, "His blood be on us, and on our children," which abides upon them as a curse unto this day. You shall either be cleansed from guilt by the blood of Jesus, or else you shall be guilty of rejecting him, and so putting yourselves in the same category as the Jews who rejected him, and who nailed him to the accursed tree. One way or other, to be sure of this, "The kingdom of God is come unto you." It is a solemn fact to have to state this, but so it is. Jesus Christ has, in some way or other, put his hand upon you, and he is now in contact with you.

II. Leaving that point, however, I feel joy in passing on to the next one. When Jesus grasped the hand of Peter's wife's mother, *he then began gently to lift her up.*

She, willingly enough, responded to his touch; and, by at once recommencing her household duties, proved that she was perfectly healed.

Now there are some poor, prostrate, desponding souls who need somebody to give them a lift; and I would that the Lord, even while I am preaching, might take some of you by the hand and lift you up. My object will be to mention a few things which may help to give you a lift. You want to be saved; you long to be saved; but you fear that you never will be, and it is that very fear which keeps you from being saved. If you could but hope, your hope would be realized; but you do not feel as if you dared even to hope. Now give me your hand, and let me try to give you a lift.

First, remember that others who were very like what you now are, have been saved. Do you not know some people who used to be very much in the condition in which you are at the present moment? If you do not, then find out the nearest Christian friend among your acquaintance, tell him what you regard as the peculiarity of your condition, and I feel almost certain that he will say to you, "Why, that is not anything peculiar; that is just how I was before I found the Savior." If you do not find it so with the first Christian person whom you meet, you ought not to be surprised, because, of course, all Christians are not alike; but I feel sure that you will not have talked to many Christian people before you will find that what you consider to be very remarkable peculiarities in yourself will turn out to have been very common, for a great many other people have been in just the same state! I challenge you who are very despondent, to see whether you cannot find some who once were as you now are, who have been saved; and when you do find them, the reasoning is very clear. If A be saved, and B is like A, then why should not B also be saved?

"Ah!" say you, "I have very few Christian acquaintances of whom I can make inquiry." Very well, then, I will give you another simple test. Take your Bible, and block out the cases of conversion, and see whether the saved ones were not very much like you now are; and if that should not satisfy you, turn to the various promises that the Lord Jesus has made to coming sinners, and see whether there is not one that is suited to such a sinner as you are. I think that you cannot go far in an honest examination of the promises of the gospel without saying, "Well, now, it really does look as if I could squeeze in there, at any rate; I think that description just exactly meets my case." I should not be surprised if you meet with some text, of which you will say, "Why, that looks as if it had been written entirely for me; it is such an accurate description of my forlorn condition." Well, then, if you find that Christ has invited such sinners as you are, and that, according to the inspired record, he has saved such as you are, why should not you also have hope! Have you been a thief? Remember that—

> The dying thief rejoiced to see
> That fountain in its day;
> And there may you, though vile as he,
> Wash all your sins away.

Have you been a sinner in a more immodest sense? Remember that there was a woman who was "a sinner" in that very sense, who washed Christ's feet with her tears, and wiped them with the hairs of her head. Have you been a swearer? I should think that Simon Peter had been a great swearer before he was converted, or else he would not have used oaths and curses so freely when he denied his Master. Yet in spite of that old habit breaking out again, Simon Peter was not only saved, but he became one of the most useful servants of our Lord Jesus Christ. I might continue to mention all sorts of sinners, and say to you, "Such a one as you now are has been saved, and has gone to heaven; is not that a lift for you? I pray the Lord to make it so. Others like you have been saved, so why should not you also be saved? Wherefore, be of good courage, poor prostrate sinner."

Let me give you another lift. Salvation is all of grace; that is to say, it is altogether of God's free favor. God does not save any man because there is anything in him that deserves salvation. The Lord saves whomsoever he wills to save; this is one of his grand prerogatives, of which he is very tenacious. His own declaration is, "I will have mercy on whom I will have mercy; and I will have compassion on whom I will have compassion"; and Paul's conclusion from that declaration is, "So then it is not of him that willeth, nor of him that runneth, but of God that sheweth mercy." Well, now, if it be God's will to bestow his mercy upon sinners, according to his own sovereign grace in Christ Jesus, irrespective of anything good in them, why should he not show mercy to you? You have been looking for some reason in yourself why he should show mercy unto you, but you cannot find any such reason; and I can tell you that there never was any reason in sinners themselves why God should save them. He has always saved them for reasons known only to himself, which he has never revealed, and which he tells us he will not reveal. He asks, like the householder in the parable, "Is it not lawful for me to do what I will with mine own?" and so he will do. No man has any right to salvation. We have all forfeited all claim of merit; so when the Lord gives his mercy, he gives it wherever he pleases. Why, then, should he not give it to you as well as to anybody else?

I may also remind you that faith in Jesus Christ always does save the soul—simply trusting him, as we were singing just now—

> Only trust him! Only trust him!
> Only trust him now!
> He will save you! He will save you!
> He will save you now!

There have been a great many who have put this to the test, and they have found that faith in Christ has saved them. There are some people, nowadays, who tell us that this is immoral doctrine; they say that we ought to preach up good works. We do preach up good works, in the most forcible manner; for we say that faith in Jesus Christ prevents men from living in sin. We do not preach good works as a ground of salvation. That would be as foolish as children who take flowers, and stick them in the ground, and say, "Oh, what a beautiful garden we have got!" We plant the seeds of the flowers, or the roots of the flowers of grace; for faith in Jesus Christ is the seed and the root of virtue, and he that believes in Jesus Christ is saved, not merely from the punishment of sin, but from the sin itself—from the power of sin, from the habit of sin. If it be still said that this is immoral doctrine, let the thousands of men who have been saved from drunkenness, and lasciviousness, and profanity, by simply believing in Jesus, rise up, and enter their solemn protest against the wicked charge that there is anything immoral in this teaching. Immoral doctrine. Why, it has brought millions to Christ, and millions to heaven. If this doctrine could truly be called immoral, then God himself might be charged with being immoral, for this gospel assuredly came from him, and it is nothing short of blasphemy to call it immoral. Hear this gospel, sinner. You have no good works, and you will never have any until you repent of sin and trust the Lord Jesus Christ. If you try to have any, they will all break down, because the motive at the back of those supposed good works will be this: you will do them in the hope of thereby saving yourself. What is that but sheer selfishness—dead selfishness, which cannot be acceptable with God?

But, sirs, if you will only trust the Lord Jesus Christ, you shall receive the immediate pardon of your sin, and with that pardon will come heartfelt gratitude to him who gives you the pardon; and with that gratitude will come intense hatred of everything that he hates, and fervent love of everything that he loves. And then you will do good works; but from what motive? Why, out of gratitude to him; and not being the result of selfishness, they will really be good works, for they will be done with the view of pleasing God, and not as a means of getting something for yourself.

Every soul, then, that has believed in Jesus has found everlasting life, and deliverance from sin. Very well, then, you also will find the same blessings if you now confide wholly in him. They did "only trust him"; do you the same— "only trust him now." They dropped into the arms of Christ; he caught them and held them fast. Do you the same; drop now into the arms of Christ, who stands beneath you, ready to catch you, and you shall most certainly be saved. This is Christ's own declaration, "He that believeth and is baptized shall be saved." The belief is to come first, and the baptism is to follow as the confession of the belief. Christ commanded his disciples to observe that order: "Go ye therefore, and teach (or make disciples of) all nations, baptizing them (those who are made disciples) into the name of the Father, and of the Son, and of the Holy Ghost." This is what Christ himself said; so if you have believed in him, and have been baptized on profession of that faith, you are saved, just as myriads of others have been saved. I have thus tried to give you a further lift up, and I pray the Lord Jesus to take you by the hand, and lift you up, you fevered and prostrate patients, who cannot rise without his power being poured into you.

Let me try to give you a lift in another way. I think I hear you say, "O sir, I know the gospel; but, somehow, I cannot get hold of it. I know what praying means, but I cannot pray as I would. I know what repenting is, but I cannot repent as I would." Here is a text which will, I hope, give you a lift: "The Spirit also helpeth our infirmities." Can you not look up to heaven, and ask that blessed Spirit to help you now? What though your heart is hard as the nether millstone? The Spirit of God can make it soft in a moment. What though it seems impossible for you to believe in Jesus? The gracious Spirit is ready now to enable you to believe in him. What if now you seem to be the very reverse of what you ought to be? The blessed Spirit can completely change your nature. He can open the blind eye, and unstop the deaf ear, and take away the stony heart out of your flesh, and give you a heart of flesh. I know that you cannot help yourself; but I also know that the Holy Spirit can help you, for nothing is impossible unto him. Come, heavenly wind, and breathe upon these dry bones; quicken them into life and activity, so that, where there was nothing but death, there may be a living army to serve the living Lord! And, blessed be his holy name, he will do it; for wherever there is a true, heartfelt prayer for his presence, he is present already, dictating that prayer; for no one really prays until the Holy Spirit teaches him how to pray. So, you who are like Peter's wife's mother, have we been able to lift you up yet? May the Lord's almighty hand be stretched out to you, for ours alone will be too weak to lift you up.

Here is another lift for you. Notwithstanding all that I have said, you still think that you deserve to be lost, and that you must be lost, for *your being punished will show the justice of God.* That is true, as far as it goes; but let me tell you something else that is equally true. Your being saved will glorify the mercy of God, and "he delighteth in mercy." I recollect the time when I thought that, if Jesus Christ saved me, it would be the biggest thing he ever did. I thought so then, and I do not know but that I think so now; and I feel sure that, when I get to heaven, I shall still have that idea. And if you, dear friend, think the same concerning yourself, I expect you are about right. Jesus Christ, however, loves to do big things; he delights to show great mercy to great sinners; and if there is one man here who seems not to have any good point about him, but whom everybody knows as being a renowned sinner—well, I pray the Lord to save you, my friend, because then the devils in hell will hear of it, and they will be angry, and I like them to be angry for such a reason as that; and the wicked men, with whom you have been accustomed to associate, will hear of it, and they will say, "What! old Jack becomes Christian? Harry turned Baptist? I never would have believed such a thing to be possible." We like to have just such converts as these, and my Lord likes to have them too, for such victories of sovereign grace cause a great stir in the camp of the Philistines, and they begin to tremble and cry, "Who will be the next to turn?" And so the kingdom of heaven grows, and Satan's fame gets dimmed, and the fame of Jesus of Nazareth grows brighter and brighter.

"Ah!" says one, "I never looked at it in that light; for, certainly, if Jesus Christ were to save me, I should be the biggest wonder on earth." Then I think it is very likely that he will save you, for he delights to do great wonders, and to work mighty marvels. How do you think that a doctor gets to have great fame? There are some physicians in London who have so many patients waiting to see them, that the poor sufferers have to wait hour after hour before they can get in. How did those doctors get to be so celebrated? If I were to tell you they got all their fame through curing chapped hands and sore fingers and warts, you would say, "Nonsense! Nobody gets fame through doing such little things as that." How did they get their honor, then? Oh, there was a poor man who was nigh unto death; he had been given up by several other doctors, but this one was enabled by God to heal him. Or there was a man whose leg was about to be amputated, and this doctor said, "I will save that man's limb." Or there was a complicated case of internal disease, and this doctor said, "I understand that case," and he cured it, and everybody talked about the wonderful cure; and now everybody goes to that doctor. He became famous through curing bad cases; one really bad case brought him more credit than fifty minor maladies might have done. So is it with the great Physician and you big sinners with such a complication of disorders that nobody but Christ can cure you. My Lord and Master has a wondrous way of healing those who appear to be incurable; and when he cures such cases as yours, heaven and earth and hell hear of it, and it makes him famous. So I would encourage you to hope that he will save even you, though you are as prostrate as Peter's wife's mother was before Christ took her by the hand, and lifted her up. May my gracious Lord and Master help you to take encouragement from what he has done for others who were in as sad a state as you are now in!

Though your case seems so hopeless to you, or, if you have any hope of recovery, you feel that it will take a long while, I want to remind you that Jesus Christ pardons sinners in an instant. A man is as black as midnight one moment, and as bright as noonday the next. Jesus Christ lifted up upon the cross has such mighty power that, if a man had all the sins of mankind resting upon him, yet, if he did but look to Christ by faith, his sins would be all gone in a moment. Did you ever see that wonderful sculpture which represents the Laocoön and his sons with the monstrous snakes twisted all about their limbs? Well, though you should be another Laocoön, and sinful habits should be twisted all about you, so that it would be impossible for you to free yourself from them, yet, if you look to Jesus by faith, these monsters shall drop dead at your feet. Jesus Christ, the Seed of the woman, sets his foot upon the monster, sin, and breaks its head; and if you believe in Jesus, that pierced foot of his shall crush the life out of your sin, and you shall be delivered from its power. Oh, that you might have grace to trust in Jesus for instantaneous pardon, instantaneous regeneration, instantaneous deliverance from nature's darkness into God's most marvelous light! If you are as prostrate as Peter's wife's mother was, you ought not to lie still any longer when Christ is ready to give you such a lift as that.

But if you do, I bid you remember, poor desponding, despairing sinner, that he who has come to save such as you are is a divine Savior. What a death blow this ought to be to every doubt! You say that there is a difficulty in your case. Yes, there is always a difficulty where there is only finite power; there always will be difficulties where there are creatures with limited capacities; but here is the Creator—the Creator in human flesh—he who made the heavens and the earth has come down to live here as a man, and to die upon the cross, in order that he may save sinners. What difficulty can there be in the presence of Omnipotence? Talk not of difficulty in the presence of the almighty God. He has but to will anything, and it is done; to speak, and it stands fast forever. Jesus Christ, my Lord and Master, is able to save unto the uttermost all them that come unto God by him, and he is able to save them with the greatest possible ease. What an easy thing it was for Christ to bless men and women and children when he was here upon earth! A poor woman came in the crowd, and just touched the hem of his garment—she could not get near enough to touch him—but she just touched the hem of his garment with her finger; there was contact between her and Christ through her finger and the hem of his garment, and she was made whole that very instant. There were other cases in which Christ healed people who were miles away from him at the time. "Go thy way," said he to the nobleman, "thy son liveth." He had not been near him; he could work the miracle just as easily at a distance. O sinner, nothing is impossible with God. If you are sick and near unto death, Jesus Christ is able to save you. If I saw you at the very gates of hell—so long as you had not actually crossed the threshold—if I saw you trembling there, and you said to me, "Can Jesus Christ save me now?" I would reply, "Aye, my brother, look unto him, and he will take you from the gates of hell to the gates of heaven in a single moment." He said when on earth, "All manner of sin and blasphemy shall be forgiven unto men," and it is just as true today. "'Come now, and let us reason together,' saith the LORD: 'though your sins be as scarlet, they shall be as white as snow; though they be red like crimson, they shall be as wool.'"

Only trust him! Only trust him!
Only trust him now!
He will save you! He will save you!
He will save you now!

Oh, that he would bless this word to you! Christ is God as well as man. He suffered in the stead of sinners on the cross, but he lives after the suffering has been accomplished, he lives as the Savior who is mighty to save; and whoever will take him as his or her own Savior shall find it to be so this very hour.

The Samaritan Woman:
Her Mission

❧❦❧

Delivered on Lord's Day morning, September 10, 1882, at the Metropolitan Tabernacle, Newington. No. 1678.

> *And upon this came his disciples, and marveled that he talked with the woman: yet no man said, "What seekest thou?" or, "Why talkest thou with her?" The woman then left her waterpot, and went her way into the city, and saith to the men, "Come, see a man, which told me all things that ever I did: is not this the Christ?" Then they went out of the city, and came unto him.*
> —JOHN 4:27–30

Behold our Lord and Master with divinely skillful art seeking after a single soul! We must have large congregations or we are disinclined for soul winning. The habit of the age is to do nothing but what is ostentatious; every work must be with beat of drum or sound of tambourine. I pray that the Lord may work in us the steadfast desire to do good on the quiet, by stealth, when no one looks on, when not a single disciple is near. Oh, that we may have such an estimate of the value of a single soul that we count whole days well spent to bring one fallen woman or one drunkard to the Savior's feet. Blessed is he who works on though he is never heard of, and looks for his reward from his Master. In the heat of the day the Lord Jesus found rest and refreshment in speaking to one whom many would scarcely look upon, except with eyes of scorn. Blessed Savior, we do not marvel as the disciples did that you did speak with the woman, but we do wonder with a higher kind of astonishment that ever you did speak to the like of us, who have so sadly fallen, and done you dishonor, and grieved your heart. We are amazed that he who is the glory of heaven, "Light of light, very God of very God," should shroud himself in the likeness of sinful flesh and, being found in fashion as a man, should seek after us unworthy ones. Oh, the compassion of the Redeemer's heart!

Read this chapter through carefully, and see the skill which that compassion taught him. How sweetly ready he was to converse with her and take up her questions. Never imagine that the thirty years of retirement at Nazareth were wasted. I would fain go, if I were young, for thirty years to learn how to talk as he did, if his own Spirit would teach me the lesson. He was a perfect Teacher, because as man he had lent a willing ear to the heavenly instruction of the Holy Ghost, and therefore grew in knowledge and fitness for his work; as says that notable Scripture, "The Lord God hath given me the tongue of the learned, that I should know how to speak a word in season to him that is weary: he wakeneth morning by morning, he wakeneth mine ear to hear as the learned. The Lord God hath opened mine ear, and I was not rebellious, neither turned away back." By communion with God in private, and by watching men in seclusion, he learned both the mind of God and the nature of man, so as to know how to handle the human mind. Men are "kittle cattle," and can only be managed by a wise hand. Many an earnest fool has driven a soul to hell in his endeavor to drag it to heaven by force; for human wills yield not to such rough force, but rebel the more. Souls have to be brought to salvation by a gentleness and wisdom such us the Savior used when he fascinated the Samaritan woman into eternal life and enticed her to the truth: so only can I describe that wondrous power which he exercised over her in the few short but blessed sentences with which he addressed her.

Now turn a moment from that glorious One, that perfect man and yet infinite God, whom we would lovingly adore before we look away from him. Here come his disciples! They have been into the city to buy food—an errand most needful—that they and their Teacher might live. But see! *When they perceive him talking with a woman they marvel,* each in his own way. Some are dumfounded, and cannot explain the phenomenon; others look as if they would interpose if they dared, and would cry to the woman, "Away, you vixen: what right have you here, speaking to such a One as our Leader, whose shoe-latchets even we are not worthy to unloose? Your approach dishonors him: take yourself away." They did say so with their eyes, though awe of their Lord restrained their tongues. For these disciples of Jesus were steeped in the customary antipathies of the age.

First, it was sufficiently offensive that the person with whom Jesus was conversing was a woman. My beloved sisters, you owe much to the gospel, for it is only by its agency that you are raised to your proper place. For what said the rabbis? "Rather burn the sayings of the law than teach them to women"; and, again, "Let no man prolong conversation with a woman; let no one converse with a woman in the streets, not even with his own wife." Women were thought to be unfit for profound religious instruction, and altogether inferior beings. My sisters, we do not think that you are superior to us, though some of you perhaps fancy so; but we are right glad to own your equality, and to know that in Christ Jesus there is neither male nor female. Jesus has lifted you up to your true place, side by side with man. Even the apostles were tainted at first with that horrible superstition which made them marvel that Jesus openly talked with a woman. Moreover, they wondered that he could talk with such a woman! I do not suppose they knew all about her character, but there is a look about the fallen which betrays them; they cannot conceal the boldness which a course of vice usually produces. They may have thought, "If he had talked with an aged matron, a saintly mother in Israel, it might not have been surprising; but how can he converse with such a woman?" They did not as yet understand his mission to rescue the perishing and save the lost.

This poor woman also had the misfortune to be a Samaritan, and above all things Jews hated Samaritans, as aliens and heretics, who dared to call Jacob their father and to believe themselves orthodox. Jews and Samaritans were much alike, and you know the sects that approach nearest to each other usually reserve their bitterest hatred for their next of kin. They will tolerate those who are far removed from them, because they are altogether in the darkness of error, and so are somewhat excusable; but those who have so much light they detest for not seeing eye to eye with themselves. We pity a dumb man, for he cannot speak at all, but we are indignant that one who can say "Sibboleth" will not take a little more trouble and pronounce it "Shibboleth," as we do. Surely he might go that other inch and be quite right. This woman was one of those Samaritan heretics who had dared to set up an opposition temple to the one at Jerusalem, and say that they also were the people of God; so the disciples shrank from her, and marveled that Jesus did not do the same. How could so good a man mix himself up with such people? I have, myself, heard a great deal of foolishness spoken about mixing up with certain people, because we dare to meet with them upon some common ground to accomplish a right purpose. I have sometimes wondered whether people ever read of Abraham when he fought for the cause of the king of Sodom. A horrible man, I have no doubt, that monarch was, yet when his country had been plundered by the invading kings, Abraham marched out on behalf of the king of Sodom; not that he cared for him, but that he desired to deliver his nephew Lot. For that reason he is found in some measure of association with Sodom's king; but when the object upon which they were united was achieved, then see how the princely Abraham washes his hands of the man. He says, "I will not take of thee from a thread even to a shoe-latchet, lest thou shouldest say, 'I have made Abraham rich.'" Thus there may be a temporary union among men, between whom there is the widest difference, and this apparent unity may be lawful and expedient because the end to be gained is altogether good. Our blessed Lord was seeking the good of this unholy woman, and therefore he was fully justified in talking with her. Thereby he rebuked the superstition of his followers more effectually than by words.

There is another side to the question. How could these disciples marvel that he spoke with anybody, after having chosen them and called them? Surely, when they frowned on others they forgot the dunghills where they grew. If they had only remembered where they were when he found them, and how often they had grieved him by their perverseness, they would have reserved their surprise for their own cases. Ah, brethren, ever since the Lord spoke with me, I have never marveled that he spoke with anybody: it has not crossed my mind to make it any subject of wonder that he should stoop to the lowest and meanest now that he has stooped to me; yet I fancy I have seen in certain brethren evident signs that they forget that they were themselves once strangers in Egypt. They forget that grace washed and cleansed them, or else they would have been filthy still, for Paul truly said, "such were some of you." I am sorry when saved ones affect superfine purity and marvelous spirituality, and turn away from such as Jesus would have welcomed. Alas, such disciples have little of the tenderness of their Master! Our divine Lord has more tenderness for sinners than the whole of us put together. There is more love in his soul toward lost ones than there is in all these thousands of believers here present, though I hope that many of your hearts beat high with a loving desire that the guilty may be delivered from the wrath to come.

But look at the disciples! See, yonder is John, that sweet-souled John, and yet he marvels: and there is Peter, good but faulty, and he marvels: and there is Thomas the thoughtful, and he marvels. They are all good men, and yet they are marveling that Jesus is gracious to a poor woman. O Peter and John and James and the rest of you, look into your own hearts, and let a glance of the Holy Spirit lighten up the darkness of your spirits, and you will renounce this self-righteous marveling which grieves the woman, and you will enter into deeper sympathy with your Lord's love. Dear friends, let us never disdain the worst of men or women, but seek with all our might to woo and win them for our Lord. Oh, to have bowels of mercies as Jesus had! This will well become the followers of the compassionate Son of man.

See, as the result of this conduct of the disciples, one of the sweetest conferences that was ever held was broken up, and brought to a close at its very climax. Just when Jesus had said, "I that speak unto thee am he," then it must end, for here they come, these cold, unsympathetic ones. Yet they were disciples, were they not? Oh, yes, and true disciples too; but alas, no breakers of communion are more blamable or more frequent in the offense than Christ's own disciples when they are out of sympathy with their Master. You see, they are thinking about the meat, and about the Savior's need of it: and these thoughts were most proper, but not very elevated or spiritual; and they come wondering that Jesus speaks with a woman, and so the holy conference ends, and the woman must go. Oh, when any of you draw near to Christ, and he is just lifting the silver veil from his dear face, and your eyes are beginning to behold him, mind that you keep your door shut. "Oh, but it is a good man at the door." Yes, but he will be just as likely to mar your fellowship as anybody else. The best of men may sometimes intrude between you and the Well Beloved, and fellowship which seemed as if it must mellow into heaven itself will come to a speedy and sorrowful close. I do not blame Peter that he wanted tabernacles in which to remain upon the top of the mount, for he was pretty well aware of what he might meet upon the plain. Do you not often wish that you could sing—

> Sequestered from the noise and strife,
> The lust, the pomp, and pride of life;
> For heaven I will my heart prepare,
> And have my conversation there.

Although the conference was thus broken up, the consequence thereof was the Lord's glory, even as often out of evil he works good. Since the woman cannot sit and gaze upon the divine face of her Lord, nor hear the strange music which flowed from his blessed lips, she will give herself to holy activity: she goes her way to the city, and she speaks to the men. This is well: there is little to deplore when men's hearts are so right that you cannot take them off from glorifying Christ, do what you may; when if you disturb their private communion they are ready at once for public service. Driven away from sitting, like Mary, at the Master's feet, let us rise to play the Martha, by preparing a table for the Lord. Always reckon, dear friends, whenever you are taken off from your usual course of life, as it were by a jerk, that the Lord has some special work for you to do. Do not fret, or try to buck the engine to get on the old lines again. No, if the switch is turned by the divine Hand, go on; he that has the management of all the railroads of your life knows better which way your soul should go than you yourself can know. I have observed Christian people jerked out of a pious family where they were extremely happy, and placed in the midst of ungodliness, a situation not of their own choosing or seeking, but appointed of the Lord, that they may bring godliness into that house, and shed light in the midst of the darkness. Friend, you, too, may be taken away from this church where your soul has flourished, and you may feel like one banished and bereaved. Well, never mind. If you are sent to some church where everything is dreary and dead, go there like a firebrand to set them on flame. Your Lord would not have permitted the breaking up of your peace unless he had some high service for you. Since you are his servant, find out his will, and do it. God will thus honor himself in you, and by and by he will honor and comfort you also.

Observe that *the woman now becomes a messenger for Christ*. She has to quit conferring with him to go and testify about him. She did not go unbidden though, for she recollected that the Lord had said at an early period of the conversation, "Go, call thy husband, and come hither." So she goes to call her husband. It is well to have a warrant for what we do. Observe, she interprets her orders very liberally. She thought as the Christ had said, "Thou hast had five husbands, and he whom thou now hast is not thy husband," he could not have limited her errand to one who was not her husband except in name, and so she might as well call any of the six men with whom she had dwelled, and therefore she might speak to all the men who were loitering about the public square, and tell them what she had seen. Remember how our Savior gave a large interpretation of his own prophetic mission. He was not sent as a teacher except to the lost sheep of the house of Israel, but he went to the very edge of his diocese, if he did not go over it. He went to the borders of Tyre and Sidon, and when a woman came out of those parts he had healing for her daughter; though he did sow most of his seed upon the acres of the Holy Land, yet he made it fly over the boundary; in fact, he sowed all the ages, and on this once barbarous island there have fallen blessed handfuls which are bringing forth fruit to his glory. Always go to the verge of your commission, never stop short of it. Try to do more good than you can, and it is very possible that you will be successful. Indeed, if you only try to do what you can do, you will do little; but when in faith you attempt what you cannot alone accomplish, God will be at your back, and in your weakness his strength shall be made clear.

Notice that *the woman leaves her waterpot*. The Spirit of God thought well to record this circumstance, and therefore I think there must be a measure of teaching in it. She left her waterpot, first, for speed. Perhaps you have got it into your head that it was an ordinary English waterpot, such as you water the garden with; possibly you so picture it, rose and all. Nothing of the sort: it was a big jar, or large pitcher of earthenware, she had to carry on her head or her shoulder, quite a load for her, and so she left it that she might run the more quickly. She was a wise woman to leave her waterpot when she wanted to move rapidly. Others think she did so because she was so taken up with her errand that she forgot her pitcher. It is blessed forgetfulness which comes of absorption in a holy design. When the King's business requires haste, it is wise to leave behind everything that would hinder. Our Lord Jesus himself forgot his hunger in his zeal to guide a soul to peace, and it is said of him in the psalm, "I forget to eat my bread." He was so absorbed in his heavenly work that he said, "I have meat to eat that ye know not of." A man has hardly felt the power of eternal things unless at times he forgets some earthly matters. If a roan [horse] is called to rush for his life through a room full of crockery there will, probably, be a number of breakages. You cannot think of everything at once; your mind is limited, and it is not advisable that you should divide the strength of your thoughts by having two or more aims. So she left her water-pot. Without thought she hit upon as good an action as thought would have suggested. The waterpot would have hindered her, but it might be useful to the Christ and his disciples. Thus they could give him to drink. He was thirsty, and probably so were they, and with her pitcher they could help themselves. Besides, it was a pledge that she was coming back. She said thereby, "I am running away on an errand, but I shall come back again. I have not listened to the great Teacher for the last time. I shall return and hear him further, till I know him better and trust him more fully." So it was significant that she left her waterpot. Sometimes you will have to leave your shop to win a soul. You will cast up a row of figures wrongly and wonder why; and the reason will be that before your mind there fluttered the soul of a swearer or the figure of a drunkard, or the image of a fallen woman, and your heart was filled with the longing to find the lost sheep. Never mind. I daresay the woman had her waterpot again, and you will get back to business again, and rectify your blunder, and attend to the shop, and set all matters right; and if a soul is saved, you will have made a profit by any loss you have sustained.

We have started the woman on her mission; now I want you to *observe particularly her mode of address,* for there is teaching here. She said to the men, "Come, see a man that told me all things that ever I did: is not this the Christ?" Observe first, when she did go back to the men she had but one aim, and that was to bring them to Jesus. She cries, "Come, see." She did not tell them anything about their sin at the time, nor try to reform their habits; she called them at once to him who could set them right. She knew that if she could bring them to Christ all things would come right inevitably. It is good for you to shoot only at one target. Choose your design and aim at it, and not at two objects. Drive away at the souls of men in the name of God to get them to Christ, and nothing short of him. Labor for this; be willing to live for this, and to die for this, that men may be saved by Emmanuel's love and blood and Spirit. This Samaritan woman aimed at this object and tried to gain it by an exceedingly earnest address. I warrant you she said it very prettily, "Come, come, come, see a man that told me all things that ever I did": perhaps with all her charms, with all the softness of her winsome tongue, with all the entreaty of her bright eyes, she cried, "Come, every one of you; come, see for yourselves, a man which told me all things that ever I did." If you go upon the Lord's errands, take your heart with you; speak every single syllable earnestly; and if you are thoroughly alive you will not need to be taught the way of doing it. The way comes naturally to those whose hearts are set upon the end.

She spoke self-forgetfully: she seemed entirely to have forgotten herself, and yet she remembered herself—a paradox, but not a contradiction. She said, "Come, see a man, which told me all things that ever I did." She quoted herself, and yet if she had thought of herself she would not have said a word on the subject of her own life. She might have feared that the men would have replied, "A pretty story that must be!" They knew her well, and might have turned around and said, "You are a beauty, to come here and talk to us in this style!" No; she let them talk of her as they pleased. "Come, see a man, which told me all things that ever I did." That putting aside of all affectation, that genuine simplicity, was part of her power. Never try to be otherwise than you are. If you have been a great sinner, be ashamed of it, but do not be ashamed of that love which saved you from it, so as to refuse to bear witness to its power. Put away the thought of what people will think of you, and only look to what they will think of Jesus for having forgiven and renewed you.

Note how short she was. Ralph Erskine calls her the female preacher. I am not so sure of the correctness of the title. If women preached just as long as she did, and no longer, no one could find fault with them; her testimony lies all in one verse, and is just an invitation and a question. There needed no more words; no, not another half a word. She said exactly enough; for she was successful in leading the men to Jesus, who could do the preaching far better than she could. I cannot call her words a sermon; at any rate, you would not care for me to preach so briefly. However, brevity is a great virtue. Do not crave to be fluent, only ask to be earnest.

Then, how vivacious she was. "Come, see a man." The words are all alive, and very far from being dull and heavy. "Come, see." It is almost as laconic as Julius Caesar's famous dispatch: "I came, I saw, I conquered." "Come, see a man, which told me all things that ever I did: is not this the Christ?"

Then, it was so sensible. There is a dispute about the exact force of what the woman said, but most of those who give us precise translations differ from our common version. It is what she meant and believed, but not exactly what she said. She probably said, "Come, see a man, which told me all things that ever I did: can this be the Christ?"—or, "This is not the Christ, is he?" She did not say he was, but she suggested it with great modesty for the men to examine. She believed that Jesus was the Christ, but she knew that men do not like to be taught by such as she, and so she humbly threw it out for their examination. "Can this be the anointed One whom we are expecting? Come and judge." She did not express all she believed, lest she should provoke them to opposition; she was adroit and wise. She fished after the manner of her Master, for she could not but feel how dexterously he had fished for her. She was an apt scholar, and humbly copied the Friend who had blessed her: "Come, see a man, which told me all things that ever I did: can this possibly be the Christ?" This led them to come, if it was only to set the woman right. Possibly they thought her a poor, mistaken body; but in their superior wisdom they would look into the matter, and so the thing she desired was granted her. Oh, to have our wits about us for Jesus!

But the argument is exceedingly strong, let her put it how she may. "This man has told me all things that ever I did." She might have said, if she thought it wise to say it, "He must be the Christ"; and that is my last point, namely, the grand argument drawn from herself, and adapted to the men. Observe the force of her reasoning. His power to read her heart and manifest her to herself was conclusive evidence to her that a special anointing was upon him.

But before I get at that, I must have you examine more fully the whole of the woman's little message, of which it was a part. It divides itself into two parts. You have been looking for "first and second" all this while, and now you shall have them. There are two parts in her sermon. The first is the invitation: "Come, see a man, which told me all things that ever I did"; the second is the argument: "Is not this the Christ?"

I. Consider at once *the invitation.*

It is a clever as well as a genuine and hearty invitation. She says, "Come, see." This was putting it most fairly, and men like a fair proposal, and the Holy Spirit works by means which suit the mind. She does not say, "You must and shall believe what I say." No, no; she is too sensible; she says, "Come and see for yourselves," and that is exactly what I want to say to every unconverted person here this morning. My Lord Jesus is the most precious Savior that I ever dreamed of. Come and test him. He is altogether lovely, and he has blessed my soul unspeakably, but I do not want you to believe because of my saying, "Come and see for yourselves." Can anything be fairer? Seek him by prayer; trust him by faith; test his gospel for yourselves. It is an old-fashioned exhortation: "O taste and see that the Lord is good," and, again, "'Prove me now,' saith the LORD of hosts." In fact, this is Christ's own word to the first disciples, "Come and see," and they used it when pleading with others, saying to them, "Come and see."

Moreover, this woman's invitation throws the responsibility upon them. She says, "Come and see." Thus would I say to you—If you do not come and see, I cannot help it, and I cannot help you either. I cannot stand sponsor for you: use your own judgments and clear your own consciences. Come and see on your own accounts. If you do not, then the blame must rest with you. If you do, then your personal investigation will be sure to end in a blessing. O dear hearers, I may preach the gospel to you, but I cannot go to Christ in your stead. It is mine to entreat and persuade, and to use every kind of means by which I may get you to the Savior; but it is a personal matter with each of you. Oh, that the Holy Spirit would lead you to come yourselves to Jesus; for it must be your own act and deed through his blessed working upon your nature. You must come; you must repent; you must believe; you must lay hold on eternal life for yourselves. Nothing but personal religion can possibly save you. The woman's call was a good exhortation in that respect.

Then, is it not pleasantly put, so as to prove the sympathy of the speaker? She does not say, as she might have said, "Go, see a man." No, "*Come,* see a man," as much as to say, "Come along; I will go with you and lead the way. You shall not say I have seen enough of him and do not care to go again, and now want to send you packing there alone because I am tired of him. No; come! Come along; come with me—we will all go together. The more I have seen of him, the more I want to see. Come, see the wondrous man." Dear friends, when you try to win a soul do not try the "go" system, but use the "come" system. When man cries, "I cannot go to Christ," or, "I will not go to Christ," look at him through your tears and cry out, "Friend, I am a sinner like yourself, and have no hope but in the precious blood of Jesus. Come, let me pray with you, let us go to Jesus together." Then, when you pray, do not say, "Lord, I am one of your saints, and come to you bringing this sinner." That may be true, but it is not a wise way of speaking. Cry, "Lord, here are two sinners that deserve your wrath, and we come to ask you in your pity to give the Savior to us, and renew our hearts by your Spirit." That is the way God helps soul winners to draw others. When we say, "Come," let us lead the way ourselves. What you wish another to do, it will be wise to do yourself, for example has more power than precept. How would you like the sinner to turn around upon you and say, "You may well give away advice when you do not intend to use it yourself." No; but, "Come, see a man, which told me all things that ever I did." A sister's heart spoke out in that word, *come.*

Again, what a blessed vanishing of the speaker there is. I have heard of brethren whose preaching is spoiled because they are so self-conscious. The man wishes you to feel that he is speaking in first-rate style, and is an eminent divine. When he has finished, the common exclamation is "I never heard such a clever man." But he was not so wise as he might have been or should have been, for he who preaches rightly makes you forget himself; in fact, the observation about him, if it comes out at all, is in this fashion: "I did not detect any eloquence; anybody might have talked like that, but somehow I have felt as I never felt before." The fish knows little about the angler, but he knows when he has swallowed the hook. When the truth has gone right home to the hearer's heart, the form of speech is of little consequence. This woman does not say anything to make the Samaritan men admire herself, but she draws to Jesus with the exhortation, "Come, see a man." What she does mention about herself is with the design of extolling the Savior. That is a grand sentence of John the Baptist, "He must increase, but I must decrease." Less, less, less of John, that there may be all the more of Christ. There is but one great universe, and Christ and you are in it. The more space you occupy, there must be so much the less for Jesus. When you get less and less, there is more for Jesus; and when you reach the vanishing point then Jesus is all in all; and that is exactly what you should aim at. This sensible woman's invitation deserves to be copied by every worker.

II. Now for *the argument*, with which I close.

An argument lies concealed here, and if you look at the text a minute or two you will discover it. She conceals it because she is persuaded that they have already agreed to it. It is this: "If Jesus be the Christ, the Anointed, then it is fit that you should come with me and see him." She does not argue that point, because every Samaritan agreed to it. If Jesus be the Christ, then we ought to go and listen to him, look at him, and become his followers. Alas, my dear hearers, I am obliged to urge that argument with many of you, because you are not so practical as these Samaritans. You believe that Jesus is the Christ; I suppose every man and woman of you does that: why, then, do you not believe in him as your Savior? You never had a doubt about his Godhead: why is he not your God? "If I tell you the truth," says Christ, "why do you not believe me?" If this be the anointed One whom God has sent to take away the sins of men, why have you not sought him that he may rid you of your sins? If this be the propitiation which God has set forth, why have you not accepted this propitiation? If this be the fountain wherein sin can be washed away, why are you not washed? There is no reason in your course of action; it is illogical and irrational. If there be a Savior, the man who is taught right reason vows that he will have him; if there be a fountain that can wash away sin, he resolves to be washed in it; if he can get right with God by any process, he hastens to be rectified. I say, this woman did not argue the point, because it did not need arguing. It goes without saying, and there let it stand.

But what she did argue was this: "This man who was just now sitting on the well, is he not the Christ?" How did she prove it? First, she did as good as say, "He must be Christ, *because he has revealed me to myself:* he has told me all things that ever I did." The words are wide. Stop, dear woman; surely he has not revealed all your life, certainly not in words. He has revealed your unchastity, but nothing else. But she was right. Were you ever out in a black and murky night when a single lightning flash has come? It has only smitten one oak in the field, but in so doing it has revealed all the landscape. It struck one object, but all around you was light as day for the moment. So when the Lord Jesus Christ revealed this woman's lustfulness, she saw clearly the whole of her life at a single view, and the Lord had indeed told her all things that ever she did. Do you wonder that she said, "Is not this the Christ?"

Beloved, no one proves himself to be truly anointed unless he begins by showing you your sins. If any teacher leads you to hope that, without repentance, or any sense of sin, you may be saved, he is not of Christ. I charge you fling away any hope which is not consistent with your own entire hopelessness apart from Jesus. If you have not known yourself a sinner, you cannot know Christ as a Savior. Some are preaching up nowadays a dry-eyed faith and men seem to jump into assurance as if there were no new birth, no conviction of sin, and no repentance. But it is not so: "Ye must be born again." That birth is not without pangs. Trust in Christ brings a hatred of sin and a mourning because of it. A man cannot hate what he does not know; but this woman was made to see her sin, and that sight proved that the Messiah was dealing with her. The non-repentance prophets cry, "Peace, peace," where there is no peace: they film [cover] the sore, but Jesus puts the lancet into it, lays it wide open, and makes the patient see the gangrene of the wound, and then he closes it up, and with his heavenly ointment makes a sure cure of it. There is no binding up the heart that was never broken: there is no comforting a man who has always been comfortable: there is no making a man righteous who always was righteous: there is no washing a man who has no filthiness. No, and this is what the Messiah does: he lays bare the disease, and this is a proof that he is sent of God, because he does not adopt the flimsy, flattering mode of deceivers, but goes straight to the truth. Her argument is, he must be the Messiah, for he has revealed me to myself.

Second, *he must be the Messiah, for he has revealed himself to me.* "No sooner did I see my filthiness than I saw at once that he was every way ready to cleanse me." A sinner's eye is never ready to see the Savior till first it has seen the sin. When the man sees despair written across the face of human strength, then he turns and sees hope mildly beaming from the kind eyes of the Son of man: but not till then. Jesus has revealed himself, and now she says, "I see that he knows me, and knows all about me." Wonderful it is how the gospel robe exactly fits a man: when he gets it and puts it on he feels that he who made this garment knew his form. Perhaps you have some special weakness or singular deformity; but you soon perceive that Jesus knew all about it, for his salvation exactly meets the lack. There is a bath: ah, he knew I was filthy. There is a robe: ah, he knew I was naked. There is eye salve: he knew that I was blind. Here is a ring for my finger: he knew I wanted a forget-me-not to keep me in memory of mercy received. Here are shoes for my bare feet, and a banquet for my griping hunger. Every want is forestalled, and this proves the omniscience of my Savior. "Therefore," said she, "he knows all about me: he must be infinitely wise; he must be the Christ." This is good arguing, is it not?

Then she seemed to say to them too, "This is more to me a great deal than it can be to you, *for he has dealt personally with me;* therefore I abide in my assurance that he is the Christ: but go and learn the same arguments for yourselves." Brethren, if the Lord Jesus Christ had told this woman all that ever her third husband did, it would have had far less power over her than telling her all she had done herself. When conviction comes personally home, and the discovery is all about your own state and character, it has a special power over your heart and mind to make you say, "This is the Christ." Also, my brethren, at the remembrance of my Lord's surgery when I was wounded and sorely broken, I am ready to cry, "See how he handles me. Never was a hand so strong and yet so tender: never a physician with such a lion's heart and such a lady's hand. I can feel his strength as he upholds me, and I can feel his tenderness as he embraces me. Surely he is the Anointed, and sent of the Lord to bind up the brokenhearted, for he has bound up my broken heart. The case is proved to me: come and experience the like conviction within yourselves."

Moreover, and perhaps there is force in this which has not been noticed, she says, "Come, see," as much as to say, *"You may come, I know,* for when I came to the well, he did not look daggers at me; and when I did not give him water, he did not grow hot with me and say, 'Disrespectful woman, I will not speak to you.' No, but I was at home with him in a moment. Come, see a man who made himself so at home with me that he told me all that ever I did. I am sure he must be the Messiah. The Messiah is to come to open the blind eyes, and he must needs be among the blind to perform the miracle. He is to fetch prisoners out of prison, and they are the lowest class that are in prison, and yet he goes to them. So, come along. I will go first and introduce you to him."

That is the woman's little speech, and how good it is! I am going to add a bit to it which she did not know, but which we know. I wish I knew how to say something that would make you unconverted ones hurry to Christ, but if anything ought to do so it is this. Suppose you never do come to Christ in this life, and die without him. God grant you may not die without having listened to him and received him; but if you do you will be wakened up at the last day from your grave with the blast of a terrible trumpet, and with the cry of "Come to judgment! Come to judgment! Come away!" Whether you will or not, you will have to come, and see a man sitting upon the great white throne, judging the nations; and do you know what he will do with you then? He will tell you all things that ever you did, and as the scenes pass before your mind's eye, and as your own words go ringing again through your ear, you will be sorely distressed. Perhaps this morning's scene will be revived before you, and conscience will tell you, "You were at the tabernacle that morning; the gospel was put plainly to you, by one who in his heart longed for you to be saved; but you did dispute to all those entreaties, and turned away." I tell you it will be your hell for Jesus to tell you all things that ever you did, and you then will see the argument: "Is not this the Christ?" But alas, he will be no Savior to you, for you refused him. He will then tell you, "I called, but you refused; I stretched out my hands, but no man regarded." Still shall proceed that awful tale of all things that ever you did, concluding with this—you refused mercy, you rejected Jesus, you turned away from salvation, you would not have this man to save you, and therefore have you come to have your past made the fuel for your everlasting burning. God grant that no one here may ever come to that. No, if I had the task to select one man out of this congregation that would have to spend an eternity in having his life rehearsed to him, where should I find him? No, I cannot see one that I dare to pitch upon, not one—not one—not even the worst man or woman here. I would not if I could. O God, of thy mercy suffer no one here to know the terror of being driven away forever from thy presence and the glory of thy power, for Jesus' sake. Amen.

The Canaanite Woman:
The Little Dogs

Delivered on Lord's Day morning, August 6, 1876, at the Metropolitan Tabernacle, Newington. No. 1309.

But he answered and said, "It is not meet to take the children's bread, and to cast it to dogs." And she said, "Truth, Lord: yet the dogs eat of the crumbs which fall from their masters' table."—MATTHEW 15:26–27

But Jesus said unto her, "Let the children first be filled: for it is not meet to take the children's bread, and to cast it unto the dogs." And she answered and said unto him, "Yes, Lord: yet the dogs under the table eat of the children's crumbs."—MARK 7:27–28

I take the two records of Matthew and Mark that we may have the whole matter before us. May the Holy Spirit bless our meditations thereon.

The brightest jewels are often found in the darkest places. Christ had not found such faith, no, not in Israel, as he discovered in this poor Canaanite woman. The borders and fringes of the land were more fruitful than the center, where the husbandry had been more abundant. In the headlands of the field, where the farmer does not expect to grow much beyond weeds, the Lord Jesus found the richest ear of corn that as yet had filled his sheaf. Let those of us who reap after him be encouraged to expect the same experience. Never let us speak of any district as too depraved to yield us converts, nor of any class of persons as too fallen to become believers. Let us go even to the borders of Tyre and Sidon, though the land be under a curse, for even there we shall discover some elect one, ordained to be a jewel for the Redeemer's crown. Our heavenly Father has children everywhere.

In spiritual things it is found that the best plants often grow in the most barren soil. Solomon spoke of trees, and discoursed concerning the hyssop on the wall and the cedar in Lebanon. So is it in the natural world, the great trees are found on great mountains and the minor plants in places adapted for their tiny roots; but it is not so among the plants of the Lord's right-hand planting, for there we have seen the cedar grow upon the wall—great saints in places where it was apparently impossible for them to exist; and we have seen hyssops growing upon Lebanon—a questionable, insignificant piety, where there have been innumerable advantages. The Lord is able to make strong faith exist with little knowledge, little present enjoyment, and little encouragement; and strong faith in such conditions triumphs and conquers, and doubly glorifies the grace of God. Such was this Canaanite woman, a cedar growing where soil was scant enough. She was a woman of amazing faith, though she could have heard but little of him in whom she believed, and perhaps had never seen his person at all until the day when she fell at his feet and said, "Lord, help me!"

Our Lord had a very quick eye for spying faith. If the jewel was lying in the mire, his eye caught its glitter; if there was a choice ear of wheat among the thorns, he failed not to perceive it. Faith has a strong attraction for the Lord Jesus; at the sight of it, "the king is held in the galleries" and cries, "Thou hast ravished my heart with one of thine eyes, with one chain of thy neck." The Lord Jesus was charmed with the fair jewel of this woman's faith, and watching it and delighting in it, he resolved to turn it around and set it in other lights, that the various facets of this priceless diamond might each one flash its brilliance and delight his soul. Therefore he tried her faith by his silence, and by his discouraging replies, that he might see its strength; but he was all the while delighting in it, and secretly sustaining it, and when he had sufficiently tried it, he brought it forth as gold, and set his own royal mark upon it in these memorable words: "O woman, great is thy faith; be it unto thee even as thou wilt."

I am hopeful this morning that perhaps some poor soul in this place under very discouraging circumstances may nevertheless be led to believe in the Lord Jesus Christ with a strong and persevering faith, and though as yet it enjoys no peace, and has seen no gracious answer to prayer, I trust that its struggling faith may be strengthened this morning by the example of the Canaanite woman.

I gather, from the story of her appeal to the Lord Jesus and her success therein, four facts. The first is, *faith's mouth cannot be closed*; the second is, *faith never disputes with God*; third, I perceive that *faith argues mightily*; and fourth, that *faith wins her suit*.

I. The mouth of faith can never be closed, for if ever the faith of a woman was tried so as to make her cease from prayer, it was that of this daughter of Tyre.

She had difficulty after difficulty to encounter, and yet she could not be put off from pleading for her little daughter, because she believed in Jesus as the great Messiah, able to heal all manner of diseases, and she meant to pray to him until he yielded to her importunity, for she was confident that he could chase the demon from her child.

Observe that *the mouth of faith cannot be closed even on account of the closed ear and the closed mouth of Christ.* He answered her never a word. She spoke very piteously, she came and threw herself at his feet, her child's case was very urgent, her motherly heart was very tender, and her cries were very piercing, and yet he answered her never a word: as if he were deaf and dumb, he passed her by; yet was she not staggered; she believed in him, and even he himself could not make her doubt him, let him try silence even if he would. It is hard to believe when prayer seems to be a failure. I would to God that some poor seeker here might believe that Jesus Christ is able and willing to save, and so fully believe it that his unanswered prayers shall not be able to make him doubt. Even if you should pray in vain by the month together, do not allow a doubt about the Lord Jesus and his power to save to cross your mind. What if you cannot yet grasp the peace which faith must ultimately bring you, what if you have no certainty of forgiveness of your sin, what if no gleams of joy should visit your spirit, yet believe you him who cannot lie. "Though he slay me," said Job, "yet will I trust in him." That was splendid faith. It would be a great deal for some if they could say, "Though he smite me, yet will I trust him," but Job said, "Though he slay me." If he put on the garb of an executioner, and come out against me as though he would destroy me, yet will I believe him to be full of love: he is good and gracious still, I cannot doubt it, and therefore at his feet I will lie down and look up, expecting grace at his hands. Oh, for such faith as this! O soul, if you have it, you are a saved man, as sure as you are alive. If even the Lord's apparent refusal to bless you cannot close your mouth, your faith is of a noble sort, and salvation is yours.

In the next place, *her faith could not be silenced by the conduct of the disciples.* They did not treat her well, but yet perhaps not altogether ill. They were not like their Master, but frequently repulsed those who would come to him. Her noise annoyed them, she kept to them with boundless perseverance, and therefore they said, "Send her away, for she crieth *after us.*" Poor soul, she never cried after *them,* it was after their Master. Sometimes disciples become very important in their own eyes, and think that the pushing and crowding to hear the gospel is caused by the people's eagerness to hear them, whereas nobody would care for their poor talk if it were not for the gospel message which they are charged to deliver. Give us any other theme, and the multitude would soon melt away. Though weary of the woman's importunate cries, they acted somewhat kindly toward her, for they were evidently desirous that she should obtain the boon she sought, or else our Lord's reply would not have been appropriate, "I am not sent save to the lost sheep of the house of Israel." It was not her daughter's healing that they cared for, but they consulted their own comfort, for they were anxious to be rid of her. "Send her away," said they, "for she crieth after us." Still, though they did not treat her as men should treat a woman, as disciples should treat a seeker, as Christians should treat everybody, yet for all that, her mouth was not stopped. Peter, I have no doubt, looked in a very scowling manner, and perhaps even John became a little impatient, for he had a quick temper by nature; Andrew and Philip and the rest of them considered her very impertinent and presumptuous; but she thought of her little daughter at home, and of the horrible miseries to which the demon subjected her, and so she pressed up to the Savior's feet and said, "Lord, help me." Cold, hard words and unkind, unsympathetic behavior could not prevent her pleading with him in whom she believed. Ah, poor sinner, perhaps you are saying, "I am longing to be saved, but such and such a good Christian man has dealt very bitterly with me; he has doubted my sincerity and questioned the reality of my repentance, and caused me the deepest sorrow; it seems as if he did not wish me to be saved." Ah, dear friend, this is very trying, but if you have true faith in the Master, you will not mind us disciples, neither the gentlest of us, nor the most crooked of us, but just urge on your suit with your Lord till he deigns to give you an answer of peace.

Her mouth, again, was not closed by exclusive doctrine, which appeared to confine the blessing to a favored few: the Lord Jesus Christ said, "I am not sent save to the lost sheep of the house of Israel," and though properly understood, there is nothing very severe in it, yet the sentence must have fallen on the woman's heart like a talent of lead. "Alas," she might have thought, "then he is not sent to me; vainly do I seek for that which he reserves for the Jews." Now the doctrine of election, which is assuredly taught in Scripture, ought not to hinder any soul from coming to Christ, for if properly understood, it would rather encourage than discourage; and yet often to the uninstructed ear the doctrine of the divine choice of a people from before the foundation of the world acts with very depressing effect.

We have known poor seekers mournfully say, "Perhaps there is no mercy for me; I may be among those for whom no purpose of mercy has been formed." They have been tempted to cease from prayer for fear they should not have been predestinated unto eternal life. Ah, dear soul, if you have the faith of God's elect in you, you will not be kept back by any self-condemning inferences drawn from the secret things of God, but you will believe in that which has been clearly revealed, and you will be assured that this cannot contradict the secret decrees of heaven. What though our Lord was only sent to the house of Israel, yet there is a house of Israel not after the flesh but after the spirit, and therefore the Syrophenician woman was included even where she thought she was shut out, and you may also be comprehended within those lines of gracious destiny which now distress you. At any rate, say to yourself, "In the election of grace others are included who were as sinful as I have been, why should not I? Others have been included who were as full of distress as I have been on account of sin, and why should not I be also?" Reasoning thus you will press forward, in hope believing against hope, suffering no plausible deduction from the doctrine of Scripture to prevent your believing in the appointed Redeemer.

The mouth of faith in this case was not even closed by a sense of admitted unworthiness. Christ spoke of dogs: he meant that the gentiles were to Israel as the dogs: she did not at all dispute it, but yielded the point by saying, "Truth, Lord." She felt she was only worthy to be compared to a dog. I have no doubt her sense of unworthiness was very deep. She did not expect to win the boon she sought for on account of any merit of her own; she depended upon the goodness of Christ's heart, not on the goodness of her cause, and upon the excellence of his power rather than upon the prevalence of her plea; yet conscious as she was that she was only a poor gentile dog, her prayers were not hindered; she cried, notwithstanding all, "Lord, help me." O sinner, if you feel yourself to be the worst sinner out of hell, still pray, believingly pray for mercy. If your sense of unworthiness be enough to drive you to self-destruction, yet I beseech you, out of the depths, out of the dungeon of self-loathing, still cry unto God; for your salvation rests in no measure or degree upon yourself, or upon anything that you are or have been or can be. You need to be saved *from* yourself, not *by* yourself. It is yours to be empty that Jesus may fill you; yours to confess your filthiness that he may wash you; yours to be less than nothing that Jesus may be everything to you. Suffer not the number, blackness, frequency, or heinousness of your transgressions to silence your prayers, but though you be a dog, yes, not worthy to be set with the dogs of the Lord's flock, yet open your mouth in believing prayer.

There was besides this a general tone and spirit in what the Lord Jesus said which tended to depress the woman's hope and restrain her prayer, yet *she was not kept back by the darkest and most depressing influences.* "It is not meet," said the Lord Jesus, "it is not becoming, it is not proper, it is hardly lawful, to take children's bread and throw it to dogs." Perhaps she did not quite see all that he might have meant, but what she did see was enough to pour cold water upon the flame of her hope, yet her faith was not quenched. It was a faith of that immortal kind which nothing can kill; for her mind was made up that whatever Jesus meant, or did not mean, she would not cease to trust him, and urge her suit with him. There are a great many things in and around the gospel which men see as in a haze, and being misunderstood they rather repel than attract seeking souls; but be they what they may, we must resolve to come to Jesus at all risks. "If I perish, I perish." Besides the great stumbling stone of election, there are truths and facts which seekers magnify and misconstrue till they see a thousand difficulties. They are troubled about Christian experience, about being born again, about inbred sin, and all sorts of things; in fact, a thousand lions are in the way when the soul attempts to come to Jesus, but he who gives Christ the faith which he deserves says, "I fear none of these things. Lord, help me, and I will still confide in thee. I will approach thee, I will press through obstacles to thee, and throw myself at thy dear feet, knowing that him that cometh to thee thou wilt in no wise cast out."

II. *Faith never disputes with the Lord.*

Faith worships. You notice how Matthew says, "Then came she and worshiped him." Faith also begs and prays. You observe how Mark says, "She besought him." She cried, "Lord, help me," after having said, "Have mercy on me, O Lord, thou Son of David." Faith pleads, but never disputes, not even against the hardest thing that Jesus says. If faith disputed—I am uttering a solecism—she would not be faith, for that which disputes is unbelief. Faith in God implies agreement with what God says, and consequently it excludes the idea of doubt. Genuine faith believes anything and everything the Lord says, whether discouraging or encouraging. She never has a "but" or an "if," or even a "yet" to put in, but she stands to it, "Thou hast said it, Lord, and therefore it is true: thou hast ordained it, Lord, and therefore it is right." She never goes beyond that.

Observe in our text that *faith assents to all the Lord says.* She said, "Truth, Lord." What had he said? "You are comparable to a dog!" "Truth, Lord; truth, Lord; so I am." "It would not be meet that the children should be robbed of bread in order to feed dogs." "Truth, Lord, it would not be fitting, and I would not have one of thy children deprived of grace for me." "It is not your time yet," said Jesus; "the children must *first* be fed, children at the mealtimes and dogs after dinner; this is Israel's time, and the gentiles may follow after. But not yet." She virtually replies, "I know it, Lord, and agree thereto."

She does not raise a question or dispute the justice of the Lord's dispensing his own grace according to his sovereign good pleasure. She fails not, as some do who cavil at divine sovereignty. It would have proved that she had little or no faith if she had done that. She disputes not as to the Lord's set time and order. Jesus said, "Let the children first be filled," and she does not dispute the time, as many do, who will not have it that now is the accepted time, but are as much for postponing as this woman was for antedating the day of grace. She entered into no argument against its being improper to take the covenant bread from the children and give it to the uncircumcised heathen: she never wished Israel to be robbed for her. Dog as she was she would not have any purpose of God nor any propriety of the divine household shifted and changed for her. She assented to all the Lord's appointments. That is the faith which saves the soul, which agrees with the mind of God, even if it seem adverse to herself, which believes the revealed declarations of God whether they appear to be pleasant or terrible, and assents to God's word whether it be like a balm to its wound or like a sword to cut and slay. If the word of God be true, O man, do not fight against it, but bow before it. It is not the way to a living faith in Jesus Christ, nor to obtain peace with God, to take up arms against anything which God declares. In yielding lies safety. Say "Truth, Lord," and you shall find salvation.

Note that she not only assented to all that the Lord said, but *she worshiped him in it*. "Truth," she said, "but yet thou art my Lord." "Thou callest me 'dog,' but thou art my Lord for all that: thou accountest me unworthy to receive thy bounties, but thou art my Lord, and I still own thee as such." She is of the mind of Job: "Shall we receive good at the hand of the Lord, and shall we not receive evil?" She is willing to take the evil and say, "Whether the Lord gives, or whether he refuses, blessed be his name; he is my Lord still." Oh, this is grand faith, which has thrown aside the disputatious spirit, and not only assents to the Lord's will, but worships him in it. Let it be what it may, O Lord, even if the truth condemns me, yet still thou art Lord, and I confess thy deity, confess thine excellence, own thy crown rights, and submit myself to thee: do with me what thou wilt.

And, you observe, when she said "Truth, Lord," *she did not go on to suggest that any alteration should be made for her*. "Lord," she said, "thou hast classed me among the dogs"; she does not say, "Put me among the children," but she only asks to be treated as a dog is. "The dogs eat the crumbs," says she. She does not want a purpose altered nor an ordinance changed, nor a decree removed: "Let it be as it is: if it be thy will, Lord, it is my will"; only she spies a gleam of hope, where, if she had not possessed faith, she would have seen only the blackness of despair. May we have such a faith as hers, and never enter into controversy with God.

III. Now I come to an interesting part of our subject, namely, that *faith argues*, though it does not dispute.

"Truth, Lord," said she, "yet the dogs eat the crumbs." This woman's argument was correct, and strictly logical throughout. It was an argument based upon the Lord's own premises, and you know if you are reasoning with a man you cannot do better than take his own statements and argue upon them. She does not proceed to lay down new premises, or dispute the old ones by saying, "I am no dog"; but she says, "Yes, I am a dog." She accepts that statement of the Lord, and uses it as a blessed *argumentum ad hominem*, such as was never excelled in this world. She took the words out of his own mouth, and vanquished him with them, even as Jacob overcame the angel. There is so much force in the women's argument, that I quite despair this morning of being able to set it all forth to you. I would, however, remark that the translators have greatly injured the text by putting in the word *yet,* for there is no "yet" in the Greek: it is quite another word. Jesus said, "It is not meet to take the children's bread and cast it to the dogs." "No," said she, "it would not be meet to do this, because the dogs are provided for, for the dogs eat the crumbs that fall from their master's table." "It would be very improper to give them the children's bread, because they have bread of their own." "Truth, Lord, I admit it would be improper to give the dogs the children's bread, because they have already their share when they eat the crumbs which fall from the children's table. That is all they want, and all I desire. I do not ask thee to give me the children's bread, I only ask for the dog's crumbs."

Let us see the force of her reasoning, which will appear in many ways. The first is this. *She argued with Christ from her hopeful position.* "I am a dog," said she, "but, Lord, thou hast come all the way to Sidon; here thou art close on the borders of my country, and therefore I am not like a dog out in the street; I am a dog under the table." Mark tells us that she said, "The dogs under the table eat of the children's crumbs." She as good as says, "Lord, thou seest my position: I was a dog in the street, far off from thee, but now thou hast come and preached in our borders, and I have been privileged to listen to thee. Others have been healed, and thou art in this very house doing deeds of grace while I look on, and therefore, though I am a dog, I am a dog under the table; therefore, Lord, let me have the crumbs." Do you see, dear hearer? You admit that you are a sinner, and a great sinner, but you say, "Lord, I am a sinner that is permitted to hear the gospel, therefore bless it to me. I am a dog, but I am under the table, deal with me as such. When there is a sermon preached for the comfort of thy people, I am there to hear it: whenever the saints gather together, and the precious promises are discussed, and they rejoice therein, I am there, looking up, and wishing that I were among them, but still, Lord, since thou hast had the grace to let me be a hearer of the gospel, wilt thou reject me now that I desire to be a receiver of it? To what end and purpose hast thou brought me so near, or rather come so near to me, if after all thou wilt reject me? Dog I am, but still I am a dog under the table. It is a favor to be privileged to be among the children, even if I may only lie at their feet. I pray thee, good Lord, then, since now I am permitted to look up to thee and ask this blessing, do not reject me." To me it seems that this was a strong point with the woman, and that she used it well.

Her next plea was *her encouraging relationship*. "Truth, Lord," she says, "I am a dog, but the dogs eat the crumbs which fall from *their masters'* table." See the stress laid there by Matthew: "from their masters' table." I cannot say that thou art my Father, I cannot look up and claim the privilege of a child, but thou art my Master, and masters feed their dogs; they give at least the crumbs to those dogs which own them as their lord." The plea is very like that suggested to the mind of the poor returning prodigal. He thought to say to his father, "Make me as one of thy hired servants": only his faith was far weaker than hers. "Lord, if I do not stand in relation to thee as a child, yet I am thy creature; thou hast made me, and I look up to thee and beseech thee not to let me perish: if I have no other hold upon thee, I have at least this, that I ought to have served thee, and therefore I am thy servant though I am a runaway. I do belong to thee at least under the covenant of works if I do not under the covenant of grace, and oh, since I am thy servant, do not utterly reject me. Thou hast some property in me by creation, at any rate; Oh, look upon me and bless me. The dogs eat what falls from their masters' table; let me do the same." She spies out a dog's relation to its master, and makes the most of it with blessed ingenuity, which we shall do well to imitate.

Notice next, she pleads *her association with the children*. Here I must tell you that it is a pity that it was not, I suppose, possible for our translators to bring clearly out what is after all the pith of the passage. She was pleading for her *little* daughter; and our Lord said to her, "It is not meet to take the children's bread and cast it to the *little* dogs." The word is a diminutive, and the woman pitched upon it. The word *dogs* could not have served her turn one half as well as that of *little dogs,* but she said, "Truth, Lord, yet the little dogs eat of the crumbs." In the East, as a rule, a dog is not allowed indoors; in fact, dogs are there looked upon as foul creatures, and roam about uncared for and half wild. Christianity has raised the dog, and made him man's companion, as it will raise all the brute creation, till the outrages of vivisection, and the cruelties of the vulgar, will be things unheard of except as horrors of a past barbarous age. In the East a dog is far down in the scale of life, a street wanderer, prowling for scanty food, and in temper little better than a reformed wolf. So the adult Easterners do not associate with dogs, having a prejudice against them, but children are not so foolish, and consequently the Eastern children associate with the little dogs. The father will not have the dog near him, but his child knows no such folly, and seeks out a little dog to join him in his sports; thus the little dog comes to be under the table, tolerated in the house for the child's sake.

The woman appears to me to argue thus—"Thou hast called me and my daughter whelps, little dogs, but then the little dogs are under the children's table; they associate with the children, even as I have been with thy disciples today. If I am not one of them, I have been associating with them and would be glad to be among them." How heartily do I wish that some poor soul would catch at this and say, "Lord, I cannot claim to be one of thy children, but I love to sit among them, for I am never happier than when I am with them. Sometimes they trouble and distress me, as little children pinch and hurt their little dogs, but oftentimes they caress me, and speak kindly and comfortably to me, and pray for me, and desire my salvation; so Lord, if I am not a child, yet thou callest me a little dog, so I am, but give me a little dog's treatment; give me the crumb of mercy which I seek."

Her argument goes further, *for the little dog eats the crumbs of the children's bread with the child's full consent.* When a child has its little dog to play with while he is eating, what does the child do? Why, of course, it gives a little bit to the dog every now and again, and the doggie himself takes great liberties and helps himself as much as he dares. When a little dog is with the children at mealtime, it is sure to get a crumb from one or other of its playmates; and none will object to its eating what it can get. So the woman seems to say, "Lord, there are the children, thy disciples; they do not treat me very well; little children do not treat little dogs always so kindly as they might; but still, Lord, they are quite willing that I should have the blessing I am seeking. They have a full portion in thee; they have thy presence; they have thy word; they sit at thy feet; they have obtained all sorts of spiritual blessings. I am sure they cannot grudge me so much less a boon; they are willing that I should have the devil cast out of my daughter, for that blessing compared with what they have is but a crumb, and they are content that I should have it. So Lord, I answer thine argument. Thou sayest it is not meet until the children are filled to give bread to dogs, but, Lord, the children are filled and are quite willing to let me have my portion, they consent to allow me the crumbs; wilt thou not give them to me?"

I think there was another point of force in her plea: it was this, *the abundance of the provision.* She had a great faith in Christ, and believed big things of him, and therefore she said, "Lord, there is no great strength in thine argument if thou dost intend to prove that I ought not to have the bread for fear there should not be enough for the children, for thou hast so much that even while the children are being fed, the dogs may get the crumbs, and there will be enough for the children still." Where it is a poor man's table, and he cannot afford to lose a crumb, dogs should not be allowed; but when it is a king's table where bread is of small account, and the children are sitting and feeding to the full, the little dogs may be permitted to feed under the table for the mere droppings—not the bread the master casts down, but the crumbs which *fall* by accident are so many that there is enough for the dogs without the children being deprived of a mouthful. "No, Lord," said she, "I would not have thee take away the bread from thine own children; God forbid that such a deed should be done for me; but there is enough for thy children in thine overflowing love and mercy, and still enough for me, for all I ask is but a crumb compared with what thou art daily bestowing upon others."

Now here is the last point in which her argument had force. *She looked at things from Christ's point of view.* "If, great Lord," said she, "thou lookest at me as a dog, then behold I humbly take thee at thy word, and plead that if I be a dog to thee then the cure I ask for my daughter is but a crumb for thy great power and goodness to bestow on me." She used a diminutive word too, and said, "a little crumb."

The little dogs eat of the little crumbs which fall from the children's table. What bold faith this was! She valued the mercy she sought beyond all price; she thought it worth ten thousand worlds to her, but yet to the Son of God she knew it to be a mere crumb, so rich is he in power to heal and so full of goodness and blessing. If a man give a crumb to a dog, he has a little the less, but if Jesus gives mercy to the greatest of sinners he has none the less, he is just as rich in condescension and mercy and power to forgive as he was before. The woman's argument was most potent. She was as wise as she was earnest, and best of all, she believed most marvelously.

I shall close this outline of the argument by saying that, at bottom, the woman was, in reality, arguing according to the eternal purpose of God—for what was the Lord's grand design in giving the bread to the children, or, in other words, sending a divine revelation to Israel? Why, it always was his purpose that through the children the dogs should get the bread; that through

Israel the gospel should be handed to the gentiles. It had always been his plan to bless his own heritage that his way might be known upon earth, his saving health among all nations; and this woman somehow or other, by a divine instinct, fell into the divine method. Though she had not spied out the secret, or at least it is not told us that she did so in so many words, yet there was the innate force of her argument. In other words, it ran thus—"It is through the children that the dogs have to be fed: Lord, I do not ask thee to cease giving the children their bread; nor do I even ask thee to hurry on the children's meal, let them be fed first, but even while they are eating let me have the crumbs which drop from their well-filled hands, and I will be content." There is a brave argument for you, poor coming sinner. I leave it in your hands, and pray the Spirit of God to help you to use it, and if you can turn it to good account you shall prevail with the Lord this day.

IV. Our last and closing head is this: *faith wins her suit.*

This woman's faith first *won a commendation for herself.* Jesus said, "O woman, great is thy faith." She had not heard of the prophecies concerning Jesus; she was not bred and born and educated in a way in which she was likely to become a believer and yet did become a believer of the first class. It was marvelous that it should be so, but grace delights in doing wonders. She had not seen the Lord before in her life, she was not like those who had associated with him for many months: and yet, with but one view of him, she gained this great faith. It was astonishing, but the grace of God is always astonishing. Perhaps she had never seen a miracle: all that her faith had to rest upon was that she had heard in her own country that the Messiah of the Jews was come, and she believed that the Man of Nazareth was he, and on this she relied. O brethren, with all our advantages, with the opportunities that we have of knowing the whole life of Christ, and understanding the doctrines of the gospel as they are revealed to us in the New Testament, with many years of observation and experience, our faith ought to be much stronger than it is. Does not this poor woman shame us when we see her with her slender opportunities nevertheless so strong in faith, so that Jesus himself commending her says, "O woman, great is thy faith."

But her faith prevailed further, that it *won a commendation for the mode of its action,* for, according to Mark, Jesus said, "Go thy way; *for this saying* the devil is gone out of thy daughter"; as if he rewarded the saying as well as the faith which suggested it. He was so delighted with the wise and prudent and humble yet courageous manner in which she turned his words against himself, that he said, "For this saying the devil is gone out of thy daughter." The

Lord who commends faith afterward commends the fruits and acts of faith. The tree consecrates the fruit. No man's actions can be acceptable with God till he himself is accepted, but the woman having been accepted on her faith, the results of her faith were agreeable to the heart of Jesus.

The woman also *gained her desire*: "The devil is gone out of thy daughter," and he was gone at once. She had only to go home and find her daughter on the bed taking a quiet rest, which she had not done since the demon had possessed her. Our Lord, when he gave her the desire of her heart, gave it in a grand manner; he gave her a sort of *carte blanche,* and said, "Be it unto thee even as thou wilt." I do not know that any other person ever had such a word said to him as this woman, "Be it unto thee even as thou wilt." It was as if the Lord of glory surrendered at discretion to the conquering arms of a woman's faith. The Lord grant to you and me in all times of our struggling to be able thus by faith still to conquer, and we cannot imagine how great will be the spoil which we shall divide when the Lord shall say, "Be it unto thee even as thou wilt."

The close of all is this: this woman is a lesson to all outsiders, to you who think yourselves beyond the pale of hope, to you who were not brought up to attend the house of God, who perhaps have been negligent of all religion for almost all your lifetime. This poor woman is a Sidonian; she comes of a race that had been condemned to die many centuries before, one of the accursed seed of Canaan, and yet for all that, she became great in the kingdom of heaven because she believed, and there is no reason why those who are reckoned to be quite outside the church of God should not be in the very center of it, and be the most burning and shining lights of the whole. O you poor outcasts and far-off ones, take heart and comfort, and come to Jesus Christ and trust yourselves in his hands.

This woman is next of all an example to those who think they have been repulsed in their endeavors after salvation. Have you been praying, and have you not succeeded? Have you sought the Lord, and do you seem to be more unhappy than ever? Have you made attempts at reformation and amendment, and believed that you made them in the divine strength, and have they failed? Yet trust in him whose blood has not lost its efficacy, whose promise has not lost its truth, and whose arm has not lost its power to save. Cling to the cross, sinner. If the earth sink beneath you, cling on; if storms should rage, and all the floods be out, and even God himself seem to be against you, cling to the cross. There is your hope. You cannot perish there.

This is a lesson, next, to every intercessor. This woman was not pleading for herself, she was asking for another. Oh, when you plead for a fellow sinner, do not do it in a coldhearted manner; plead as for your own soul and your own life. That man will prevail with God as an intercessor who solemnly bears the matter upon his own heart and makes it his own, and with tears entreats an answer of peace.

Last, recollect that this mighty woman, this glorious woman, is a lesson to every mother, for she was pleading for her little daughter. Maternal instinct makes the weakest strong, and the most timid brave. Even among poor beasts and birds, how powerful is a mother's love. Why, the poor little robin, which would be frightened at the approach of a footstep, will sit upon its nest when the intruder comes near when her little ones are in danger. A mother's love makes her heroic for her child; and so when you are pleading with God, plead as a mother's love suggests to you, till the Lord shall say to you also, "O woman, great is thy faith; the devil is gone out of thy daughter; be it unto thee even as thou wilt." I leave that last thought with parents as an encouragement to pray. The Lord stir you up to it, for Jesus' sake. Amen.

The Infirmed Woman: The Lifting Up of the Bowed Down

Delivered on Lord's Day morning, July 14, 1878, at the Metropolitan Tabernacle, Newington. No. 1426.

> And he was teaching in one of the synagogues on the sabbath. And, behold, there was a woman which had a spirit of infirmity eighteen years, and was bowed together, and could in no wise lift up herself. And when Jesus saw her, he called her to him, and said unto her, "Woman, thou art loosed from thine infirmity." And he laid his hands on her: and immediately she was made straight, and glorified God.—LUKE 13:10–13

I believe that the infirmity of this woman was not only physical but spiritual: her outward appearance was the index of her deep and long-continued depression of mind. She was bent double as to her body, and she was bowed down by sadness as to her mind.

There is always a sympathy between body and soul, but it is not always so plainly seen as in her case; many sad sights would meet us on all hands if it were so. Imagine for a moment what would be the result upon the present congregation if our outward forms were to set forth our inward states. If someone having an eye like that of the Savior could gaze upon us now, and could see the inward in the outward, what would be the appearance of this crowd? Very deplorable sights would be seen, for in many a pew dead persons would be sitting, looking forth from the glassy eyes of death, bearing the semblance of life and a name to live, but all the while being dead as to spiritual things. My friend, you would shudder as you found yourself placed next to a corpse. Alas, the corpse would not shudder, but would remain as insensible as ungodly persons usually are, though the precious truth of the gospel rings in their ears—ears which hear but hear in vain. A large number of souls will be found in all congregations, "dead in trespasses and sins," and yet sitting as God's people sit, and not to be discerned from the living in Zion. Even in those cases in which there is spiritual life, the aspect would not be altogether lovely. Here we should see a man blind, and there another maimed; and a third twisted from perfect uprightness.

Spiritual deformity assumes many forms, and each form is painful to look upon. A paralyzed man with a trembling faith, set forth by a trembling body, would be an uncomfortable neighbor, and a person subject to fits of passion or despair would be equally undesirable if his body suffered from fits also. How sad it would be to have around us persons with a fever upon them, or shivering with ague, hot and cold by turns, burning almost to fanaticism at one moment and then chilled as with a northern wind with utter indifference. I will not try to sketch in further detail the halt [crippled], lame, blind, and impotent folk who are assembled in this Bethesda. Surely if the flesh were shaped according to the spirit, this tabernacle would be turned into a hospital, and each man would flee from his fellow, and wish to run from himself. If to any one of us our inward ailments were to be set forth upon our brow, I warrant you we should not linger long at the glass, nor scarcely dare to think upon the wretched objects which there our eyes would behold. Let us quit the imaginary scene with this consoling thought, that Jesus is among us notwithstanding that we be sick folk, and although he sees nothing to delight his eye if he judges us according to the law, yet, since his mercy delights to relieve human misery, there is abundant scope for him here in the midst of these thousands of ailing souls.

In that synagogue on the Sabbath, this poor woman described in the text must have been one of the least observed. Her particular disease would render her very short in stature; she was dwarfed to almost half her original height, and in consequence, like other very short persons, she would be almost lost in a standing crowd. A person so bent down as she was might have come in and gone out and not have been noticed by anyone standing upon the floor of the meeting place; but I can imagine that our Lord occupied a somewhat elevated position, as he was teaching in the synagogue, for he had probably gone to one of the higher places for the greater convenience of being seen and heard, and for this reason he could more readily see her than others could. Jesus always occupies a place from which he can spy out those who are bowed down. His quick eye did not miss its mark. She, poor soul, was naturally the least observed of all the people in the company, yet was she the most observed, for our Lord's gracious eye glanced over all the rest, but it lighted upon her with fixed regard. There his tender look remained till he had worked the deed of love.

Peradventure, there is someone in the crowd this morning the least observed of anybody, who is yet noticed by the Savior; for he sees not as man sees, but observes most those whom man passes over as beneath his regard. Nobody knows you, nobody cares for you; your peculiar trouble is quite unknown, and you would not reveal it for the world. You feel quite alone; there is no solitude like that which is to be found in a dense throng; and you are in that solitude now. Be not, however, quite despairing, for you have a friend left. The preacher's heart is going after you, but that will little help you: there is far more joy in the fact that, as our Master observed most the least-observed one on that Sabbath in the synagogue, so we trust he will do this day, and his eye shall light on you, even you. He will not pass you by, but will deal out a special Sabbath blessing to your weary heart. Though by yourself accounted to be among the last, you shall now be put upon the first by the Lord's working a notable miracle of love upon you. In the hope that this may be so, we will proceed, by the help of the Holy Spirit, to look into the gracious deed which was done to this poor woman.

I. Our first subject for consideration is, *the bowing down of the afflicted.*

We read of this woman that "she had a spirit of infirmity and was bowed together, and could in no wise lift up herself." Upon which we remark first, that she had lost all her natural brightness. I can imagine that when she was a girl, she was light of foot as a young roe, that her face was dimpled with many a smile, and that her eyes flashed with childish glee. She had her share of the brightness and beauty of youth, and walked erect like others of her race, look-ing up to the sun by day, and to the sparkling stars at night, rejoicing in all around her, and feeling life to be a joy. But there gradually crept over her an infirmity which dragged her down, probably a weakness of the spine: either the muscles and ligatures began to tighten so that she was bound together, and drawn more and more toward herself and toward the earth; or else the mus-cles commenced to relax, so that she could not retain the perpendicular posi-tion, and her body dropped forward more and more. I suppose either of these causes might cause her to be bowed together, so that she could in no wise lift herself up.

At any rate, for eighteen years she had not gazed upon the sun; for eigh-teen years no star of night had gladdened her eye; her face was drawn down-ward toward the dust, and all the light of her life was dim: she walked about as if she were searching for a grave, and I do not doubt she often felt that it would have been gladness to have found one. She was as truly fettered as if bound in iron, and as much in prison as if surrounded by stone walls. Alas, we know certain of the children of God who are at this moment in much the same condition. They are perpetually bowed down, and though they recollect happier days, the memory only serves to deepen their present gloom. They sometimes sing in the minor key:

Where is the blessedness I knew
When first I saw the Lord?
Where is the sweet refreshing view
Of Jesus and his word?

What blissful hours I then enjoyed!
How sweet their memory still!
But they have left an aching void
The world can never fill.

They seldom enter into communion with God now; seldom or never behold the face of the Well Beloved. They try to hold on by believing, and they succeed; but they have little peace, little comfort, little joy: they have lost the crown and flower of spiritual life, though that life still remains. I feel certain that I am addressing more than two or three who are in such a plight at this moment, and I pray the Comforter to bless my discourse to them.

This poor woman was *bowed toward herself and toward that which was depressing*. She seemed to grow downward; her life was stooping; she bent lower and lower and lower, as the weight of years pressed upon her. Her looks were all earthward; nothing heavenly, nothing bright could come before her eyes; her views were narrowed to the dust, and to the grave. So are there some of God's people whose thoughts sink evermore like lead, and their feelings run in a deep groove, cutting evermore a lower channel. You cannot give them delight, but you can readily cause them alarm: by a strange art they squeeze the juice of sorrow from the clusters of Eshcol; where others would leap for joy, they stoop for very grief, for they draw the unhappy inference that joyous things are not meant for the likes of them. Cordials expressly prepared for mourners they dare not accept, and the more comforting they are, the more are they afraid to appropriate them. If there is a dark passage in the Word of God, they are sure to read it, and say, "That applies to me"; if there is a thundering portion in a sermon, they recollect every syllable of it, and although they wonder how the preacher knows them so well, yet they are sure that he aimed every word at them. If anything occurs in providence, either adverse or propitious, instead of reading it as a token for good, whether they might rationally do so or not, they manage to translate it into a sign of evil. "All these things are against me," say they, for they can see nothing but the earth, and can imagine nothing but fear and distress.

We have known certain prudent, but somewhat unfeeling, persons blame these people, and chide them for being low spirited; and that brings us to notice next, that *she could not lift up herself.* There was no use in blaming her.

There may have been a time, perhaps, when her older sisters said, "Sister, you should keep yourself more upright; you should not be so round shouldered; you are getting quite out of figure; you must be careful or you will become deformed." Dear me, what good advice some people can give! Advice is usually given gratis, and this is very proper, since in most cases that is its full value. Advice given to persons who become depressed in spirit is usually unwise, and causes pain and aggravation of spirit. I sometimes wish that those who are so ready with their advice had themselves suffered a little, for then, perhaps, they would have the wisdom to hold their tongues. Of what use is it to advise a blind person to see, or to tell one who cannot lift up herself that she ought to be upright, and should not look so much upon the earth? This is a needless increase of misery. Some persons who pretend to be comforters might more fitly be classed with tormentors. A spiritual infirmity is as real as a physical one. When Satan binds a soul it is as truly bound as when a man binds an ox or an ass. It cannot get free, it is of necessity in bondage; and that was the condition of this poor woman. I may be speaking to some who have bravely attempted to rally their spirits: they have tried change of scene, they have gone into godly company, they have asked Christian people to comfort them, they have frequented the house of God, and read consoling books; but still they are bound, and there is no disputing it. As one that pours vinegar upon niter, so is he that sings songs to a sad heart: there is an incongruity about the choicest joys when forced upon broken spirits. Some distressed souls are so sick that they abhor all manner of meat, and draw near unto the gates of death. Yet if any one of my hearers be in this plight, he may not despair, for Jesus can lift up those who are most bowed down.

The worst point, perhaps, about the poor woman's case was that *she had borne her trouble for eighteen years,* and therefore her disease was chronic and her illness confirmed. Eighteen years! It is a long, long time. Eighteen years of happiness!—the years fly like Mercuries, with wings to their heels: they come, and they are gone. Eighteen years of happy life—how short a span! But eighteen years of pain, eighteen years of being bowed down to the earth, eighteen years in which the body approximated rather to the fashion of a brute than to that of a man, what a period this must be! Eighteen long years—each with twelve dreary months dragging like a chain behind it! She had been eighteen years under the bond of the devil; what a woe was this! Can a child of God be eighteen years in despondency? I am bound to answer, yes. There is one instance, that of Mr. Timothy Rogers, who has written a book upon *Religious Melancholy,* a very wonderful book too, who was, I think, twenty-eight years in despondency: he tells the story himself, and there can be no question as to his accuracy. Similar instances are well known to those familiar with religious biographies. Individuals have been locked up for many years in the gloomy den of despair, and yet after all have been singularly brought out into joy and comfort. Eighteen years' despondency must be a frightful affliction, and yet there is an escape out of it, for though the devil may take eighteen years to forge a chain, it does not take our blessed Lord eighteen minutes to break it. He can soon set the captive free. Build, build your dungeons, O fiend of hell, and lay the foundations deep, and place the courses of granite so fast together that none can stir a stone of your fabric; but when *he* comes, your Master who will destroy all your works, *he* does but speak, and like the unsubstantial fabric of a vision your Bastille vanishes into thin air. Eighteen years of melancholy do not prove that Jesus cannot set the captive free; they only offer him an opportunity for displaying his gracious power.

Note further about this poor woman, that bowed down as she was both in mind and body, *she yet frequented the house of prayer.* Our Lord was in the synagogue, and there was she. She might very well have said, "It is very painful for me to go into a public place; I ought to be excused." But no, there she was. Dear child of God, the devil has sometimes suggested to you that it is vain for you to go any more to hear the word. Go all the same. He knows you are likely to escape from his hands so long as you hear the word, and therefore if he can keep you away, he will do so. It was while in the house of prayer that this woman found her liberty, and there you may find it; therefore still continue to go up to the house of the Lord, come what may.

All this while, too, she was a daughter of Abraham. The devil had tied her up like an ox or an ass, but he could not take away her privileged character. She was still a daughter of Abraham, still a believing soul trusting in God by humble faith. When the Savior healed her, he did not say, "Thy sins be forgiven thee." There was no particular sin in the case. He did not address her as he did those whose infirmity had been caused by sin; for, notwithstanding her being thus bowed down, all she needed was comfort, not rebuke. Her heart was right with God. I know it was, for the moment she was healed, she began to glorify God, which showed that she was ready for it, and that the praise was waiting in her spirit for the glad opportunity. In going up to the house of God, she felt some measure of comfort, though for eighteen years she was bowed down. Where else should she have gone? What good could she have gained by staying at home? A sick child is best in its father's house, and she was best where prayer was wont to be made.

Here, then, is a picture of what may still be seen among the sons of men, and may possibly be your case, dear hearer. May the Holy Spirit bless this description to your hearts' encouragement.

II. I invite you, second, to notice *the hand of Satan in this bondage.*

We should not have known it if our Lord had not told us, that it was Satan who had bound this poor woman for eighteen years. *He must have bound her very cunningly to make the knot hold all that time,* for he does not appear to have possessed her. You notice in reading the Evangelists that our Lord never laid his hand on a person possessed with a devil. Satan had not possessed her, but he had fallen upon her once upon a time eighteen years before, and bound her up as men tie a beast in its stable, and she had not been able to get free all that while. The devil can tie in a moment a knot which you and I cannot unloose in eighteen years. He had in this case so securely fastened his victim that no power of herself or others could avail: in the same way, when permitted he can tie up any one of God's own people in a very short time, and by almost any means. Perhaps one word from a preacher, which was never meant to cause sadness, may make a heart wretched; one single sentence out of a good book or one misunderstood passage of Scripture, may be quite enough in Satan's cunning hand to fasten up a child of God in a long bondage.

Satan had bound the woman to herself and to the earth. There is a cruel way of tying a beast which is somewhat after the same fashion: I have seen a poor animal's head fastened to its knee or foot, and somewhat after that fashion Satan had bound the woman downward to herself. So there are some children of God whose thoughts are all about themselves: they have turned their eyes so that they look inside and see only the transactions of the little world within themselves. They are always lamenting their own infirmities, always mourning their own corruptions, always watching their own emotions. The one and only subject of their thoughts is their own condition. If they ever change the scene and turn to another subject, it is only to gaze upon the earth beneath them, to groan over this poor world with its sorrows, its miseries, its sins, and its disappointments. Thus they are tied to themselves and to the earth and cannot look up to Christ as they should, nor let the sunlight of his love shine full upon them. They go mourning without the sun, pressed down with cares and burdens. Our Lord uses the figure of an ox or an ass tied up, and he says that even on the Sabbath its owner would loose it for watering.

This poor woman was restrained from what her soul needed. She was like an ass or an ox which cannot get to the trough to drink. She knew the promises; she heard them read every Sabbath day; she went to the synagogue and heard of him who comes to loose the captives; but she could not rejoice in the promise or enter into liberty. So are there multitudes of God's dear people who are fastened to themselves and cannot get to watering, cannot drink from the river of life, nor find consolation in the Scriptures. They know how precious the gospel is, and how consolatory are the blessings of the covenant, but they cannot enjoy the consolations or the blessings. Oh, that they could. They sigh and cry, but they feel themselves to be bound.

There is a saving clause here. Satan had done a good deal to the poor woman, but *he had done all he could do*. You may rest assured that whenever Satan smites a child of God, he never spares his strength. He knows nothing of mercy, neither does any other consideration restrain him. When the Lord delivered Job into Satan's hand for a time, what destruction and havoc he made with Job's property. He did not save him chick or child or sheep or goat or camel or ox; but he smote him right and left, and caused ruin to his whole estate. When, under a second permit, he came to touch him in his bone and in his flesh, nothing would satisfy the devil but covering him from the sole of his foot to the crown of his head with sore boils and blains. He might have pained him quite sufficiently by torturing one part of his body, but this would not suffice, he must glut himself with vengeance. The devil would do all he could, and therefore he covered him with running sores. Yet, as in Job's case, there was a limit, so was there here; Satan had bound this woman, but he had not killed her. He might bend her toward the grave, but he could not bend her into it; he might make her droop over till she was bent double, but he could not take away her poor feeble life: with all his infernal craft, he could not make her die before her time. Moreover, she was still a woman, and he could not make a beast of her, notwithstanding that she was thus bowed down into the form of the brute. Even so the devil cannot destroy you, O child of God. He can smite you, but he cannot slay you. He worries those whom he cannot destroy and feels a malicious joy in so doing. He knows there is no hope of your destruction, for you are beyond shot of his gun; but if he cannot wound you with the shot, he will frighten you with the powder if he can. If he cannot slay, he will bind, as if for the slaughter; yes, and he knows how to make a poor soul feel a thousand deaths in fearing one. But all this while Satan was quite unable to touch this poor woman as to her true standing: she was a daughter of Abraham eighteen years before when first the devil attacked her, and she was a daughter of Abraham eighteen years afterward, when the fiend had done his worst. And you, dear heart, if you should never have a comfortable sense of the Lord's love for eighteen years, are still his beloved; and if never once he should give you any token of his love which you could sensibly enjoy, and if by reason of bewilderment and distraction you should keep on writing bitter things against yourself all this while, yet still your name is on the hands of Christ, where none can erase it. You belong to Jesus, and none shall pluck you out of his hands. The devil may bind you fast, but Christ has bound you faster still with cords of everlasting love, which must and shall hold you to the end.

That poor woman was being prepared, even by the agency of the devil, to glorify God. Nobody in the synagogue could glorify God as she could when she was at last set free. Every year out of the eighteen gave emphasis to the utterance of her thanksgiving. The deeper her sorrow, the sweeter her song. I should like to have been there that morning, to have heard her tell the story of the emancipating power of the Christ of God. The devil must have felt that he had lost all his trouble, and he must have regretted that he had not let her alone all the eighteen years, since he had only been qualifying her thereby to tell out the more sweetly the story of Jesus' wondrous power.

III. I want you to notice in the third place *the Liberator at his work.*

We have seen the woman bound by the devil, but here comes the Liberator, and the first thing we read of him is that he saw her. His eyes looked round, reading every heart as he glanced from one to another. At last he saw the woman. Yes, that was the very one he was seeking. We are not to think that he saw her in the same common way as I see one of you, but he read every line of her character and history, every thought of her heart, every desire of her soul. Nobody had told him that she had been eighteen years bound, but he knew all about it—how she came to be bound, what she had suffered during the time, how she had prayed for healing, and how the infirmity still pressed upon her. In one minute he had read her history and understood her case. He saw her; and oh, what meaning there was in his searching glance. Our Lord had wonderful eyes; all the painters in the world will never be able to produce a satisfactory picture of Christ, because they cannot copy those expressive eyes. Heaven lay calmly reposing in his eyes; they were not only bright and penetrating, but they were full of a melting power, a tenderness irresistible, a strength which secured confidence. As he looked at the poor woman, I doubt not the tears started from our Lord's eyes, but they were not tears of unmingled sorrow, for he knew that he could heal her, and he anticipated the joy of doing so.

When he had gazed upon her, he called her to him. Did he know her name? Oh, yes, he knows all our names, and his calling is therefore personal and unmistakable. "I have called thee by thy name," says he, "thou art mine."

See, there is the poor creature, coming up the aisle; that pitiful mass of sorrow, though bowed to the earth, is moving. Is it a woman at all? You can hardly see that she has a face, but she is coming toward him who called her. She could not stand upright, but she could come as she was, bent and infirm as she was. I rejoice in my Master's way of healing people, for he comes to them where they are. He does not propose to them that if they will do somewhat, he will do the rest, but he begins and ends. He bids them approach him as they are, and does not ask them to mend or prepare. May my blessed Master this morning look on some of you till you feel, "The preacher means me, the preacher's Master means me," and then may there sound a voice in your ears saying, "Come to Jesus just as you are." Then may you have grace to reply—

> Just as I am—poor, wretched, blind,
> Sight, riches, healing of the mind,
> Yea, all I need, in thee to find,
> O Lamb of God, I come.

When the woman came, *the great Liberator said to her, "Woman, thou art loosed from thine infirmity."* How could that be true? She was still as bent as she was before. He meant that the spell of Satan was taken off from her, that the power which had made her thus to bow herself was broken. This she believed in her inmost soul, even as Jesus said it, though as yet she was not at all different in appearance from her former state.

Oh, that some of you who are God's dear people would have power to believe this morning that the end of your gloom has come, power to believe that your eighteen years are over, and that your time of doubt and despondency is ended. I pray that God may give you grace to know that when this morning's sun first gilded the east, light was ordained for you. Behold, I come today to publish the glad message from the Lord. Come forth, you prisoners; leap, you captives, for Jesus comes to set you free today.

The woman was liberated, but she could not actually enjoy the liberty, and I will tell you why directly. Our Lord proceeded to give her full enlargement in his own way: *he laid his hands on her.* She suffered from want of strength, and by putting his hands upon her, I conceive that the Lord poured his life into her. The warm stream of his own infinite power and vitality came into contact with the lethargic stream of her painful existence, and so quickened it that she lifted up herself. The deed of love was done: Jesus himself had done it. Beloved mourners, if we could get you away this morning from thinking about yourselves to thinking about our Lord Jesus, and from looking down upon your cares to thinking of him, what a change would come over you. If his hands could be laid upon you, those dear pierced hands which bought you, those mighty hands which rule heaven and earth on your behalf, those blessed hands which are outstretched to plead for sinners, those dear hands which will press you to his bosom forever: if you could feel these by thinking of him, then would you soon recover your early joy, and renew the elasticity of your spirit, and the bowing down of your soul would pass away like a night dream, to be forgotten forever. O Spirit of the Lord, make it to be so.

IV. I will not linger there, but invite you now to notice *the loosing of the bound.*

She was made straight we are told, and that at once. Now, what I want you to notice is this, that she must have lifted herself up—that was her own act and deed. No pressure or force was put upon her, she lifted up herself; and yet she was "made straight." She was passive insomuch as a miracle was worked upon her, but she was active too, and, being enabled, she lifted up herself. What a wonderful meeting there is here of the active and the passive in the salvation of men.

The Arminian says to the sinner, "Now, sinner, you are a responsible being; you must do this and that." The Calvinist says, "Truly, sinner, you are responsible enough, but you are also unable to do anything of yourself. God must work in you both to will and to do." What shall we do with these two teachers? They fell to fighting, a hundred years ago, most frightfully. We will not let them fight now, but what shall we do with them? We will let both speak, and believe what is true in both their testimonies.

Is it true what the Arminian says, that there must be an effort on the sinner's part or he will never be saved? Unquestionably it is. As soon as ever the Lord gives spiritual life, there is spiritual activity. Nobody is ever lugged into heaven by his ears or carried there asleep on a feather bed. God deals with us as with responsible, intelligent beings. That is true, and what is the use of denying it?

Now what has the Calvinist to say? He says that the sinner is bound by the infirmity of sin and cannot lift up himself, and when he does so, it is God that does it all, and the Lord must have all the glory of it. Is not that true too? "Oh," says the Arminian, "I never denied that the Lord is to have the glory. I will sing a hymn with you to the divine honor; and I will pray the same prayer with you for the divine power." All Christians are thorough Calvinists when they come to singing and praying, but it is a pity to doubt as a doctrine what we profess on our knees and in our songs. It is most true that Jesus alone saves the sinner, and equally true that the sinner believes unto salvation. The Holy Ghost never believed on behalf of anybody: a man must believe for himself and repent for himself, or be lost; but yet there never was a grain of true faith or true repentance in this world except it was produced by the Holy Ghost. I am not going to explain these difficulties, because they are not difficulties, except in theory. They are plain facts of practical everyday life. The poor woman knew at any rate where to put the crown; she did not say, "I straightened myself," no, but she glorified God, and attributed all the work to his gracious power.

The most remarkable fact is that *she was made straight immediately;* for there was something beyond her infirmity to be overcome. Suppose that any person had been diseased of the spine, or of the nerves and muscles, for eighteen years, even if the disease which occasioned his being deformed could be entirely removed, what would be the effect? Why, that the result of the disease would still remain, for the body would have become set through long continuance in one posture. You have doubtless heard of the fakirs and others in India: a man will hold his hand up for years in pursuance of a vow, but when the years of his penance are over, he cannot bring his hand down: it has become fixed and immovable. In this case the bond which held the poor bowed body was taken away, and at the same time the consequent rigidity was removed, and she in a moment stood up straight; this was a double display of miraculous power. O my poor, tried friend, if the Lord will visit you this morning, he will not only take away the first and greatest cause of your sadness, but the very tendency to melancholy shall depart; the long grooves which you have worn shall be smoothed, the ruts in the road of sorrow which you have worn by long continuance in sadness shall be filled up, and you shall be strong in the Lord and in the power of his might.

The cure being thus perfect, *up rose the woman to glorify God.* I wish I had been there; I have been wishing so all the morning. I should have liked to have seen that hypocritical ruler of the synagogue when he made his angry speech: I should have liked to have seen him when the Master silenced him so thoroughly; but especially I should have rejoiced to have seen this poor woman standing upright, and to have heard her praise the Lord. What did she say? It is not recorded, but we can well imagine. It was something like this: "I have been eighteen years in and out among you; you have seen me, and know what a poor, miserable, wretched object I was; but God has lifted me up all in a moment. Blessed be his name, I have been made straight." What she spoke with her mouth was not half of what she expressed. No reporter could have taken it down; she spoke with her eyes, she spoke with her hands, she spoke with every limb of her body. I suppose she moved about to see if she was really straight, and to make sure that it was not all a delusion. She must have been all over a living mass of pleasure, and by every movement she praised God from the sole of the foot to the crown of the head. Never was there a more eloquent woman in the universe. She was like one newborn, delivered from a long death, joyous with all the novelty of a fresh life. Well might she glorify God.

She made no mistake as to how the cure was worked; she traced it to a divine power, and that divine power she extolled. Brother, sister, cannot you glorify Christ this morning that he has set you free? Though bound so long, you need not be bound any longer. Christ is able to deliver you. Trust him, believe him, be made straight, and then go and tell your kinsfolk and acquaintances, "You knew how depressed I was, for you cheered me in my sorrow as best you could, but now I have to tell you what the Lord has done for my soul."

V. Fifth, let us reflect upon *our reason for expecting the Lord Jesus to do the same thing today* as he did eighteen hundred years and more ago.

What was his reason for setting this woman free? According to his own statement, it was, first of all, *human kindness*. He says, "When you have your ox or your ass tied up, and you see that it is thirsty, you untie the knot, and lead the poor creature away down to the river, or the tank, to water. None of you would leave an ox tied up to famish." This is good reasoning, and leads us to believe that Jesus will help sorrowing ones. Tried soul, would you not loose an ox or an ass if you saw it suffering? "Yes," you say. And do you think the Lord will not loose you? Have you more bowels of mercy than the Christ of God? Come, come, think not so meanly of my Master. If your heart would lead you to pity an ass, do you think his heart will not lead him to pity you? He has not forgotten you: he remembers you still. His tender humanity moves him to set you free.

More than that, there was *special relationship*. He tells this master of the synagogue that a man would loose his ox or his ass. Perhaps he might not think it his business to go and loose that which belonged to another man, but it is his own ass, his own ox, and he will loose him. And do you think, dear heart, that the Lord Jesus will not loose you? He bought you with his blood, his Father gave you to him, he has loved you with an everlasting love: will he not loose you? You are his property. Do you not know that he sweeps his house to find his lost goat, that he runs over hill and dale to find his lost sheep? And will he not come and loose his poor tied-up ox or ass? Will he not liberate his captive daughter? Assuredly he will. Are you a daughter of Abraham, a child of faith, and will he not set you free? Depend upon it, he will.

Next, there was *a point of antagonism* which moved the Savior to act promptly. He says, "This woman being a daughter of Abraham, whom Satan hath bound." Now, if I knew the devil had tied anything up I am sure I would try to unloose it, would not you? We may be sure some mischief is brewing when the devil is working, and, therefore, it must be a good deed to undo his work. But Jesus Christ came into the world on purpose to destroy the works of the devil; and so when he saw the woman like a tied-up ox he said, "I will unloose her if for nothing else that I may undo what the devil has done." Now, dear tried friend, inasmuch as your sorrow may be traced to satanic influence, Jesus Christ will prove in your case more than a match for the devil, and he will set you free.

Then think of *her sorrowful condition.* An ox or an ass tied up to the manger without water would soon be in a very sad plight. Pity it, poor thing. Hear the lowing of the ox, as hour after hour its thirst tells upon it. Would you not pity it? And do you think the Lord does not pity his poor, tried, tempted, afflicted children? Those tears, shall they fall for nothing? Those sleepless nights, shall they be disregarded? That broken heart which fain would but cannot believe the promise, shall that forever be denied a hearing? Hath the Lord forgotten to be gracious? Hath he in anger shut up the bowels of his mercy? Ah no, he will remember your sorrowful estate and hear your groanings, for he puts your tears into his bottle.

Last of all, there was this reason to move the heart of Christ, that *she had been eighteen years in that state.* "Then," said he, "she shall be loosed at once." The master of the synagogue would have said, "She has been eighteen years bound, and she may well wait till tomorrow, for it is only one day." "No," says Christ, "if she has been bound eighteen years, she shall not wait a minute; she has had too much of it already; she shall be set free at once." Do not, therefore, argue from the length of your despondency that it shall not come to an end, but rather argue from it that release is near. The night has been so long, it must be so much nearer the dawning. You have been scourged so long that it must be so much nearer the last stroke, for the Lord does not afflict willingly, nor grieve the children of men. Therefore take heart and be of a good courage. Oh, that my divine Master would now come and do what I fain would do but cannot, namely, make every child of God here leap for joy.

I know what this being bound by Satan means. The devil has not tied me up for eighteen years at a stretch, and I do not think he ever will, but he has brought me into sad bondage many a time. Still, my Master comes and sets me free, and leads me out to watering: and what a drink I get at such times! I seem as if I could drink up Jordan at a draft when I get to his promises, and quaff my fill of his sweet love. I know by this that he will lead other poor souls out to the watering; and when he does so to any of you, I pray you drink like an ox. You may be tied up again; therefore drink as much as you can of his grace, and rejoice while you may. Eat that which is good, and let your soul delight in fatness. Be glad in the Lord, you righteous, and shout for joy all you that are upright in heart, for the Lord looses the prisoners. May he loose many now. Amen.

Mary of Bethany: To Lovers of Jesus—An Example

Intended for reading on Lord's Day, April 12, 1885; delivered on November 2, 1884, at the Metropolitan Tabernacle, Newington. No. 1834.

She hath wrought a good work on me.—MARK 14:6

This holy woman had *displeased the disciples*. She must have been very sorry to do that. She would not have willfully grieved the least servant of her Lord. But she did so without the slightest blame on her part: it was the unexpected consequence of a most blessed action, and the fault lay with those who complained of her holy deed, and not with her. I do not know whether all the disciples felt grieved, but we are told by Matthew that "they had indignation," and he seems to speak of them as a body; from which I gather that those who love Jesus much must not measure their conduct by that of Christ's ordinary disciples, indeed it might fare ill with them even if apostles became their judges. They must not tone down the fervor of their zeal to the lukewarmness of the general order of Christian men: they must not measure the consecration of their lives by the little which many professors present upon the altar to God. No, my brother or sister, you must not be too much distressed if the best of the household misjudge you, for it has happened to many favored sons before you. You, O man, greatly beloved, cannot abide to be lukewarm, and be not surprised if the lukewarm cannot agree with you! Count it no strange thing if, in your ardor, you should come to be accused of fanaticism, want of prudence, rashness, forwardness. Do not break your heart over it if they should even call you mad, or suspect that you have more zeal than knowledge; for Mary, whom we would be glad to imitate, came under this kind of censure; and David, and your Lord, the Son of David, were each thought to be madmen.

This honored woman performed a notable act, which is to be rehearsed wherever the gospel is preached, and yet thereby she stirred the wrath of the brotherhood of the disciples: of how small account is the judgment of men!

Chiefly, she called down upon her head the censure of Judas. As far as Judas was known to his brethren, he was reckoned among the best of them. They never suspected him of playing the traitor, or they would have caviled at his being their treasurer: they once had indignation at James and John, but the canny Judas had their respect. I should think he was the most businesslike man of the whole company—which is not saying much for business, is it? He was a leading spirit among that little band. He was one who would be selected because of his prudence—and that is not saying much for prudence, is it? Doubtless Judas abounded in that cool, calculating shrewdness which makes a man fit to deal with monies and purchases. He had far more business ability than impetuous Peter, or affectionate John, or thoughtful Thomas. He was the right man in the right place, if he had but happened to have been an honest man. Wonderful it was that he could conceal the deep meanness of his spirit from all his fellows during the years in which they lived together; but he had done so, and therefore his opinion carried weight with it. Among the apostles, the censure of Judas meant the calm condemnation of a judicious person. His judgment was not what you and I would esteem it to be, for we should think nothing of his censure now, because we know that he betrayed his Lord; but the disciples could not foresee this, and in their judgment that which Judas would condemn must be very censurable; at least it must be unbusinesslike; it must lack common sense; it must be imprudent and wasteful. Was not Judas the perfect model of economy? Was he not the sort of man who in these days many a father would point out to his boy as an example? Hear him say, "Boy, if you want to get on in the world, imitate Judas Iscariot; he is the model man, he is a Christian, and yet he has a keen eye for his own advantage, and is a sharp man of business."

It was a hard thing for a timid woman to bear such a censure from one so highly respected in the college of apostles; but she had this solace, which I will warrant you, put quite out of her mind all care about the censure of disciples, even of the biggest of them: she pleased her Master. She could see by the very look of him that he accepted what his followers condemned. She knew in her conscience that she had the approbation of the Lord, even though she had the disapprobation of the servants. O brothers and sisters, let us always carry our case into the highest court, and live before the Lord, and not as the slaves of men! If we are conscious that we have sincerely done what we have done as unto the Lord, and if we feel sure that he has approved our service, it is of the smallest consequence possible what men shall say of us. Let us never provoke our brethren to be ill-tempered to us, neither let us do anything that can be rightly censured out if we have gone somewhat beyond common custom in the fervor of our spirit; let us reply with young David to his envious brethren,

"Is there not a cause?" The opinions of other men are no rule to us: we have our own obligations to discharge, and as our debt of love is larger than usual, let us take liberty to be as full of love and zeal as we can be, only regretting that we cannot go still further in the way of sacred service.

"Well," says one, "but do those who love Christ encounter the frowns of men at this time?" Oh yes, and of their own Christian brethren too! If you consort with the common ruck of brethren, and travel on the road to heaven so slowly that it is a question whether you are going there at all, then you will escape criticism: if you keep with those who practice the snail's march they will call you a good easy man, a right respectable person. But if you run for it, if you put out all the energy of your nature, and are determined to live at a high pitch for Christ, you will get the cold shoulder, even from many of his disciples, for you will be practically condemning their halfheartedness; and who are you to be such a troubler in Israel? The more prudent among your brethren will say that your pride and the naughtiness of your heart make you so forward and presumptuous, and they will try to put you down or put you out. You cannot commit a greater crime against some people than to be more useful than they are. When a person reckons himself to be the standard of holiness, he looks upon one who excels him as guilty of a kind of blasphemy. If you outrun others, do not reckon upon smiles, but count upon black looks. You will be called impudent and thought impertinent. Bear it all and fret not. Go to your Lord, and tell him that you have done and are doing all you can as unto him, and entreat him to smile upon you. Crave his acceptance of your poor doings, and then go about your business, occupying till he shall come. Sow the seed of duty, and care not whether in human judgment it shines or rains. "He that regardeth the clouds shall not reap"; if you regard not the clouds at all, you will do your sowing and your reaping with the comfort of true faith, and God will bless you.

I am going to talk about this blessed woman at this time with this hopeful desire—that you and I may imitate her ever-memorable example. I shall have nothing to say but to open up the meaning of our Lord, as far as I know it, when he said, "She hath wrought a good work on me" or "in me." The passage might be rendered—only the translators do not like to use the term—"She hath wrought a beautiful work on me"—a comely work. "A thing of beauty is a joy forever" [John Keats]. This was a thing of beauty, which is a joy forever to the church of God, in that constant memorial of her which is blended with the preaching of the gospel of Christ; for as long as the gospel is proclaimed, this Mary of Bethany shall have a memorial, because of what she did.

What was there beautiful about her work—the breaking of the alabaster vase, and the pouring out of the liquid nard? What was there beautiful about that? I will try to show you.

I. There were seven beauties in it, and the first and chief beauty, perhaps, was that *it was altogether glorifying of Jesus.*

She meant when she poured that ointment on his head to honor *him* personally; every drop of it was for himself, out of reverence for his actual personality.

She was not so much thinking of his deeds of love, or of his words of truth, as of his own unrivaled and most precious self. She had seen his deeds of love when Lazarus was raised; she had heard his words of truth when she sat at his feet: but now she felt an adoring reverence for his thrice-blessed Person, and she brought that box of precious spikenard, and offered it to him as her Teacher, her Friend, her Lord, her all. Suggestion was made that she should have sold it and given it to the poor; but she longed to present one offering *to him* directly, and not by any roundabout method. Doubtless she was not behindhand in her gifts to the poor, but she felt that when she had done *that* she had not satisfied the cravings of her grateful heart toward *him* who had become poorest of the poor for her sake. She wanted to give something *to him*—something suitable for such a One as she conceived him to be—something suitable for the time and circumstances then present with regard to him.

I think this holy woman knew more about our Lord than all his apostles put together. Her eyes had peered within the veil. You remember that only a day or two after this, he rode in triumph through Jerusalem a proclaimed king. Should he not first be anointed? And who would anoint him to the kingdom visibly with oil but this consecrated woman? She was come to give him a royal anointing preparatory to his proclamation in the streets of his capital city. At any rate her spikenard must be poured out alone *for him.* She forgot the poor just then as she quite forgot the disciples. Martha was busy at the table waiting upon them all, disciples and Master; but Mary had concentrated all her thoughts on Jesus. She "saw no man save Jesus only." Blessed exclusiveness of vision! What she did must not be for Peter and James and John with Jesus, but it must be for him alone, who indeed is alone, above and beyond all others, worthy of a homage all his own. Because she had a love for him beyond all others that she had ever heard of, her heart must find expression in a deed of love which must be entirely, wholly, only toward himself.

Now this is, as we have read the text, a beautiful thing. It will be beautiful on your part and mine if, having taken care of the poor according to our ability, having discharged the claims of our relationships to our fellowmen, we then feel that we must do something for Jesus—distinctly for our Lord. Do you ask me what you shall do for him? No, but, sister, I must not tell you; your own heart must originate the thought, as your own hand must carry it out. "Oh," cries a brother, "tell me what I could do for Jesus!" No, but, brother, I must not tell you. The better part of the whole matter will lie in the hallowed ingenuity of your spirit in inventing something for him out of your own fervent soul. The holy woman's deed had been somewhat spoiled if there had been a command for her to bring the alabaster box, and pour the ointment on his head: her love commanded her, and that was better than a formal precept. Her deed had not possessed half its worth if Simon had suggested to her, "I have not sufficient spikenard to anoint our guests; fetch you a box from home." The very glory of it lay in the spontaneous suggestion of her own heart that she must do something which should be all for Jesus.

She must do it herself personally, and not by proxy; and she must do it unto him distinctly, directly, openly. Others might smell the spikenard. That she did not wish to prevent; but still the perfume was never meant for them, but for him exclusively. She poured it on *his* head; she poured it on *his* feet; she would anoint *him* from head to foot with this token of her intense and reverent gratitude, and her boundless love: she felt wrapped up in *him*, her Lord and her God, and so her willing offering was for him, and for him alone. What a joy to be permitted to do anything for him whose great love holds us fast! I feel as if I would fain at once retire from you all to indulge my heart in this rare luxury.

Alas, good Lord, how little have you of this devotion in these calculating days! Instead of "all for Jesus," how seldom we do anything for Jesus! Brethren, when you sing your hymns, do you "sing a hymn to Jesus"? When you are in prayer, do you pray *to* Jesus, and *for* Jesus? Is it not written, "Prayer also shall be made for him continually, and daily shall he be praised"? When you come to this communion table, I pray that you may forget all that come with you in this assembly, and cry, "I will remember *thee*." In the chief place, at any rate, let Jesus fill your thoughts. Set him alone upon the throne, and think only of eating his flesh and drinking his blood, and receiving him into your very self, that there may be a vital union between the Christ of God and your own souls. To my mind this is the beauty of our fellowship in the holy Supper, that we feed on Jesus only. Let us make him our soul's sole meat and drink; and then let us live for him. My heart craves now to know what I shall do that I may imitate her who gave to "Jesus only" that box of spikenard, very costly. O you lovers of my Lord who have been washed in his precious blood, who owe your all to him, think of his matchless beauties now, and as you look up into that face where shines your heaven, think to yourselves, "What can we do for him—for him absolutely, directly, and personally?" There is the first beauty of this woman's act of homage: it was for Jesus, for Jesus only, for Jesus wholly.

II. A second beauty lay in this: that *it was an act of pure love*, altogether of love to Jesus.

The other woman—blessed was she also among women—I refer to that woman who was a sinner: she also came and brought an alabaster box, and did much the same thing as this Mary of Bethany. But she did what Mary did not do: she mingled weeping with her ointment: she washed his feet with tears, and wiped them with the hairs of her head. That was a beautiful act in its own way, but Mary's deed is a beautiful thing in another way. In this lies the distinction: there does not seem to have been in Mary's act any remembrance of personal sin, though, doubtless, that feeling was in her heart, and had brought her to the higher stage of adoration of her pardoning Lord. Her sin was put away long ago. Mary had sat at Jesus' feet, and had chosen the good part, and the matter of pardon for sin had been transacted a long while before; and now, although in her heart there is deep gratitude for it, and for the raising of her dear brother Lazarus, yet it seems to be quite absorbed in the deeper thought of her soul, for she had attained to an all-consuming love of himself. She never would have known that kind of love if she had not learned to sit at his feet, but to sit long there has a wonderful operation on the human mind; it causes even things that are good in themselves to be overshadowed by matters that are less and less in relation to self. It is a blessed thing to love Christ because we escape from hell by him; it is a blessed thing to love Christ because he has opened the kingdom of heaven to all believers; but it is a still higher thing to forget yourself, and to contemplate with delight the ineffable perfections of him whom heaven and earth acknowledge to be chief among ten thousand, and altogether lovely. "We love him because he first loved us"; here we begin, and this beginning always remains; but on it we pile tier after tier of precious stones of love, which are crowned with pinnacles of inexpressible affection for the great Lord himself. He in himself has won our hearts, and carried our spirits by storm, and now we must do something which will express our love to him. That love is not alone a gratitude for benefits received from him, but an intense affection for his glorious, adorable person.

Come, dear friends, do you feel that kind of emotion in your hearts at this time? Do you even now feel that so perfectly has Christ won the verdict of

your understanding, so completely has he bound in silken fetters every movement of your affections, that you want to be doing something which shall have
but this one aim, to express your love to him who has made you what you are?
Indulge the emotion, crown it with action, continue it through life. In this
point be not slow to be imitators of the sister of Martha and Lazarus. O sweet
love of Jesus, come and fill our souls to the brim, and run over in delicate personal service!

III. The third beauty of the action was that *it was done with considerable sacrifice.*

There was an expense about it, and that of no trifling character to a
woman who was neither queen nor princess. I shall always feel obliged to Judas
for figuring up the price of that box of costly nard. He did it to blame her, but
we will let his figures stand, and think the more of her the more he put down
to the account of waste. I should never have known what it cost, nor would
you either, if Judas had not marked down in his pocket book that it "might have
been sold for much." How he grudged that "much." He calculated the value at
three hundred pence. He did well to put it in pence, for his sordid soul reveled
in small monies which make up the pounds. Pence, indeed, when the expense
is for him to whom the silver and the gold belong! Yet I like his calculation in
pence, for it is suggestive, since a Roman penny was a day's wages; and take a
day's wages now—say four shillings—and you get some £60. It was a large
sum of money for a woman in her state of life in Bethany. It was £10 of their
money, but money then was of a different value from what it is now, and it was
a great sum for her to expend in one single deed of love.

Her gift was costly, and the Lord Jesus deserved to be served at the best
rate, and at the highest cost. There was a woman who served the Lord at a
higher rate than this: she only spent two mites in the doing of it, but then you
know it was all that she had. I do not know how much Mary had, but I feel persuaded that it was pretty well all she had, and that all she could get together
seemed to her to be far too little for the Lord Jesus Christ. If his head was to
be anointed, plenty of ordinary oil might have been procured at Bethany. The
Mount of Olives was hard by. But she would have scorned the thought of
pouring common olive oil on him: she must find an imperial unguent such as
Caesar might have accepted. If he is to be anointed, there is nard to be bought
in the bazaars at Jerusalem at a very reasonable rate. Why must you, Mary,
seek after this liquid ointment of the East, this oil distilled from myriads of
roses, of which it needs leagues of gardens to make a drop? Why must you
buy the "very precious" nard, and spend such a deal of money upon that

which will only last half an hour, and then the wind will have carried it away, and its perfume will have vanished? Yes, but the glory of service to Christ is to serve him with the best of the best!

He deserves, if we serve him with sermons, that we preach the best discourses mind can frame or tongue deliver; or if we serve him with teaching in the class, he deserves that we teach in the tenderest fashion, and feed his lambs with the best of the grass; or if we serve him with the pen, that we write not a line that may need to be erased; or if we serve him with money, that we give with liberality of the best we have, and much of it. We must see to it that in everything we do not serve Christ with the lean sheep of the flock, or with such as are wounded, and broken, and torn by beasts; but that he has the fat of our offerings. We should not be content if we are rich to give him out of our estate the cheese parings and candle ends, such as we dare not keep back for very shame. Usual donations have little beauty in them—those monies dragged out of people by importunity—that guinea dribbled out by custom because it is a respectable amount. There is nothing to satisfy love in the slender oblations which come forth like an unwilling taxation, which a miser could scarcely withhold. But oh, to give to the Lord Jesus freely, richly, whatever it is with which he has entrusted us, whether it be gold or genius, time or words— whether it be the minted coinage of the purse, or the living courage of a loving heart, or the labor of an earnest hand! Let us give our Well Beloved the best we have, and he will call it beautiful. Mary's gift was all for him, and all for love, and it was done at great expense, and therefore it was beautiful.

IV. Next, remember, that part of the beauty of Mary's action lay in this, that *it was done with preparation.*

We are told by John what we should not else have known, "Against the day of my burying hath she kept this." "Kept this." It was not that seeing Jesus there at the feast, and being seized with a sudden thought, she rushed back to her stores, and fetched out the little vase of spikenard, and broke it in a passion of affection, which in cooler moments she might regret. Far from it: she was now consummating the long thought of weeks and months. We have known warm-spirited brethren and sisters both say and do and give grandly, under a certain spur and impulse, what they never thought of doing when they entered into the assembly. I shall not blame them; rather do I commend them for obeying gracious impulses; but it is not the best way of doing service to our ever-blessed Master. Passion seldom gives so acceptably as principle. Mary did not perform a thoughtless action under a tempestuous force of unusual zeal. No, she had kept this. She had kept this choice unguent on purpose till a fitting time should come for putting it to its most appropriate use. My own belief is that, when she sat at Jesus' feet, she learned much more than any of the disciples had ever gathered from his public preaching. She had heard him say that the Son of man would be delivered to the scribes and Pharisees, and that he would be spat upon and scourged, and they would put him to death, and the third day he would rise again; and she believed it. She thought it over, and she studied it, and made out more of the meaning of it than any one of the apostles had done. She said to herself—he is going to die as a sacrifice at the hands of wicked men, and I will, therefore, render him special honor. I should not wonder if she began to read the Old Testament with that light, "This is he whom God hath sent, upon whom he hath laid the iniquities of us all, and he shall be given up to judgment, and he shall bear the sin of man." Then she thought within herself, "If that is so, I will get the spikenard ready to anoint him for his burial." Perhaps she intended as much as that, for so the Lord himself interpreted the deed. At any rate, she thought, "Alas, for my Lord! If he dies he will need to be embalmed, and I will be ready to aid in his burial." Therefore she kept this.

"Against the day of my burying hath she kept this." Brethren, there is great beauty in an action which is the outcome of a long time of loving careful consideration. It is ill to delay a good deed which might be done at once; but if a deed must be delayed, it is well to be doing it at once by preparing for it. When a person feels, "The time is not yet, but I will be prepared when it does come," it shows that the heart is occupied with a love of a very engrossing character. We sing—

> *Oh, what shall I do*
> *My Savior to praise?*

And it were well if the question were constantly in our minds. Let each man resolve in his heart—I will not offer my Lord the hasty fruit of impulse, or that which shall cost me nothing, but I will consider what I can do for him. Of what will there be a need? In what direction can I do him homage where else he might lack that honor? I will turn it over and meditate and consider, and then I will perform. This last the preacher would repeat with emphasis, for o my brothers, it is a custom with many of us to get a grand thought and then, as we turn it over, to let it evaporate without its leaving even a drop of practical result behind! This holy woman was no mere planner and purposer, but a doer of holy deeds. She could keep her alabaster box as long as was prudent, and yet she did not arrive at the tempting conclusion to keep it altogether. She allowed her heart to weigh the project; and the more she weighed it, she became the more resolved to do it—to do it when the due time came. When she believed that the hour had come, she did not delay for an instant. She was as prompt as she had been thoughtful. The Passover was drawing very near; it was within six days, and so she brought out what she had held in reserve. Blessed are the punctualities of service which are the result of earnest endeavor to honor the Lord in the best possible way.

There is something beautiful in seeing, as we have seen, some poor woman saving her little bits, and putting them by for years till she could accomplish a secret purpose by which Jesus would be glorified. It is striking to see, as you and I did see, a woman of moderate wealth discarding all the comforts of life that she might save sufficient that there might be an orphanage in which children might be cared for; not, as she said, for the children's sake, but for Christ's sake, that he might be glorified. The Stockwell Orphanage is the alabaster box which a devout woman presented to her Lord. Her memory is blessed. Its perfume is recognized in all parts of the earth at this moment, to the glory of the Lord she loved. Such a thoughtful deed is what Jesus would call a beautiful thing. Let us abound in such beautiful things. For a man to say, "There will come a crisis when I shall have to stand out for God and his truth, and it will be a serious loss to me," and then so to ponder it as to be almost eager for the occasion, is a beautiful thing. To feel like the Lord Jesus, "I have a baptism to be baptized with, and how am I straitened till it be accomplished!" is a beautiful thing. A courageous, self-sacrificing decision for the truth is a beautiful thing, when its action is well considered, and carried out with enthusiasm. God give us to mix thought and impulse, reason and affection, and thus serve him both with the mind and the heart!

V. There is a fifth point of beauty. *Mary did her great deed without a word.*

Dear sisters, you will pardon me for commending this holy woman for her wise and fitting silence all through her gracious act. She did not talk about it beforehand, she said not a word while she did it, and she said nothing afterward. Martha was the worker, and rather the talker too; but I think that all you will find Mary saying is, "Lord, if thou hadst been here, my brother had not died"; and she was so scant of words that she had to borrow those from Martha. Martha said a great deal more than that; but Mary was quite satisfied to be as brief as possible. She was a great thinker, a great sitter at Jesus' feet, and a great learner, but not a great talker. When the time came, she was a great worker, for it is very curious, though Martha bears the palm for work in our ordinary talk, yet Mary, the thinker, did more than Martha, the worker. "She," said Christ, "hath wrought a good work on me," which he never said of Martha, good as Martha was. He a little censured the elder sister for being cumbered with much serving; but Mary's work he commended, and decreed that it should be remembered as long as the world stands. Though she does not bear the name of a worker in the vulgar judgment, yet is she the queen in the kingdom of good works.

Yet, I remind you, she did not say a word. There is such a thing as spoiling what you do by making so great a fuss before you do it, that when the mouse is born people are only astonished that such a small creature should be the only fruit of the dreadful throes of the mountain. Moreover, there is such a thing as talking so much afterward of what we have done that it spoils it all. It seems as if we must let all the world know something about ourselves; whereas the joy and bliss of it all is not to let yourself be seen, but to let the oil go streaming upon the Master till he is anointed with perfume, and we ourselves sink back into our natural insignificance. Silent acts of love have musical voices in the ear of Jesus. Sound no trumpet before you, or Jesus will take warning and be gone.

If we could all *do* more and *talk* less, it might be a blessing to ourselves at least, perhaps to others. Let us labor in our service for the Lord to be more and more hidden; as much as the proud desire to catch the eye of man, let us endeavor to avoid it.

"I should like to know," says one, "how to do holy work." Go and do it, and consult not with flesh and blood. "I have done my work, and now I should dearly like to hear what you think of it." You should rise above such idle dependence upon man's opinion; what matters it to you what your fellow servant thinks? To your own Master you stand or fall. If you have done a good thing, do it again. You know the story of the man who comes riding up to the captain, and says, "Sir, we have taken a gun from the enemy." "Go and take another," said the matter-of-fact officer. That is the best advice which I can render to a friend who is elated with his own success. So much remains to be accomplished that we have no time to consider what has been done. If we have done holy service, let us do it a second time, and do it a third time, and continue to do it, ever praying the Lord to accept our persevering service. In any case let our consecrated life be for our Lord's eye alone, a spring shut up, a fountain sealed. Anything like sounding a trumpet before us is hateful to the lowly Lord; secrecy has a charm for Jesus, and the more carefully we preserve it, the better.

VI. Next, and sixth, there was this beauty about the action of Mary—that *she did it in reference to our Lord's death.*

The disciples shrank from thinking of that sad subject. Peter said, "That be far from thee, Lord." But Mary, bearing her Master's heart very near her own, and sympathizing with him in his glorious enterprise, instead of drawing back from the thought of that death, performed her work in connection with it. I am not certain to what degree she was conscious that it was so, but there is the fact—the anointing had reference to the burial of the Lord. It seems to me that the best and tenderest duty that Christians do for their Lord Jesus is that which is touched with the blood mark—which bears the stamp of the cross. The best preaching is "We preach Christ crucified." The best living is "We are crucified with Christ." The best man is a crucified man. The best style is a crucified style: may we drop into it! The more we live beholding our Lord's unutterable griefs, and understanding how he has fully put away our sin, the more holiness shall we produce. The more we dwell where the cries of Calvary can be heard, where we can view heaven and earth and hell, all moved by his wondrous passion—the more noble will our lives become. Nothing puts life into men like a dying Savior. Get you close to Christ, and carry the remembrance of him about you from day to day, and you will do right royal deeds. Come, let us slay sin, for Christ was slain. Come, let us bury all our pride, for Christ was buried. Come, let us rise to newness of life, for Christ has risen. Let us be united with our crucified Lord in his one great object—let us live and die with him, and then every action of our lives will be very beautiful.

VII. The seventh beauty, to my mind, is this: you may think it a little far-fetched, but I cannot help mentioning it, for it touches my heart. I believe that *Mary had in this anointing of the Savior some little glimpse of his resurrection from the dead,* **and of his after existence.**

For I would ask of you—Why do nations at all embalm their dead? Why not consume them in the fire? A mysterious something makes the ordinary Christian man shudder at the thought of cremation. That must surely be an acquired taste: unsophisticated nature does not court the furnace or covet the flame; we prefer to lie beneath the green hillock with our fathers. Many nations of antiquity, and especially the Egyptians and other Orientals, took great care to anoint the bodies of the departed with precious perfumes, and to lay them asleep in gems and fine linen. What for? Because there darkly shone upon their minds some thought of the hereafter. There remained with man, long after the fall, a glimmering, undefined belief in immortality. That truth was so universally received that the Old Testament takes it for granted. The existence of God and the immortality of the soul lie at the basis of Old Testament teaching. The afterlife of the body was accepted also in a manner more or less clear. Immortality was not brought to light, but there it was, and they who reject that doctrine go back into a darkness denser than that in which the heathens themselves dwelled. Why did the Egyptian king embalm his father and lay him in spices, but that he thought that somehow or other there was another life, and he would, therefore, take care of the body? They would not have wasted precious linen and gems and spices, if they had thought that the body was mere rottenness for worms to consume forever. Mary had deeper and clearer thoughts than that, for she expected that something would happen to that blessed body after Christ had died; and she must, therefore, anoint it, and bring the most precious spices that she could procure for his burial. At any rate, let your service of the Lord Jesus be the service of a risen Christ. Come not hither to worship one who died years ago—a hero of the past; but come to adore the ever-living Jesus.

> *He lives, your great Redeemer lives.*

He will certainly come in his own person to reward his saints; and ere he comes he sees what you are doing. "We live," said one, "in the great Taskmaster's eye." I care not for that title. I have no Taskmaster. It is far more an impulse to my life that I live within the sight of him whom, having not seen, I love, because he loved me and gave himself for me. If this does not quicken you, what will? If this does not nerve you to tireless diligence in holy service, what can? Our Lord Jesus Christ lives. Let us find some way of anointing his dear and reverend head—some way of crowning him who wore the crown of thorns for our sake. Ours it is to know that he lives, and that we live in him. On him would we expend the full force of our being, counting it all joy to spend and to be spent for his sake.

I am not going to stir you up, my fellow Christians, to do anything for Christ, for I fear to spoil the freeness of your love's life. I do not want to be pleading with you to enter into his service more fully; for the work of pressed men is never so much prized as that of happy volunteers. Yet as I love you, I would have you love your Lord more and more. It is so sweet to belong to Christ, that the more fully we can belong to him the more free we are. I like that of Paul, where he calls himself the *doulos* of Christ, the slave of Jesus. He says exultingly, "Let no man trouble me. I bear in my body the marks of the Lord Jesus," as if he gloried to think of himself as the branded slave of his

Lord. He had been beaten and scourged, and he retained upon his back the marks of his lashings, and therefore he was wont to say to himself, and smile all the while, "These are my Master's marks. I am branded with his name." Oh, sweet service, in which if it could be slavery it would be joy! I would not have a hair of my head that was not my Lord's if I could help it, nor a drop of my blood that did not flow for him if I could help it. My liberty—and I speak for you all—my liberty, if I might choose it, would be liberty never to sin again; freedom to do Christ's bidding, and that alone. I would fain lose my free will in his sweet will, and find it again as I never found it before in having yielded it up completely to his command.

I will not, therefore, so much intrude upon the sanctity of your heart's love as to suggest what you can do for Jesus. As the best juice flows from the cluster with the least pressure, so shall the best service be that which is most spontaneous. Do not let me push you on, or draw you on, or drag you on; but be eager on your own account. Say to the Lord himself, "Draw me: I will run after thee." Have you not a certain private reason why you should love your Lord better than any other of his redeemed? I repeat it; I will not pry into your sacred secrets, but leave you to commune with your own heart, and with your Lord. Only let us so love him that when we look at him he shall say, "Thou hast ravished my heart, my sister, my spouse; thou hast ravished my heart with one of thine eyes, with one chain of thy neck." Then shall we know what to do for our Well Beloved, and, what is better, we shall do it without further exhortation.

There I leave it. May the Holy Ghost bless the word!

As for you that do not love the Lord Jesus, God be merciful to you! I will not pronounce upon you an "Anathema Maranatha," but I tremble lest it fall upon you. I am sorely grieved for your sakes. I am, moreover, sorely vexed for Christ's sake, that he should be deprived of your love and service. What has he done that you should slight him? O blind eyes, that cannot see his beauties, and deaf ears, that cannot hear the charms of his voice! God be merciful to you, and help you to trust your Savior, and then you will love him for his salvation! It is no wonder that the saved ones love their Lord: it is a marvel that they do not love him ten thousand times more. The Lord be with you for Christ's sake! Amen.

A Repentant Woman:
A Gracious Dismissal

⟡

Intended for reading on Lord's Day, January 11, 1891; delivered at the Metropolitan Tabernacle, Newington. No. 2183.

And he said to the woman, "Thy faith hath saved thee; go in peace."
—LUKE 7:50

The main part of my subject will be that gracious dismissal, "Go in peace." To her who had been so lately blessed, the word *go* sounded mournfully; for she would fain have remained through life with her pardoning Lord; but the added words *in peace* turned the wormwood into honey—there was now peace for her who had been so long hunted and harried by her sins. Rising from the feet she had washed with tears, she went forth to keep her future footsteps such as those of a believing, and therefore saved, woman ought to be.

We like a motto to begin the year with, and it has been useful to some spirits to choose a motto with which to enter on a new course of life. We climb the hill of enterprise, or dare the wave of trial, with an inspiring word upon our lip. To certain young men a word has come in life's early morning, wet with the dew of heaven, and that word of their day dawn has kept with them. The echoes of that life-evoking word have followed them long after it was spoken; amid strange scenes it has come to them like a voice from the unseen. It has whispered to them within the curtains of their dying bed: it has murmured consolation amid Jordan's swelling waves. That first word of joy and peace from Jesus with which they began the new life came to them over again just as they were melting away into the invisible land: so they began the service of the Redeemer, and so he declared that their work was finished. Perhaps that love note will be their welcome at the very gates of heaven.

Our Lord, in the instance before us, sent a penitent away from the chill atmosphere of self-righteous caviling, and thus relieved her of a controversy for which she was not fitted; but I see more than that in this benediction. It looks to me as if our divine Master, when he found this poor sinner so full of love to him that she washed his feet with tears, and wiped them with the hairs of her head, having by a parable explained to the Pharisee the reason for the greatness of her love, then said to her, "Go in peace"—meaning that word not only to be cheering for the necessary purpose of the moment, but to go with her, and to attend her all the rest of her life, until, when she came into the dark valley, she should fear no evil, for she would still hear that sweet voice saying, "Go in peace." What music to have heard! What music still to hear!

Now, I would to God that the word which I shall speak at this time might be honored of the Lord to serve that sacred purpose to some here present. May it be a life-word to certain of you! May it be to others of us who have long known the Savior a revival of our rest, and may we get such a draft of peace from Jesus that we may never thirst again! The lips of our divine Lord are a wellspring of delight; each word is a chalice brimmed with sweetness. Imbibing this, we shall go our way henceforth even to our journey's end, after the manner of the hymn which we sang just now—

> Calm in the hour of buoyant health,
> Calm in my hour of pain;
> Calm in my poverty or wealth,
> Calm in my loss or gain;
>
> Calm me, my God, and keep me calm,
> Soft resting on thy breast;
> Soothe me with holy hymn and psalm,
> And bid my spirit rest.

Oh, that our life may be as a sea of glass! May the sacred circle of our fellowship be within the golden line of the peace of God! You who did bid us come to you and rest, now bid us "go in peace."

I am going to say a little in my opening upon a *delightful assurance* which constituted the reason why the woman went in peace: "Thy faith hath saved thee"; or, as in verse 48, "Thy sins are forgiven thee." Upon the strength of the assurance that she was saved, she might safely go in peace. When we have talked a little upon that subject, we will then come to a *considerate precept*: the Savior directed her, in the moment of trial, to "go in peace." There was an assurance for her comfort, and a precept for her guidance.

I. First, then, consider *a delightful assurance.*

The ground upon which the penitent woman might go in peace was that she had been saved. The Savior assured her: "Thy faith hath saved thee."

She was not saved otherwise than we are saved; but she received the common salvation by like precious faith. The way of salvation to her was faith in Christ. There is the same way for us, but she had what some of you, no doubt, would greatly like to have: she had *an assurance that she was saved, from the Lord's own mouth.* I think I hear some saying, "I should go in peace, I am sure, if the Lord Jesus would but appear to me, and speak, and say with his own lips, 'Thy faith hath saved thee.'" It is natural that you should think so; it must have been rapture to receive a benediction from the mouth of our King, our Savior. Yet, dear friends, we must not hang our confidence upon a mere circumstance. For a mere circumstance it is, whether Christ shall literally stand before you in the flesh, and say, "Thy faith hath saved thee," or whether he shall say it to you by the infallible record of his own Word. It does not make much difference as to my faith in what my father says to me, whether I meet the venerable man in the morning in my garden, and there hear his voice, or whether I get a letter by post in his handwriting, and he says to me upon that paper just what he would have said if I had met him face to face. I do not require him always to come up the hill to my house to tell me everything that he has to say: I should think myself an idiot if I did. If I were to say, "My dear father, you have assured me of your love by letter; but somehow, I cannot credit it unless you come and look me in the face, and take my hand, and assure me of your goodwill," surely he would say to me, "My dear son, what ails you? You must be out of your mind. I never knew you to be so childish before: my handwriting has always been enough. I can hardly think you mean it when you say that you cannot credit me unless I stand manifest before your eyes, and with your ears you hear me speak."

Now what I would not do to my earthly father, I certainly would not do to my heavenly Savior. I am perfectly satisfied myself to believe what he writes to me; and if it be so written in his Book, it seems to me to be quite as true and sure as if he had actually come from heaven, and had talked with me, or had appeared to me in the visions of the night. Is not this the reasoning of common sense? Do you not at once agree with me?

"Well," say you, "we go with you there, dear sir; but, then, he spoke that word to her personally. We should never have any more doubts, but should go in peace, if he said that word of assurance to us. You see, it is not merely that Jesus himself spoke, and said, 'Thy faith hath made thee whole,' but he looked that way; he turned toward her, and she knew that he referred to her. There was no mistaking to whom the assurance was given. There were other people in the room, but he did not say it to Simon; he did not say it to Peter; he did not say it to James and John. She knew by the look of him that he meant it for her, and for her alone, for she was the only person to go, and consequently the only one to 'go in peace.' Our Lord put it in the singular number, and said, 'Thy faith hath saved thee.' I want it to come home just so to me."

Yes, but I think that this is a little unreasonable too; is it not? Because if my father (to carry on my figure) were to speak to me, and to my brothers and to my sisters, and were to say, "Dear children, I have loving thoughts concerning you, and I have laid up in store for your needs," I do not think that I should say to him by and by, "Now, Father, do you know that I did not believe you, or derive any pleasure from what you said, because you spoke to others besides myself? I did not think your statement of love could be true, because you included my brothers and my sisters. You did not use the singular, but you put it in the plural; and you spoke to all my brothers and sisters, as well as to myself; and therefore I felt that I could not take any comfort out of your tender assurances." I should be a most unreasonable kind of body if I were to talk in that way; and my father would begin to think that his son was qualifying for a lunatic asylum. If he did not attribute it to unkindness of heart, he certainly would ascribe it to imbecility of head. Why, surely, surely, if my father says the same to each one of his children as he says to me, his words are all the more likely to be true, instead of being less worthy of belief; and therefore I derive comfort from his promises of love being put in the plural rather than in the singular. Surely, it should not be less easy to believe that God would deal graciously with me in company with thousands of others than that he should pursue a solitary plan with me as the lone object of his love. Is it not so?

"Ah yes!" says one, "but you have not hit on it yet. I want to know that I am one that is in that plural, and I want to know that I really am one of those to whom Jesus speaks in his Word." My anxious friend, you may know it; and you may know it most certainly. It is written, "He that believeth on him hath everlasting life." It need never be a question whether you believe in him or not; if you trust him, that is the gist of the matter. You can readily ascertain whether you do really trust him, or do not trust him. If you do trust him, you are his, and every promise of his covenant is made to you. You have faith, and when the Lord lays it down as a general statement that faith saves—the statement is applicable to all the world, in every place, and in all time, until the present age shall end, and men shall have passed into the fixed state of retribution, where no gospel of faith is preached. "Thy faith hath saved thee": if you have faith at all—if you believe that Jesus is the Christ—you are born of God. If you can say to the Lord Jesus,

> All my trust on thee is stayed,
> All my help from thee I bring,

that is faith, and Jesus testifies, "Thy faith hath saved thee." Now, because the infallible Witness says this of all who have faith, I do not think you ought to doubt it. It is true you do not hear his voice, because he says it rather by the written Word than by word of mouth; but surely this does not affect your faith. We believe a true man whether he writes or speaks: indeed, if there be any choice, we prefer that which he has deliberately put upon paper; for this remains when the sound of the voice is clean gone. It is most profitable for us that we should read our Lord's declaration over and over again, and put it in all sorts of shapes, and see how it remains evermore faithful and true. It is more assuring to you to find it in the volume of the Book than it would be if the Savior met you tonight, and said to you, "Thy sins are forgiven thee. Thy faith hath saved thee." The record excels the voice.

"No," say you, "I cannot see that." Well now, Peter was with Christ on the Mount of Transfiguration, and nothing could shake Peter's conviction that he had been there in the midst of that heavenly glory; and yet, for all that, Peter says, concerning the inspired Word, "We have a more sure word of testimony [prophecy]." He felt that even the memory of that vision, which he had assuredly seen, did not always yield to him so much assurance as did the abidingly inspired Word of God. You ought to feel the same. If I were conscious tonight that, at some period of my life, I had seen the Lord, and that he had spoken to me, the very spot of ground on which it occurred would be exceedingly dear and sacred to my spirit; but I am certain that when I grew depressed, when darkness rushed over my soul, as it does sometimes, I should be sure to say to myself, "You never saw anything of the kind. It was a delusion, a figment of imagination, a delirium, and nothing more." But, beloved, when I get to this Book, and see before me the sacred lines, I know that I am not deluded. There it stands, "God so loved the world, that he gave his only begotten Son, that whosoever believeth in him should not perish, but have everlasting life." I am sure about that, and I am sure that I believe, and therefore I am sure that I am saved. I like to put my finger right down on the passage, and then say, "Lord, I know you cannot lie. I have never had a question about this being your Book. Whatever other doubts have plagued me, this has not. You have so spoken it home to my soul, that I am as assured that this is your Book as I am assured of my own existence; and, hence, you have done better for the removal of my doubts, and for the assurance of my soul's eternal salvation, by putting your promise in your Book, than if you had yourself personally appeared to me, and spoken with your own voice."

O my hearer, the written Word is most sure! If you believe, you are saved, as surely as you are alive. If you believe, heaven and earth may pass away, but the Word of the Lord shall stand fast for you. "He that believeth in him hath everlasting life." He has eternal life in present possession. Our Lord has put it thus: "He that believeth and is baptized shall be saved." "He that with his heart believeth, and with his mouth maketh confession of him, shall be saved." There are no "ifs" or "buts" about these words of promise. Salvation is put as a present thing, and as an abiding thing, but in every case as a certain thing; and why should we be worried and worn about the matter? It is so, and let us take the comfort of the fact. We must either throw away this Book by beginning to talk about "degrees of inspiration" and all that foul rubbish, or else we are logically bound to be sure of our hope, and to rejoice in it. I warrant you, O my hearer, that as long as you stand fast by the belief that this is a sure word of testimony, you will know that you are saved! If this Book be true, every believer in Jesus is as safe as Jesus himself. To say "I believe, but I am afraid I am not saved" is to say, only in a roundabout way, that you do not believe at all; for, if you believe, then you believe that God speaks the truth; and this is the testimony, that "God hath given us eternal life, and that life is in his Son." This is the testimony of the great Father, and the testimony of the eternal Spirit; and we must not dare to doubt it. You may doubt whether you believe or not; but given that you do really and unfeignedly put your trust in the Lord Jesus, then, as effect follows cause, it is certain that the cause of faith will be followed by its sure effect—salvation. "Thy faith hath saved thee: go in peace."

Do not worry any longer: go in peace. Have done with questioning; end debate; go in peace. Go about your business, for the work of salvation is done. You are a saved soul: go and rejoice in finished salvation, and ask no more questions. "Wherefore criest thou unto me?" said God to Moses. "Speak unto the children of Israel, that they go forward." Wherefore do you question and doubt any longer? Go forward to enjoy what God has prepared for you; and as you are saved and justified in Christ, now seek sanctification, and all the other blessings of the covenant of grace which lie before you in Christ Jesus your Lord. The promise is sure; be sure that it is so, and in perfect rest of soul enjoy the good which God provides you.

I think I have thus brought out as clearly as I can that delightful assurance which is the ground of the command, "Go in peace."

II. We come, second, to hearken to *a considerate precept.*

Our Lord, with wise tenderness, dismissed the beloved object of his pardoning love, and bade her "go in peace." May the Holy Spirit bless this to us!

This precept divides itself into two parts. There is, first, "go," and then there is "go in peace."

There is "*go.*" Now in "*go,*" there are two things: to go *from* and to go *to*. *Where was she to go from?* First, she was *to go from these quibblers.* Simon and the Pharisees are as full of objections as a swarm of bees is full of stings. They say in their hearts one to another, "Who is this that forgiveth sins also?" They have even dared to question the character of the perfect One, and have hinted a suspicion of his purity for allowing such a woman to come so near him, and to wash his feet with her tears. Therefore the Savior says to her "*go.*" This was not a happy place for a childlike love to linger in. Her soul would have been among lions. Jesus seems to say, "Do not stay to be tormented by these cavilers. Thy faith hath saved thee; go. You have gained a great blessing; go home with it. Let these people argue with each other; you have a rich prize, take it out of the reach of these pirates."

Oftentimes I believe that the child of God would find it to be his greatest wisdom, whenever he is in company that begins to assail his Lord, or to denounce his faith, just to go about his business, and let the scoffers have their scoffing to themselves. Some of us have thought it our miserable duty to read certain books that have been brought out against the truth, that we might be able to answer them; but it is a perilous calling. The Lord have mercy upon us when we have to go down into these sewers; for the process is not healthy!

"Oh," says a man, "but you must prove all things!" Yes, so I will; but if one should set a joint of meat on his table, and it smelled rather high, I would cut a slice, and if I put one bit of it in my mouth, and found it far gone, I should not feel it necessary to eat the whole round of beef to test its sweetness. Some people seem to think that they must read a bad book through; and they must go and hear a bad preacher often before they can be sure of his quality. Why, you can judge many teachings in five minutes! You say to yourself, "No, sir, no, no, no! This is good meat—for dogs. Let them have it, but it is not good meat for me, and I do not intend to poison myself with it." The Savior does not tell the woman, "Stop, now, and hear what Simon has got to say. Dear good woman, you have been washing my feet with tears, and here is a highly intelligent gentleman, a Pharisee, who has a very learned prelection to deliver; give him a fair hearing. You have to prove all things; therefore, stop and hear him. And here are more gentlemen who object to my pardoning your sins; and their objections are fetched from deep veins of thought. Listen to them, and then I will meet their questions, and have peace: do not stop till you lose it. You have your comfort and joy: refuse to be robbed of them." Why, if you were in a room, and you saw a certain number of gentlemen of a suspicious character, and you had your watch with you, you would not feel it necessary to stop and see whether they were able to extract your watch from you, but you would say to yourself, "No; I am best out of this company." We are safest out of the society of those whose great object it is to rob us of our faith. "Thy faith hath saved thee. Go home. Leave them. Go in peace."

I think that he meant, besides going away from the men, "*Go away from the publicity into which you have unwillingly stepped.*" If our Savior had been like some excellent people of the present day, he would have said, "Stand before all these men, and tell your experience. I shall require you to be at half a dozen meetings this week, and you must speak at every one of them." A splendid woman, was she not, who washed the Savior's feet with tears, and wiped them with the hairs of her head? She might have exhibited her eyes and her hair, and told their gracious story. Who can tell but several would have been impressed by the narrative? The Savior said to the woman—so excitable, for she was all that, as well as grateful, "Thy faith hath saved thee: go in peace." As much as to say, "There are certain of your own sex that you can speak to. You will find some poor fallen woman to whom you can quietly tell of my pardoning grace. But yours is a case in which the very beauty of your character will lie in the quietude of your future life. 'Thy faith hath saved thee.' That is enough for you. You have come upon the stage of action by that splendid act of your love; but do not acquire the habit of winning publicity. Do not aspire to display yourself in a bold and heroic attitude, but go in peace." He almost seems to say, "Subside now into your family. Take your place with the rest of your sisters. Adorn by your future purity my doctrine, and let all men see what a change has been worked in you; for, maybe, that very weakness of yours, which made you what you were as a sinner, may put you in danger even as a saint. Therefore I do not ask you to tarry here, and join my disciples, and follow me publicly through the streets, but your faith has saved you: go in peace."

I think that the Master taught a great deal of wisdom here, which some of those who are leaders in the church of God would do well to copy. Yes, I think that I shall go a little further, and say, that *I think the Savior there and then dismissed her from that high ministry which, for once in her life, she had carried out.* She washed his feet with tears, and wiped them with the hairs of her head. It was the action of a love which had risen to a passion. It was an action such as shall be told for a memorial of her everywhere; and we may well imitate her penitence, and her heroic courage, as well as her love to Christ. But, at the same time, we cannot always be doing heroic actions: life is mainly made up of common deeds. It would not be possible to be always washing feet with tears, nor to be always unbraiding tresses to use them as a towel. The difficulty with some people is that they are always wanting to practice the sublime. Alas! they often fail by just one step, and become ridiculous. They are always straining after effect; and hearing of what has been done once, by one choice person, they must do it themselves, and they must keep on doing it.

O my sister! there may come a time when you will have to speak for Christ, and speak openly before many; but tomorrow you had better go home, and see to the children, and make home happy for your husband. You will glorify Christ by darning stockings, and mending the socks of the little ones, quite as surely as by washing his feet with tears. You make a great mistake if you have not a piety which will take you into domestic life—which will help you to make the common drudgery of life a divine service.

We want men that can serve God with the axe and plane or behind a counter or by driving a quill. These are the men we want; but there are many that crave to vault at once into a conspicuous place and perform an astounding deed. Having done it once, they become unsettled all the rest of their lives; and do not seem as if they ever could take to plainly keeping the Ten Commandments, and walking in the steps of Jesus. I wish that those who must flash and blaze would hear the Lord Jesus say to them, "Go in peace." I mean any of you who really did distinguish yourselves on one occasion, and deserved much praise from your Christian friends. I fear lest you should pine for unusual and even undesirable forms of service and become useless in the ordinary course of life. Now do not be spoiled for life by having been allowed in one unusual deed, but hear the Master say, "Thy faith hath saved thee: go in peace. Serve me in the daily avocations of life, and bring glory to my name at home. Go from the strain of publicity to the gentler pressures of family duty."

Do you not think that he even meant that she was now to cease *from that singular fellowship with him that she had enjoyed*? She had been very close to him; but she was, perhaps, never to be quite so near to him again. In spirit she should be; but certainly not physically. It happens that those who take to the contemplative life—and there is no life higher than that—are apt to think that they must forget the practical life. But it must not be so. We must do that which the Master bids us do, as well as sit at his feet.

I am tempted to tell a story which most of you must know concerning the famous man of God, who, in his cell, thought he saw the Lord Jesus, and under that persuasion he worshiped with rapt delight. But just then the bell at the convent gate rang, and it was his turn to stand at the door and deal out bread to the hungry. There was a little battle in his mind as to which he should do—tarry with his Lord or go to hand out bread to the poor mendicants. At last, he felt that he must do his duty even at the cost of the highest spiritual bliss. He went and distributed the bread, and when he came back, to his great delight, the vision was still there, and a voice said to him, "If you had stayed, I would have gone; but as you have gone, I have therefore stayed still to commune with you." The path of duty must be followed, and no spiritual enjoyment can excuse us from it. Never offer one duty to God stained with the blood of another. Balance your duties and let not one press out another. "Thy faith hath saved thee: go in peace." Do not think that you need to be all day long at your Bible, or all the evening at your prayer. There is time for everything. Let every holy work have its place, that your life may be a fair mosaic of brilliant colors, all set according to the divine pattern, to make up a perfect character. "Thy faith hath saved thee. Go in peace, and do the next thing, and the next, without weariness."

That leads me to speak of *what she was to go to*. It seems to me that the Savior said, "Now go home. You have been a fallen woman: home is the place for you. Go home to your mother and father, or other relatives. Seek a home. Be domesticated. *Attend to your own work*. Whatever your place is, go to it. Leaving daily duty was the source of your temptation; return to walks of usefulness, and habits of order, and this will be your safety. You will be less likely to be led away if you have work to occupy head and heart and hands."

Did he not mean, *"Go now to your ordinary life-trial"*? Do you think yourself a very peculiar person—a sort of saint, that has to float in the air, or live upon roses? Do not fancy such a thing. I have heard of the Chinese, that they sell shoes with which you can walk on the clouds; and I believe that some people must have bought a pair of these remarkable articles; for their lives are spent in cloudland, walking as in a dream, upon high stilts of fond imaginations. Do not think great things of yourself. You are but a commonplace man or woman. Do such duty as your fellow Christians do, and do not think yourself a superior person. The worst people in the world to work with are superior people. Those are of no importance who think they are of great importance. Poor creature! it is not the grace of God which turns your brain, but your own silly conceit.

Go forth to your further service: "Go in peace. There are some to whom you can tell of my love. Oh, how you will tell it! You that have washed my feet with your tears, go and shower those tears over fallen ones like yourself. Go, use those eyes, that you may look my love right into their hearts as you are speaking to them. Go all your life in peace, and do for me all that I shall put in your way to do for me." That is what I think our Lord meant. Brethren, do not think of sitting here to enjoy yourselves; but go off, and glorify your Redeemer's name. Go!

But then here is the point of it: he said, *"Go in peace."* O my brethren, I desire that all of us who love the Lord may go henceforth all the rest of our life journey in peace. May pardoning love put us at peace concerning all our sins! O pardoned one, you love much, for you have had much forgiven; let your thoughts all run to love, and none to fear. Fret not about the past—the dark, dishonorable past. The hand that was pierced has blotted it all out. The great Lord has frankly forgiven you all your debt. Let not that disturb you any longer. Go in peace. What a rest it is to be rid of the burden of sin, and to know of a certainty, from the teaching of God's own Word, that your sins are forgiven you! This is peace which passeth all understanding.

Our Lord meant, next, *"go in peace" in reference to all the criticisms of all these people who have looked at you.* Do not mind them. Do not trouble about them. What have they to do with you? It is enough for a servant if his master accepts him: he need not mind what others have to say about his service. Your faith has saved you. Forget all the unkind things they have said, and do not trouble your heart about the cruel speeches they may yet make. Go in peace, and be under no alarm as to upbraiding tongues.

And then I think he meant, *"Go in peace about what thou hast done."* I know the mood of a word like that. I have preached the gospel: I have thrown my whole soul into it; and after it is all over, I have felt bound to chide myself that I did not do much better as to style or spirit or length, or some other matter. Oh, but if the Master accepts it, one may go in peace about it! This woman had done a very extraordinary thing in washing Christ's feet with tears, and wiping them with the hairs of her head; and when she got away, she might have said to herself, "I wonder that I was so bold. Was I not immodestly conspicuous? How could I have done it? How must I have looked when I was bathing his feet? For me, too—such a sinner as I am—for me to have done it to the blessed and holy One! I fear he must have felt vexed at my rudeness!" Have you not sometimes done a brave thing for Christ, and then afterward felt just like that. "I was a bold minx," say you, "after all, to push myself so forward." The good young man, who has just preached for the first time, says, "Well, I got through it this time, but I will never attempt it again, for I am sure that I am not fit for such holy work." So the Master says to this woman, "Go in peace. I have accepted thee and thy loving service. Do not trouble about what thou hast done. It is all sweet to me, and has a rich perfume of thy great love. Never fret about what you have done. You have done the right thing. Thy faith hath saved thee. Go in peace." I want us to have just that kind of peace— peace about what we have done for our Lord, even as we have peace about sin forgiven, and peace about human criticisms. "Go in peace." Oh, to possess, from this time forth, a holy quiet! We are so apt to grow fretful. I know some good brethren who have a swollen vein of suspicion about them, that bleeds every now and then, and pains them greatly, and alarms other people. I know some sisters: they are very good, but unreasonably fearful. They say that they are "nervous." Perhaps that is the fact; and so I will say no more. But oh, that we could get them cured of this disease of the nerves! I would they could be quieted! I admire the members of the Society of Friends for this virtue beyond almost any other which they exhibit: they seem to be so steady, self-contained, and equable. They are a little slow, perhaps; but then they are very sure and firm and steadfast and calm. We are some of us too much in a hurry to go fast. If we were a little slower, we should be quicker. If we left our affairs more entirely with God, our peace might be like a river.

Yes, I would to God, dear friends, that we might feel henceforth a constant joy. Why not? Nothing ought to trouble us, for we know that all things work together for good. If we live by faith, nothing can trouble us; for between here and heaven we shall keep company with you, you blessed One! And if the way you take be rough, the fact of your being with us shall make it smooth to us. We will travel merrily with this as our march music: "Thy faith hath saved thee; go in peace."

Still, to come back to where I began, I daresay that the good woman thought that she would like to speak a word for the Lord. When they said that he could not forgive sin, would not she have liked to say, "But he did forgive my sin, and he changed my nature. How dare you speak thus"?

But the Savior said, go. She was not called to contend. Thank God every child of God is not called to fight with the adversary: those of us who are men of war from our youth up take no pleasure in strife. We wish that, like this holy woman, we could be exempt from this warfare. She might well rejoice in her escape from the sacred conscription. Many a cuff and blow she thus avoided; and as her Captain sent her off the field, she might go home right happily.

She might have lost the blessed frame of mind in which she then was, and this would have been a real injury to her. She was sweetly wrapped up in love, and there her Lord would have her abide.

He seems to say, "You are too precious to be battered and bruised in battle. Go—go in peace. Dear soul, you are so full of love to me that I do not want you to be worried with fighting and contending and controverting. Go in peace." She would have done no good, I dare say, if she had ventured into a fray for which she was so unfitted. If she had spoken, she would have said something which the cruel Pharisees would have turned into a jest. So he said to her, "Go in peace." Why should her feebleness give them an occasion for unholy triumph? All true hearts are not fit for fight. Besides, she had her Lord to be her Advocate, and there was no need for her to speak. Therefore he said, "I can manage them without your presence. Go in peace." When we may believingly leave a difficulty with our Lord, it is faith's duty to go home quietly. No doubt, by going in peace, she would be doing greater service than she would by using her tongue upon these ungodly men. A quiet, happy life is often the noblest witness that we can bear for Christ. Therefore I say to everyone who loves the Lord, there are times when he will say to us, "Do not enter into any of this conflict and turmoil and muddle. Thy faith hath saved thee. Go in peace."

The last word I have to say is this. There are many poor souls who talk about coming to Christ who are not yet saved; and they are always hearing about faith, and thinking of it, and yet they never do, in very truth, believe. Now do not hear or debate any more about faith, but *believe*. Trust Jesus Christ, and think no more about your own trusting. You shall think of it as a thing done, I mean, but not as a thing to be done. God help you now to believe in Jesus, and so pass over the bridge of belief to the golden shore of Jesus himself!

Well, but I notice some say that they believe, but it is not believing, because if it were believing, they would "go in peace." A person comes to the bank with a check. He believes it to be honestly his, and the signature to be correct. He puts it down on the counter, and the clerk puts out the money. But see! The man does not take it. He stands and loafs about; and the clerk looks at him, and wonders what he is at. At last, when the person has been there long enough to wear the good man's patience out, the clerk says, "Did you bring that check to have the money?" "Yes, I handed it in." "Well, then, why do you not take the money and go about your business?" If he is a sensible man, he delays no longer; no, he would not have delayed so long. He takes the money, and departs in peace. Now, dear soul, if you have a promise from God—"He that believeth is not condemned," or, "He that believeth hath everlasting life"—do you believe? Then take the blessing, and go about your business. Do not keep on saying, "Perhaps it is so," and, "Perhaps it is not so." Do you believe that God speaks the truth? If so, then take the promised blessing and enjoy it; for you are a saved man. "But I have been going to a place of worship for years, and I have been believing in a sort of a way; but I have never dared to say that I was saved." Then you are acting the part of an unbeliever.

If you do not know that you are saved, how dare you go to sleep tonight? How should a man dare to eat his meals, and go about his business, and yet say, "I do not know whether I am saved or not"? You may know it, and you ought to know it. If you believe, you are saved: if you doubt that fact, you are rather an unbeliever than a believer. Take up your money and go home. "O thou of little faith, wherefore didst thou doubt?" Trust Jesus! Your faith has saved you. Go in peace.

The Lord help you truly to believe, for Jesus' sake! Amen.

Mary and Martha:
The Master Calls

Delivered at the Metropolitan Tabernacle, Newington. No. 1198.

She . . . called Mary her sister secretly, saying, "The Master is come, and calleth for thee."—JOHN 11:28

I suppose by Martha's whispering the words "the Master" in Mary's ear, that it was the common name by which the sisters spoke of our Lord to one another in his absence. Perhaps it was his usual name among all the disciples, for Jesus said, "Ye call me Master and Lord: and ye say well; for so I am." It often happens that for persons whom we love, we have some special title by which we speak of them familiarly when we are in the circle of those who join in our esteem of them. Instead of always using their official titles or their actual names, there is some one name which we have attached to them, which calls up happy associations, or reminds us of endearing traits in their character, and therefore it is very sweet in our mouths. So I suppose that most of the disciples called Jesus "the Master," many of them coupling with it the word Lord.

Mary, I should suppose, was peculiarly given to the use of the term—it was *her* name for the Lord. I fancy that she called him "*my* Master," only, of course, Martha could not say to her, "your Master is come," for that would have been to cast suspicion on her own loyalty to Jesus, and perhaps she did not feel exactly in a frame of mind to say, "our Master," remembering that he was Master of so many more besides, and half hoping that he might be Master over death himself. She therefore said, "*the* Master." It was an emphatic title, "*The* Master is come."

Very remarkable is it that minds of a kindred spirit to Mary have always loved this title of "the Master," and more especially that wondrous, sweet, mystic poet and dear lover of his Lord, George Herbert, who, whenever he heard the name of Jesus mentioned, would always say "my Master." He has given us that quaint poem, called "The Odor," which begins,

How sweetly doth my Master sound, my Master.

There must needs be something exceedingly precious about the title for a Mary and a Herbert thus to be enamored of it above all others. Jesus has many names, all full of music; this must be choice indeed to be selected before them all as the title which his best beloved prefer to apply to him. There are many among us who are ourselves accustomed to speak of the Lord as the Master, and, though there are many other titles, such as the Well Beloved, the Good Shepherd, the Friend, the Bridegroom, the Redeemer, and the Savior, yet we still cherish a very special affection for this one name, which gives forth to us "an oriental fragrancy," with which "all day [we] do perfume our mind" [George Herbert].

You are aware that the word might just as well be translated the "Teacher," the authoritative Teacher, for that is the gist of its meaning. I am glad to pronounce it Master, because usage and sweet association have enshrined the word, and also because we have still among us the custom of calling the chief teacher in a school or college *the master*, but still, had our version given us "the Teacher is come," it would have been nearer the mark.

I. I shall speak a few words, first, upon *the deep propriety of this title as applied to our Lord.*

He is, indeed, the Master—the Teacher. What if I put the two together, and say the Master-Teacher? He has a peculiar fitness for this office. To be a master-teacher a man must have *a masterly mind.* Certainly all minds are not cast in the same mold and are not possessed with the same vigor, depth, force, and quickness of action. Some mental organizations are princely by their very formation; though they may belong to plowboys, the imperial stamp is on them. These minds cannot be smothered by a peasant's smock frock, nor kept down by the load of poverty; master minds are recognized by an innate superiority, and force their way to the front. I say nothing of the moral qualities of Napoleon, but a mind so vast as his could not have been forever hidden away among the soldiers in the ranks; he must become a captain and a conqueror. So, too, a Cromwell or a Washington must rise to be masters among men, because the caliber of their minds was masterly. Such men see a thing quickly; they hold it with a comprehensive grasp; and they have a way of infusing faith into others about it which, before long, pushes them into a master's position, with the common consent of all around them. You cannot have for a master-teacher a man with a little soul. He may insinuate himself into the chair of the teacher, but everyone will see that he is out of place and no one will delight to think of him as his master. Many painters there are, but there have been few Raphaels or Michelangelos, few who could found schools to perpetuate their names. Many songsters have there been, but few poets have founded schools of tuneful thought in which they have been the beloved choirmasters. Many philosophers have there been, but a Socrates or an Aristotle will not be found every day; for great teachers must have great minds, and these are rare among men. The teacher of all teachers, the master of all the teachers must needs be a grand, colossal spirit, head and shoulders above other men.

Such a soul Mary saw in her Lord Jesus Christ, and such we see there also, and we therefore challenge for our Lord the name of the Master. There we have divinity itself, with its omniscience and infallibility, and at the same time a complete, full-orbed manhood, harmonious in all its qualities, a perfect equilibrium of excellence, in which there is no excess and no deficiency. You find in him a perfect mind, and that mind so human, as to be intensely manly, and sweetly womanly also. In Jesus there was all the tenderness and sympathy of woman, joined with the strength and courage of man. His love was feminine, but not effeminate; his heart was masculine, but not hard and stern. He was *the* complete man, unfallen manhood in its perfectness.

Our Lord was a man who impressed all who came near him; they either hated him intensely or loved him fervently. Wherever he was, he was seen to be a prince among the sons of men. The devil recognized him and tempted him beyond all others. He saw in him a foeman worthy of his steel, and took him into the wilderness to have a duel with him, hoping to defeat the race by vanquishing its manifest chief. Even scribes and Pharisees, who despised everyone who made not broad the borders of his garment, could not despise this man; they could hate him, but their hate was the unconscious reverence which evil is forced to render to superlative goodness and greatness. Jesus could not be ignored and overlooked. He was a force in every place, a power wherever he might be. He is a master, yes, "the Master." There is a grandeur about his whole human nature, so that he stands out above all other men, like some mighty Alpine peak, which overtops the minor hills, and casts its shadow all down the vales.

But to make a master teacher, a man must not only have a master mind, but he must have *a master knowledge* of that which he has to teach; and it is best if that be acquired by experience rather than by instruction. Such was the case with our Lord Jesus. He came to teach us the science of life, and in him was life; he experienced life in all its phases, and was tempted in all points like as we are, though without sin. The highest were not above him, the lowest he did not regard as beneath him, but he condescended to their infirmities and sorrows. There are no dreary glens of melancholy which his feet have not trodden, nor lofty peaks of joy which he has not scaled; wondrous was the joy as well as the sorrow of our Lord Jesus Christ. He leads his people through the wilderness, and, like Hobab of old, he knows where they should encamp in the wilderness, and understands all the way which they must traverse to reach the Promised Land. He was made "perfect through suffering." He teaches us no truth as mere theory, but as matter of actual experiment on his own person. The remedy he gives to us he has tested. If there be bitterness for us, he has quaffed full bowls of it, and if there be sweetness in his cup he gives us of his joy; all things that have to do with this life and godliness, the whole science of salvation from the gates of hell up to the throne of God, he understands right well, by personal acquaintance therewith. There is not a single chapter of the book of revelation which he does not comprehend, nor a solitary page of the book of experience which he does not understand; and therefore he is fit to teach, having both a master mind and a master knowledge of that which he comes to inculcate.

Moreover, our great Master while here below had *a masterly way of teaching*, and this also is essential, for it is not every man of vast knowledge and great mind that can teach others. Aptness to teach is required. We know some whose utterances never seem to be in the tongue of ordinary men. If they have anything to say, they say it in a jargon of their own, which they probably comprehend, and a few of their disciples, but it is Greek to commonplace people. Blessed is that teacher who teaches what he understands himself in a way which enables others to understand him. I like the style of old Cobbett when he said, "I not only speak so that men can understand me, but so that they *cannot misunderstand* me"; and such a teacher was Christ to his own disciples. When they sat at his feet, he made truth so clear that wayfaring men, though fools, need not err therein. By homely parables and phrases which caught the ear and won the heart, he brought down celestial truths to ordinary comprehensions, when the Spirit of God had once cleansed those comprehensions, and made them able to receive the truth. He taught, moreover, not only plainly, but lovingly. So gently did he open up things to his own disciples that it must have been a pleasure to be ignorant, in order to require to be taught, and a greater pleasure still to learn—to learn in such a way. The way in which he taught was as sweet as the truth he taught. Everybody that came into Christ's school felt at home, felt pleased with their Master, and confident that if they could learn anywhere, they must learn at his feet.

The Master gave, in connection with his teaching, a measure of the Holy Spirit—not the full measure, for that was reserved until he had ascended up on high, and the Spirit should baptize the church, but he gave to each of his people a measure of the Spirit of God, by which truths were not taught to their ears only but to their hearts also. Ah, my brethren, we are not such teachers as Christ; for, when we have done our best, we can only reach the ear. We cannot give the Holy Spirit, but he can; and when the Spirit this day comes from Christ, and takes of his things and reveals them unto us, then we see yet more of our Lord's masterly modes of teaching and learn what a Master Jesus is, who writes his lessons, not on the blackboard, but on the fleshy tablets of the heart; who gives us school books, no, is himself the Book; who sets us lessons, yes, is himself the Lesson; who performs before us that which he would have us do, so that when we know him we know what he has to teach, and when we imitate him we have followed the precepts which he gives. Our Lord's way of embodying his instruction in himself is a right royal one, and none can rival him in it. Do not children learn infinitely more by example than ever they do by precept? And this is how our Master teaches us. "Never man spake like this man" is a grand Christian proverb; but it might be eclipsed by another: "Never man *acted* like this man"; for this man's deeds and words tally with each other, the deeds embody and enforce the words, give them life, and help us to understand them. He is a prophet like unto Moses, because he is mighty both in word and in deed, and so he is of prophets and teachers *the Master*. Here a master mind, a master experience, and a master mode of teaching: well is he called the Master.

Withal, dear friends, there was, over and above this—if I have not comprehended it in what I have already said—*a master influence* which Jesus, as a teacher, had over those who came within his range. They did not merely see, but feel; they did not only know, but love; they did not merely prize the lesson, but they worshiped the Teacher. What a master was this Christ, whose very self became the power by which sin was checked, and ultimately cast out, and by which virtue was implanted, and the new life commenced, nourished, and brought to perfection. To have one to teach you who is very dear to you is to make lessons easy. No child learns better than from a mother qualified to teach, who knows how to make her lessons sweet, by crystallizing them in the sugar of her own affection. Then it is pleasure, as well as duty, to learn.

But no mother ever won her child's heart (and there have been tender and affectionate mothers too) so thoroughly as Jesus won the heart of Mary; or, I may say, as Jesus has won your heart and mine, if you feel as my heart feels to my Lord. From him we want no reasonings to prove what he says; he is himself instead of reason and of argument. His love is the logic which proves everything to us. With him we hold no debate; what he has done for us has answered every question we could raise. If he tells us what we do not understand, we believe it. We ask if we may understand it, and if he tells us no, we stay where we are and believe the mystery. We love him so that we are as glad *not* to know as *to* know, if such should be his will; we believe his silence to be as eloquent as his speech, and that which he conceals to be as kindly intended as that which he reveals. Because we love him he exercises such an influence over us that, straightaway, we prize his teaching and receive it; and the more we know him, and the more his inexpressibly delightful influence dominates our nature, the more completely we yield up imagination, thought, reason, everything, to him.

Men may call us fools for it, but we have learned at Jesus' feet that "the world by wisdom knew not God," and that except we be converted, and become as little children, we shall in no wise enter the kingdom of heaven, and therefore we are not confounded when the world thinks us childish and credulous. The world is growing more manly and more foolish, and we are growing more childlike and more wise. We reckon that to grow downward into our Lord Jesus is the surest and truest growth; and when we shall have grown clean down to nothing, and lower still, till we are less than nothing, then we shall be full grown in the school of Jesus, and shall take a high degree in true learning, knowing the love of Christ which passes knowledge.

We may well call him Master who has a masterly mind, a masterly experience, and a masterly way of teaching; and, moreover, wields a masterly influence over his pupils, so that they are forever bound heart and soul to him, and count him to be himself his own highest lesson, as well as the chief of all instructors.

Having proved that our beloved Lord is fairly entitled to the name, let me add that he is by office the sole and alone Master of the church. There is in the Christian church no authority for a doctrine but Christ's Word. The inspired Book which he has left us, charging us never to diminish a letter or add a syllable, that is our code imperial, our authorized creed, our settled standard of belief. I hear a great deal said of sundry "bodies of divinity," but my own impression is that there never was but one Body of divinity, and there never will be but one, and that is Jesus Christ, in whom "dwelleth all the fullness of the Godhead bodily." To the true church, her body of divinity is Christ. Some churches refer to other standards, but we know no standard of theology but our Master. "I, if I be lifted up," says he, "will draw all men unto me"; we feel no drawings toward any other master. He is the standard—"Unto him shall the gathering of the people be."

We are not of those who will go no further than Martin Luther. Blessed be God for Martin Luther! God forbid that we should say a word in depreciation of him. But were we baptized unto Martin Luther? I believe not. Some can never budge an inch beyond John Calvin, whom I reverence first of all merely mortal men; but still John Calvin is not our master, but only a more advanced pupil in the school of Christ. He teaches, and, as far as he teaches as Christ taught, he is authoritative, but where Calvin goes apart from Jesus, he is no more to be followed than Voltaire himself. There be brethren whose one reference for everything is to the utterances of John Wesley. "What would Mr. Wesley have said?" is a weighty question with them. We think it a small matter what he would have said, or what he did say for the guidance of Christians, now so many years after his departure; far better is it to inquire what Jesus says in his Word. One of the grandest of men that ever lived was Wesley, but he is no master of ours. We were not baptized in the name of John Wesley or John Calvin or Martin Luther. "One is our Master, even Christ." And now the parliament of our country is about to set apart a learned judge to decide what is right in a so-called church of Christ, and he is to say, "This garment you may wear, and that you shall not; hitherto your ritual shall go but no further." In his person the House of Commons is to be recognized as the creator and lord and master of the Church of England, to whom he will say, "do this," and she will do it, or, "refrain," and she will stay her hand. She must crouch and bend, and take her meat like any dog from the hand that patronizes her, and her collar, made of what brass or leather Caesar chooses to ordain, shall bear this motto, "His servants ye are whom ye obey." Why, the poorest minister in the most despised of our churches, whose poverty is thought to make him contemptible, but whose poverty is his glory if he bears it for Christ's sake, would scorn to have any spiritual act of his church submitted to the judgment of the state, and would sooner die than be dictated to in the matter of divine worship. What has the church to do with the state? Our Master and Lord has set up a kingdom which owns no other King but himself; and we cannot bow, and will not bow, before decrees of Parliament and lords and kings in spiritual things. Christ's church has but one head, and that is Christ, and the doctrines which the church has to teach cannot be tested by a Court of Arches, or a bench of bishops, or a synod of ministers, or a presbytery, or a conference.

The Lord Jesus Christ has taught us this and that: if his teaching be contradicted, the contradiction is treason against his crown. Though the whole church were assembled, and that church the true one, if it should contradict the teaching of Christ, its decrees ought to be no more to a Christian than the whistling of the wind upon the mountain wilds, for Christ is Master, and none but Christ. Though an apostle or an angel from heaven preach any other doctrine than that of our Lord, "let him be accursed." I would God that all Christians stood up for this. Then would

Sects and names and parties fall,
And Jesus Christ be all in all.

He is the sole Teacher and the sole Legislator. A church has a right to execute Christ's laws, but she has no right to make a law. The ministers of Christ are bound to carry out the rules of Christ, and when they so do, what is bound on earth is bound in heaven; but if they have acted upon any rules but those of this Book, their laws are only worthy of contempt; be they what they may, they bind no Christian heart. The yoke Christ puts on us, it shall be our joy to wear, but the yoke which prelates would thrust upon us it shall be our glory to trample on. "If the Son make you free, you shall be free indeed." "Stand fast therefore in the liberty wherewith Christ hath made you free, and be not entangled again with the yoke of bondage."

"*The Master.*" That is the name Christ should receive throughout the whole church, and he should be regarded always, and on all occasions, and in reference to all spiritual subjects, as the last court of appeal, whose inspired word is

The judge that ends the strife
Where wit and reason fail.

Thus much upon the propriety of the title.

II. But now, second, let us consider *the peculiar recognition which Mary gave to Christ as the Master.*

How did she give that recognition? *She became his pupil:* she sat right reverently at his feet. Beloved, if he be our Master, let us do the same. Let us take every word of Jesus, weigh it, read it, mark it, learn it, feed on it, and inwardly digest it. I am afraid we do not read our Bibles as we should, or attach such importance as we ought to every shade of expression which our Master uses. I should like to see a picture of Mary sitting at the Master's feet. Great artists have painted the virgin Mary so often that they might take a change, and sketch this Mary looking up with a deep, fixed gaze, drinking all in, and treasuring all up; sometimes startled by a new thought and a fresh doctrine, and then inquiringly waiting till her face beams with unspeakable delight as new light floods her heart. Her attentive discipleship proved how truly Jesus was her Master.

Then, mark, she was not only his disciple, but *she was a disciple of nobody else.* I do not know whether Gamaliel was in fashion then, but she did not sit at his feet. I daresay there was some Rabbi Ben Simon, or other famous doctor of the period, but Mary never spent an hour with him, for every moment she could set apart was joyously spent at the feet of a far dearer Rabbi. I wonder whether she was a little deaf, and so sat close to the teacher for fear of losing a word! Perhaps she feared she might be slow of heart, and so she got as near the preacher as others do who have a little deafness in their ears; anyhow, her favorite place was close at his feet. That shows us, since we are always dull of hearing in our souls, that it is good to get very close to Jesus when we are hearing him, and commune while we listen. She did not change from him to someone else for variety's sake. No, the Master, her Master, her only Master, was the Nazarene, whom others despised, but whom she called her Lord.

She was a willing scholar, for "Mary hath chosen the good part," said Jesus. Nobody sent her to sit at Jesus' feet. Jesus drew her, and she could not help coming, but she loved to be there. She was a willing and delighted listener. Never was she so happy as when she had her choice, that choice being always to learn of him. Children at school always learn well if they want to learn. If they are driven to school, they learn but little comparatively, but when they want to go, and when they love the teacher, it is quick learning with them; and happy is the teacher who has a class that has chosen him to teach them. Mary could well call him "the Master," for she rendered him her sole attention, her loving and delighted attention. And, mark you, in choosing Christ for Master, *she perseveringly stuck to him*. Her choice was not taken away from her, and she did not give it up. Martha looked very cross one day. How was she to see to the roast meat and the boiled at once? How could she be expected to prepare the table, and to look to the fire in the kitchen too? Why could not Mary come? And she scowled, I do not doubt. But it did not signify. Mary sat there still. Perhaps she did not even notice Martha's face; I think she did not, for the saints do not notice other countenances when Christ's beauty is to be seen: there is something so absorbing about him. He takes you all into himself, and bears you right away, drawing not only all men, but all *of* men to himself, when he does draw; and so she sat there still, and listened on. Those children will learn who stick to their books, who come not sometimes to study, but are always learning. So Mary recognized the Lord Jesus Christ's master-teachership by giving to him that persevering attention which such a Master-Teacher had a right to claim.

She went humbly to him; for while she sat at his feet for nearness, she sat there too out of deep humiliation of spirit. She felt it her highest honor to be sitting in the lowest place, for lowly was her mind. They shall learn most of Christ who think least of themselves. When a place at his feet seems to be too good for us, or at any rate we are more than content with it, then will his speech distill as the rain and drop as the dew, and we shall be as the tender herbs that drink in sweet refreshment, and our souls shall grow.

Blessed were you, O Mary! And blessed is each one of you, if you can call Christ your Master and prove it as she did. You shall have the good part which shall not be taken away from you.

III. Now I come to my third point, which is this—*the special sweetness of the name to us.*

I have shown why it was peculiarly recognized by Mary, and now I would show that it has a peculiar sweetness for us also. *"The Master"* or *"My Master"* or *"My Teacher."*

I love that name in my own soul, because it is *as a teacher* that *Jesus Christ is my Savior.* The best illustration I can give you is that of one of those poor little boys in the street, an urchin without father and mother, or with parents worse than none; the poor child is covered with filth and rags, he is well known to the policemen, and has seen the inside of many a jail; but a teacher of a ragged school has laid hold of him, and instructs him, and he is now washed and clothed and happy. Now that poor boy does not know the sweetness of "my father" or "my mother"; he does not recognize anything in those titles. Perhaps he never knew them or only knew such a form of them as to disgust him. But with what a zest does he say, *"My teacher!"* These little children say, "My teacher," with quite as much affection as others speak of their mother. Where there has been a great moral change worked by the influence of a teacher, the name "my teacher" has great sweetness in it. Now hear the parable of the ragged boy and his teacher! I was that ragged child. Truly, I did not think myself ragged, for I was foolish enough to think my rags were fine garments, and that my filth was my beauty. I knew not what I was. My Teacher saw me, he knew how foul I was and how ragged I was, and he taught me to see myself, and also to believe that he could wash me whiter than the snow. Yes, he went further and actually washed me till I was clean before the Lord. My Teacher showed me a wardrobe of snow-white linen garments, and clothed me in them. My Teacher has taught me a thousand things and worked innumerable good works upon me; I owe my salvation wholly to my Teacher, my Master, my Lord. Cannot you say the same?

I know you can if you are indeed disciples of Jesus. "My Teacher" means to you "my Savior," for he saved you by teaching you your disease and your remedy, teaching you how wrong you were, and making you right by his teaching. The word master or teacher has to us a delightful meaning, for it is by his teaching that we are saved.

Let me tell you how as a preacher I love that name, "my Master." I like to feel that what I said to those people on Sunday was not mine. I preached my Master, and I preached what my Master told me. Some find fault with the doctrine; I do not mind that, because it was none of mine, it was my Master's. If I were a servant and went to the front door with a message, and the gentleman to whom I took it did not like the message, I should say, "Do not be vexed with me, sir. I have told you my master's message to the best of my ability, and I am not responsible for it. It is my master's word, not mine." When there are no souls converted, it is dreary work, and one's heart is heavy, but it is sweet to go and tell your Master; and when souls are converted, and your heart is glad, it is a happy and a healthy thing to give all the glory to your Master. It must be an awkward thing to be an ambassador from the English court in some far-off land where there is no telegraph, and where the ambassador has to act on his own responsibility. He must feel it a serious burden. But, blessed be God, between every true minister and his Master there is a telegraphic communication; he need never do anything on his own account. He may imitate the disciples of John, who, when they had taken up the Baptist's mangled body, went and told Jesus. That is the thing to do. There are difficulties in all churches, troubles in all families, and cares in all businesses, but it is good to have a Master to whom you can go as a servant, feeling, "He has the responsibility of the whole concern—not I; I have only to do what he bids me." If we once step beyond our Lord's commands, the responsibility rests on us, and our trouble begins, but if we follow our Lord we cannot go astray.

And is not this a sweet name to quote when you are troubled, dear friends? Perhaps some of you are in trouble now. How it removes fear when you find out that he who sent the trouble is the Teacher who teaches you by the trouble—the Master who has a right to use what form of teaching he likes. In our schools much is learned from the blackboard, and in Christ's school much is learned from affliction. You have heard the story often, but I venture to repeat it again, of the gardener who had preserved with great care a very choice rose; and one morning when he went into the garden it was gone, and he scolded his fellow servants and felt very grieved, till someone said, "I saw the master coming through the garden this morning, and I believe he took the rose." "Oh, then," said he, "if the master took it, I am content." Have you lost a dear child or a wife or a friend? It was he that took your flower. It belonged to him. Would you wish to keep what Jesus wants? We are asked to pray sometimes for the lives of good people, and I think we may, but I have not always exercised faith while pleading, because it seemed to me that Christ pulled one way and I pulled the other. I said, "Father, let them be here," and Jesus said,

"Father, I will that they be with me where I am"; and one could not pull very hard then. Only feel that Christ is drawing the other way, and you give up directly. You say, "Let the Master have it. The servant cannot oppose the Master." It is the Lord; let him do what seemeth him good. I was dumb with silence; I opened not my mouth because thou didst it.

Our Master learned that lesson himself which he teaches to us. That is a very striking expression, "Father, I thank thee that thou hast hid these things from the wise and prudent, and hast revealed them unto babes; even so, Father, for so it seemed good in thy sight." It pleased God to pass by the wise and prudent, and therefore it pleased Christ that it should be so. It is well to have our hearts like that poor shepherd to whom a gentleman said, "I wish you a good day." Said he, "I never knew a bad day." "How is that, my friend?" "The days are such as God chooses to make them, and therefore they are all good." "Well," said the other, "but some days please you more than others?" "No," said he, "what pleases God pleases me." "Well, but have you not a choice?" said the other. "Yes, I have a choice, and that is, I choose that God should choose for me." "But have you not a choice whether you would live or die?" "No," said he, "for if I am here Christ will be with me, and if I am in heaven I shall be with him." "But suppose you had to choose." "I would ask God to choose for me," said he. Oh, sweet simplicity which leaves everything with God; this is calling Jesus Master to perfection:

Pleased with all the Lord provides,
Weaned from all the world besides.

Once again, dear friends, is it not sweet to us to call Jesus Master, because in so doing we take a position easy to reach, and yet most delightful. To call him Bridegroom—what an honor is it to be so near akin to the Son of God! Friend is a familiar and honorable title; to call him Master, however, is often easier, and it is quite as sweet, for his service, if we take no higher place, is pure delight to us. If our hearts are right, to do the Lord's bidding is as much as we can ask for. Though we are sons now and not slaves, and therefore our service is of a different character from what it ever was before, yet service is delight. What will heaven be but perpetual service? Here we labor to enter into rest; there they enter into rest while they labor. Their rest is the perfect obedience of their fully sanctified spirits. Are you not panting for it? Will it not be one of your greatest joys in heaven to feel that you are his servants? The glorified ones are called his servants in heaven. "His servants shall serve him, and they shall see his face, and his name shall be on their foreheads." Rid us of sin, and we should be in heaven now; earth would be heaven to us.

I want you, dear brethren in Christ, to go away rolling this sweet word under your tongue: "my Master, my Master." You will never hear better music than that: "my Master, my Master." Go and live as servants should live. Mind you make him truly your Master, for he says, "If I be a Master where is my honor?" Speak well of him, for servants should speak well of a good master, and no servant ever had so dear a Master as he is.

But there are some of you who cannot say this. I wish you could. Jesus is not your Master. Who is, then? You have a master somewhere, for "his servants you are whom ye obey." Now, if you obey the lusts of the flesh, your master is your flesh, and the wages will be corruption; for that is what flesh comes to—corruption, and nothing better. Or your master is the devil, and his wages must be death. Run away from such a master. Mostly when servants leave their masters, they are bound to give notice, but here is a case in which no notice should ever be given. When the prodigal son ran away from feeding the swine, he never stopped to give notice that he was going to leave the pigs, but started off directly, and I recommend every sinner to run by the grace of God straightaway from his sins. Stopping to give notice is the ruin of many. They mean to be sober, but they must treat their good resolution to another glass or two; they intend to think about divine things, but they must go to the theater once more; they would fain serve Christ, but tomorrow, not tonight. If I had such a master as you have—you who live in sin—I would up and away at once, by the grace of God, and say, "I will have Christ for my Lord." Look at your black master. Look at his cunning eyes! Can you not see that he is a flatterer? He means your ruin. He will destroy you as he has destroyed myriads already. That horrid leer of sin, that painted face, consider them and abhor them. Serve not a master who, though he gives you fair promises, labors for your destruction! Up and away, you slaves of sin! Eternal Spirit, come and break their chains! Sweet star of liberty, guide them to the free country, and let them find in Jesus Christ their liberty! My Master rejoices to receive runaways. His door is open to vagrants and vagabonds, to the scum of the earth and the offscouring of all things, to men that are dissatisfied with themselves, to wretches who have no joy of their lives, and are ready to lie down and die. "This man receiveth sinners." He is like David, who went into Adullam, and every man that was in debt and discontented came to him, and he became a captain over them. As Romulus and Remus gathered the first population of new Rome by harboring escaped slaves and robbers, whom they trained into citizens and made to be brave soldiers, so my Master has laid the foundation of the new Jerusalem, and he looks for his citizens—yes, the noblest of them, over yonder there, where sin and Satan hold them captive; and he bids us sound out the silver trumpet, and tell the slaves of sin that if they flee to him he will never give them up to their old master, but he will emancipate them, make them citizens of his great city, sharers of his bounties, partakers in his triumphs; and they shall be his in the day when he makes up his jewels.

I recollect preaching in this strain once, and an old sea captain told me after the sermon that he had served under the black flag for fifty years, and by the grace of God he would tear the old rag down, and run up the bloodred cross at the masthead. I recommended him not merely to change his flag, but to see that the vessel was repaired, but he wisely replied that repairing would be of no use to such an old waterlogged hulk, and he had better scuttle the old ship and have a new one. I reckon that is the best thing to do, to be dead indeed unto sin and made alive in Christ Jesus; for you may do what you will with the old wreck of fallen nature, you will never keep it afloat. The old man must be crucified with Christ. It must be dead and buried and sunk fifty thousand fathoms deep, never to be heard of again. In the new vessel which Jesus launches in the day of our regeneration, with the blessed flag of atoning blood above us, we will sail to heaven convoyed by irresistible grace, giving God the glory forever and ever. Amen.

Two Marys: "Over Against the Sepulcher"

༄ཉྫༀ

Delivered on Lord's Day morning, March 24, 1878, at the Metropolitan Tabernacle, Newington. No. 1404.

Sitting over against the sepulcher.—MATTHEW 27:61

Mary Magdalene and the other Mary were last at the Savior's grave. They had associated themselves with Joseph and Nicodemus in the sad but loving task of placing the body of their Lord in the silent tomb, and after the holy men had gone home they lingered still near the grave. Sitting down, perhaps upon some seat in the garden, or on some projection of the rock, they waited in mournful solitude. They had seen where and how the body was laid, and so had done their utmost, but yet they sat watching still: love has never done enough, it is hungry to render service. They could scarcely take their eyes away from the spot which held their most precious treasure, nor leave, till they were compelled to do so, the sacred relics of their Best Beloved.

The virgin Mary had been taken by John to his own home. She had sustained too great a shock to remain at the tomb, for in her were fulfilled the words, "Yea, a sword shall pierce through thine own heart also." She was wise to leave to others those sorrowful offices which were beyond her own power; exceedingly wise, also, from that hour to her life's end, to remain in the shade, modestly bearing the honor which made her blessed among women. The mother of Zebedee's children, who also lingered late at the tomb, was gone home too, for as she was the mother of John it is exceedingly probable that John resided with her, and had taken the Virgin to her home: hence she was needed at home to act as hostess and assist her son, and thus she would be obeying the last wish of her dying Lord when he said, "Son, behold thy mother," and explained his meaning by a look. All having thus departed, the two Marys were the sole watchers at the tomb of Christ at the time of the going down of the sun. They had work yet to do for his burial, and this called them away, but they stayed as long as they could—last to go and first to return.

This morning we shall with the women take up the somewhat unusual post of "sitting over against the sepulcher." I call it unusual, for as none remained save these two women, so few have preached upon our Redeemer's burial. Thousands of sermons have been delivered upon his death and resurrection, and in this I greatly rejoice, only wishing that there were thousands more; but still the burial of our Lord deserves a larger share of consideration than it generally obtains. "He was crucified, dead, and buried," says the creed, and therefore those who wrote that summary must have thought his burial an important truth; and so indeed it is. It was the natural sequence and seal of his death, and so was related to that which went before; it was the fit and suitable preparation for his rising again, and so stood in connection with that which followed after. Come, then, let us take our seat with the holy women "over against the sepulcher," and sing—

> Rest, glorious Son of God: thy work is done,
> And all thy burdens borne;
> Rest on that stone till the third sun has brought
> Thine everlasting morn.

> How calmly in that tomb thou liest now,
> Thy rest how still and deep!
> O'er thee in love the Father rests: he gives
> To his beloved sleep.

> On Bethel pillow now thy head is laid,
> In Joseph's rock-hewn cell;
> Thy watchers are the angels of thy God,
> They guard thy slumbers well.

I. Supposing ourselves to be sitting in the garden with our eyes fixed upon the great stone which formed the door of the tomb, we first of all *admire that he had a grave* at all.

We wonder how that stone could hide him who is the brightness of his Father's glory; how the Life of all could lie among the dead; how he who holds creation in his strong right hand could even for an hour be entombed. Admiring this, we would calmly reflect, first, upon the testimony of his grave that he was really dead. Those tender women could not have been mistaken, their eyes were too quick to suffer him to be buried alive, even if anyone had wished to do so. Of our Lord's actual death, we have many proofs connected with his burial. When Joseph of Arimathaea went to Pilate and begged the body, the Roman ruler would not give it up till he was certified of his death. The centurion, a man under authority, careful in all that he did, certified that Jesus was dead. The soldier who served under the centurion had by a very conclusive test established the fact of his death beyond all doubt, for with a spear he pierced his side, and forthwith there came out blood and water. Pilate, who would not have given up the body of a condemned person unless he was sure that execution had taken place, registered the death and commanded the body to be delivered to Joseph. Both Joseph of Arimathaea and Nicodemus and all the friends who aided in the interment were beyond all question convinced that he was dead. They handled the lifeless frame, they wrapped it in the bands of fine linen, they placed the spices about the sacred flesh which they loved so well: they were sadly assured that their Lord was dead.

Even his enemies were quite certain that they had slain him; they never had a suspicion that possibly a little life remained in him, and that it could be revived, for their stern hate allowed no doubt to remain upon that point; they knew even to the satisfaction of their mistrustful malice that Jesus of Nazareth had died. Even when in their anxiety they went to Pilate, it was not that they might obtain stronger proofs of death, but to prevent the disciples from stealing his dead body and giving out that he had risen from the dead.

Yes, Jesus died, literally and actually died, and his body of flesh and bones was really laid in Joseph's grave. It was no phantom that was crucified, as certain heretics dreamed of old. We have not to look to a spectral atonement or to a visionary sacrifice, though some in our own times would reduce redemption to something shadowy and unsubstantial. Jesus was a real man, and truly tasted the bitter pangs of death; and therefore he in very deed lay in the sepulcher, motionless as the rock out of which it was hewn, shrouded in his winding sheet. Remember as you think of your Lord's death that the day will come, unless the second advent should intervene, in which you and I shall lie low among the dead, as once our Master did. Soon to this heart there will be left no pulsing life, to this eye no glance of observation, to this tongue no voice, to this ear no sensibility of sound. We naturally start from this, yet must it be. We shall certainly mingle with the dust we tread upon and feed the worm. But as we gaze on Jesus' tomb and assure ourselves that our great Lord and Master died, each thought of dread is gone, and we no longer shudder: we feel that we can safely go where Christ has gone before.

Sitting down over against the sepulcher, after one has ruminated upon the wondrous fact that he who only has immortality was numbered with the dead, the next subject which suggests itself is *the testimony of the grave to his union with us.* He had his grave hard by the city, and not on some lone mountain peak where foot of man could never tread. His grave was where it could be seen; it was a family grave which Joseph had no doubt prepared for himself and his household. Jesus was laid in a family vault where another had expected to lie. Where was Moses buried? No man knows of his sepulcher unto this day. But where Jesus was buried was well known to his friends. He was not caught away in a chariot of fire, nor was it said of him that God took him, but he was laid in the grave, "as the manner of the Jews is to bury." Jesus found his grave among the men he had redeemed. Hard by the common place of execution there was a garden, and in that garden they laid him in a tomb which was meant for others; so that our Lord's sepulcher stands, as it were, among our homes and gardens, and is one tomb among many. Before me rises a picture. I see the cemetery, or sleeping place, of the saints, where each one rests on his lowly bed. They lie not alone, but like soldiers sleeping around their captain's pavilion, where he also spent the night, though he is up before them. The sepulcher of Jesus is the central grave of God's acre; it is empty now, but his saints lie buried all around that cave in the rock, gathered in ranks around their dear Redeemer's resting place. Surely it robs the grave of its ancient terror when we think that Jesus slept in one of the chambers of the great dormitory of the sons of men.

Very much might be said about the tomb in which Jesus lay. It was a *new* tomb, wherein no remains had been previously laid, and thus if he came forth from it there would be no suspicion that another had arisen, nor could it be imagined that he arose through touching some old prophet's bones, as he did who was laid in Elisha's grave. As he was born of a virgin mother, so was he buried in a virgin tomb, wherein never man had lain. It was a rocky tomb, and therefore nobody could dig into it by night or tunnel through the earth. It was a borrowed tomb; so poor was Jesus that he owed a grave to charity; but that tomb was spontaneously offered, so rich was he in the love of hearts which he had won. That tomb he returned to Joseph, honored unspeakably by his temporary sojourn therein. I know not whether Joseph ever used it for any of his house; but I see no reason why he should not have done so. Certainly, our Lord when he borrows always makes prompt repayment, and gives a bonus over: he filled Simon's boat with fish when he used it for a pulpit, and he sanctified the rocky cell wherein he had lodged, and left it perfumed for the next who should sleep therein.

We, too, expect, unless special circumstances should intervene, that these bodies of ours will lie in their narrow beds beneath the greensward, and slumber till the resurrection. Nor need we be afraid of the tomb, for Jesus has been there. Sitting over against his sepulcher we grow brave, and are ready, like knights of the holy sepulcher, to hurl defiance at death. At times we almost long for evening to undress that we may rest with God, in the chamber where "he giveth to his beloved sleep."

Now, note that our Lord's tomb was in a garden; for this is typically *the testimony of his grave to the hope of better things.* Just a little beyond the garden wall you would see a little knoll, of grim name and character, the Tyburn of Jerusalem, Golgotha, the place of a skull, and there stood the cross. That rising ground was given up to horror and barrenness; but around the actual tomb of our Savior there grew herbs and plants and flowers. A spiritual garden still blooms around his tomb; the wilderness and the solitary place are glad for him, and the desert rejoices and blossoms as the rose. He has made another paradise for us, and he himself is the sweetest flower therein. The first Adam sinned in a garden and spoiled our nature; the second Adam slept in a garden and restored our loss. The Savior buried in the earth has removed the curse from the soil; henceforth blessed is the ground for his sake. He died for us that we ourselves might become in heart and life fruitful gardens of the Lord. Let but his tomb, and all the facts which surround it, have due influence upon the minds of men, and this poor blighted earth shall again yield her increase: instead of the thorn shall come up the fir tree, and instead of the brier shall come up the myrtle tree, and it shall be to the Lord for a name.

Sitting over against the sepulcher perhaps the best thought of all is that now it is empty and *so bears testimony to our resurrection.* It must have made the two Marys weep, when before they left the grave they saw it filled with so beloved a treasure, so surely dead, they ought to have rejoiced to find it empty when they returned, but they knew not as yet the angel's message—"He is not here, for he is risen." Our Christ is not dead now; he ever lives to make intercession for us. He could not be held by the bands of death. There was nothing corruptible about him, and therefore his body has left the abode of decay to live in newness of life. The sepulcher is spoiled and the spoiler has gone up to glory, leaving captivity captive. As you sit over against the sepulcher, let your hearts be comforted concerning death, whose sting is gone forever. There shall be a resurrection. Be sure of this, for if the dead rise not then is Christ not risen; but the Lord is risen indeed, and his rising necessitates that all who are in him should rise as he has done.

Yet another thought comes to me: can I follow Christ as fully as these two women did? That is to say, can I still cling to him though to sense and reason his cause should seem dead and laid in a rocky sepulcher? Can I like Joseph and Magdalene be a disciple of a dead Christ? Could I follow him even at his lowest point? I want to apply this practically. Times have come upon the Christian church when truth seems to be fallen in the streets, and the kingdom of Christ is in apparent peril. Just now the Lord Jesus is betrayed by not a few of his professed ministers. He is being crucified afresh in the perpetual attacks of skepticism against his blessed gospel; and it may be things may wax worse and worse. This is not the first occasion when it has been so, for at various times in the history of the church of God his enemies have exulted, and cried out that the gospel of past ages was exploded, and might be reckoned as dead and buried. For one I mean to sit over against the very sepulcher of truth. I am a disciple of the old-fashioned doctrine as much when it is covered with obloquy and rebuke as when it shall again display its power, as it surely shall. Skeptics may seem to take truth and bind it, and scourge it, and crucify it, and say that it is dead, and they may endeavor to bury it in scorn, but the Lord has many a Joseph and a Nicodemus who will see honor done even to the body of truth, and will wrap the despised creed in sweet spices, and hide it away in their hearts. They may, perhaps, be half afraid that it is really dead, as the wise men assert, yet it is precious to their souls, and they will come forth right gladly to espouse its cause, and to confess that they are its disciples. We will sit down in sorrow but not in despair, and watch until the stone is rolled away, and Christ in his truth shall live again, and be openly triumphant. We shall see a divine interposition and shall cease to fear; while they who stand armed to prevent the resurrection of the grand old doctrine shall quake and become as dead men, because the gospel's everlasting life has been vindicated, and they are made to quail before the brightness of its glory.

This, then, is our first meditation: we admire that Jesus ever had a grave, and we sit in wonder over against the sepulcher.

II. Second, sitting here, *we rejoice in the honors of his burial.*

The burial of Christ was, under some aspects of it, the lowest step of his humiliation: he must not merely for a moment die, but he must be buried a while in the heart of the earth. On the other hand, under other aspects our Lord's burial was the first step of his glory: it was a turning point in his great career, as we shall hope to show you. Our Lord's body was given up by Pilate to Joseph, and he went with authority to receive it from those who were appointed to see him take it down. I yesterday had a glimpse at a work of art by one of our own Lambeth neighbors, exhibited by Mr. Doulton; it is a fine piece of work in terra-cotta, representing the taking down of Christ from the cross. I could have wished to have studied it more at leisure, but a mere glimpse has charmed me. The artist represents a Roman soldier at the top of the cross taking down the parchment upon which the accusation was written;

he is rolling it up to put it away forever. I thought of the taking away of the handwriting which was against him, even as he had taken away that which was against us. The Roman soldier by authority is thus represented as removing the charge which was once nailed over the ever-blessed head; there is no accusation against him now: he died, and the law is satisfied, it can no longer accuse the man who has endured its penalty. Another soldier is represented with a pair of pincers drawing out one of the big nails from the hands; the sacred body is free now, law has no further claims upon it, and withdraws its nails. A disciple, not a soldier, has mounted a ladder on the other side, and with a pair of scissors is cutting away the crown of thorns; and I think the artist did well to represent his doing so, for henceforth it is our delight to remove all shame from the name of Jesus, and to crown him in another fashion. Then the artist has represented certain of his disciples as gently taking hold of the body as it is gradually being unloosed by the soldiers, while Joseph of Arimathaea stands there with his long linen sheet ready to receive him. Jars of precious myrrh and spices are standing there, and the women ready to open the lids and to place the spices around the holy flesh. Every part of the design is significant and instructive, and the artist deserves great praise for it: it brought before my mind the descent from the cross with greater vividness than any painting I have ever seen. The nails are all extracted; he is held no longer to the cross; the body is taken down, no longer to be spit upon, and despised, and rejected, but tenderly handled by his friends; for all and everything that has to do with shame, and suffering, and paying of penalty is ended once for all.

What became of the cross of wood? You find in Scripture no further mention of it. The legends concerning it are all false upon the face of them. The cross is gone forever; neither gibbet, nor nail, nor spear, nor thorny crown can be found; there is no further use for them. Jesus our Lord has gone to his glory; for by his one sacrifice he has secured the salvation of his own.

But now as to his burial. Beloved, there were many honorable circumstances about it. Its first effect was *the development of timid minds*. Joseph of Arimathaea occupied a high post as an honorable counselor, but he was a secret disciple. Nicodemus, too, was a ruler of the Jews, and though he had spoken a word for the Master now and then, as probably Joseph had done (for we are told that he had not consented to their counsel and deed), yet he had never come out boldly till now. He came to Jesus by night aforetime, but he came by daylight now. At the worst estate of the Savior's cause, we should have thought that these two men would remain concealed, but they did not. Now that the case seemed desperate, they show their faith in Jesus and pluck up courage to honor their Lord. Lambs become lions when the Lamb is slain. Joseph went boldly in unto Pilate and begged the body of Jesus. For a dead Christ, he risks his position, and even his life, for he is asking the body of a reputed traitor, and may himself be put to death by Pilate; or else the members of the Sanhedrin may be enraged at him, and bind themselves with an oath that they will slay him for paying honor to the Nazarene, whom they called "that deceiver." Joseph can venture everything for Jesus, even though he knows him to be dead.

Equally brave is Nicodemus; for publicly at the foot of the cross he stands with his hundred pounds weight of spices, caring nothing for any who may report the deed. I cheerfully hope, dear brethren, that one result of the ferocious attacks made upon the gospel at this time will be that a great number of quiet and retiring spirits will be roused to energy and courage. Such works of evil might move the very stones to cry out. While, perhaps, some who have spoken well in other days and have usually done the battling may be downcast and quiet, these who have kept in the rear rank, and have only in secret followed Jesus, will be brought to the front, and we shall see men of substance and of position avowing their Lord. Joseph and Nicodemus both illustrate the dreadful truth that it is hard for them that have riches to enter into the kingdom of God; but they also show us that when they do enter they frequently excel. If they come last they remain to the last. If cowards when others are heroes, they can also be heroes when even apostles are cowards. Each man has his turn, and so while the fishermen-apostles were hiding away, the wealthy noncommittal brethren came to the front: though bred in luxury, they bore the brunt of the storm, and avowed the cause whose leader lay dead. Brave are the hearts which stand up for Jesus in his burial. "Sitting over against the sepulcher," we draw comfort from the sight of the friends who honored the Lord in his death.

I like to remember that the burial of the Lord *displayed the union of loving hearts.* The tomb became the meeting place of the old disciples and the new, of those who had long consorted with the Master, and those who had but newly avowed him. Magdalene and Mary had been with the Lord for years and had ministered to him of their substance; but Joseph of Arimathaea, as far as his public avowal of Christ is concerned, was, like Nicodemus, a new disciple: old and new followers united in the deed of love, and laid their Master in the tomb. A common sorrow and a common love unite us wondrously. When our great Master's cause is under a cloud and his name blasphemed, it is pleasant to see the young men battling with the foe and aiding their fathers in the stern struggle. Magdalene with her penitent love, and Mary with her deep

attachment to her Lord, join with the rabbi and the counselor who now begin
to prove that they intensely love the Man of Nazareth. That small society, that
little working meeting, which gathered around our Master's body, was a type
of the whole Christian church. When once aroused, believers forget all differ-
ences and degrees of spiritual condition, and each one is eager to do his part
to honor his Lord.

Mark, too, that the Savior's death *brought out abundant liberality.* The
spices, one hundred pounds in weight, and the fine linen, were furnished by
the men; and then the holy women prepared the liquid spices with which to
carry out what they might have called his great funeral, when they would
more completely wrap the body in odoriferous spices as the manner of the
Jews was to bury. There was much of honor intended by all that they
brought. A very thoughtful writer observes that the clothes in which our
Lord was wrapped are not called grave clothes but "linen cloth," and that the
emphasis would seem to be put upon their being linen; and he reminds us
that when we read of the garments of the priests in the Book of the Law we
find that every garment must be of linen. Our Lord's priesthood is, therefore,
suggested by the sole use of linen for his death robes. The Apostle and High
Priest of our profession in his tomb slept in pure white linen, even as now
today he represents himself to his servants as clothed with a garment down
to the foot. Even after death he acted as a priest, and poured out a libation of
blood and water; and it was, therefore, meet that in the grave he should still
wear priestly garments.

"He made his grave with the wicked"—there was his shame; "but with
the rich in his death"—there was his honor. He was put to death by rough soldiery, but he was laid in his grave by tender women. Persons of honorable
estate helped gently to receive, and reverentially to place in its position his
dear and sacred frame; and then, as if to do him honor, though they meant it
not, his tomb must not be left unsentineled, and Caesar lends his guards to
watch the couch of the Prince of peace. Like a king he slumbers, till as the
King of kings he wakes at daybreak.

To my mind it is very pleasant to see all this honor come to our Lord
when he is in his worst estate—dead and buried. Will we not also honor our
Lord when others despise him? Will we not cleave to him, come what may?
If the church were all but extirpated, if every voice should go over to the
enemy, if a great stone of philosophic reasoning were rolled at the door of
truth, and it should seem no longer possible for argument to remove it, yet
would we wait till the gospel should rise again to confound its foes. We will
not be afraid, but keep our position; we will stand still and see the salvation

of God, or "sitting over against the sepulcher," we will watch for the Lord's coming. Let the worst come to the worst, we would sooner serve Christ while he is conceived to be dead than all the philosophers that ever lived when in their prime. Even if fools should dance over the grave of Christianity, there shall remain at least a few who will weep over it, and brushing away their tears from their eyes expect to see it revive, and put forth all its ancient strength.

III. I must now pass to a third point. While sitting over against the sepulcher *we observe that his enemies were not at rest.*

They had their own way, but they were not content. They had taken the Savior, and with wicked hands they had crucified and slain him, but they were not satisfied. They were the most uneasy people in the world, though they had gained their point. It was their Sabbath day, and it was a high day, that Sabbath of Sabbaths, the Sabbath of the Passover. They kept a preparation for it and had been very careful not to go into the place called the pavement, lest they should defile themselves—sweet creatures! And now have they not gained all they wanted? They have killed Jesus and buried him: are they not happy? No: and what is more, their humiliation had begun—they were doomed to belie their own favorite profession. What was that profession? Their boast of rigid Sabbath keeping was its chief point, and they were perpetually charging our blessed Lord with Sabbath breaking, for healing the sick, and even because his disciples rubbed a few ears of wheat between their hands when they were hungry on the Sabbath day. Brethren, look at these men and laugh at their hypocrisy. It is the Sabbath day, and they come to Pilate, holding counsel on the Sabbath with a heathen! They tell him that they are afraid that Jesus' body will be spirited away, and he says, "Ye have a watch; go your way, make it as sure as you can"; and they go and seal the stone on the Sabbath. O you hypocritical Pharisees, here was an awful breaking of your Sabbath by your own selves! According to their superstitious tradition the rubbing ears of wheat between the hands was a kind of threshing, and therefore it was a breach of the law; surely, by the same reasoning, the burning of a candle to melt the wax must have been similar to the lighting of a furnace, and the melting of wax must have been a kind of foundry work, like that of the smith who pours metal into a mold; for in such a ridiculous fashion their rabbis interpreted the smallest acts. But they had to seal the stone and break their own absurd laws to satisfy their restless malice. One is pleased to see either Pharisees or Sadducees made to overturn their own professions and lay bare their hypocrisy. Modern-thought gentlemen will, before long, be forced to the same humiliation.

Next, they had to retract their own accusation against our Lord. They charged Jesus with having said, "Destroy this temple, and I will build it in three days," pretending that he referred to the temple upon Zion. Now they come to Pilate and tell him, "This deceiver said, 'After three days I will rise again.'" O you knaves, that is your new version, is it? You put the man to death for quite another rendering! Now you understand the dark saying? Yes, you deceivers, and you understood it before; but now you must eat your leek, and swallow your own words. Truly, he scorns the scorners, and pours contempt upon his enemies.

And now see how these kill-Christs betray their own fears. He is dead, but they are afraid of him! He is dead, but they cannot shake off the dread that he will vanquish them yet. They are full of agitation and alarm.

Nor was this all, they were to be made witnesses for God—to sign certificates of the death and resurrection of his Anointed. In order that there might be no doubt about the resurrection at all, there must be a seal, and *they* must go and set it; there must be a guard, and *they* must see it mustered. The disciples need not trouble about certifying that Jesus is in the grave, these Jews will do it, and set their own great seal to the evidence. These proud ones are sent to do drudges' work in Christ's kitchen, to wait upon a dead Christ, and to protect the body which they had slain. The lie which they told afterward crowned their shame: they bribed the soldiers to say that his disciples stole him away while they slept; and this was a transparent falsehood; for if the soldiers were asleep how could they know what was done? We cannot conceive of an instance in which men were more completely made to contradict and convict themselves. That Sabbath was a high day, but it was no Sabbath to them, nor would the overthrow of the gospel be any rest of soul to its opponents. If ever we should live to see the truth pushed into a corner, and the blessed cause of Christ fastened up as with rationalistic nails, and its very heart pierced by a critic's spear, yet, mark you, even in the darkest night that can ever try our faith, the adversaries of the gospel will still be in alarm lest it should rise again.

The old truth has a wonderful habit of leaping up from every fall as strong as ever. In Dr. Doddridge's days men had pretty nearly buried the gospel. Socinianism was taught in many if not most Dissenting pulpits, and the same was true of the Church of England: the liberal thinkers dreamed that they had won the victory and extinguished evangelical teaching; but their shouting came a little too soon. They said, "We shall hear no more of this miserable justification by faith, and regeneration by the Holy Ghost." They laid the gospel in a tomb cut out in the cold rock of Unitarianism, and they set the seal of their learning upon the great stone of doubt which shut in the gospel. There it was to lie forever; but God meant otherwise. There was a potboy [server of drinks in a tavern] over in Gloucester called George Whitefield, and there was a young student who had lately gone to Oxford called John Wesley, and these two passed by the grave of the gospel and beheld a strange sight, which they began to tell; and as they told it, the sods of unbelief and the stones of learned criticism began to move, and the truth which had been buried started up with Pentecostal power. Aha! you adversaries, how greatly had you deceived yourselves! Within a few months all over England the work of the devil and his ministers was broken to pieces, as when a tower is split by lightning, or the thick darkness scattered by the rising sun. The weight of ignorance and unbelief fled before the bright day of the gospel, though that gospel was for the most part proclaimed by unlettered men. The thing which has been is the thing which shall be.

History repeats itself. O generation of modern thinkers, you will have to eat your own words and disprove your own assertions. You will have to confute each other and yourselves, even as the Moabites and Elamites slew each other. It may even happen that your infidelities will work themselves out into practical evil of which you will be the victims. You may bring about a repetition of the French Revolution of 1789, with more than all its bloodshed, and who will wonder. You, some of you calling yourselves ministers of God, with your insinuations of doubt, your denials of future punishment, your insults of the gospel, your ingenious speeches against the Bible, are shaking the very foundation of society. I impeach you as the worst enemies of mankind. In effect you proclaim to men that they may sin as they like, for there is no hell, or if there be, it is but a little one: thus you publish a gospel of licentiousness, and you may one day rue the result. You may live to see a reign of terror of your own creating, but even if you do, the gospel of Jesus will come forth from all the filth you have heaped upon it, for the holy gospel will live as Christ lives, and its enemies shall never cease to be in fear. Your harsh speeches against those who preach the gospel, your bitterness and your sneers of contempt, all show that you know better than you say, and are afraid of the very Christ whom you kill. We who cleave to the glorious gospel will abide in peace, come what may, but you will not.

IV. And now our last thought is that while these enemies of Christ were in fear and trembling *we note that his followers were resting.*

It was the seventh day, and therefore they ceased from labor. The Marys waited, and Joseph and Nicodemus refrained from visiting the tomb; they obediently observed the Sabbath rest. I am not sure that they had faith enough to feel very happy, but they evidently did expect something, and anxiously awaited the third day. They had enough of the comfort of hope to remain quiet on the seventh day.

Now, beloved, sitting over against the sepulcher while Christ lies in it, my first thought about it is, *I will rest, for he rests.* What a wonderful stillness there was about our Lord in that rocky grave. He had been daily thronged by thousands: even when he ate bread they disturbed him. He scarcely could have a moment's stillness in life; but now how quiet is his bed! Not a sound is heard. The great stone shuts out all noise, and the body is at peace. Well, if he rests, I may. If for a while the Lord seems to suspend his energies, his servants may cry unto him, but they may not fret. He knows best when to sleep and when to wake.

As I see the Christ resting in the grave, my next thought is, *he has the power to come forth again.* Some few months ago, I tried to show you that when the disciples were alarmed because Jesus was asleep they were in error, for his sleep was the token of their security. When I see a captain on board ship pacing anxiously up and down the deck, I may fear that danger is suspected; but when the captain turns into his cabin, then I may be sure that all is right, and there is no reason why I should not turn in too. So if our blessed Lord should ever suffer his cause to droop, and if he should give no marvelous manifestations of his power, we need not doubt his power; let us keep our Sabbath, pray to him, and work for him, for these are duties of the holy day of rest; but do not let us fret and worry, for his time to work will come.

The rest of the Christian lies in believing in Christ under all circumstances. Go in for this, beloved. Believe in him in the manger, when his cause is young and weak. Believe in him in the streets, when the populace applaud him, for he deserves their loudest acclamations. Believe in him when they take him to the brow of the hill to cast him headlong, he is just as worthy as when they cry "hosanna." Believe in him when he is in an agony, and believe in him when he is on the cross; and if ever it should seem to you that his cause must die out, believe in him still. Christ's gospel in any circumstances deserves our fullest trust. That gospel which has saved your souls, that gospel which you have received, and which has been sealed upon your hearts by the Holy Ghost, stand fast in it, come what may, and through faith, peace and quiet shall pervade your souls.

Once more, it will be well if we can obtain peace by having fellowship with our Lord in his burial. Die with him, and be buried with him; there is nothing like it. I desire for my soul while she lives in the Lord that, as to the world and all its wisdom, I may be as a dead man. When accused of having no power of thought, and no originality of teaching, I am content to own the charge, for my soul desires to be dead to all but that which is revealed and taught by the Lord Jesus. I would lie in the rocky tomb of the everlasting truth, not creating thought, but giving myself up to God's thoughts. But, brethren, if we are ever to lie in that tomb, we must be wrapped about with the fine linen of holiness: these are the shrouds of a man who is dead to sin. All about us must be the spices, the myrrh, and aloes of preserving grace, that being dead with Christ we may see no corruption, but may show that death to be only another form of the new life which we have received in him. When the world goes by, let it know concerning our heart's desire and ambition, that they are all buried with Christ, and it is written on the memorial of our spiritual grave, "Here he lies"; as far as this world's sin and pleasure and self-seeking and wisdom are concerned, "Here he lies buried with his Master."

Know, you who are not converted, that the way of salvation is by believing in Christ, or trusting in him, and if you do so trust you shall never be confounded, world without end, for he that trusts Christ, and believes in him even as a little child, the same shall enter into his kingdom, and he that will follow him, even down to his grave, shall be with him in his glory, and shall see his triumphs forever and ever. Amen.

Mary Magdalene: A Handkerchief

꧁꧂

Published on Thursday, October 5, 1905; delivered on Lord's Day evening, June 13, 1875, at the Metropolitan Tabernacle, Newington. No. 2956.

Jesus saith unto her, "Woman, why weepest thou? whom seekest thou?"
—JOHN 20:15

In the garden of Eden, immediately after the Fall, the sentence of sorrow, and of sorrow multiplied, fell upon the woman. In the garden where Christ had been buried, after his resurrection, the news of comfort—comfort rich and divine—came to a woman through the woman's promised Seed, the Lord Jesus Christ. If the sentence must fall heavily upon the woman, so must the comfort come most sweetly to her. I will not say that the resurrection reversed the curse of the Fall; but, at any rate, it took the sting out of it, lifted it up, and sanctified it. There was reason enough for the woman to weep after the sentence had been pronounced upon her; but there is no reason for her to weep now that Jesus Christ has fulfilled the promise which followed upon man's disobedience, namely, that the Seed of the woman should bruise the serpent's head.

Observe the wise method followed by the divine Consoler. In order to comfort Mary Magdalene, our Lord put a question to her. It is often the wisest way to relieve minds that are swollen through grief to allow them to find the natural end of their sorrow by asking them why they are weeping. We have to do this with ourselves sometimes; we inquire, "Why art thou cast down, O my soul? and why art thou disquieted within me?" The soul begins to ask for the reason of its grief, and often finds that it is insufficient to justify so bitter a sorrow; and perhaps it even discovers that the sources of its sorrow have been misunderstood, and that, if they had been rightly comprehended, they would have been sources of joy instead. He who would be wise in dealing with the daughters of grief must let them tell their own story; and, almost without a single sentence from you, their own story will be blessed by God to the relieving of their grief.

Moreover, it is always wise, before we attempt to comfort anyone, to know what is the peculiar form and fashion which grief has taken. The physician who, without investigation, should at once proceed to apply a remedy to his patient, might be giving the wrong medicine for the disease. He has to make his diagnosis of the malady, to see whence it came, what are its symptoms, and how it works, and then the physician adapts his medicine to the case. Sit down with your sorrow, my friend, and let us hear what ails you. What causes you to fret? What causes your soul to travail? Possibly, the sorrowing ones will themselves direct you to the right remedy for their malady, and so you shall be able to speak a word in season, and "a word spoken in due season, how good it is!" You are at present like a man groping in the dark, and you will be as one pouring vinegar upon niter if you do sing songs to a heavy heart, and you will make matters worse which you had hoped to make better unless you do find out the cause of the mourner's tears.

My one object, at this time, is to take this question of our Lord to Mary, and apply it to all who are sorrowing here; and although I shall keep to the text, and repeat the question, "Woman, why weepest, thou?" I shall hope that other sorrows besides [those of] the women here will find comfort from the words which the Holy Spirit will teach me to speak. I shall ask, first, *is it natural sorrow?* And, second, *is it spiritual sorrow?*

I. We will, first, inquire about that which is common to us all without exception: *is it natural sorrow?*

Is it sorrow which springs from our human nature, and is common to all who are born of woman, to whom sorrow comes as a portion of our heritage?

Well, my friend, what is the cause of your grief? What ails you? *Is it because you are bereaved?* Have you lost someone who was very dear to you? Then your grief is not unusual, and your weeping is not unpardonable, for Jesus wept as he stood at the grave of his friend Lazarus. But let not your weeping go beyond due bounds. Your tears are right enough so far, but they may be wrong if they go any further. There is a weeping of regret, and of a lacerated spirit, upon which God looks with pity; but there may come a weeping of rebelliousness upon which even our heavenly Father may feel that he must look with anger. "Why weepest thou?" Will you look into your heart, beloved, and see whether the cause of your grief is such as does fully justify it, or see whether you have carried it too far already? You have lost a child—a lovely child; but, my sister, you have not really lost your child. Call you that lost which is in Christ's keeping? Call you that babe lost which is up among the angels? If your child had been taken to be a prince in a palace, you would not have said that he was lost; inasmuch as he has been caught away to be with Jesus, say not that he is lost. You are the mother of one who can see the face of God, and thus says the Lord unto you, "Refrain thine eyes from weeping, for thy children shall come again from the land of their captivity."

Have you lost your husband? It is a heavy blow, and well may you weep; but, still, who took him from you? Was it not he who lent him to you? Bless the Lord that you have had all those years of comfort and joy, and say with Job, "The LORD gave, and the LORD hath taken away; blessed be the name of the LORD." The loss of your husband has made a great void in your life, but the Lord will fill that void. Do you know him? Then, he will be a Husband unto you, and a Father to your fatherless children. He has said, "Leave thy fatherless children, I will preserve them alive; and let thy widows trust in me." You are a widow; then, trust in the Lord. If you are a widow without faith in God, then yours is a sorrow indeed; but if the widow's sorrow shall drive her to trust in Christ as her Savior, if she shall look up, and in her deep sorrow trust herself with the great Helper of the helpless, she shall find her loss to be a gain.

"Woman, why weepest thou?" Whatever relative or friend you have lost, your God will be more to you than the loved one could ever be. The Well Beloved, the Lord Jesus Christ is better to us than all earthly friends; and when they are taken away from us, he more than fills the space which once they occupied; so that, if we have less of human love, we have more of the divine, and thus we are gainers rather than losers. Look forward to the resurrection and be comforted. Remember that the worm has not consumed the beauty forever, neither has the precious temple of the body been given up to everlasting will. If they fell asleep in Christ as surely as they were buried, they shall rise again in beauty, in the image of Jesus Christ; so let us not sorrow as those who are without hope. Brush away your tears; or, if they must fall, smile through them in sweet resignation to the divine will, and be still.

"Why weepest thou?" Is there another reason for your sorrow? *Do you weep because you are very poor?* There are some who do not know the sorrow of poverty, who will, perhaps, blame you; but I know that there are some of you who have a hard task to find a livelihood—a task at which a slave might be pitied. In this great city, how many toil till they wear themselves almost to skeletons, and even then scarcely find food enough to keep body and soul together! There are some of the choicest sons and daughters of the Lord who seem to be the lowest of all in the scale of this world's possessions, and their lot, from morning to night, is one of incessant drudgery. Were it not for these sweet Sabbaths, to live on earth would be to them altogether a bondage. But weep not, my poor sister; weep not, my poor brother; there is One who was poorer than you are, who will bear your burdens for you. Jesus Christ was poorer than poverty, because he had once been so exceedingly rich; and none are so poor as those who come down from wealth to poverty. You know that, though he was rich, yet, for our sakes, he became poor, that we, through his poverty, might become rich. Poor mourner, remember the promise to him that walks righteously, and speaks uprightly, "Bread shall be given him, his waters shall be sure." Recollect also how the Lord Jesus said to his disciples, "Consider the lilies of the field, how they grow; they toil not, neither do they spin; and yet I say unto you, that even Solomon in all his glory was not arrayed like one of these. Wherefore, if God so clothe the grass of the field, which today is, and tomorrow is cast into the oven, shall he not much more clothe you, O ye of little faith?" "Behold the fowls of the air; for they sow not, neither do they reap, nor gather into barns; yet your heavenly Father feedeth them." So will he not feed you also? Wipe away your tears; bend your back to the burden which God has laid upon you, "and be content with such things as ye have, for he hath said, 'I will never leave thee, nor forsake thee.'"

"Woman, why weepest thou?" Suppose that neither of these causes should account for your sorrow. *Have you a beloved sick one at home?* Yes, and you may well weep if that sickness has been long, and if it wears away the beauty from the cheek, and the brightness from the eye, and if it costs innumerable pains and anguish only to be understood by those who suffer it, and those who watch, hour by hour, by the sufferer. I can understand your weeping; and yet, beloved, your case is in Christ's hands, and you may safely leave your dear ones in his hands. He never sent a trial to any child of his unless it was so necessary that, to have withheld it would have been unkind. Accept it as the Lord's love token. Besides, remember that he can recover our loved ones if he deems it wise, or he can sustain them in their sickness if he does not see fit to recover them, and he can give them a joyful exit from this world, and an abundant entrance into his everlasting kingdom. So do not weep too much; but say, "It is the LORD; let him do what seemeth him good."

Possibly, however, the weeping may come to us because *we have sickness in our own bodies.* While we are sitting or standing here, some of us little know the amount of suffering that may be felt by the person who is sitting next to us. I have often wondered how some of my beloved hearers ever manage to get here at all; yet they are here, although full of pain. They find a sweet forgetfulness, at least for a little time, while the Word is being preached; and they cannot forgo the pleasure of mingling with the people of God, even though it costs them many a sharp pang. Yet I would urge even such sufferers to dry their tears; it may be that the dreaded disease of consumption is gradually wearing away the life; but, my sister, it is no ill thing just to swoon away into heaven, and gently to pass from this life to another and a brighter day. Perhaps you are suffering from some painful disease which is known to be fatal. Well, that is only another way of bringing a King's messenger to take you swiftly home. If you have no Christ, you may well weep if you have received your death wound, for after death comes judgment. This disease is a messenger sent to bid you prepare to meet your God. Suppose you were smitten down today, God has given you a timely warning. Take it, I pray you; and, instead of weeping over your sickness, may the Holy Spirit enable you to weep over your sin, and to trust in Christ as your Savior, for then all shall be well. If we have believed in Jesus, we need not weep, even though the dread archer may have lodged the fatal shaft quite near our heart. What is there to weep about?

When a Christian has received an intimation that he is soon to be with his Savior in glory, we may congratulate him that he is the sooner to be out of the strife and the sin, and to wear the crown of victory and glory forever, so we will not weep about that.

Perhaps I am addressing one who says, "My sorrow is neither bereavement, nor personal sickness, nor the sickness of friends, nor poverty; I sometimes think I could bear any or all of those trials; but I have been the victim of a treacherous friend; *I trusted and have been deceived.* I gave my heart's best affections and have been betrayed." You, too, dear friend, are not alone in that trial. There was One, better far than you, on whose cheek came the hot kiss from the betrayer's lips, so that Jesus said to Judas, "Betrayest thou the Son of man with a kiss?" Many have had so-called friends, who, in the time of testing, have been more cruel than avowed foes. They have been as the cunning fowler who spreads his net so warily that he may catch the little birds. Well, if your case is like that of the birds, fly away to Jesus; trust him, for he will never deceive you. If Jesus shall fill that vacancy in your heart, it will have been a blessed vacancy. A broken heart is best healed by a touch of the pierced hand of Jesus. Get you away to him, you Hannah, you woman of a sorrowful spirit; go you to the "Man of sorrows, and acquainted with grief," and he will find a balm for your spirit.

I cannot go further into these natural sorrows; they are so many, and the river of grief is so deep and rapid; but, whatsoever your sorrow may be, one piece of advice I have to give to every weeping one—find then the divine Comforter; and, whatever your griefs may be, they shall be assuaged.

II. Now I come to our main question, which is this: *is it spiritual sorrow?*

If so, is it sorrow for others, or sorrow for yourselves?

I will begin with the nobler form. "Woman, why weepest thou?" *Do you weep for others?* Are there some whom you love, and for whom you have often prayed, who remain in the gall of bitterness, and in the bonds of iniquity? This is a suitable subject for mourning. Weep not for those who have gone to be "forever with the Lord," for all is well with them; but weep for those who are living in sin—for the young man, in his unbridled lust, who has dishonored his father's name, for the daughter who, in her willfulness, has gone astray into the paths of transgression. Weep for the heart that will not break. Weep for the eyes that will not weep. Weep for the sinners who will not confess their sins, but are resolutely seeking their own damnation. Ah, my dear friends, when you are weeping like that, you are weeping as your Savior did when he wept over Jerusalem, and God will put your tears into his bottle. Be comforted, for those tears of yours are omens of good to the souls you pity; for, as surely as you groan and sigh and cry over these beloved ones, you are doing what you can to bring them the blessing, and I think that is a token that the blessing of God is on its way to them. You remember that it is written that "the power of the Lord was present to heal" on a certain occasion: why was it more present then than at any other time? Was it not because there were four men who were breaking up the roof to let down a sick one into the room where Christ was? Wherever there is real concern for souls, although it be only in four persons, there is about the ministry a power of an unusual kind. Go on, then, and still weep, but not hopelessly, not with the bitterness of despair. The Lord will see your tears, and will hear your prayers, and will grant your petition, even though you may not live to see it. Peradventure, when you are in heaven, your son, your husband, your sister, over whom you now are weeping, shall be brought to Christ.

Possibly, however, the sorrow for others relates to the church with which this mourner is connected. It is often my lot to meet with brethren and sisters coming from country towns who say to me, "What are we to do? The place of worship where we attend might almost as well be pulled down, for there is no life, no energy, no power there." Oh, it is wretched work indeed when that is the case! Many towns and villages would be all the better if the meeting house and the parish church, too, were utterly demobilized, because then they would feel that they had not any religious means at all, and would, perhaps, be stirred up to seek them. But now there is dead formalism in both places. There is nothing worse than sluggishness in the pastors and members of church. What is the use of a dead church? It is no use at all. The fact is, the better a church is, the sooner it rots when it is dead. The man who is very stout is the very worst person to keep in the house when once he is dead, and the church that seems to be most packed with divine truth is the most obnoxious to all when once the life goes out of it. Well, my dear friends, if you are sorrowing over the low condition of the church to which you belong, and the state of religion in general in the neighborhood where you live, I would not stay your tears, yet I would try to comfort you, and I would advise you to take the case to your Lord. He is the Head of the church, so carry that burden to him. Do not go about finding fault; do not try to sow dissension and dissatisfaction, or you will do hurt instead of good; but lay the matter before your Lord and Master, and give him no rest till once again he puts forth his almighty power and raises his church to life.

Now I must leave this point; but I think that it is a grand thing to sorrow and weep for others. We ought to make it a rule of our life to bear the sorrows of other people. If sinners will not repent, we cannot repent for them; if they will not believe, we cannot believe for them; true religion can never be a matter of sponsorship, but we can do this for sinners. We can say to the Lord, "O Lord, these sinners will not themselves feel their sin, but we feel it, it grieves us, and cuts us to the heart! O Lord, will you not give them repentance? Will you not cause these sinners to believe in you? We confess their iniquity before you, for we know the guiltiness of their hearts in rejecting you. We weep and mourn that they will not admire your beauty, and will not yield their hearts to you; but, dear Savior, *do* win their hearts in answer to our prayer. They are far away from God by their wicked works; bring them near by your precious blood." That is what I mean; and if you can do this, appropriating, as it were, the sins and sorrows of mankind to yourself, you will be showing your sympathy with them in the best possible way. Woman, if you weep thus for others, blessed are you among women.

But, now, "why weepest thou?" *Is it for yourself?* Are these spiritual sorrows on your own account? Are you a sorrowing child of God? Do you know yourself to be a Christian, and yet do you weep? Then, what is the cause of your grief? Do you miss your Lord's presence? If so, there is reason enough for your weeping; yet why should you weep? He is present even now; you have not seen him, but he has seen you, and is gazing upon you at this very moment. Beloved mourner, do not say, "I am out of fellowship with Christ, and I am afraid I cannot return to that blessed experience for months." Listen to this text: "Behold, I stand at the door, and knock: if any man hear my voice, and open the door,"—that is all—"I will come in to him, and will sup with him, and he with me." It was to the angel of the church of the Laodiceans, the lukewarm Laodiceans, that these words were written, and they are also written to you, my sister, and to you, my brother, if you have grown lukewarm. Be willing for Christ to come to you; and, before ever you are aware, your soul shall make you like the chariots of Amminadib. Do not imagine that restoration to communion with Christ need occupy a longer time than conversion, and conversion is often worked instantaneously. So you may be lifted up from the depths of despondency to the heights of sacred fellowship with your Lord before this present service closes. Be of good cheer, and let your joy be renewed this very hour.

But perhaps you say, "I weep because I have grieved my Lord." Those are blessed tears, although the offense which caused them is grievous. Well may we be grieved when Christ has been grieved by us; but, mourning soul, though he is rightly grieved with you, remember this gracious declaration, "He will not always chide: neither will he keep his anger forever"; and this comforting promise, "'For a small moment have I forsaken thee; but with great mercies will I gather thee. In a little wrath I hid my face from thee for a moment; but with everlasting kindness will I have mercy on these,' saith the LORD thy Redeemer." Only confess that you have transgressed against the Lord your Redeemer, and you may come back to him at once; no, even now he comes to meet with you, and he brings with him the basin and the towel, that he may wash your soiled feet, for he has washed you once in his blood, and now he will again wash your feet, and you shall be clean every whit, and shall walk with cleansed feet in renewed fellowship with your Lord.

Possibly, some of you say that your sorrow is that you are not as holy as you wish to be. Ah! that is a sorrow which I share with you, for I can say with the apostle Paul, "When I would do good, evil is present with me"; and though I hear of some who do not find that evil is present with them, I suspect that the reason is, because they do not know themselves as they really are, or they would find that it was so with them, at least at times. If I could, I would be without one sinful thought or word or deed or imagination or wish, and so would you; and because you cannot be so at present, you weep. It is well that such tears should fall, only do not let these tears dim your view of Christ. Do not let those longings prevent your knowing that you are perfect and complete in Christ Jesus. Do not let your struggles hinder you from believing that Christ has conquered sin for you, and that he will yet conquer sin in you. Do not let anything take away from you the full conviction that sin shall be altogether destroyed in you, and that Christ will present you to his Father "without spot, or wrinkle, or any such thing," "holy and unblamable and unreprovable in his sight."

Perhaps you say that your sorrow is because you can do so little for Christ. Ah! there again, I have sympathy with you; but do not fret about that. Those of us who have the largest opportunities are often those who most regret that we can so little avail ourselves of them. But I know some godly women who are confined to the house with the care of a numerous family, or, worse still, are confined to their bed, in constant pain, and one of their greatest griefs is that they can do so little for Christ. But, brother, sister, do you not know the rule of David, and the rule of David's Lord? They that abide by the stuff shall have the same portion as they who go out to the battle. You are like the soldiers who have to keep in the rear and guard the baggage; but when the King comes back, with all the active troops who have been doing the fighting, you will share the victory with them. You who are at home keeping the camp preserve many things which might be forgotten if we were all on active service. Be you comforted, then, if you are called to suffer or to be in obscurity; you shall be equal to the man and woman who are called to labor more prominently. Do what you can; I do not know that Christ himself ever praised anybody more than he did that woman of whom he said, "She hath done what she could." I daresay she wanted to do a great deal more, but she did what she could; and if you have done what you could, it is well.

"Ah!" says another, "but I am conscious of a great deal of weakness. What I do is done so badly. Even in prayer, I do not always prevail; my petitions often seem to come back to me unanswered." Well, dear friend, do not altogether regret your weakness, for there was one who said that when he was weak, he was strong. If you have many infirmities which make you weak, there is a way of glorying in infirmities because the power of Christ does rest upon you. Suppose that you are not only weak, but that you are weakness itself—that you are nothing and nobody; for when you have reached that point, the cause of your weeping will have vanished, because, where you end, there God begins; and when you have done with self, then Christ will be all in all to you, and you will lift up your voice in praise of him who has done such great things for you.

Many strange things happen to young Christians between the time of their conversion and their entrance into heaven. Their program of life is seldom carried out. The map which they make of the route is not according to the true geography of it. They reckon that, as soon as they have believed in Jesus, they will enter into sweet peace and rest, which is probably correct, but they also suppose that this peace and rest will always continue, and probably increase, that they will go to heaven, singing all the way, along pleasant roads and paths of peace, and that the light upon their way will get brighter and brighter, till it comes to the perfect day. They feel so happy, and they sing so sweetly, that they imagine it will always be with them just as it was in the first hours of their Christian experience. They are like persons who have, for the first time in their lives, come into the bright light of day, after having lived in a deep mine, or been immured in a dark dungeon. They ask what season of the year it is, and they are told that it is springtime, that the flowers have begun to bloom, but that there are more to follow. They hear the birds singing, but they are told that there are brighter days to come, that May is a fairer month than April, and June brighter still, and then will come the months of harvest, when the sickle shall be thrust in among the golden grain.

All this is very cheering, so this new beginner plans that, tomorrow, he will be out all day upon the green grass, or in the gardens admiring the bursting buds, and gathering for himself many a delightful garland of flowers; but, perhaps, when he gets up tomorrow morning, the heavens are all black with clouds, and a torrent of rain is falling. "Oh!" says he, "I never reckoned upon this." Then, perhaps, in June, there comes such a hurly-burly in the sky as he never thought of, flames of fire and loud thunders out of the heavens, and dreadful drenching showers intermixed with rattling hail. "Oh!" says he, "I never calculated upon this; I thought the months were to grow brighter and brighter, and that, at last, there would come the golden harvest." We tell him that these rains and storms all conduce to the very result which we promised him, and that they are by no means contrary to our statement. We were only giving him a brief outline of the year's history, and these things are by no means contrary to our outline, nor need he fear but that the month of harvest will come in due season. It is true, young Christian, that you will have a light upon your road, and that it will grow more and more bright unto the perfect day. It is true that the ways of wisdom "are ways of pleasantness, and all her paths are peace." Your highest conception of the joy to be found in Christ is not an exaggerated one. However much delight you may anticipate, you shall have all that, and you shall also have even more, as you are able to bear it; but intermittent times will come—strange times to you—in which your joy will seem to be dead, and your peace will be fearfully disturbed. Your soul will be "tossed with tempest, and not comforted." You will sorrowfully sit in sackcloth and ashes, and you will not go to the table of feasting, but to the house of mourning. There will you be made to drink the water of tears, and have your bread salted with grief. Be not surprised, then, when this comes to pass, as though some strange things had happened to you. Remember that we have told you of it; we, who have gone further on the road to heaven than you have gone, tell you that there will come dark times, and stormy times, and we bid you prepare for them.

Now I must turn to others in our assembly. "Woman, why weepest thou?"

Perhaps you say, "O sir, I dare not put myself down among the saints!" Well, then, will you put yourself down among the sinners? "Yes, I am a sinner," you reply; "yet I think—I hope—I am not altogether without some little faith in Christ. I sometimes feel myself inclined to love him; but, oftentimes, I am of another mind, averse to all that is good." Ah, my friend, I know you; and I have met with many like your class. I said once to one of your sort, "You say that you are not a Christian." "No," she said, "I fear I am not." "Then," I asked, "why do you go to the home of God on the Sabbath? Why don't you stop at home, or go where sinners go?" "Oh, no, sir!" she answered, "I could not do that; when I hear people blaspheme the name of Christ it cuts me to the quick; and I am never so happy as when I am with the people of God. I enjoy the hymns that they sing; and, while I am with them, my heart gets so warm that I feel as if I must praise the Lord. I think it is a great mercy that I cannot help blessing and praising God." "Well, then," I said, "I think that you must really have some faith in Christ, or you would not feel and act as you do."

I remember hearing of a minister, who wrote down these words, "I do not believe on the Lord Jesus Christ," and asked a person, who was full of doubt, to sign her name to that declaration, but she would not do that. She did believe in Christ though she did not think that she believed. I once offered a person who said she had no faith, a £5 note if she would give up her faith, but she said that she would not take a thousand worlds for it! Mrs. Much-Afraid and Mr. Despondency and Mr. Feeble-Mind and Mr. Ready-to-Halt—there are plenty of that family still living; and I know why you weep, good woman, for you also belong to that tribe. Well, then, if you cannot come to Christ as a saint, come to him as a sinner. If you have made a mistake, and have never trusted in Christ, do it now. If you really have not repented, and have not believed, and have not been renewed in heart, remember that it is still written, "Him that cometh to me I will in no wise cast out"; "and whosoever will, let him take the water of life freely." If the title deeds of your spiritual estate are not genuine, but forgeries, do not dispute the question with one who is wiser than yourself; but come straightaway to Jesus Christ empty handed, in the manner in which he bids all sinners come to him, and then I shall not have to ask, "Why weepest thou?"

But, last of all, is this person who is weeping a seeking sinner? Christ not only said to Mary Magdalene, "Why weepest thou?" but also, "Whom seekest thou?" for he knew that she was seeking *him*. I would give all I possess if I might always preach to weeping sinners who are seeking Christ. I sometimes think that I would like to be always weeping on account of sin, if I might be always sure that I was seeking Jesus. It is possible that there has come into this place someone who is seeking a Savior. Ah, weeping woman! Do you weep because sin burdens you? Do you weep because sweet sin has become bitter to you? Do you weep because the things wherein your soul once delighted have now become your torment and your grief? Then I rejoice over your tears, for they are precious in God's sight; they are more valuable than the finest diamonds in the world. Blessed is the soul that can repent of sin.

But, possibly, your weeping is because you are afraid of being rejected by Christ. Put every tear of that kind away, for there is no fear of one sinner who comes to Christ being rejected by him. As I reminded you just now, he has said, "Him that cometh to me I will in no wise cast out." Come, then, you burdened sinner; come, you heavily laden soul; and trust yourself with Jesus, and then he cannot—unless he can completely change, and that is impossible—he cannot reject you. Come and trust him even now, and you shall be saved this very hour.

But, perhaps, your weeping is for this reason; you say, "Alas! I have been aroused before this, and I thought that I would seek the Lord, and I did get some hope, and I fancied that I was relieved of sin; but I have gone back, and my last end has been worse than the first." Well may you weep if that is really the case, and I cannot forbid you to do so. But, my dear friend, if you came falsely once, that is only one more reason why you should come truly now. If you built on the sand once, and that house is gone, it is but another argument for building on the rock. If you were excited, and mistook a transient emotion for the work of the Spirit of God—if you put presumption in the place of faith, do not do so again; but come, just as you now are, and rest your weary soul on Christ's atoning sacrifice, and you shall find peace, immediate and permanent peace.

But, possibly, you weep because you say, "If I came to Christ I fear I should not hold on to him to the end." I know you would not by yourself, but I also know that he will hold you on if you will but come and trust him. It is not you who have to keep Christ; it is Christ who has to keep you. I should not wonder if your former failure arose from your having so much to do with it. So have nothing to do with it this time. If you are very weak, lean all the more heavily on your Beloved; no, if you are nothing, let Christ be all the more to you because of your nothingness. If you are black, give all the more praise to the blood that can make you whiter than snow. If you realize that you are lost, and fear that you will be found among the damned, flee the more eagerly to those bleeding wounds which give life, not merely to perishing sinners, but to sinners dead in trespasses and sins.

"Ah!" says one, "I think you have invited me, but I feel as though I could not come, and I weep because I cannot come for I do not properly understand the matter." Well, then, dry your tears, and listen while I tell you the story again, and we who believe in Jesus will pray the Holy Spirit to lead you to understand the truth. The Father, whom you have offended, does not ask you to do anything to make him pleased with you; he does not wish you to contribute either good works or right feelings in order to make an atonement for your sin. His dear Son, Jesus Christ, has made the only atonement for sin that can ever be made; what the Father bids you do is to accept of what his Son has done, and trust alone to that. Can you not do this? What more do you need, you doubting, sorrowing seekers, but that you trust in Jesus Christ, the Son of God, who was nailed to Calvary's cross, but is now risen from the dead, and gone back to his glory with the Father? We sometimes sing, in one of our hymns—

> *What more can he say than to you he hath said,*
> *You who unto Jesus for refuge have fled?*

And I say the same to you who are seeking Christ, "What more can he say to you?" What sort of a promise would you like him to make to you? Shall it be one like this, "Though your sins be as scarlet, they shall be as white as snow"? You say that you would like such a promise as that; well, there is that very one in the Bible. Or would this one suit you, "Let the wicked forsake his way, and the unrighteous man his thoughts: and let him return unto the LORD, and he will have mercy upon him; and to our God, for he will abundantly pardon"? Or would this one meet your case, "The blood of Jesus Christ his Son cleanseth us from all sin"? Surely this one must suit you, "Whosoever shall call on the name of the Lord shall be saved." Or this message, "If we confess our sins, he is faithful and just to forgive us our sins, and to cleanse us from all unrighteousness." Or this, "Seek ye the LORD while he may be found, call ye upon him while he is near." If these do not meet your case, I do not know what you would wish to have. My Lord, by his blessed Spirit, seems to have put the gospel into all sorts of lights to suit all sorts of eyes, and he tells us, his ministers, to labor for this end, to get you to look at Jesus Christ. I have tried to do this, and I beseech you not to be content with your weepings or your feelings or your Bible searchings; do not be content even with prayer. This way of salvation is "Believe on the Lord Jesus Christ"; so rest you in him; that is believing. Trust in him, depend upon him; that is another way of believing in him; and when you have done that, you are saved—saved the moment you believe in Jesus. The great work of salvation then commences in you, as the work of salvation for you is already complete, and you shall be saved from your sins, made new creatures, and made holy creatures, through the power of that blessed Spirit whom Jesus Christ bestows upon those who believe in him.

May God bless the words I have spoken to the comfort of some! I believe he will; I expect he will; I know he will; and he shall have the glory. Amen.

Mary, Mother of Mark: The Special Prayer Meeting

~⚬~

Delivered on Lord's Day morning, July 20, 1875, at the Metropolitan Tabernacle, Newington. No. 1247.

When he had considered the thing, he came to the house of Mary the mother of John, whose surname was Mark; where many were gathered together praying.—ACTS 12:12

It was a great wonder that the infant church of Christ was not destroyed. Truly, she was like a lone lamb in the midst of furious wolves, without either earthly power or prestige or patronage to protect her, yet, as though she wore a charmed life, she escaped from the hosts of her cruel foes. Had not this child been something more than others, it had been slain like the innocents at Bethlehem: but being heaven-born it escaped the fury of the destroyer.

It is worthwhile asking, however—with what weapons did this church protect herself? For *we* may very wisely use the same. She was preserved in her utmost danger from overwhelming destruction, what was her defense? Where found she shield and buckler? The answer is—in prayer: "many were gathered together praying." Whatever may be the danger of the times, and each age has its own peculiar hazard, we may rest in calm assurance that our defense is of God, and we may avail ourselves of that defense in the same manner as the early church did, namely, by abounding in prayer. However poisonous the viper, prayer can extract its sting; however fierce the lion, prayer can break its teeth; however terrible the fire, prayer can quench the violence of the flame.

But this is not all: the newborn church not only escaped, but it multiplied: from being as a grain of mustard seed, when it could all assemble in the upper room, it has now become a great tree; lo, it covers the nations, and the birds of the air in flocks find shelter in its branches. Whence this wondrous increase? What made it grow? Outward circumstances were unfavorable to its progress; upon what nourishment has it been fed? What means were taken with this tender shoot that has been so speedily developed? For, whatever means were used of old, we may wisely use them today also to strengthen which things remain and are ready to die, and to develop that which is hopeful in our midst. The answer is—the fact that on all occasions "many were gathered together praying." While praying, the Spirit of God came down upon them; while praying, the Spirit often separated this man and that for special work; while praying, their hearts grew warm with inward fire; while praying, their tongues were unloosed, and they went forth to speak to the people; and while praying, the Lord opened to them the treasures of his grace. By prayer they were protected, and by prayer they grew; and if our churches are to live and grow they must be watered from the selfsame source. "Let us pray," is one of the most needful watchwords which I can suggest to Christian men and women, for if we will but pray, prayer will fill up the pools in the valley of Baca, yes, and open to us all the channels of that river of God which is full of water, the streams whereof make glad the city of our God.

We have heard a great deal of talk in certain sections of the church about going back to primitive times, and they are introducing to us all sorts of superstitious inventions, under cover of the customs of the early church. The plea is cunningly chosen, for primitive practices have great weight with true Christians; but the weak point of the argument is that unfortunately what they call the early church is not early enough. If we must have the early church held up as a model, let us have the earliest church of all; if we are to have fathers, let us go back to apostolic fathers; and if we are to have ritual and rule and ceremonial modeled on strict precedent, let us go back to the original precedent recorded in the holy Scriptures. We who are called Baptists, have not the slightest objection to go back in everything to the apostolic habit and practice; we reverence the real primitive method, and desire to follow the customs of the true early church: and if we could see every ordinance restored to the exact mode in which it was practiced by the saints immediately after the ascension of our Lord, and during apostolic times, we would clap our hands with delight. 'Tis a consummation devoutly to be wished. To see the early church alive again would cause us unfeigned satisfaction. Especially upon this point would we imitate the early church: we would have it said of us—"Many were gathered together praying." May we have much prayer, much household prayer, much believing prayer, much prevalent prayer, and then we shall obtain great blessings from the Lord.

I. This morning my earnest desire is to stir up the church of Jesus Christ to increased prayerfulness, and I have taken this text as it furnishes me with one or two points of great interest and is full of practical suggestions. The first is this: *let us notice the importance which the early church attributed to prayer,* and to prayer meetings.

Let this be *a lesson* to us. As soon as we begin to read in the Acts, and continually as we read on in that record, we note that meetings for prayer had become *a standing institution in the church.* We read nothing of masses, but we read much of prayer meetings. We hear nothing of church festivals, but we read often of meeting together for prayer. It is said that Peter considered the thing: I fancy that he considered it all around, and thought, "Where shall I go?" and he recollected that it was prayer meeting night down at John Mark's mother's house, and there would he go, because he felt that there he should meet with true brethren.

In those days they did things by plan and order, according to that text, "Let all things be done decently and in order," and I have no doubt that it had been duly arranged that the meeting should be held that evening at the house of John Mark's mother, and therefore Peter went there, and found, as he probably expected, that there was a prayer meeting going on. They were not met to hear a sermon. It is most proper that we should very frequently assemble for that purpose, but this was distinctly a meeting where "many were gathered together praying." Praying was the business on hand. I do not know that they even had an address, though some will come to the prayer meeting if the pastor is present to speak; but you see James, who is generally thought to have been pastor of the church at Jerusalem, was not there, for Peter said, "Go show these things to James," and most probably none of the apostles were there, because Peter added, "and to the brethren," and I suppose by that he meant the brethren of the apostolic college. The eminent speaking brethren seem to have been all away, and perhaps no one expounded or exhorted that night, nor was there any need, for they were all too much engrossed in the common intercession. The meeting was convened for praying, and this, I say, was a regular institution of the Christian church, and ought always to be kept up.

There should be meetings wholly devoted to prayer, and there is a serious flaw in the arrangements of a church when such gatherings are omitted or placed in a secondary position. These prayer meetings should be kept to their object, and their great attraction should be prayer itself. An address if you like, a few burning words to stir up prayer if you like, but if you cannot have them, do not look upon speech making as at all necessary. Let it be a standing ordinance in the church that at certain times and occasions many shall meet together to pray, and supplication shall be their sole object. The private Christian will read and hear and meditate, but none of these can be a substitute for prayer. The same truth holds good upon the larger scale. The church should listen to her teachers, and receive edification from gospel ordinances, but she must also pray; nothing can compensate for the neglect of devotion.

It appears, however, that while prayer meetings were a regular institution, the *prayer was sometimes made special*, for we read that prayer was made without ceasing of the church unto God "for him," that is, for Peter. It adds greatly to the interest, and not a little to the fervency, of prayer when there is some great object to pray for. The brethren would have prayed if Peter had been out of prison, but seeing that he was in prison, and likely to be put to death, it was announced that the prayer meeting would be specially to pray for Peter, that the Lord would deliver his servant, or give him grace to die triumphantly; and this special subject gave enthusiasm to the assembly. Yes, they prayed fervently, for I find the margin of the fifth verse runs thus, "Instant and earnest prayer was made of the church for him." They prized the man, for they saw what wonders God had worked by his ministry, and they could not let him die if prayer would save him. When they thought of Peter, and how his bleeding head might be exhibited to the populace on the morrow, they prayed heart and soul, and each succeeding speaker threw more and more fervency into his pleading. The united cry went up to heaven, "Lord, spare Peter"; I think I can hear their sobs and cries even now. God grant that our churches may often turn their regular prayer meetings into gatherings with a special object, for then they will become more real. Why not pray for a certain missionary or some chosen district or class of persons or order of agencies? We should do well to turn the grand artillery of supplication against some special point of the enemy's walls.

It is clear that these friends *fully believed that there was power in prayer*; for, Peter being in prison, they did not meet together to arrange a plan for getting him out. Some wise brother might have suggested the bribing of the guards, and another might have suggested something else; but they had done with planning, and took themselves to praying. I do not find that they met to petition Herod. It would have been of no avail to ask that monster to relent: they might as well request a wolf to release a lamb which he has seized. No, the petitions were to Herod's Lord and Master, to the great invisible God. It looked as if they could do nothing, but they felt they could do everything by prayer. They thought little of the fact that sixteen soldiers had him in charge. What are sixteen guards? If there had been sixteen thousand soldiers, these believing men and women would still have prayed Peter out. They believed in

God, that he would do wonders; they believed in prayer, that it had an influence with God, and that the Lord did listen to the believing petitions of his servants. They met together for prayer in no dubious mood. They knew what they were at, and had no question as to the power which lay in supplication. Oh, let it never be insinuated in the Christian church that prayer is a good thing and a useful exercise to ourselves, but that it would be superstition to suppose that it affects the mind of God. Those who say this have foolishly thought to please us by allowing us their scientific toleration to go on with our devotions, but do they think we are idiots, that we would continue asking for what we knew we should not receive; that we would keep on praying if it would be of no more use than whistling to the winds? They must think us devoid of reason if they imagine that we shall be able to keep up prayer as a pious exercise if we once concede that it can have no result with God. As surely as any law of nature can be ascertained and proved, we know both by observation and experiment that God assuredly hears prayer; and, instead of its being a doubtful agency, we maintain prayer to be the most potent and unfailing force beneath the skies. We say in the proverb, "man proposes but God disposes," and here is the power of prayer, that it does not dally with the proposer but goes at once to the Disposer, and deals with the First Cause. Prayer moves that arm which moves all things else. O brethren, may we gather power in prayer by having faith in it. Let us not say, "What can prayer do?" but, "What cannot it do?" for all things are possible to him that believes. No wonder prayer meetings flag if faith in prayer be weak; and no wonder if conversions and revivals are scarce where intercession is neglected.

This prayer in the early church we remark, in the next place, was *industriously continued*. As soon as Herod had put Peter into prison, the church began to pray. Herod took care that the guards should be sufficient in number to keep good watch over his victim, but the saints of God set their watches too. As in times of war, when two armies lie near each other, they both set their sentries, so in this case Herod had his sentries of the night to keep the watch, and the church had its pickets too. Prayer was made of the church without ceasing; as soon as one little company were compelled to separate to go to their daily labor, they were relieved by another company, and when some were forced to take rest in sleep, others were ready to take up the blessed work of supplication. Thus both sides were on the alert, and the guards were changed both by day and by night. It was not hard to foresee which side would win the victory, for truly "except the LORD keep the city, the watchman waketh but in vain"; and when, instead of helping to keep the castle, God sends angels to open doors and gates, then we may be sure that the watchmen will wake in vain, or fall into a dead slumber. Continually, therefore, the people of God pleaded at his mercy seat; relays of petitioners appeared before the throne. Some mercies are not given to us except in answer to importunate prayer. There are blessings which, like ripe fruit, drop into your hand the moment you touch the bough; but there are others which require you to shake the tree again and again, until you make it rock with the vehemence of your exercise, for then only will the fruit fall down. My brethren, we must cultivate importunity in prayer. While the sun is shining and when the sun has gone down, still should prayer be kept up and fed with fresh fuel, so that it burns fiercely, and flames on high like a beacon fire blazing toward heaven.

I would fain pause here a minute and urge my dear brethren to attach as much importance to prayer as the early church did. You cannot think too much of it. Believing prayer, dictated of the Spirit, and presented through Jesus Christ, is today the power of the church, and we cannot do without it. Some look at her active agencies, and prize them, but they suppose that prayer might be dispensed with. You have seen the threshing machine going along the country road from farm to farm: in front there is a huge, black engine which toils along the road, and then behind you see the machine which actually does the threshing. A novice might say, "I will hire the threshing machine, but I do not want your engine; that is an expensive affair which consumes coal and makes smoke; I do not require it. I will have the machine which actually does the work, but I do not want the engine." Such a remark would be absurd, for of what use would the machine be to you if the motive power were gone? Prayer in the church is the steam engine which makes the wheels revolve, and really does the work, and therefore we cannot do without it.

Suppose a foreman were employed by some great builder, and sent out to manage works at a distance. He has to pay the men their wages weekly, and he is very diligent in doing so; he neglects none of his duty toward the men, but he forgets to communicate with headquarters. He neither writes to his employer, nor goes to the bank for cash to go on with. Is this wise? When the next pay night comes round, I am afraid he will find that, however diligent he may have been toward the men, he will be in a queer position, for he will have no silver or gold to hand out, because he has forgotten to apply to headquarters. Now, brethren, the minister does, as it were, distribute the portions to the people, but if he does not apply to his Master to get them, he will have nothing to distribute. Never sunder the connection between your soul and God. Keep up a constant communication with heaven, or your communications with earth will be of little worth. To cease from prayer is to stop the vital stream upon which all your energy is dependent; you may go on preaching and teaching, and giving away tracts, and what you like, but nothing can possibly come of it when the power of almighty God has ceased to be with you.

Thus much on our first point. May the Holy Spirit use it and arouse the churches to unanimous, intense, importunate intercession.

II. Next we notice *the number assembled*, which is a rebuke to some here present.

The text says, *"Many* were gathered together praying." Somebody said the other day of prayer meetings, that two or three thousand people had no more power in prayer than two or three. I think that is a grave mistake in many ways; but clearly so in reference to each other; for have you never noticed that when many meet together praying, warmth of desire and glow of earnestness are greatly increased. Perhaps two or three might have been all dull, but out of a larger number someone at least is a warmhearted brother, and sets all the rest on a flame. Have you not observed how the requests of one will lead another on to ask for yet greater things? How one Christian brother suggests to another to increase his petition, and so the petitions grow by the mingling of heart with heart, and the communion of spirit with spirit? Besides, faith is a cumulative force. "According to thy faith so be it done unto thee" is true to one, to two, to twenty, to twenty thousand; and twenty thousand times the force will be the result of twenty thousand times the faith. Rest assured that while two or three have power with God in their measure, two or three hundred have still more. If great results are to come, they will be accompanied by the prayers of many; no, the brightest days of all will never come except by the unanimous prayer of the entire church, for as soon as Zion travails—not one or two in her midst, but the whole church travails—then shall she bring forth her children.

Therefore I do earnestly pray, brethren, to make the numbers gathered in prayer as great as they can be. Of course, if we come together listlessly, if each heart be cold and dead, there is only so much more coldness and deadness; but taking for granted that each one comes in the spirit of prayer, the gathering of numbers is like adding firebrand to firebrand, and piling on the burning coals, and we are likely to have a heat like that of coals of juniper, which have a most vehement flame.

Now this is *not a very common occurrence*, and why is it that so many prayer meetings are so very thin? I know some places in London where they talk about giving up the prayer meeting, where instead of two services during the week they have compassion on their poor, overworked minister, and only wish him to hold forth for a few minutes at a sort of mongrel service, half prayer meeting and half lecture. Poor dear things, they cannot manage to get out to worship more than once in the week, they are so much occupied. This is not in poor churches, but in respectable churches. Gentlemen who do not get home from the city and have their dinner till seven o'clock cannot be expected to go out to a prayer meeting; who would have the barbarity to suggest such a thing? They work so extremely hard all the day, so much harder than any of the working men, that they say, "I pray thee have me excused." Churches in the suburbs, as a general rule, have miserable prayer meetings, because of the unfortunate circumstances of the members who happen to be burdened with so much riches that they cannot meet for prayer as poor people do. Some of you who have your delightful villas are very careful of your health and never venture out into the evening air at prayer meetings, though I rather suspect that your parties and soirees are still kept up. I say not this with particular reference to anybody, except it happens to refer to him, and if it does refer to him the reference is very special.

After all, dear friends, this is a personal matter. It is of no use my standing here or your sitting there and complaining that so few come to the prayer meeting: how are we to increase the number? I would suggest to you a way of increasing it, namely, by coming yourself. You may be aware, perhaps, that one and one make two, and that another one will make three, so that by accretions of ones we shall gradually get up to thousands. The largest numbers are made up of units; so that the practical point of all is, if choice blessings are to be gained by numbers coming together for prayer, the way for me to increase the number is to go there myself, and if I can induce a friend to go also, so much the better.

I have a very high opinion of the early church, but I am not sure that quite so many would have been gathered together that night if it had not been that Peter was in prison. They said to one another, "Peter is in prison, and in danger of his life, let us go to the prayer meeting and plead for him." Did you ever know a minister who was often laid aside by illness and always found his people pray better when he was ill? Did it never strike you that one reason for his being afflicted was God's desire to stir the hearts of his people to intercede for him? Their prayers are better than his preaching; and so his Lord says to him, "I can do without you; I will put you on the bed of pain and make the people pray." Now I have an opinion that the best way for these people really to do good to their pastor is to pray that they may be kept in a right condition, and may not need his sickness as a stimulus to prayer. If churches become slack in prayer, those whom they most value may be laid aside, or even taken away by death, and then they will cry to God in the bitterness of their souls. Could not we do without such flogging? Some horses want to be reminded now and then with a little touch of the whip; if they did not need the lash they would not get it; and so it may be with us, that we need church trials to keep us up to the mark in prayer, and if we need them we shall have them; but if we are alive and earnest in prayer, it may be that Peter will not get into prison, and some other trying things will not happen besides.

III. The third thing in my text is *the place of assembly.* That we will dwell upon this morning as *a suggestion.*

"The house of Mary, the mother of John, whose surname was Mark." This was a prayer meeting held in a private house, and I want to urge upon my brethren here to consecrate their houses by frequently using them for prayer meetings. This would have an advantage about it: it would avoid all savor of superstition. There still lingers among people the notion that buildings may be consecrated and rendered holy. Well, it is so babyish an idea, that I should have hoped the manliness of this generation, let alone anything else, would have given up the notion. How can it be that inside four brick walls there should be more holiness than outside, or that prayer offered in some particular seat should be more acceptable than prayer offered anywhere else. Behold, this day, God hears prayer wherever there is a true heart.

> Where'er we seek him, he is found,
> And every place is hallowed ground.

Meetings for prayer, held at the house of the mother of Mark, at *your* mother's house, at your brother's house, at your own house, will do much to be a plain protest against the superstition which reverences holy places. There was a meetness in their meeting in this particular house, the house of Mark's mother, for that family stood in a very dear relationship to Peter. Do you know who Mark was, in reference to Peter? If you turn to 1 Peter 5, you will read, "Marcus, my son." Ah, I am sure Mark would pray for Peter, because Peter was his spiritual father. I should not wonder but what Mark and his mother were both converted on the day of Pentecost, when Peter preached that famous sermon. Anyhow, Mark was converted under Peter, and so both he and his mother often invited Peter to their house, and when he was imprisoned they had the special prayer meetings at their house, because they loved him greatly. There is sure to be prayer for the pastor in the house where the pastor has been blessed to the family. He need not be afraid but what his own sons and daughters in the faith will be sure to pray for him.

These meetings had a good effect upon Mrs. Mark's house. She, herself, no doubt, had a blessing, but her son Mark obtained peculiar favor of the

Lord. Naturally he was not all we should like him to have been, for though his uncle Barnabas was very fond of him, Paul, who was a very good judge, could not put up with his instability. But he obtained so great a blessing from the Lord that he became, according to the unanimous tradition of the church, the writer of the gospel of Mark. He might have been a very weak and useless Christian if it had not been that the prayer meetings at his mother's house warmed his heart, and he might never have used his graphic pen for the Lord had not the conversation of the good people who came to his house instructed him as to the facts, which he afterward recorded in the precious gospel which bears his name.

The house received a blessing, and so will you, too, if your house shall be every now and then opened for special prayer. I urge upon the followers of Jesus Christ to use their own houses more frequently than they now do for holy purposes. How largely might the Sunday schools in London be extended if all the better instructed gathered together Bible classes in their own houses and taught them during the Sabbath day; and what a multitude of prayers would go up to heaven if Christians who have suitable rooms would frequently call together their brethren and neighbors to offer prayer. Many an hour is wasted in idle talk, many an evening frittered away in foolish amusements, degrading to Christians, when the time might be occupied in exercises calculated to bring down untold blessings upon the family and upon the church.

Prayer meetings at private houses are very useful, because friends who would be afraid to pray before a large assembly, and others who if they did so would be very much restricted in language, are able to feel free and easy in a smaller company in a private house. Sometimes, too, the social element is consecrated by God to promote a greater warmth and fervor, so that prayer will often burn in the family when perhaps it might have declined in the public assembly. I never knew the little church of which I was pastor before I came here to be in such a happy condition as when the members took it into their heads to hold prayer meetings in their own houses. I have sometimes myself attended six or seven in an evening, running from one to another just to look in upon them, finding twelve in a kitchen, ten or a dozen in a parlor, two or three met together in a little chamber. We saw a great work of grace then; the biggest sinners in the parish felt the power of the gospel, the old saints warmed up and began to believe in young people being converted, and we were all alive by reason of the abundance of prayer.

Brethren, we must have the like abundance of prayer; do pray that we may have it. We have been distinguished as a church for prayerfulness, and I am jealous with a godly jealousy lest we should go back in any degree, and I do affectionately suggest to you with much earnestness of heart that we should try to increase the number of the places where many shall be met together praying. I do not know where the mother of John Mark is this morning, but I hope she will start a prayer meeting in her large room. She is well to do, I believe, because her brother Barnabas had land, and sold it, and I suppose she had property also; we will use her drawing room. If a poorer friend has a smaller and poorer room, we shall be glad of the loan of it, for it will be more suitable for persons of another class to go to. Perhaps they would not like to go to Mrs. Mark's drawing room, but they will come to your kitchen. All sorts will have an opportunity of praying when all sorts of chambers are dedicated to prayer.

IV. I have a little to say about *the time of this prayer meeting*.

It was held at dead of night. I suppose they prayed all through the night. They could say, "We have been waiting, we have been waiting, all the night long." After midnight the angel set Peter free. Peter went to the house, and they were not gone to bed, but many were met together praying. Now, as to the time for prayer meetings, let me say this. If it happens to be an inconvenient hour, and I should think the dead of night was rather inconvenient, nevertheless go. Better hold prayer meetings at twelve o'clock at night than not at all; better that we should be accused, as the Christians were of old, of holding secret conventicles under the shadow of night, than not meet together for prayer.

But there is another lesson. The dead of the night was chosen because it was the most suitable hour, since they could not safely meet in the day because of the Jews. It becomes those who appoint the times for prayer meetings to select as good an hour as they can, a quiet hour, a leisure hour, an hour suited to the habits of the people. Still let us remember that whatever hour is appointed, if we come together with true hearts, it will be an acceptable hour. Better still, it would be well if there could be meetings for prayer at all hours. Then every hour would be an acceptable hour, and if one happened to be unseasonable, another would be convenient, and all classes of believers could thus meet together at some time or other to pour out their hearts in prayer to God. O brethren, if your business will not let you meet in the middle of the day, meet in the middle of the night; if you cannot come together for prayer at the times that are generally appointed, then have prayer meetings at such times as will suit yourselves; but do let there be a unanimous resolve throughout the whole church of Christ, that much prayer shall be presented to the most High.

V. Notice, in the last place, the *success of the prayer meetings as an encouragement to us.*

They prayed, and they were heard at once. The answer came so speedily that they were themselves surprised. It has sometimes been said that they did not expect Peter to be set free, and that their astonishment was the result of unbelief. Perhaps so; but I doubt it, for you must remember that their prayer did set Peter free, and therefore it does not look as if it could have been unbelieving prayer. I trace their surprise to another cause. I think they expected that God would somehow or other deliver Peter, but they did not think he would deliver him in the dead of the night. They very likely had appointed in their own minds that something would happen next day, and so their surprise arose, not from the fact that Peter was free, so much as from his being out of the dungeon at that particular time, and in that particular manner, for I cannot judge that to have been an unbelieving prayer which really did win the day with the God of heaven.

Dear friends, the Lord Jesus waits to give us great boons in answer to prayer. He can send us surprises quite as great as those which astonished the assembly at midnight. We may pray for some sinner, and while we are yet praying we may hear him cry, "What must I do to be saved?" We may offer our prayers for the sleeping church, and while we pray it may be answered. True, the church sleeps still; she has had a smiting on the side of late, but has not yet girded herself and come out of the prison house of her coldness and conventionality; but if we continue in prayer we may see with astonishment the church rouse herself from sleep and come forth to liberty. We cannot tell what will happen, prayer operates in so many ways, but operate it will, and we shall assuredly have our reward.

I selected this topic just now for this reason. The American evangelists who have been so useful in this great city have gone from us, and the great assemblies which they gathered are no more. There must have been many converted: I cannot but believe that many thousands have the Lord Jesus Christ, and I have no sympathy whatever with the remarks of those who alarm that our friends have not touched the lowest class of society. I believe they have touched every class of society. At any rate their business was to preach the gospel to every creature, and they have done so with great impartiality and earnestness. If the poorest did not go, it was not because they were not welcome. But they did go; I am an eyewitness to it. I know that many who went nowhere before did attend the Bow and Camberwell Halls, and the fact that the congregation looked respectable by no means proves that they were not of the working classes; for what workingman is there among us but tries to dress as neatly as he can when he goes to a place of worship? There are plenty of friends here who work hard for their daily bread, but looking around they all seem by their dress to be well-to-do. No one has a right to judge that because a man does not come to worship in rags he cannot therefore belong to the lower portion of the working class, for it is not the habit of the working-men of London to go to places of worship in their everyday clothes or in rags. I saw with my own eyes that multitudes assembled there were of that class which did not habitually hear the gospel. I am sure that good was done, and I do not care who cavils. The practical point is—What is to be done now? We must keep up this work. And how? Not by those large assemblies, but by all the churches being revived all round, and the numbers in all the places of worship becoming more numerous, and at the same time becoming more prayerful.

Let us pray *now.* We want prayer to train the converts, to keep God's people warm now they are warm, and to make them yet more so. What wonders we have obtained in the tabernacle in answer to prayer. We began this work with a little handful of Christian men. I remember the first Monday night after I came to London; there was a slender audience on the Sabbath, but thank God there was almost as many at the prayer meeting as on the Sunday; and I thought, "This is all right; these people can pray." They did pray, and as we increased in prayer we increased in numbers. Sometimes, at prayer meetings, my heart was almost ready to break for joy because of the mighty supplication that was offered. We wanted to build this great house: we were poor enough, but we prayed for it, and prayer built it. Praying gave us everything we have. Praying brings us all manner of supplies, spiritual and temporal. Whatever I am in the church of God, this day I owe, under God's blessing, to your prayers. As long as your prayers sustain me, I shall not flag nor fail, but if your prayers be gone, then my power is gone, for the Spirit of God is gone, and what can I do? All through the church of God the true progress is in proportion to the prayer. I do not care about the talent of the speaker; I am glad if he has talent. I do not care about the wealth of the congregation, though I am glad if they have wealth. But I do care beyond everything for the deep, real, earnest prayer, the darting up of the souls of Christians to God, and the bringing down of the blessing upon men from God. And if this were the last word I had to address to this congregation, I would say to you, dear brethren, abound in prayer, multiply the petitions that you put up, and increase the fervor with which you present them to God.

When my venerable predecessor, Dr. Rippon, was growing old, this was one of the things everybody noticed about him, that he always prayed earnestly for his successors. He did not know who they might be, but his prayer was that God would bless the church and his successors in years to come, and I have heard old Christians say that our present prosperity might be traced to Dr. Rippon's prayers. Oh, let us pray. I believe we have had a revival very much in answer to the multitudinous fervent prayers that were put up here and elsewhere; and now that God is beginning to bless the church in answer to prayer, if she stays her hand she will be like that king of old, who had the arrows and the bow put into his hands, and shot once or twice, whereas, if he had shot many times, God would have destroyed Syria before him, and established his people. Take down your quivers full of desires, and grasp the mighty bow of faith. Now shoot again and again the arrow of the Lord's deliverance, and God will give us multitudes of converts all over London, and throughout the world. "'Prove me now herewith,' saith the LORD of hosts, 'and see if I do not open the windows of heaven and pour you out a blessing that ye shall not have room enough to receive it.'" God bless you, for Christ's sake.

Lydia: The First European Convert

◆◆◆

Intended for reading on Lord's Day, September 20, 1891; delivered at the Metropolitan Tabernacle, Newington. No. 2222.

And a certain woman named Lydia, a seller of purple, of the city of Thyatira, which worshiped God, heard us: whose heart the Lord opened, that she attended unto the things which were spoken of Paul.—ACTS 16:14

We may laudably exercise curiosity with regard to the first proclamation of the gospel in our own quarter of the globe. We are happy that history so accurately tells us, by the pen of Luke, when first the gospel was preached in Europe, and by whom, and who was the first convert brought by that preaching to the Savior's feet. I half envy Lydia that she should be the leader of the European band; yet I feel right glad that a woman led the vanguard, and that her household followed so closely in the rear.

God has made great use of women, and greatly honored them in the kingdom of our Lord and Savior Jesus Christ. Holy women ministered to our Lord when he was upon the earth, and since that time much sacred work has been done by their patient hands. Man and woman fell together; together they must rise. After the resurrection, it was a woman who was first commissioned to carry the glad tidings of the risen Christ; and in Europe, where woman was in future days to be set free from many of the trammels of the East, it seems fitting that a woman should be the first believer. Not only, however, was Lydia a sort of firstfruit for Europe, but she probably also became a witness in her own city of Thyatira, in Asia. We do not know how the gospel was introduced into that city; but we are informed of the existence of a church there by the message of the ascended Christ, through his servant John, to "the angel of the church in Thyatira." Very likely Lydia became the herald of the gospel in her native place. Let the women who know the truth proclaim it; for why should their influence be lost? "The Lord giveth the word; the women that publish the tidings are a great host." Woman can be as powerful for evil as for good: we see it in this very church of Thyatira, where the woman Jezebel, who called herself a prophetess, sought to seduce many from the truth. Seeing, then, that the devil employs women in his service, let those women whom God has called by his grace be doubly earnest in seeking to prevent or undo the mischief that others of their sex are working. If not called to public service, all have the home sphere wherein they can shed forth the aroma of a godly life and testimony.

If the gospel does not influence our homes, it is little likely to make headway among the community. God has made family piety to be, as it were, a sort of trademark on religion in Europe; for the very first convert brings with her all her family. Her household believed, and were baptized with her. You shall notice in Europe, though I do not mean to say that it is not the same anywhere else, that true godliness has always flourished in proportion as family religion has been observed. They hang a bell in a steeple, and they tell us that it is our duty to go every morning and every evening into the steeple house there to join in prayer; but we reply that our own house is better for many reasons; at any rate, it will not engender superstition for us to pray there. Gather your children together, and offer prayer and supplication to God in your own room.

"But there is no priest." Then there ought to be. Every man should be a priest in his own household; and, in the absence of a godly father, the mother should lead the devotions. Every house should be the house of God, and there should be a church in every house; and when this is the case, it will be the greatest barrier against priestcraft and the idolatry of holy places. Family prayer and the pulpit are the bulwarks of Protestantism. Depend upon it, when family piety goes down, the life of godliness will become very low. In Europe, at any rate, seeing that the Christian faith began with a converted household, we ought to seek after the conversion of all our families, and to maintain within our houses the good and holy practice of family worship.

Lydia, then, is the first European convert, and we will review her history so far as we have it in Holy Writ. Toward her conversion four things cooperated, upon which we will speak briefly. First, *the working of Providence*; second, *the working of Lydia herself*; third, *the working of Paul*; and fourth, *the working of the Holy Spirit*.

I. First, notice *the working of Providence.*

When I was in Amsterdam, I visited the works of a diamond cutter, where I saw many large wheels and much powerful machinery at work; and I must confess that it seemed very odd that all that great array of apparatus should be brought to bear upon a tiny bit of crystal, which looked like a fragment of glass. Was that diamond worth so much that a whole factory should be set to work to cut its facets, and cause it to sparkle? So the diamond cutter believed. Within that small space lay a gem which was thought worthy of all this care and labor. That diamond may be at this time glistening upon the finger or brow of royalty! Now when I look abroad upon Providence, it seems preposterous to believe that kingdoms, dynasties, and great events should all be cooperating and working together for the accomplishment of the divine purpose in the salvation of God's people. But they are so working. It might have seemed preposterous, but it was not so, that these great wheels should all be working for the cutting of a single diamond; and it is not preposterous, however it may seem so, to say that all the events of providence are being ordered by God to effect the salvation of his own people, the perfecting of the precious jewels which are to adorn the crown of Christ forever and ever.

In the case before us, the working of God's providence is seen, first of all, in bringing Paul to Philippi. Lydia is there. I do not know how long she had been there, nor exactly what brought her there; but there she is, selling her purple, her Turkey-red cloth. Paul must come there, too, but he does not want to come; he has not, indeed, had any desire to come there. He has a kind of prejudice hanging about him still, so that, though he is willing to preach to the gentiles, he scarcely likes to go out of Asia among those gentiles or the gentiles over in Europe. He wants to preach the word in Asia. Very singularly, the Spirit suffers him not, and he seems to have a cold hand laid on him to stop him when his heart is warmest. He is gagged; he cannot speak. "Then I will go into Bithynia," he says; but when he starts on the journey, he is distinctly told that there is no work for him to do there. He must not speak for his Master in that region, at least not yet: "the Spirit suffered him not." He feels himself to be a silenced man. What is he to do? He gets down to Troas on the verge of the sea, and there comes to him the vision of a man of Macedonia, who prayed him, saying, "Come over into Macedonia, and help us." He infers that he must go across to Macedonia. A ship is ready for him; he has a free course, a favorable passage, and he soon arrives at Philippi. God brings Paul to the spot where Lydia was, in this strange and singular manner.

But the working of Providence was quite as much manifested in bringing Lydia there; for Lydia was not originally at Philippi. She was a seller of purple, of Thyatira. Thyatira was a city famous for its dyers. They made a peculiar purple, which was much prized by the Romans. Lydia appears to have carried on this business. She was either a widow, or perhaps had had no husband, though she may have gathered a household of servants about her. She comes over to Philippi across the sea. I think I see them bringing the great rolls of red cloth up the hill, that she may sell at Philippi the cloth which she has made and dyed at Thyatira. Why does she come just at this season? Why does she come just when Paul is coming? Why does she come to Philippi? Why not to Neapolis? Why not press on to Athens? Why not sell her cloth over at Corinth? Whatever reason she might have given for her choice, there was one cause, of which she was ignorant, which shaped her action, and brought her to Philippi at that time. God had a surprise in store for her. She and Paul have to meet. It does not matter what their will is; their wills shall be so moved and actuated by the providence of God that they shall cross each other's path, and Paul shall preach the gospel to Lydia. I think it never entered into Lydia's heart, when she left Thyatira with her purple bales, that she was going to find Jesus Christ over at Philippi; neither did Paul guess, when he saw, in a vision, a man of Macedonia, and heard him say, "Come over into Macedonia, and help us," that the first person he would have to help would not be a man of Macedonia at all, but a woman of Thyatira, and that the congregation he should preach to would be just a handful of women gathered by the side of the little stream that runs through Philippi. Neither Paul nor Lydia knew what God was about to do; but God knew. He understands the end from the beginning, and times his acts of providence to meet our deepest needs in the wisest way.

> His wisdom is sublime,
> His heart profoundly kind;
> God never is before his time,
> And never is behind.

What an odd thing it seemed that this woman should be a woman of Thyatira in Asia, and Paul must not go and preach in Asia; and yet, when he comes to Macedonia, the first person who hears him is a woman of Asia! Why, you and I would have said, "If the woman belongs to Thyatira, let her stop at home, and let Paul go there; that is the shortest cut." Not so. The woman of Thyatira must go to Philippi, and Paul must go to Philippi too. This is God's plan; and if we knew all the circumstances as God knows them, we should doubtless admire the wisdom of it. Perhaps the very peculiarity of the circumstances made Paul more alert to seize the opportunity at Philippi than he would have been had he gone on to Thyatira; perhaps the isolation of the strange city made Lydia yearn more after spiritual things. God can answer a dozen ends by one act.

One of our evangelists tells of a man who was converted in a small Irish town, and it was afterward discovered that he, and the preacher who led him to Christ, resided but a few hundred yards from each other in London. They had never met in this great city, where neighbors are strangers to each other; nor was it likely that they ever would have been brought into contact with one another here; for the man, who was a commercial traveler, was too careless ever to attend a place of worship in London. But to sell his goods he went to Ireland, where, also, went the evangelist to preach the gospel; and being somewhat at a loss to know what to do with his time, he no sooner saw the name of a preacher from London announced, than he determined to attend the service, and there he met with Christ. We can see how natural this was in the case of which we know all the particulars, and it was doubtless as well arranged in the case of Lydia and Paul.

Now I should not wonder tonight if there are a number of providences that have worked together to bring some of my hearers into their places at this time. What brought *you* to London, friend? It was not your intention to be in this city. Coming to London, what brought you to this part of it? What led you to be at this service? And why was it that you did not come on one of the Sundays when the preacher would have been here if he could, but could not be here by reason of his weakness? Because, it may be, that only from these lips can the word come to you, and only tonight, and you must come to this place. Perhaps there is someone who preaches the gospel much better in the town where you live; or, peradventure, you have had opportunities of hearing the same preachers near your own door, and you did not avail yourself of them; and yet God has brought you here. I wish we watched providences more. "Whoso is wise, and will observe these things, even they shall understand the lovingkindness of the LORD." If the Lord should meet with you, and convert you tonight, I will warrant you that you will be a believer in Providence, and say, "Yes, God guided my steps. He directed my path, and he brought me to the spot where Jesus met with me, and opened my heart that I might receive the gospel of his grace." Be of good courage, you ministers of the gospel! Providence is always working with you while you are working for God. I have often admired the language of Mahomet, when in the battle of Ohod he said to his followers, pointing to their foes, "Charge them! I can hear the wings of the angels as they hasten to our help." That was a delusion on his part, for he and his men were badly beaten; but it is no delusion in the case of the servants of Christ. We *can* hear the wings of the angels. We may hear the grinding of the great wheels of Providence as they revolve for the help of the preacher of the gospel. Everything is with us when we are with God. Who can be against us? The stars in their courses fight for the servants of God; and all things, great and small, shall bow before the feet of him who trod the waves of the Sea of Galilee, and still is Master of all things, and rules all things to the accomplishment of his divine purposes.

So much, then, for the working of Providence.

II. The next thing is, *the working of Lydia.*

God's intention is that Lydia shall be saved. Yet, you know, no woman was ever saved against her will. God makes us willing in the day of his power, and it is the way of his grace not to violate the will, but sweetly to overcome it. Never will there be anybody dragged to heaven by the ears: depend upon that. We shall go there with all our hearts and all our desires. What, then, was Lydia doing?

Having by God's grace been made willing, the first thing was that *she kept the Sabbath.* She was a proselyte, and she kept the seventh day. She was away from Thyatira, and nobody would know what she would do, yet she observed the Lord's Day carefully. She was abroad when she was at Philippi, but she had not left God behind her. I have known some English people, when they once reached the Continent, go rattling along, Sundays and weekdays, as if God did not live on the Continent, and as if at home they only observed the Sabbath because they happened to be in England, which is very probably the case with a good many. When they get away, they say, "When you are at Rome, you must do as Rome does"; and so they take their pleasure on God's day. It was not so with Lydia. There was no selling of purple that day; she regarded the Sabbath. Oh, I would to God that everyone would regard the Sabbath! May God grant that it may never be taken away from us! There is a plot now to make some of you work all the seven days of the week, and you will not get any more pay for seven days than you get for six. Stand out against it, and preserve your right to rest upon God's day. The observance of one day in seven as a day of rest materially helps toward the conversion of men, because then they are inclined to think. They have the opportunity to hear, and, if they choose to avail themselves of it, the probabilities are that God will bless the hearing, and they will be saved.

Now notice next that, not only did Lydia observe the Sabbath, but *she went up to the place of worship.* It was not a very fine place. I do not suppose there was any building. It may have been a little temporary oratory put up by the riverside; but very probably it was just on the bank of the river that they met together. It does not appear that there were any men, but only a few women. They only held a prayer meeting: "where prayer was wont to be made." But Lydia did not step away from the gathering. She might easily have excused herself after her long journey, and the wearying work of setting up a new establishment; but her heart was in this matter, and so she found it no drudgery to meet where prayer was offered. She did not say, "I can read a sermon at home," or, "I can read in the Book of the Law indoors." She wished to be where God's people were, however few, or however poor they might be. She did not go to the gorgeous heathen temple at Philippi, but she sought out the few faithful ones that met to worship the true God.

Now, dear friends, do the same. You that are not converted, still attend the means of grace, and do not go to a place simply because it is a fine building, and because there is a crowd, but go where they are truly worshiping God in spirit and in truth. If they should happen to be very few and very poor, yet go with them, for in so doing you are in the way of blessing. I think you will yet have to say, "Being in the way, God met with me." If it is what some call "only a prayer meeting," you will do well to go. Some of the best blessings that men have ever gained have been received at prayer meetings. If we would meet with God, let us seek him diligently, "not forsaking the assembling of ourselves together, as the manner of some is." Though you cannot save yourself or open your own heart, you can at least do what Lydia did: observe the Sabbath, and gather together with God's people.

Lydia, being there with the assembly, when Paul began to speak, we find that *she attended to the things that were spoken*, which is another thing that we can do. It is very ill when people come up to the house of God, and do not attend. I have never had to complain of people not attending in this house since the day I first preached in it; but I have been in places of worship where there seemed to be anything but attention. How can it be expected that there will be a blessing when the pew becomes a place to slumber in, or when the mind is active over the farm or in the kitchen or in the shop, forgetting altogether the gospel which is being preached to the outward ear? If you want a blessing, attend with all your might to the word that is preached; but of that we will speak more by and by.

So far we have spoken upon the working of Providence and the working of Lydia.

III. Now, next, *the working of Paul*; for this was necessary too.

In order to the conversion of men, it is necessary that the person who aims at their conversion should work as if it all depended upon him, though he knows that he cannot accomplish the work. We are to seek to win souls with as much earnestness and prudence and zeal, as if everything depended upon ourselves; and then we are to leave all with God, knowing that none but the Lord can save a single soul.

Now notice, Paul, wishing for converts, is *judicious in the choice of the place* where he will go to look after them. He goes to the spot where there should be a synagogue. He thinks that where people have a desire to pray, there he will find the kind of people who will be ready to hear the word. So he selects devout people, devout worshipers of the one God, that he may go and speak to them about Christ. It is sometimes our plain duty to publish the word from the housetop to the careless crowd; but I think you will generally find that more success comes when those, on whose hearts the Spirit of God has already begun to work, are sought out and instructed. When Christ sent out his disciples on their first journey, he told them, when they entered a town, to "inquire who in it is worthy; and there abide till ye go thence"; evidently showing that, even among those who do not know the truth, there are some whose hearts are prepared to receive it, who are of a devout spirit, and in that sense are worthy. These are the people who should first be sought after. In the same limited sense was Cornelius, to whom Peter was sent, worthy to hear the glad tidings of great joy. His reverent spirit was well pleasing to God; for we read, "Thy prayer is heard, and thine alms are had in remembrance in the sight of God." We must not, of course, think that these things give any claim to salvation; but rather that they are the expression of hearts prepared to receive the message of salvation, seeking the Lord, "if haply they might feel after him, and find him."

One of our greatest difficulties in these days is that so many have lost all reverence for authority of any kind, even God's: having risen against human despotism, they also foolishly try to break God's bands asunder. We are cast back on the infinite power of God when we come to deal with such people; but when we meet with others who are willing to listen and pray, we know that God has already begun to work. Now, dear worker, choose the person who is evidently pointed out to you by God's gracious providence. Choose judiciously, and try to speak with those with whom you may hopefully speak, and trust that God will bless the word.

When Paul goes down to the river, you notice that he is very *judicious as to his manner* of introducing his subject. He did not preach at all. He found only a few women; and to stand up and preach to them, as he did to the crowds at Corinth, or at Athens, might have seemed absurd; but we read this: "We sat down, and spake unto the women which resorted thither." He took his seat on the river's bank, where they were all sitting still, and at prayer, and he began just to have a talk. A sermon would have been out of place; but a talk was the right sort of thing. So he talked the gospel into them. Now be careful of the way in which you go to work with people; for much of the result must depend upon that. Some people can be preached right away from Christ; for the moment you begin to preach they say, "Oh, thank you, I do not want any of your sermon!" Perhaps you could slip a word in edgewise; just drop a seed in a crack; or leave a word with them, just one word. Say at once, "If you do not want any preaching, I do not want to preach to you: I am not so fond of preaching as all that; but I read a very curious story in the newspapers the other day!" And then tell the story, and wrap the gospel up in it. If they do not want pills, do not give them pills. Give them a bit of sugar. They will take the sugar, and when they get it, there will be a pill inside. I mention this, because we may miss opportunities of doing good through not being wide awake. "Be ye wise as serpents, and harmless as doves." Paul therefore just sits down, and has a friendly talk with the women who resorted thither.

But whether Paul preached, or whether Paul talked, it was all the same: he was *judicious as to the matter* of his discourse. He had but one subject, and that was Christ; the Christ who had met him on the way to Damascus, and changed his heart; the Christ who was able still to save; the Christ who bled upon the cross, to bring men to God, and cleanse them in his blood; the Christ in heaven, interceding for sinners; the Christ waiting to be gracious. Paul would not end his talk without saying, "Trust him: trust him. He that believeth in him hath everlasting life." So whether he preached or whether he talked, it was the same story of Jesus Christ, and him crucified. That is how Paul worked. He might have acted very differently. If his heart had not been all aflame for Jesus, he would very likely not have spoken at all, or if he had, it would have been a commonplace remark about the weather. He might have been eager to learn the method by which the beautiful purple dye was obtained, and not have remembered that gospel message, written by Isaiah long ago, which would come with special force to the hearts of his hearers: "Though your sins be as scarlet, they shall be as white as snow; though they be red like crimson, they shall be as wool." He might have been so interested in his inquiries about Thyatira as to forget to speak of the way to the city of light. A dozen subjects might have claimed attention, if his heart had not been set upon one object. He could have spoken of his journeys, and even of his plans, without actually preaching Christ to her.

He might have spoken about the gospel, as I fear we often do, and not have spoken the gospel itself. Some sermons which I have heard, though faultlessly orthodox, have contained nothing that could convert anybody; for there has been nothing to touch the conscience or heart. Others, though very clever and profound, have had no possible bearing on the needs of the hearers; and so it was little wonder that they were without result.

But I am sure Paul's talk would aim straight at the center of the target: it was evidently addressed to the heart, for we are told that it was with the heart Lydia heard it. After all, it is not our most orderly discourses, nor our aptest illustrations, which bring people to Christ; but some little sentence which is slipped in unawares, or some burning word which comes straight out of our own heart's experience. There would be sure to be many such that day in that earnest simple talk by the riverside. Let us multiply such conversations, if we would win more Lydias for the church.

IV. But, now, fourth—and here is the main point—let us notice *the working of the Spirit of God*.

Providence brings Paul and Lydia together. Lydia comes there because she observes the Sabbath, and loves the place of worship. Paul comes there because he loves to win souls, and, like his Master, is on the watch for stray sheep. But it would have been a poor meeting for them if the Spirit of God had not been there also. So we next read of Lydia, "whose heart the Lord opened, that she attended unto the things which were spoken of Paul." It is not a wonder that the Lord can open a human heart; for he who made the lock knows well what key will fit it. What means he made use of in the case of Lydia, I do not know; but I will tell you what might have happened. Perhaps she had lost her husband; many a woman's heart has been opened by that great gash. The joy of her soul has been taken away, and she has turned to God. Perhaps her husband was spared to her; but she had lost a child. Oh, how many a babe has been sent here on purpose to entice its mother to the skies; a lamb taken away that the sheep might follow the Shepherd! Perhaps she had had bad trade; the price of purple may have fallen. She may have been half afraid she would fail in business. I have known such trouble to open some people's hearts. Perhaps she had had prosperity; possibly the purple had gone up in price. I have known some so impressed with God's temporal blessings that they have been ready to think of him, and to turn to him. I do not know; I cannot guess, and I have no right to guess what it was. But I know that God has very wonderful plows, with which he breaks up the hard soil of human hearts. When I have been through the Britannia Iron Works, at Bedford, I have wondered at the strange clod crushers, clod breakers, and plows, made there by the Messrs. Howard; and God has some marvelous machines in his providence for turning up the soil of our hearts. I cannot tell what he has done to you, dear friend, but I do trust that whatever has happened has been opening the soil, so that the good seed may drop in. It was the Spirit of God who did it, whatever the instrument may have been, and Lydia's heart was "opened."

Opened to what? To attend. "She attended unto the things which were spoken of Paul."

So, first, her heart was opened *to listen very intently*. She wanted to catch every word. She did as some of you do, put her hand to her ear, for fear she should not hear all that was spoken. There are many ways of listening. Some people listen with both their ears, allowing it to go in at one ear and out at the other; like that wit who, when he was being seriously spoken to, and yet seemed very inattentive, at length wearied the friend who was discoursing. "I am afraid it is not doing you much good," he said. "No," came the reply, "but I think it will do this gentleman some good," pointing to one who sat beside him, "for as it has gone in at this side it has gone out at the other." Oh, how I wish that you had only one ear, so that the truth you hear could never get out again after it had once got in! Well did the Lord speak through Isaiah the prophet unto the people, "Hearken *diligently* unto me, and eat ye that which is good." Many people can listen for an hour or two to a scientific lecture, or a political speech, without feeling in the least weary; they can even go to the theater, and sit there a whole evening without dreaming of being tired; yet they complain if the sermon is a minute beyond the appointed time. They seem to endure the preaching as a sort of penance, scarcely hearing the words, or, at least, never imagining that the message can have any application to their own case.

Lydia's heart was so opened "that she attended"; that is, she listened to the word of salvation until she began *to desire it*. It is always a pleasure to entertain guests who relish the food placed before them; and it is a great joy to preach to those who are eagerly hungering after the truth. But how heartbreaking a task it is to keep continually praising the pearl of great price to those who know not its value, nor desire its beauty! Daniel was a man "greatly beloved"; the Hebrew word there employed means "a man of desires." He was not one of your conceited, self-satisfied individuals. He longed and yearned for better things than he had yet attained, and hence was "greatly beloved." God loves people to thirst after him, and to desire to know his love and power. Let us explain the gospel as we may, if there is no desire in the heart, our plainest messages are lost. A man said, about something he wished to make clear, "Why, it is as plain as A B C!" "Yes," said a third party, "but the man you are talking to is D E F." So, some of our hearers seem to turn away from the Word of God. But when a person says, "I want to find salvation; I want to get Christ this very day; and I am going to listen with the determination that I will find out the way of salvation"; surely, if the things spoken are the same things that Paul spoke of, few in that condition will go out of the house without finding salvation. Lydia's heart was opened to attend to the gospel, that is, to desire it.

But, next, her heart was opened to understand it. It is wonderful how little even well-educated people sometimes understand of the gospel when it is preached in the simplest manner. One is constantly being astounded by the misapprehensions that persons have as to the way of salvation. But Lydia had grasped the truth. "Thanks be to God," she said, "I see it. Jesus Christ suffered in our stead; and we, by an act of faith, accept him as our Substitute, and we are saved thereby. I have it. I never saw it before. I read about a paschal lamb, and the sprinkling of the blood, and the passing over of the houses where the blood was sprinkled. I could not quite make it out. Now I see, if the blood be sprinkled upon me, God will pass over me, according to his word, 'When I see the blood, I will pass over you.' " She attended unto the things which were spoken of Paul, so as to understand them.

But more than that; her heart was so opened that she attended to the gospel so as to accept it. "Ah!" she said, "now I understand it, I will have it. Christ for me! Christ for me! That blessed Substitute for sinners! Is that all I have to do, simply to trust him? Then I will trust him. Sink or swim, I will cast myself upon him now." She did so there and then. There was no hesitating. She believed what Paul said; that Jesus was the Son of God, the appointed propitiation for sin, and that whosoever believed on him should then and there be justified; and she did believe in him, and she was justified; as you will be, my friend, if you will believe in him at this moment. You, too, shall have immediate salvation, my dear sister sitting yonder, if you will come, like this Lydia of old, and just take Christ to be yours, and trust him now. She attended unto the things which were spoken of Paul, so that she accepted Christ.

Having done that, she went further: her heart was so won, that she was, by the Spirit, led to obey the word, and avow her faith. Paul told her that the gospel was this—"He that believeth and is baptized shall be saved." He said to her, "My commission is, 'Go ye into all the world, and preach the gospel to every creature. He that believeth and is baptized shall be saved.'" Perhaps she said, "But why must I be baptized?" He said, "As a testimony of your obedience to Christ, whom you take to be your Master and your Lord; and as a type of your being one with him in his burial. You are to be buried in water as he was buried in the tomb of Joseph; and you are to be raised up out of the water even as he rose again from the dead. This act is to be a token and type to you of your oneness with him in his death and burial and resurrection." What did Lydia say? Did she say, "Well, I think I must wait a little while: the water is cold"? Did she say, "I think I must ask about it; I must consider it"? No, not at all. Paul tells her that this is Christ's ordinance, and she at once replies, "Here am I, Paul, let me be baptized, and my servants, too, and all that belong to my household, for they also believe in Jesus Christ. Let us have the baptism at once." There and then "she was baptized, and her household." She did at once obey the heavenly message, and she became a baptized believer. She was not ashamed to confess Christ. She had not known him long; but what she did know of him was so blessed and joyous to her soul, that she would have said, if she had known the hymn—

> Through floods and flames, if Jesus lead,
> I'll follow where he goes;
> "Hinder me not," shall be my cry,
> Though earth and hell oppose.

You can imagine her saying, "Did he go down into the Jordan, and say, 'Thus it becometh us to fulfill all righteousness'? Then I will go where he leads the way, and be obedient to him, and say to all the world, 'I, too, am a follower of the crucified Christ.'"

Now, last, after Lydia was baptized, *she became an enthusiastic Christian.* She said to Paul, "You must come home with me. I know you have not anywhere to go. Come along; and there is your friend Silas. I have plenty of room for him; and Timothy too; and Luke also. We can make room for the four of you among the purple bales, or somewhere; but, at any rate, I have house room for you four, and I have heart room for forty thousand of you. I wish I could take in the whole church of God." Dear good woman that she was, she felt that she could not do too much for the men who had been made a blessing to her; for she regarded what she did to them as done to their Lord and Master. They might have said, "No, really, we cannot trouble you. You have the household. You have all this business to look after." "Yes," she would answer, "I know that. It is very kind of you to excuse yourselves; but you must come." "No," Paul might urge, "my dear good woman, I am going to find out some tent makers, and make tents with them. We will find a lodging where we have been." "Ah!" she would say, "but I mean to have you. You must come to my home." "She constrained us." She would probably put it thus: "Now, I shall not think that you fully believe in me if you do not come home with me. Come, you baptized me, and by that very act you professed that you considered that I was a true believer. If you do really believe it, come and stay in my house as long as you like, and I will make you as comfortable as ever I can."

So at last Paul yields to her constraint, and goes to her home. How glad they would all be, and what praise to Christ would rise from that household! I hope that the generous spirit, which glowed in the heart of the first convert in Europe, will always continue among the converts of Europe till the last day. I trust that when they are called not merely to entertain God's ministers, but to help all God's people of every sort, they may be ready and willing to do it for Christ's sake; for love shall fill them with a holy hospitality, and an earnest desire to bless the children of God. Love one another, brothers and sisters, and do good to one another, as you have opportunity; for so will you be worthy followers of Lydia, the first European convert, whose heart the Lord opened.

The Lord open your hearts, for his name's sake! Amen.

The Women in Rome: Romans, but Not Romanists

Delivered at the Metropolitan Tabernacle, Newington. No. 1113.

I commend unto you Phebe our sister, which is a servant of the church which is at Cenchrea: that ye receive her in the Lord, as becometh saints, and that ye assist her in whatsoever business she hath need of you: for she hath been a succorer of many, and of myself also.

Greet Priscilla and Aquila my helpers in Christ Jesus: who have for my life laid down their own necks: unto whom not only I give thanks, but also all the churches of the gentiles. Likewise greet the church that is in their house. Salute my well-beloved Epaenetus, who is the firstfruits of Achaia unto Christ.

Greet Mary, who bestowed much labor on us. Salute Andronicus and Junia, my kinsmen, and my fellow prisoners, who are of note among the apostles, who also were in Christ before me. Greet Amplias my beloved in the Lord. Salute Urbane, our helper in Christ, and Stachys my beloved. Salute Apelles approved in Christ. Salute them which are of Aristobulus' household. Salute Herodion my kinsman.

Greet them that be of the household of Narcissus, which are in the Lord. Salute Tryphena and Tryphosa, who labor in the Lord. Salute the beloved Persis, which labored much in the Lord. Salute Rufus chosen in the Lord, and his mother and mine. Salute Asyncritus, Phlegon, Hermas, Patrobas, Hermes, and the brethren which are with them. Salute Philologus, and Julia, Nereus, and his sister, and Olympas, and all the saints which are with them. Salute one another with a holy kiss. The churches of Christ salute you.
—ROMANS 16:1–16

This chapter contains Paul's loving salutation to the various Christians dwelling at Rome. Remember that it is an inspired passage: although it consists of Christian courtesies addressed to different individuals, yet it was written by an apostle, and written not as an ordinary letter but as a part of the inspired volume. Therefore there must be valuable matter in it; and though, when we read it, it may appear to be uninstructive, there must be edifying matter beneath the surface, because all Scripture is given by inspiration, and is meant to benefit us in one way or another. It shows to us one thing, at any rate, that Paul was of a most affectionate disposition, and that God did not select as the apostle of the gentiles a man of a coarse, unfeeling, selfish turn of mind. His memory, as well as his heart, must have been in good condition to remember so large a number of names, and these were but a few of his many beloved brethren and spiritual children all over the world whom he mentions by name in his other epistles. His warm heart, I doubt not, quickened his memory, and secured to his remembrance the form, condition, history, character, and name of each one of his friends. He loved them too well to forget them. Christians should love one another, and should bear one another's names upon their hearts, even as the great High Priest wears the names of all his saints upon his jeweled breastplate. A Christian because of the love he bears to others is ever anxious to please by courtesy, and desires never to pain by rudeness. Grace makes the servant of God to be in the highest sense a true gentleman. If we learn nothing more from this passage than the duty of acting lovingly and courteously the one to the other, we shall be all the better for it, for there is none too much tender consideration and gentle speech among professors at this time.

I. Beyond this, our text is singularly full of instructive matter, as I shall hope to show you. Without preface, let us notice first, that *this passage illustrates remarkably the various relations of families to the church.*

Note in the third verse that the apostle says, "Greet Priscilla and Aquila my helpers in Christ Jesus." Here you have a household, in which both the father and the mother, or say the husband and the wife, were joined to the church of God. What a happy circumstance was this! Their influence upon the rest of the household must have been very powerful, for when two loving hearts pull together, they accomplish wonders. What different associations cluster around the names of "Priscilla and Aquila" from those which are awakened by the words "Ananias and Sapphira"! There we have a husband and a wife conspiring in hypocrisy, and here a wife and a husband united in sincere devotion. Thrice happy are those who are not only joined in marriage, but are one in the Lord Jesus Christ; such marriages are made in heaven. This couple appear to have been advanced Christians, for they became instructors of others; and not merely teachers of the ignorant, but teachers of those who already knew much of the gospel, for they instructed young Apollos, an eloquent man and mighty in the Scriptures. They taught him the way of God more perfectly, and therefore we may be sure were deep-taught Christians themselves. We must usually look for our spiritual fathers and nursing mothers to those households where husband and wife are walking in the fear of God; they are mutually helpful, and therefore grow in grace beyond others.

I do not know why Paul in this case wrote "Priscilla and Aquila," thus placing the wife first, for in the Acts we read of them as Aquila and Priscilla. I should not wonder but he put them in order according to quality rather than according to the rule of sex. He named Priscilla first because she was first in energy of character and attainments in grace. There is a precedence which, in Christ, is due to the woman when she becomes the leader in devotion, and manifests the stronger mind in the things of God. It is well when nature and grace both authorize our saying "Aquila and Priscilla," but it is not amiss when grace outruns nature and we hear of "Priscilla and Aquila." Whether the wife be first or second matters little if both be truly the servants of God. Dear husband, is your wife unconverted? Never fail to pray for her. Good sister, have you not yet seen the partner of your joys brought in to be a partaker in grace? Never bow your knee for yourself without mentioning that beloved name before the throne of mercy. Pray unceasingly that your life companions may be converted to God. Priscilla and Aquila were tent makers, and were thus of the same trade with the apostle, who for this reason lodged with them at Corinth; they had lived in Rome at one time, but had been obliged to leave owing to a decree of Claudius which banished the Jews from the imperial city. When that decree was no longer carried out, they seem to have gone back to Rome, which from the vast awnings used in the great public buildings must have afforded a fine sphere for the tent-makers' craft. It is very likely that their occupation of tent making necessitated their having a large room in which to carry on their work, and therefore they allowed the Christians to meet in it. Paul spoke of the church that was in their house.

It is a great privilege when a Christian family can accommodate the church of God. It is well when they judge that the parlor will be honored by being used for a prayer meeting, and consider that the best room in the house is none too good for the servants of God to meet in. Such a dwelling becomes like the house of Obededom, where the ark of God tarried and left a permanent blessing behind.

To pass on; in the seventh verse you have another family. "Salute Andronicus and Junia, my kinsmen, and my fellow prisoners, who are of note among the apostles, who also were in Christ before me." Now, if I understand this passage right, we have here a case of two men, perhaps they are both male names, Andronicus and Junius, or else a husband and wife or a brother and sister—

Andronicus and Junia; but at any rate they represent part of a household, and part of a very remarkable household too, for they were kinsmen of Paul, and they were converted to God before Paul was, which interesting fact slips out quite incidentally. I have wondered in my own mind whether the conversion of his relatives helped to irritate Paul into his murderous fury against the church of Christ, whether when he saw Andronicus and Junia his relatives, converted to what he thought to be the superstition of Nazareth—whether that excited in him the desperate animosity which he displayed toward the Lord Jesus Christ. I may leave that as a matter of question, but I feel certain that the prayers of his two relations followed the young persecutor, and that if you were to look deep into the reason for the conversion of Saul of Tarsus on his way to Damascus, you would find it at the mercy seat in the prayers of Andronicus and Junia, his kinsmen, who were in Christ before him.

This should act as a great encouragement for all of you who desire the salvation of your households. Perhaps you have a relative who is very much opposed to the gospel of Jesus Christ; for that very reason pray the more importunately for him! There is nonetheless hope for him because of his zealous opposition, the man is evidently in a thoughtful condition, and the grace of God is able to turn his ignorant zeal to good account when his heart has been enlightened and renewed. There is something to be made out of a man who has enough stuff in him to be opposed to the gospel; a good sword will make a good plowshare. Out of persecutors God can make apostles. Nowadays the world swarms with milksops of men who neither believe in the gospel, nor thoroughly disbelieve it; they are neither for nor against, neither true to God nor the devil. Such men of straw will never be worth their salt even if they should become converted. An out-and-out honest hater of the gospel is the man who with one touch of divine grace may be made into an equally sincere lover of the truth which once he despised. Pray on, pray hard, pray believingly for your relatives, and you may live to see them occupy the pulpit and preach the faith which now they strive to overturn. It is a happy and hopeful token for good to a family when a part of the household is joined to the church of God.

Passing on again, we meet with a third family in relation to the church, but in this case the master of the house was not a Christian—I suppose not, from the tenth verse, "Salute them which are of Aristobulus' household." Not "Salute Aristobulus," no, but they that are of his household. Why leave Aristobulus out? It is just possible that he was dead, but far more likely that he was unsaved. He was left out of the apostle's salutation because he had left himself out; he was no believer, and therefore there could be no Christian salutation sent to him. Alas for him, the kingdom of God was near to him, yes, in his house, and yet he was unblessed by it! Am I not speaking to a man in this condition? Where are you, Aristobulus? That is not your name, perhaps, but your character is the same as that of this unregenerate Roman, whose family knew the Lord. I might speak in God's name good words and comfortable words to your wife and to your children, but I could not so speak to you, Aristobulus! The Lord sends a message of grace to your dear child, to your beloved wife, but not to you; for you have not given your heart to him. I will pray for you, and I am happy to know that those of your household who love the Lord are interceding for you both day and night. It is a hopeful connection that you have with the church, though perhaps you do not care much about it. Yet be sure of this—the kingdom of God has come near unto you. This fact will involve dreadful responsibility, if it does not lead to your salvation, for if like Capernaum you are exalted to heaven by your privileges, it will be all the more dreadful to be thrust down to hell. It is a sad thing in a family when one is taken and another left. Oh, think you how wretched will be your condition if you continue in unbelief, for when your child is in heaven and your wife is in heaven, and you see your mother who is there already, and you yourself are cast far off into hell, you will remember that you were called but refused, were bidden but would not come. You shut your eyes to the light and would not see; you rejected Christ and perished willfully, a suicide to your own soul.

Another instance of this, and I think a worse one, is to be seen further on in our text where the apostle speaks of the "household of Narcissus," in the eleventh verse: "Greet them that be of the household of Narcissus, which are in the Lord." Now I fancy that Narcissus was the master of the house, and that the converts in the house were his servants or his slaves. There was a Narcissus in the days of Nero, who was put to death by Nero's successor. He was Nero's favorite, and when I have said that, you may conclude that he was a man of no very commendable character. It is said of him that he was extremely rich, and that he was as bad as he was rich. Yet while the halls of the house of Narcissus echoed to blasphemous songs, and while luxurious gluttony, mingled with unbridled licentiousness, made his mansion a very hell, there was a saving salt in the servants' hall and the slaves' dormitory. Perhaps under the stairs, in the little place where the slave crept in to sleep, prayer was made unto the living God, and when the master little dreamed of it, the servants about his house sang hymns in praise of one Jesus Christ, the anointed Savior, whom they adored as the Son of God. Wonderful are the ways of electing love, which passes by the rich and great to have respect unto the man of low degree.

It may be there is some bad master within reach of my voice; he is himself utterly irreligious, but yet in his house there are those who wait upon the

Lord in prayer. He who blacks your shoes may be one of the beloved of the Lord, while you who wear them may be without God and without hope in the world. The little maid in your house fears the Lord, though you are forgetful of his praises; an angel received unawares waits upon you at table. There was a good man some years ago who used to sit up for a certain king of ours of wretched memory—let his name rot! This king was called a gentleman, but other titles might better describe him. While his master would be rioting, this man was communing with God, and reading Boston's *Crook in the Lot,* or some such blessed book, to while away the weary hours. There are still at this day in the halls of the great, and wicked, and in the abodes of transgressors of all classes, God's hidden ones, who are the salt of the earth, and cry unto God day and night against the iniquity of their masters. There shall be an inquisition concerning all this; the godly shall not always be forgotten, the golden nuggets shall not always lie hidden in the dust. Think you, O masters, how will it fare with you when your humblest menials shall be crowned with glory and you yourselves shall be driven into the blackness of darkness forever? Seek ye also the Lord, ye great ones, and he will be found of you.

We cannot afford to stay with Narcissus. Let us turn to the twelfth verse, and you have another instance of a family in connection with Christ's people: "Salute Tryphena and Tryphosa, who labor in the Lord"—I suppose two sisters, the names sound very like it. Where were their brothers? Where was their father? Where was their mother? "Tryphena and Tryphosa," how often have I seen them in the church, two humble, earnest, faithful women, the lone ones of the family, and all the rest far off from God! O brother, let not your sister go to heaven alone. Father, if your daughters be children of God, do not yourself remain his enemy. Let the examples of your godly children help you, O parents, to be yourselves decided for the Redeemer! Hail to you, you gracious women who keep each other company on the road to heaven! The Lord make you a comfort to one another. May you shine both here and hereafter like twin stars, shedding a gentle radiance of holiness on all around. There is work for you in your heavenly Father's house, and though you may not be called to public preaching, yet, in spheres appropriate, you may with much acceptance "labor in the Lord."

Further down, in the fifteenth verse, we have a brother and his sister, "Nereus, and his sister." It is pleasant to see the stronger and weaker sex thus associated. "They grew in beauty side by side" in the field of nature, and now they bloom together in the garden of grace. It is a sweet relationship, that of a godly brother and sister; they are as the rose and the lily in the same posy; but had they no other relatives? Were there no others remaining of their kindred? Had they no trouble in spirit concerning others dear to them? Depend upon it, they often prayed together, and sighed because their relatives were not in Christ, for concerning all the rest of the family the record is blank. God hear your prayers, my dear friends, when you, like Nereus and his sister, unite in brotherly prayer and sisterly intercession.

One other very beautiful instance of a family connection with the church is in the thirteenth verse: "Salute Rufus chosen in the Lord, and his mother and mine." Now, this is a case of a mother and her son. I would not wish to say anything that is far-fetched, but I think there is no vain conjecture in supposing that this good woman was the wife of Simon the Cyrenian, who carried the cross of Christ. You will remember he is said by Mark to be the father of Alexander and Rufus, two persons who evidently were well known in the church of God at that time. And here we have familiar mention of Rufus and his mother. Whether she was the wife of Simon or not, she seems to have been a kind, good, lovable soul, one of those dear matrons who are at once an ornament and a comfort to the Christian church; and such an excellent woman was she that Paul when he calls her the mother of Rufus adds, "and mine"—she had been like a mother to him. I do not wonder that such choice mothers have choice sons—"chosen in the Lord." If those whom we deeply love carry their religion about with them set in a frame of affectionate cheerfulness, it is hard to resist the charms of their lovely piety. When a godly woman is a tender mother, it is no wonder if her sons, Rufus and Alexander, become believers in Jesus Christ too, for their mother's love and example draw them toward Jesus.

There is a legend connected with Rufus and Alexander; I have never read it, but I have seen it set forth in glowing colors by an artist in a cathedral in Belgium. I saw a series of paintings which represented Christ bearing his cross through the streets of Jerusalem, and among the crowd the artist has placed a countryman looking on, and carrying with him his mattock and spade, as if he had just come into the town from laboring in the fields. In the next picture this countryman is evidently moved to tears by seeing the cruelties practiced upon the Redeemer, and he shows his sympathy so plainly that the cruel persecutors of our Lord who are watching the spectators observe it, and gather angrily around him. The countryman's two boys are there too, Alexander and Rufus; Rufus is the boy with the red head; he is ardent and sanguine, bold and outspoken, and you can see that one of the rough men has just been cuffing him about the head for showing sympathy with the poor cross-bearing Savior. The next picture represents the father taken and compelled to bear the cross, while Alexander holds his father's pick, and Rufus is carrying his father's spade, and they are going along close by the Lord Jesus, pitying him greatly. If they cannot bear the cross, they will at least help their father by carrying his tools.

Of course it is but a legend, but who marvels if Alexander and Rufus saw their father carry Christ's cross so well, that they, too, should afterward count it their glory to be followers of the crucified One, so that Paul should say when he wrote down the name of Rufus, that he was a choice man, for so we may translate of the passage, "chosen in the Lord," or, "the choice one of the Lord"! He was a distinguished Christian, with great depth of Christian experience, and in all respects a fit descendant of a remarkable father and mother.

Thus have we observed the different ways in which families come in contact with Christ, and I pray God that every family here may make up a part of the whole family in heaven and earth, which is named by the name of Jesus. May all your sons and your daughters, your brethren and your sisters, your servants and kinsfolk, but chiefly yourselves, take up the cross of Jesus, and be saved in the Lord with an everlasting salvation.

II. The interesting passage before us shows *what are points of interest among Christians.*

Now, among worldly people points of interest are very many and characteristic. In any worldly community one very important point of interest is, how much is a man worth? That is an important point with Christians, too, in the right sense, but the worldly man means by that, "How much money has the man scraped into his own till?" He may have gained his pelf in the worst way in the world, but nobody takes account of that, the one all-important question among mammonites is, "What is his balance at the bankers?" Now Paul does not in his salutation make a single reference to any one on account of his wealth or poverty. He does not say, "To Philologus, our brother, who has £10,000 a year, and Julia, our sister, who keeps a carriage and pair"—nothing of the sort. He makes no account of position or property, except so far as those may be implied in the service which each person rendered to the cause of God. Neither is there any allusion made to their holding important offices under government, or being what is called exceedingly respectable people or persons of good family. The points of interest with Paul, as a Christian, were very different from those.

The first matter of which he made honorable mention was their service for the church. Phebe, in the first verse, is "a servant of the church, which is at Cenchrea. She hath been a succorer of many, and of myself also." It is a distinction and honor among Christians to be allowed to serve, and the most menial employment for the church of God is the most honorable. Every man who seeks honor after God's fashion seeks it by being abased, by undertaking that ministry which will involve the most self-denial, and will secure the greatest reproach. Foremost in the ranks of the divine peerage are the martyrs, because they were the most despised; they suffered most, and they have the most of honor. So Phebe shall have her name inscribed in this golden book of Christ's nobility, because she is the servant of the church, and because, in being such, she succored the poor and needy. I doubt not she was a nurse among the poorer Christians, or as some call them, a deaconess, for, in the olden time, it was so, that the elder women who had need were maintained by the church, and in return occupied themselves with the nursing of sick believers; and it were well if such were the case again, and if the old office could be revived.

Another special point for remark among Christians is their labor. Kindly refer to your Bibles, and read the sixth verse: "Greet Mary, who bestowed much labor on us." This is the sixth Mary mentioned in the Bible. She appears to have been one who laid herself out to help the minister. "She bestowed much labor *on us*," says the apostle, or, "on me"—she was one of those useful women who took personal care of the preacher, because she believed the life of God's servant to be precious, and that he should be cared for in his many labors and perils. What she did for Paul and his fellow laborers we are not told, but it was something which cost her effort, amounting to "much labor." She loved much and therefore toiled much. She was "always abounding in the work of the Lord." Sister Mary, imitate your namesake.

Then follow the two good women, Tryphena and Tryphosa, of whom it is said, "who labor in the Lord," and Persis, of whom it is written she "labored *much* in the Lord." I do not suppose Tryphena and Tryphosa were angry because the apostle made this distinction, but it is certainly a very plain and explicit one; the first two "labored," but Persis "labored much." So there are distinctions and degrees in honor among believers, and these are graduated by the scale of service done. It is an honor to labor for Christ; it is a still greater honor to labor much. If, then, any, in joining the Christian church, desire place or position, honor or respect, the way to it is this—labor, and labor much. Persis had probably been a slave, and was of a strange race from the far-off land of Persia, but she was so excellent in disposition that she is called "the beloved Persis," and for her indefatigable industry she receives signal mention. Among believers the rewards of affectionate respect are distributed according to the self-denying service which is rendered to Christ and to his cause. May all of us be helped to labor much, by the power of the Holy Spirit.

At the same time, another point of interest is *character*, for as I have already said, Rufus in the thirteenth verse is said to be "chosen in the Lord," which cannot allude to his election, since all the rest were chosen too, but must mean that he was a choice man in the Lord, a man of peculiarly sweet spirit, a devout man, a man who walked with God, a man well instructed in the things of God, and a man whose practice was equal to his knowledge. "Salute" him, says the apostle. He who would be noted in the church of God must have real character: there must be holiness unto the Lord, there must be faith; a man must have it said of him, "he is full of faith and of the Holy Ghost." This shall get him commemoration, but nothing else will do it. Apelles is described as "approved in Christ," a tried, proved, and experienced believer. Christians value those who have been tested and found faithful; tried saints are had in honor among us.

Character, you see, is the one noteworthy point in the society of the church, and nothing else. Yes, there is one thing else. I find one person here noted in the church as a person around whom great interest centered, because of the time of his conversion. It is in the fifth verse: "Salute my well-beloved Epaenetus, who is the firstfruits of Achaia unto Christ." You know what that means. When Paul began to preach in Achaia, Epaenetus was one of his first converts, and while every minister feels a peculiar attachment to all his converts, he has the tenderest memory of the first ones. What parent does not prize above all others his first child? I can speak from experience. I remember well the first woman who professed to be brought to Christ when I began to preach the gospel. I have the house in my mind's eye at this moment, and though I cannot say that it was a picturesque cottage, yet it will always interest me. Great was the joy I felt when I heard that peasant's story of repentance and of faith. She died, and went to heaven a short time after her conversion, being taken away by consumption, but the remembrance of her gave me more comfort than I have ordinarily received by the recollection of twenty or even a hundred converts since then. She was a precious seal set upon my ministry to begin with, and to encourage my infant faith. Some of you were the firstfruits of my ministry in London, in Park Street, and very precious people you were. How gladly would I see some of you in this tabernacle become the firstfruits of this present year; there would be something very interesting about you, for it would encourage us all through the year. If you are brought to seek the Lord just now, I shall always view you with love, and think of you as I read this chapter so full of names. I shall be as thankful for those born to God tonight as for those regenerated at any other time, for my heart is earnestly going out after you.

So I have shown you that there are points of interest about individual persons in the church of God, and what they are.

III. But as time has fled, though I have much to say I must close with the third point, which is this. This long passage *reveals the general love which exists* (must I say which ought to exist?) *in the church of God.*

For, first, the whole passage shows the love of the apostle toward the saints and brethren at Rome. He would not have taken the trouble to write all this to them if he had not really loved them. And it shows that there were Christians in those days who were full of love to each other. Their salutation, the holy kiss, marked their fervor of love, for they were by no means a people given to use outward signs unless they had something to express thereby. Oh, that Christian love reigned among all Christians now to a greater extent! "Ah!" says one, "there is very little of it." I know you, my friend, very well indeed; you are the man who is forever grumbling at others for want of love, when the truth is that you are destitute of it yourself. I always find that those who say there is no love among Christians now, judge by what they see at home in their own hearts, for those who love Christians believe that Christians also love one another; and you shall find the man of loving heart, though he will say, "I wish there were more love," will never be the man to say that there is none. Brethren, it is a lie that there is no love among Christians: we love each other still, and we will show it by the grace of God even more, if the Spirit of God shall help us.

Note according to this passage the early Christians were accustomed to show their love to one another by practical help; for in the second verse Paul says of Phebe, "Receive her in the Lord, as becometh saints, and assist her in whatever business she hath need of you, for she hath been a succorer of many, and of myself also." I do not think that the apostle alluded to any church business, but to her own business, whatever that may have been; she may have had monies to gather in, or some complaint to make at headquarters of an exacting tax gatherer. I do not know what it was; and it is quite as well that Paul did not tell us. It is no part of an apostle's commission to tell us other people's business; but whatever business it was, if any Christian in Rome could help her, he was to do so. And so if we can help our Christian brethren in any way or shape, "as much as lieth in us" we are to endeavor to do it. Our love must not lie in words alone or it will be unsubstantial as the air. Mark you, you are not called upon to become sureties for your brethren, or to put your name on the back of bills for them; do that for nobody, for you have an express word in

Scripture against it—"He that hateth suretyship is sure," says Solomon, and "he that is a surety shall smart for it." I could wish that some brethren had been wise enough to have recollected the teaching of Scripture upon that point, for it might have saved them a sea of troubles. But for your fellow Christians, do anything that is lawful for you to do, do it for one another out of love to your common Lord, bearing one another's burdens, and so fulfilling the law of Christ.

We are bound to show our love to each other, even when it involves great sacrifices; for in the fourth verse the apostle says of Priscilla and Aquila that for his life "they laid down their own necks." They went into great peril to save the apostle. Such love exists in our churches still. This is denied, but I know it is so. I know Christians who could say honestly that if their minister's life could be spared, they would be willing to die in his stead. It has been said by some here, and I have heard it, and have felt that they who said it meant what they said. I know the prayer has gone up from some lips here that they might sooner die than I should. When your pastor has been in danger, many of you have lovingly declared that if your life could stand for his life, it should be freely rendered before God. Christians love each other still, and they make sacrifices for one another still. I speak this to the honor of many of you, that your love to your pastor has not been in word only, but in deed and in truth; and for this may the Lord reward you.

Christian love in those days had an intense respect for those who had suffered for Christ. Read the seventh verse. Paul says that Andronicus and Junia were his fellow prisoners, and he speaks of them with special unction because of that. No one was thought more of among the early Christians than the prisoner for Christ, the martyr, or the almost martyr. Why, there was even too much made of such sufferers, so that while Christians were in prison, expecting to be martyred, they received attentions which showed almost too great a reverence for their persons. Now, brethren, whenever any man in these times is laughed at for following Christ fully, or ridiculed for bearing an honest testimony for the truth, do not be ashamed of him and turn your backs upon him. Such a man may not expect you to give him double honor, but he may claim that you shall stand shoulder to shoulder with him, and not be ashamed of the reproach which he is called to bear for Christ his Lord.

So was it with the church in the olden time, the men who went first in suffering were also first in their love and esteem. They never failed to own that they were brothers to the man who was doomed to die; on the contrary, the Christians of the apostolic times used to do what our Protestant forefathers did in England. The young Christian people of the church, when there was a martyr to be put to death, would go and stand with tears in their eyes to see him die, and what think you for? To learn the way! One of them said when his father asked him why he stole out to see his pastor burned, "Father, I did it that I might learn the way"; and he did learn it so well that when his turn came he burned as well, and triumphed in God as gloriously as his minister had done. Learn the way, young man, to bear reproach. Look at those who have been lampooned and satirized, and say, "Well, I will learn how to take my turn when my turn comes, but as God helps me, I will speak for the truth faithfully and boldly."

Again, that love always honored workers. For Paul says, "Mary, who bestowed much labor on us"; and he speaks of the laborers over and over again, with intense affection. We ought to love much those who do much for Christ, whether they are Christian men or women. Alas, I know some who, if anybody does a little more than another, straightaway begin to pick holes in his coat. "Mr. So-and-So is very earnest, but—ah—yes! And Mrs. So-and-So, yes—God blesses her, but—but—yes." For want of anything definite to say, they shrug their shoulders and insinuate. This is the reverse of the spirit of Paul, for he recognized holy industry and praised it. Dear friend, do not become a faultfinder; it is as bad a trade as a pickpocket's. Till you can do better, hold your tongue! Did you ever know a man or woman whom God blessed that was perfect? If God were to work by perfect instruments, the instruments would earn a part of the glory. Take it for granted that we are all imperfect; but when you have taken that for granted, love those who serve God well, and never allow anybody to speak against them in your hearing. Silence cavilers at once by saying, "God honors them; and whom God honors, I dare not despise!" We cannot be wrong in putting our honor where God is pleased to place his.

Still, Christian love in Paul's days—though it loved all the saints—had its specialties. Read down the chapter, and you will find Paul saying, "my well-beloved Epaenetus," "Amplias my beloved in the Lord," "Stachys my beloved." All these were persons whom he especially esteemed. There were some whom he liked better than others, and you must not blame yourself if you judge some Christians to be better than others, and if you therefore love them better; for even the Lord himself had a disciple whom he loved more than the rest. I desire to love all the Lord's people, but there are some of them whom I can love best while I know the least about them, and feel the most comfort in them when I have not seen them for a month or so. There are Christian people whom you could live with in heaven comfortably enough, but it is a severe trial to bear with them on earth, although you feel that they are good people, and since God puts up with them, so ought you. Since there are such peculiar people, do not be always getting in their way to irritate them—leave them alone, and seek peace by keeping out of their way. Brethren, let us love one another; by all means let us love one another, for love is of God. But let us all try to be lovable, so as to make this duty as easy as possible to our brethren.

Once more, love among Christians in those early days was wont to respect seniority in spiritual life; for Paul speaks of some who were in Christ before himself. Among us I hope there always will be profound esteem for those who have been longest in Christ, for those who have stood the test of years, for our aged members, the elders and the matrons among us. Reverence to old age is but a natural duty, but reverence to advanced Christians is a privilege as well. Let it always be so among us.

And the last word is this: love to all Christians should make us recollect even the most obscure and mean members of the church. When the apostle Paul wrote, "Salute Asyncritus, Phlegon, Hermas," why, many of us say, "whoever were these good people?" And when he goes on to mention, "Patrobas, Hermes," we ask, "And who were they? What did these men attempt or perform? Is that all? Philologus, who was he? And who was Olympas? We know next to nothing about those good people." They were like the most of us, commonplace individuals; but they loved the Lord, and therefore as Paul recollected their names he sent them a message of love which has become embalmed in the holy Scriptures. Do not let us think of the distinguished Christians exclusively so as to forget the rank and file of the Lord's army. Do not let the eye rest exclusively upon the front rank, but let us love all whom Christ loves; let us value all Christ's servants. It is better to be God's dog than to be the devil's darling. It were better to be the meanest Christian than to be the greatest sinner. If Christ is in them, and they are in Christ, and you are a Christian, let your heart go out toward them.

And now, finally, may grace, mercy, and peace be with all them that love our Lord Jesus Christ; and may we labor to promote unity and love among his people. The God of peace shall bruise Satan under our feet shortly. May we therefore in patience possess our souls. Oh, that those who are not yet numbered among the people of the Lord may be brought in through faith in Jesus Christ to his glory! Amen.

Sermons on Women in the Bible

Charles H. Spurgeon

The text of this book is set in Dante 11/14 and Delphin IA,
with Poetica® Ornaments.

Typeset in QuarkXPress.

Preface by Patricia Klein.

These sermons by Charles Spurgeon have been
gently edited and updated for the modern reader.

Interior design and typesetting by Rose Yancik, of Y Designs.
www.ydesigns.us